Nutshell Series
Hornbook Series
and
Black Letter Series
of
WEST PUBLISHING COMPANY
P.O. Box 64526
St. Paul, Minnesota 55164–0526

Accounting

FARIS' ACCOUNTING AND LAW IN A NUTSHELL, 377 pages, 1984. Softcover. (Text)

Administrative Law

AMAN AND MAYTON'S HORNBOOK ON ADMINISTRATIVE LAW, Approximately 750 pages, 1993. (Text)

GELLHORN AND LEVIN'S ADMINISTRATIVE LAW AND PROCESS IN A NUTSHELL, Third Edition, 479 pages, 1990. Softcover. (Text)

Admiralty

MARAIST'S ADMIRALTY IN A NUTSHELL, Second Edition, 379 pages, 1988. Softcover. (Text)

SCHOENBAUM'S HORNBOOK ON ADMIRALTY AND MARITIME LAW, Student Edition, 692 pages, 1987 with 1992 pocket part. (Text)

Agency—Partnership

REUSCHLEIN AND GREGORY'S HORNBOOK ON THE LAW OF AGENCY AND PARTNERSHIP, Second Edition, 683 pages, 1990. (Text)

STEFFEN'S AGENCY-PARTNERSHIP IN A NUTSHELL, 364 pages, 1977. Softcover. (Text)

NOLAN–HALEY'S ALTERNATIVE DISPUTE RESOLUTION IN A NUTSHELL, 298 pages, 1992. Softcover. (Text)

RISKIN'S DISPUTE RESOLUTION FOR LAWYERS VIDEO TAPES, 1992. (Available for purchase by schools and libraries.)

List current as of January, 1993

STUDY AIDS

American Indian Law

CANBY'S AMERICAN INDIAN LAW IN A NUTSHELL, Second Edition, 336 pages, 1988. Softcover. (Text)

Antitrust—see also Regulated Industries, Trade Regulation

GELLHORN'S ANTITRUST LAW AND ECONOMICS IN A NUTSHELL, Third Edition, 472 pages, 1986. Softcover. (Text)

HOVENKAMP'S BLACK LETTER ON ANTITRUST, Second Edition approximately 325 pages, April 1993 Pub. Softcover. (Review)

HOVENKAMP'S HORNBOOK ON ECONOMICS AND FEDERAL ANTITRUST LAW, Student Edition, 414 pages, 1985. (Text)

SULLIVAN'S HORNBOOK OF THE LAW OF ANTITRUST, 886 pages, 1977. (Text)

Appellate Advocacy—see Trial and Appellate Advocacy

Art Law

DUBOFF'S ART LAW IN A NUTSHELL, Second Edition, approximately 325 pages, 1993. Softcover. (Text)

Banking Law

LOVETT'S BANKING AND FINANCIAL INSTITUTIONS LAW IN A NUTSHELL, Third Edition, 470 pages, 1992. Softcover. (Text)

Civil Procedure—see also Federal Jurisdiction and Procedure

CLERMONT'S BLACK LETTER ON CIVIL PROCEDURE, Third Edition, approximately 350 pages, May, 1993 Pub. Softcover. (Review)

FRIEDENTHAL, KANE AND MILLER'S HORNBOOK ON CIVIL PROCEDURE, Second Edition, approximately 1000 pages, May 1993 Pub. (Text)

KANE'S CIVIL PROCEDURE IN A NUTSHELL, Third Edition, 303 pages, 1991. Softcover. (Text)

KOFFLER AND REPPY'S HORNBOOK ON COMMON LAW PLEADING, 663 pages, 1969. (Text)

SIEGEL'S HORNBOOK ON NEW YORK PRACTICE, Second Edition, Student Edition, 1068 pages, 1991. Softcover. (Text) 1992 Supplemental Pamphlet.

SLOMANSON AND WINGATE'S CALIFORNIA CIVIL PROCEDURE IN A NUTSHELL, 230 pages, 1992. Softcover. (Text)

Commercial Law

BAILEY AND HAGEDORN'S SECURED TRANSACTIONS IN A NUTSHELL, Third Edition, 390 pages, 1988. Softcover. (Text)

HENSON'S HORNBOOK ON SECURED TRANSACTIONS UNDER THE U.C.C., Second Edition, 504

STUDY AIDS

Commercial Law—Continued pages, 1979, with 1979 pocket part. (Text)

MEYER AND SPEIDEL'S BLACK LETTER ON SALES AND LEASES OF GOODS, Approximately 300 pages, 1993. Softcover. (Review)

NICKLES' BLACK LETTER ON COMMERCIAL PAPER, 450 pages, 1988. Softcover. (Review)

STOCKTON AND MILLER'S SALES AND LEASES OF GOODS IN A NUTSHELL, Third Edition, 441 pages, 1992. Softcover. (Text)

STONE'S UNIFORM COMMERCIAL CODE IN A NUTSHELL, Third Edition, 580 pages, 1989. Softcover. (Text)

WEBER AND SPEIDEL'S COMMERCIAL PAPER IN A NUTSHELL, Third Edition, 404 pages, 1982. Softcover. (Text)

WHITE AND SUMMERS' HORNBOOK ON THE UNIFORM COMMERCIAL CODE, Third Edition, Student Edition, 1386 pages, 1988. (Text)

Community Property

MENNELL AND BOYKOFF'S COMMUNITY PROPERTY IN A NUTSHELL, Second Edition, 432 pages, 1988. Softcover. (Text)

Comparative Law

FOLSOM, MINAN AND OTTO'S LAW AND POLITICS IN THE PEOPLE'S REPUBLIC OF CHINA IN A NUTSHELL, 451 pages, 1992. Softcover. (Text)

GLENDON, GORDON AND OSAKWE'S COMPARATIVE LEGAL TRADITIONS IN A NUTSHELL. 402 pages, 1982. Softcover. (Text)

Conflict of Laws

HAY'S BLACK LETTER ON CONFLICT OF LAWS, 330 pages, 1989. Softcover. (Review)

SCOLES AND HAY'S HORNBOOK ON CONFLICT OF LAWS, Student Edition, 1160 pages, 1992. (Text)

SIEGEL'S CONFLICTS IN A NUTSHELL, 470 pages, 1982. Softcover. (Text)

Constitutional Law—Civil Rights

BARRON AND DIENES' BLACK LETTER ON CONSTITUTIONAL LAW, Third Edition, 440 pages, 1991. Softcover. (Review)

BARRON AND DIENES' CONSTITUTIONAL LAW IN A NUTSHELL, Second Edition, 483 pages, 1991. Softcover. (Text)

ENGDAHL'S CONSTITUTIONAL FEDERALISM IN A NUTSHELL, Second Edition, 411 pages, 1987. Softcover. (Text)

MARKS AND COOPER'S STATE CON-

STUDY AIDS

Constitutional Law—Civil Rights—Continued

STITUTIONAL LAW IN A NUTSHELL, 329 pages, 1988. Softcover. (Text)

NOWAK AND ROTUNDA'S HORNBOOK ON CONSTITUTIONAL LAW, Fourth Edition, 1357 pages, 1991. (Text)

VIEIRA'S CONSTITUTIONAL CIVIL RIGHTS IN A NUTSHELL, Second Edition, 322 pages, 1990. Softcover. (Text)

WILLIAMS' CONSTITUTIONAL ANALYSIS IN A NUTSHELL, 388 pages, 1979. Softcover. (Text)

Consumer Law—see also Commercial Law

EPSTEIN AND NICKLES' CONSUMER LAW IN A NUTSHELL, Second Edition, 418 pages, 1981. Softcover. (Text)

Contracts

CALAMARI AND PERILLO'S BLACK LETTER ON CONTRACTS, Second Edition, 462 pages, 1990. Softcover. (Review)

CALAMARI AND PERILLO'S HORNBOOK ON CONTRACTS, Third Edition, 1049 pages, 1987. (Text)

CORBIN'S TEXT ON CONTRACTS, One Volume Student Edition, 1224 pages, 1952. (Text)

FRIEDMAN'S CONTRACT REMEDIES IN A NUTSHELL, 323 pages, 1981. Softcover. (Text)

KEYES' GOVERNMENT CONTRACTS IN A NUTSHELL, Second Edition, 557 pages, 1990. Softcover. (Text)

SCHABER AND ROHWER'S CONTRACTS IN A NUTSHELL, Third Edition, 457 pages, 1990. Softcover. (Text)

Copyright—see Patent and Copyright Law

Corporations

HAMILTON'S BLACK LETTER ON CORPORATIONS, Third Edition, 732 pages, 1992. Softcover. (Review)

HAMILTON'S THE LAW OF CORPORATIONS IN A NUTSHELL, Third Edition, 518 pages, 1991. Softcover. (Text)

HENN AND ALEXANDER'S HORNBOOK ON LAWS OF CORPORATIONS, Third Edition, Student Edition, 1371 pages, 1983, with 1986 pocket part. (Text)

Corrections

KRANTZ' THE LAW OF CORRECTIONS AND PRISONERS' RIGHTS IN A NUTSHELL, Third Edition, 407 pages, 1988. Softcover. (Text)

Creditors' Rights

EPSTEIN'S DEBTOR-CREDITOR LAW IN A NUTSHELL, Fourth Edition,

STUDY AIDS

Creditors' Rights—Continued
401 pages, 1991. Softcover. (Text)

EPSTEIN, NICKLES AND WHITE'S HORNBOOK ON BANKRUPTCY, Approximately 1000 pages, January, 1992 Pub. (Text)

NICKLES AND EPSTEIN'S BLACK LETTER ON CREDITORS' RIGHTS AND BANKRUPTCY, 576 pages, 1989. (Review)

Criminal Law and Criminal Procedure—see also Corrections, Juvenile Justice

ISRAEL AND LAFAVE'S CRIMINAL PROCEDURE—CONSTITUTIONAL LIMITATIONS IN A NUTSHELL, Fourth Edition, 461 pages, 1988. Softcover. (Text)

LAFAVE AND ISRAEL'S HORNBOOK ON CRIMINAL PROCEDURE, Second Edition, 1309 pages, 1992 with 1992 pocket part. (Text)

LAFAVE AND SCOTT'S HORNBOOK ON CRIMINAL LAW, Second Edition, 918 pages, 1986. (Text)

LOEWY'S CRIMINAL LAW IN A NUTSHELL, Second Edition, 321 pages, 1987. Softcover. (Text)

LOW'S BLACK LETTER ON CRIMINAL LAW, Revised First Edition, 443 pages, 1990. Softcover. (Review)

SUBIN, MIRSKY AND WEINSTEIN'S THE CRIMINAL PROCESS: PROSECUTION AND DEFENSE FUNCTIONS, Approximately 450 pages, February, 1993 Pub. Softcover. Teacher's Manual available. (Text)

Domestic Relations

CLARK'S HORNBOOK ON DOMESTIC RELATIONS, Second Edition, Student Edition, 1050 pages, 1988. (Text)

KRAUSE'S BLACK LETTER ON FAMILY LAW, 314 pages, 1988. Softcover. (Review)

KRAUSE'S FAMILY LAW IN A NUTSHELL, Second Edition, 444 pages, 1986. Softcover. (Text)

MALLOY'S LAW AND ECONOMICS: A COMPARATIVE APPROACH TO THEORY AND PRACTICE, 166 pages, 1990. Softcover. (Text)

Education Law

ALEXANDER AND ALEXANDER'S THE LAW OF SCHOOLS, STUDENTS AND TEACHERS IN A NUTSHELL, 409 pages, 1984. Softcover. (Text)

Employment Discrimination—see also Gender Discrimination

PLAYER'S FEDERAL LAW OF EMPLOYMENT DISCRIMINATION IN A NUTSHELL, Third Edition, 338 pages, 1992. Softcover. (Text)

STUDY AIDS

Employment Discrimination—Continued

PLAYER'S HORNBOOK ON EMPLOYMENT DISCRIMINATION LAW, Student Edition, 708 pages, 1988. (Text)

Energy and Natural Resources Law—see also Oil and Gas

LAITOS AND TOMAIN'S ENERGY AND NATURAL RESOURCES LAW IN A NUTSHELL, 554 pages, 1992. Softcover. (Text)

Environmental Law—see also Energy and Natural Resources Law; Sea, Law of

FINDLEY AND FARBER'S ENVIRONMENTAL LAW IN A NUTSHELL, Third Edition, 355 pages, 1992. Softcover. (Text)

RODGERS' HORNBOOK ON ENVIRONMENTAL LAW, 956 pages, 1977, with 1984 pocket part. (Text)

Equity—see Remedies

Estate Planning—see also Trusts and Estates; Taxation—Estate and Gift

LYNN'S INTRODUCTION TO ESTATE PLANNING IN A NUTSHELL, Fourth Edition, 352 pages, 1992. Softcover. (Text)

Evidence

BROUN AND BLAKEY'S BLACK LETTER ON EVIDENCE, 269 pages, 1984. Softcover. (Review)

GRAHAM'S FEDERAL RULES OF EVIDENCE IN A NUTSHELL, Third Edition, 486 pages, 1992. Softcover. (Text)

LILLY'S AN INTRODUCTION TO THE LAW OF EVIDENCE, Second Edition, 585 pages, 1987. (Text)

MCCORMICK'S HORNBOOK ON EVIDENCE, Fourth Edition, Student Edition, 672 pages, 1992. (Text)

ROTHSTEIN'S EVIDENCE IN A NUTSHELL: STATE AND FEDERAL RULES, Second Edition, 514 pages, 1981. Softcover. (Text)

Federal Jurisdiction and Procedure

CURRIE'S FEDERAL JURISDICTION IN A NUTSHELL, Third Edition, 242 pages, 1990. Softcover. (Text)

REDISH'S BLACK LETTER ON FEDERAL JURISDICTION, Second Edition, 234 pages, 1991. Softcover. (Review)

WRIGHT'S HORNBOOK ON FEDERAL COURTS, Fourth Edition, Student Edition, 870 pages, 1983. (Text)

First Amendment

GARVEY AND SCHAUER'S THE FIRST AMENDMENT: A READER, 527 pages, 1992. Softcover.

STUDY AIDS

First Amendment—Continued (Reader)

Future Interests—see Trusts and Estates

Gender Discrimination—see also Employment Discrimination

THOMAS' SEX DISCRIMINATION IN A NUTSHELL, Second Edition, 395 pages, 1991. Softcover. (Text)

Health Law—see Medicine, Law and

Human Rights—see International Law

Immigration Law

WEISSBRODT'S IMMIGRATION LAW AND PROCEDURE IN A NUTSHELL, Third Edition, 497 pages, 1992. Softcover. (Text)

Indian Law—see American Indian Law

Insurance Law

DOBBYN'S INSURANCE LAW IN A NUTSHELL, Second Edition, 316 pages, 1989. Softcover. (Text)

KEETON AND WIDISS' INSURANCE LAW, Student Edition, 1359 pages, 1988. (Text)

International Law—see also Sea, Law of

BUERGENTHAL'S INTERNATIONAL HUMAN RIGHTS IN A NUTSHELL, 283 pages, 1988. Softcover. (Text)

BUERGENTHAL AND MAIER'S PUBLIC INTERNATIONAL LAW IN A NUTSHELL, Second Edition, 275 pages, 1990. Softcover. (Text)

FOLSOM'S EUROPEAN COMMUNITY LAW IN A NUTSHELL, 423 pages, 1992. Softcover. (Text)

FOLSOM, GORDON AND SPANOGLE'S INTERNATIONAL BUSINESS TRANSACTIONS IN A NUTSHELL, Fourth Edition, 548 pages, 1992. Softcover. (Text)

Interviewing and Counseling

SHAFFER AND ELKINS' LEGAL INTERVIEWING AND COUNSELING IN A NUTSHELL, Second Edition, 487 pages, 1987. Softcover. (Text)

Introduction to Law—see Legal Method and Legal System

Introduction to Law Study

HEGLAND'S INTRODUCTION TO THE STUDY AND PRACTICE OF LAW IN A NUTSHELL, 418 pages, 1983. Softcover. (Text)

KINYON'S INTRODUCTION TO LAW STUDY AND LAW EXAMINATIONS IN A NUTSHELL, 389 pages, 1971. Softcover. (Text)

Judicial Process—see Legal Method and Legal System

SINHA'S JURISPRUDENCE (LEGAL PHILOSOPHY) IN A NUTSHELL.

STUDY AIDS

Judicial Process—Continued

Approximately 350 pages, 1993. Softcover. (Text)

Juvenile Justice

Fox's Juvenile Courts in a Nutshell, Third Edition, 291 pages, 1984. Softcover. (Text)

Labor and Employment Law—see also Employment Discrimination, Workers' Compensation

Leslie's Labor Law in a Nutshell, Third Edition, 388 pages, 1992. Softcover. (Text)

Nolan's Labor Arbitration Law and Practice in a Nutshell, 358 pages, 1979. Softcover. (Text)

Land Finance—Property Security—see Real Estate Transactions

Land Use

Hagman and Juergensmeyer's Hornbook on Urban Planning and Land Development Control Law, Second Edition, Student Edition, 680 pages, 1986. (Text)

Wright and Wright's Land Use in a Nutshell, Second Edition, 356 pages, 1985. Softcover. (Text)

Legal Method and Legal System—see also Legal Research, Legal Writing

Kempin's Historical Introduction to Anglo-American Law in a Nutshell, Third Edition, 323 pages, 1990. Softcover. (Text)

Reynolds' Judicial Process in a Nutshell, Second Edition, 308 pages, 1991. Softcover. (Text)

Legal Research

Cohen and Olson's Legal Research in a Nutshell, Fifth Edition, 370 pages, 1992. Softcover. (Text)

Cohen, Berring and Olson's How to Find the Law, Ninth Edition, 716 pages, 1989. (Text)

Legal Writing and Drafting

Mellinkoff's Dictionary of American Legal Usage, 703 pages, 1992. Softcover. (Text)

Squires and Rombauer's Legal Writing in a Nutshell, 294 pages, 1982. Softcover. (Text)

Legislation—see also Legal Writing and Drafting

Davies' Legislative Law and Process in a Nutshell, Second Edition, 346 pages, 1986. Softcover. (Text)

STUDY AIDS

Local Government

McCarthy's Local Government Law in a Nutshell, Third Edition, 435 pages, 1990. Softcover. (Text)

Reynolds' Hornbook on Local Government Law, 860 pages, 1982 with 1990 pocket part. (Text)

Mass Communication Law

Zuckman, Gaynes, Carter and Dee's Mass Communications Law in a Nutshell, Third Edition, 538 pages, 1988. Softcover. (Text)

Medicine, Law and

Hall and Ellman's Health Care Law and Ethics in a Nutshell, 401 pages, 1990. Softcover (Text)

Jarvis, Closen, Hermann and Leonard's AIDS Law in a Nutshell, 349 pages, 1991. Softcover. (Text)

King's The Law of Medical Malpractice in a Nutshell, Second Edition, 342 pages, 1986. Softcover. (Text)

Military Law

Shanor and Terrell's Military Law in a Nutshell, 378 pages, 1980. Softcover. (Text)

Mining Law—see Energy and Natural Resources Law

Mortgages—see Real Estate Transactions

Natural Resources Law—see Energy and Natural Resources Law, Environmental Law

Teply's Legal Negotiation in a Nutshell, 282 pages, 1992. Softcover. (Text)

Office Practice—see also Computers and Law, Interviewing and Counseling, Negotiation

Hegland's Trial and Practice Skills in a Nutshell, 346 pages, 1978. Softcover (Text)

Oil and Gas—see also Energy and Natural Resources Law

Hemingway's Hornbook on the Law of Oil and Gas, Third Edition, Student Edition, 711 pages, 1992. (Text)

Lowe's Oil and Gas Law in a Nutshell, Second Edition, 465 pages, 1988. Softcover. (Text)

Partnership—see Agency—Partnership

Patent and Copyright Law

Miller and Davis' Intellectual Property—Patents, Trademarks and Copyright in a Nutshell, Second Edition, 437 pages, 1990. Softcover. (Text)

Products Liability

Phillips' Products Liability in

STUDY AIDS

Products Liability—Continued

A NUTSHELL, Third Edition, 307 pages, 1988. Softcover. (Text)

Professional Responsibility

ARONSON AND WECKSTEIN'S PROFESSIONAL RESPONSIBILITY IN A NUTSHELL, Second Edition, 514 pages, 1991. Softcover. (Text)

LESNICK'S BEING A LAWYER: INDIVIDUAL CHOICE AND RESPONSIBILITY IN THE PRACTICE OF LAW, 422 pages, 1992. Softcover. Teacher's Manual available. (Coursebook)

ROTUNDA'S BLACK LETTER ON PROFESSIONAL RESPONSIBILITY, Third Edition, 492 pages, 1992. Softcover. (Review)

WOLFRAM'S HORNBOOK ON MODERN LEGAL ETHICS, Student Edition, 1120 pages, 1986. (Text)

WYDICK AND PERSCHBACHER'S CALIFORNIA LEGAL ETHICS, 439 pages, 1992. Softcover. (Coursebook)

Property—see also Real Estate Transactions, Land Use, Trusts and Estates

BERNHARDT'S BLACK LETTER ON PROPERTY, Second Edition, 388 pages, 1991. Softcover. (Review)

BERNHARDT'S REAL PROPERTY IN A NUTSHELL, Second Edition, 448 pages, 1981. Softcover. (Text)

BOYER, HOVENKAMP AND KURTZ' THE LAW OF PROPERTY, AN INTRODUCTORY SURVEY, Fourth Edition, 696 pages, 1991. (Text)

BURKE'S PERSONAL PROPERTY IN A NUTSHELL, Second Edition, approximately 400 pages, May, 1993 Pub. Softcover. (Text)

CUNNINGHAM, STOEBUCK AND WHITMAN'S HORNBOOK ON THE LAW OF PROPERTY, Second Edition, approximately 900 pages, May, 1993 Pub. (Text)

HILL'S LANDLORD AND TENANT LAW IN A NUTSHELL, Second Edition, 311 pages, 1986. Softcover. (Text)

Real Estate Transactions

BRUCE'S REAL ESTATE FINANCE IN A NUTSHELL, Third Edition, 287 pages, 1991. Softcover. (Text)

NELSON AND WHITMAN'S BLACK LETTER ON LAND TRANSACTIONS AND FINANCE, Second Edition, 466 pages, 1988. Softcover. (Review)

NELSON AND WHITMAN'S HORNBOOK ON REAL ESTATE FINANCE LAW, Second Edition, 941 pages, 1985 with 1989 pocket part. (Text)

STUDY AIDS

Regulated Industries—see also Mass Communication Law, Banking Law

GELLHORN AND PIERCE'S REGULATED INDUSTRIES IN A NUTSHELL, Second Edition, 389 pages, 1987. Softcover. (Text)

Remedies

DOBBS' HORNBOOK ON REMEDIES, Second Edition, approximately 1000 pages, April, 1993 Pub. (Text)

DOBBYN'S INJUNCTIONS IN A NUTSHELL, 264 pages, 1974. Softcover. (Text)

FRIEDMAN'S CONTRACT REMEDIES IN A NUTSHELL, 323 pages, 1981. Softcover. (Text)

O'CONNELL'S REMEDIES IN A NUTSHELL, Second Edition, 320 pages, 1985. Softcover. (Text)

Sea, Law of

SOHN AND GUSTAFSON'S THE LAW OF THE SEA IN A NUTSHELL, 264 pages, 1984. Softcover. (Text)

Securities Regulation

HAZEN'S HORNBOOK ON THE LAW OF SECURITIES REGULATION, Second Edition, Student Edition, 1082 pages, 1990. (Text)

RATNER'S SECURITIES REGULATION IN A NUTSHELL, Fourth Edition, 320 pages, 1992. Softcover. (Text)

Sports Law

CHAMPION'S SPORTS LAW IN A NUTSHELL,. Approximately 300 pages, January, 1993 Pub. Softcover. (Text)

SCHUBERT, SMITH AND TRENTADUE'S SPORTS LAW, 395 pages, 1986. (Text)

Tax Practice and Procedure

MORGAN'S TAX PROCEDURE AND TAX FRAUD IN A NUTSHELL, 400 pages, 1990. Softcover. (Text)

Taxation—Corporate

SCHWARZ AND LATHROPE'S BLACK LETTER ON CORPORATE AND PARTNERSHIP TAXATION, 537 pages, 1991. Softcover. (Review)

WEIDENBRUCH AND BURKE'S FEDERAL INCOME TAXATION OF CORPORATIONS AND STOCKHOLDERS IN A NUTSHELL, Third Edition, 309 pages, 1989. Softcover. (Text)

Taxation—Estate & Gift—see also Estate Planning, Trusts and Estates

MCNULTY'S FEDERAL ESTATE AND GIFT TAXATION IN A NUTSHELL, Fourth Edition, 496 pages, 1989. Softcover. (Text)

PEAT AND WILLBANKS' FEDERAL ESTATE AND GIFT TAXATION: AN ANALYSIS AND CRITIQUE, 265 pages, 1991. Softcover. (Text)

STUDY AIDS

Taxation—Individual

Dodge's The Logic of Tax, 343 pages, 1989. Softcover. (Text)

Hudson and Lind's Black Letter on Federal Income Taxation, Fourth Edition, 410 pages, 1992. Softcover. (Review)

McNulty's Federal Income Taxation of Individuals in a Nutshell, Fourth Edition, 503 pages, 1988. Softcover. (Text)

Posin's Federal Income Taxation, Second Edition, approximately 650 pages, May, 1993 Pub. Softcover. (Text)

Rose and Chommie's Hornbook on Federal Income Taxation, Third Edition, 923 pages, 1988, with 1991 pocket part. (Text)

Taxation—International

Doernberg's International Taxation in a Nutshell, 325 pages, 1989. Softcover. (Text)

Bishop and Brooks' Federal Partnership Taxation: A Guide to the Leading Cases, Statutes, and Regulations, 545 pages, 1990. Softcover. (Text)

Burke's Federal Income Taxation of Partnerships in a Nutshell, 356 pages, 1992. Softcover. (Text)

Schwarz and Lathrope's Black Letter on Corporate and Partnership Taxation, 537 pages, 1991. Softcover. (Review)

Taxation—State & Local

Gelfand and Salsich's State and Local Taxation and Finance in a Nutshell, 309 pages, 1986. Softcover. (Text)

Torts—see also Products Liability

Kionka's Black Letter on Torts, 339 pages, 1988. Softcover. (Review)

Kionka's Torts in a Nutshell, Second Edition, 449 pages, 1992. Softcover. (Text)

Prosser and Keeton's Hornbook on Torts, Fifth Edition, Student Edition, 1286 pages, 1984 with 1988 pocket part. (Text)

Trade Regulation—see also Antitrust, Regulated Industries

McManis' Unfair Trade Practices in a Nutshell, Third Edition, approximately 450 pages, 1993. Softcover. (Text)

Schechter's Black Letter on Unfair Trade Practices, 272 pages, 1986. Softcover. (Review)

Trial and Appellate Advocacy—see also Civil Procedure

Bergman's Trial Advocacy in a

STUDY AIDS

Trial and Appellate Advocacy—Continued

NUTSHELL, Second Edition, 354 pages, 1989. Softcover. (Text)

CLARY'S PRIMER ON THE ANALYSIS AND PRESENTATION OF LEGAL ARGUMENT, 106 pages, 1992. Softcover. (Text)

DESSEM'S PRETRIAL LITIGATION IN A NUTSHELL, 382 pages, 1992. Softcover. (Text)

GOLDBERG'S THE FIRST TRIAL (WHERE DO I SIT? WHAT DO I SAY?) IN A NUTSHELL, 396 pages, 1982. Softcover. (Text)

HEGLAND'S TRIAL AND PRACTICE SKILLS IN A NUTSHELL, 346 pages, 1978. Softcover. (Text)

HORNSTEIN'S APPELLATE ADVOCACY IN A NUTSHELL, 325 pages, 1984. Softcover. (Text)

JEANS' HANDBOOK ON TRIAL ADVOCACY, Student Edition, 473 pages, 1975. Softcover. (Text)

Trusts and Estates

ATKINSON'S HORNBOOK ON WILLS, Second Edition, 975 pages, 1953. (Text)

AVERILL'S UNIFORM PROBATE CODE IN A NUTSHELL, Second Edition, 454 pages, 1987. Softcover. (Text)

BOGERT'S HORNBOOK ON TRUSTS, Sixth Edition, Student Edition, 794 pages, 1987. (Text)

MCGOVERN, KURTZ AND REIN'S HORNBOOK ON WILLS, TRUSTS AND ESTATES–INCLUDING TAXATION AND FUTURE INTERESTS, 996 pages, 1988. (Text)

MENNELL'S WILLS AND TRUSTS IN A NUTSHELL, 392 pages, 1979. Softcover. (Text)

SIMES' HORNBOOK ON FUTURE INTERESTS, Second Edition, 355 pages, 1966. (Text)

TURANO AND RADIGAN'S HORNBOOK ON NEW YORK ESTATE ADMINISTRATION, 676 pages, 1986 with 1991 pocket part. (Text)

WAGGONER'S FUTURE INTERESTS IN A NUTSHELL, 361 pages, 1981. Softcover. (Text)

Water Law—see also Environmental Law

GETCHES' WATER LAW IN A NUTSHELL, Second Edition, 459 pages, 1990. Softcover. (Text)

Wills—see Trusts and Estates

Workers' Compensation

HOOD, HARDY AND LEWIS' WORKERS' COMPENSATION AND EMPLOYEE PROTECTION LAWS IN A NUTSHELL, Second Edition, 361 pages, 1990. Softcover. (Text)

Advisory Board

CURTIS J. BERGER
Professor of Law, Columbia University

JESSE H. CHOPER
Dean and Professor of Law,
University of California, Berkeley

DAVID P. CURRIE
Professor of Law, University of Chicago

YALE KAMISAR
Professor of Law, University of Michigan

MARY KAY KANE
Professor of Law, University of California,
Hastings College of the Law

WAYNE R. LaFAVE
Professor of Law, University of Illinois

RICHARD C. MAXWELL
Professor of Law, Duke University

ARTHUR R. MILLER
Professor of Law, Harvard University

GRANT S. NELSON
Professor of Law, University of California, Los Angeles

ROBERT A. STEIN
Dean and Professor of Law, University of Minnesota

JAMES J. WHITE
Professor of Law, University of Michigan

CHARLES ALAN WRIGHT
Professor of Law, University of Texas

UNFAIR TRADE PRACTICES

IN A NUTSHELL

Third Edition

By

CHARLES R. McMANIS
Professor of Law
Washington University in St. Louis

ST. PAUL, MINN.
WEST PUBLISHING CO.
1993

Nutshell Series, In a Nutshell, the Nutshell Logo and the WP symbol are registered trademarks of West Publishing Co. Registered in the U.S. Patent and Trademark Office.

COPYRIGHT © 1983, 1988 WEST PUBLISHING CO.
COPYRIGHT © 1992 By WEST PUBLISHING CO.
610 Opperman Drive
P.O. Box 64526
St. Paul, Minnesota 55164-0526

All rights reserved
Printed in the United States of America

Library of Congress Cataloging-in-Publication Data

McManis, Charles R., 1941–
    Unfair trade practices in a nutshell / by Charles R. McManis. —
3rd ed.
    p.   cm. — (Nutshell series)
  Includes index.
  ISBN 0-314-01122-6
  1. Competition, Unfair—United States. I. Title. II. Series.
KF1610.M354 1993
343.73'072—dc20
[347.30372]
                                            92-34509
                                              CIP

ISBN 0-314-01122-6

McManis, Unfair Trade Prac. 3rd, NS

To Christopher and Kevin

PREFACE

The subject of this book has been aptly described by my former colleague and fellow Nutshell writer, the late Wax Malone, as "a hybrid area where common law doctrine tends to lose its identity as it merges with statutory and constitutional material in the estuary of public law." See Malone, *Torts in a Nutshell: Injuries to Family, Social and Trade Relations* (1979) (Preface). In that fertile estuary, it might be added, a new and distinct body of law has spawned. The birth announcement appears in an introductory note to Volume 4 of the Restatement, Second, of Torts (1979), which observes that although the "rules relating to liability for harm caused by unfair trade practices developed doctrinally from established principles in the law of Torts," the fields of Unfair Competition and Trade Regulation have been rapidly developing into independent bodies of law, so that today "the law of Unfair Competition and Trade Regulation is no more dependent upon Tort law than it is on many other general fields of the law and upon broad statutory developments, particularly at the federal level."

This new body of law is entitled to its own name. Although it could be called "Unfair Competition and Trade Regulation," so as to identify both

V

PREFACE

its common-law and statutory ancestry, that title is unwieldy and inaccurately identifies parents and offspring alike. The term "Unfair Competition" is an overly narrow description of the relevant common law, for it fails to encompass unfair bargaining or marketing practices that adversely affect non-competing businesses. The term "Trade Regulation," on the other hand, is so broad that it arguably encompasses the statutory law of antitrust, consumer protection, regulated industries and perhaps labor law as well. Thus I prefer to call the offspring the Law of Unfair Trade Practices.

The identity of this new body of law is further complicated because it encompasses another, more narrowly defined body of law, called the Law of Intellectual Property, which is likewise comprised of both statutory and common-law elements—specifically the federal statutory law of patents and copyrights, the largely common law of trade secrets, and the mixed federal and state law of trademarks and unfair competition. This book covers all of these areas, but extends as well to the law governing interference with contractual and non-contractual relations, trade disparagement, and deceptive advertising, promotional and pricing practices. It is thus suitable for use in courses having a wide variety of titles—Business or Commercial Torts, Intellectual Property, Trade Regulation, Unfair Competition and Unfair Trade Practices, to mention only some of them. The book is specifically designed for use with

PREFACE

three casebooks: Weston, Maggs, and Schecter, *Unfair Trade Practices and Consumer Protection* (5th ed. 1992); Goldstein's *Copyright, Patent, Trademark and Related State Doctrines* (3d ed. 1990); and Kitch and Perlman's *Legal Regulation of the Competitive Process* (4th ed. 1989). For a detailed treatment of the federal statutory law of patents, copyrights and trademarks, see Miller & Davis, *Intellectual Property in a Nutshell: Patents, Trademarks and Copyright* (2d ed. 1990).

A third edition of "Unfair Trade Practices" was made necessary by continuing case-law developments and a number of significant statutory changes affecting several areas of law covered by this book. In addition, the international dimension of the law of unfair trade practices has continued to grow in importance, and has thus been given even greater emphasis than it received in earlier editions.

This edition is joyfully dedicated to my two little associates, Christopher and Kevin, who in addition to lighting up their father's life, continually challenge him with their intuitive understanding of such fundamental legal concepts as procedural due process, distributional equality, the sanctity of promises, and the principle of mine and thine. I am glad they are mine.

C.R.M.

St. Louis, Missouri
October, 1992

*

OUTLINE

	Page
PREFACE	V
TABLE OF CASES	XIX
TABLE OF STATUTES	XXXVII

Chapter One. Introduction to the Law of Unfair Trade Practices 1

A. Sources of The Law of Unfair Trade Practices 2
  1. Common–Law Sources 2
    a. Tortious Interference With Advantageous Relations Generally 4
    b. Unfair Competition 5
      (1) Palming Off and Trademark Infringement 6
      (2) Misappropriation 8
      (3) Malicious Competition 9
    c. Prima Facie Tort 12
  2. Statutory, Constitutional and Treaty Sources 15
    a. Federal Trade Regulation 18
      (1) Preemptive Federal Legislation: Patent, Copyright, and Labor Law 19
      (2) Non-preemptive Federal Legislation: Trademark and Antitrust Law 22

OUTLINE

Chapter One. Introduction to the Law of Unfair Trade Practices—Continued

		Page
	(3) Constitutional Limits on State and Federal Trade Regulation	24
b.	State Trade Regulation	26
c.	International Trade Regulation	27
	(1) International Agreements	28
	(2) U.S. Foreign Trade Legislation	29

B. Objectives of the Law of Unfair Trade Practices 33
   1. Trade Relations and Relational Interests Protected 34
   2. Actionable and Privileged Interference with Trade Relations 36

C. A Suggested Approach: The Law of Unfair Trade Practices in Functional Context .. 38

PART I. INTERFERENCE WITH PROSPECTIVE AND EXISTING CONTRACTUAL RELATIONS

Chapter Two. Interference With Precontractual and Non-contractual Relations 40

A. Trade Relations and Relational Interests Protected 42
B. Actionable and Privileged Interference 43
   1. Improper Business Methods 44
      a. Physical Interference 45

OUTLINE

Chapter Two. Interference With Precontractual and Non-contractual Relations—Continued Page
    b. Injurious Speech: Deceit, Defamation, Disparagement 49
    c. Coercive and Other Improper Conduct 53
  2. Improper Business Objectives............... 55
    a. Anticompetitive Conduct 56
    b. Malicious or Predatory Conduct.... 57
    c. Refusals to Deal With Another Business 61
  3. Concerted Group Conduct..................... 65
C. Affirmative Defenses and Remedies........... 72

Chapter Three. Interference With Contractual Relations................................... 73
A. Contractual Relations Protected................. 74
  1. Express Contracts: Term, Terminable at Will, and Unenforceable Contracts 76
  2. Implied Contracts and the Obligation of Fair Dealing 81
B. Actionable and Privileged Interference...... 83
  1. Inducing Breach of Contract 84
  2. Coercing Modification of Contracts and Abuse of Trust or Confidence 89
  3. Concerted Group Interference with Contractual Relations............................. 92
  4. Other Improper Interference................. 93
C. Affirmative Defenses and Remedies........... 94

OUTLINE

PART II. PRODUCT, SERVICE AND BUSINESS MISIDENTIFICATION

Page

Chapter Four. Use of Similar Trademarks and Trade Names 97

A. Trade Relations and Trade Symbols Protected 99
   1. Marks and Names Protected 99
      a. Common-Law Trademarks and Trade Names 101
      b. Statutory Trademarks, Service Marks and Trade Names 104
      c. A Note on Nomenclature 109
   2. Acquiring Rights in a Mark or Name .. 110
      a. Actual Use/Intended Use/Foreign Registration 116
      b. Inherent and Acquired Distinctiveness 118
         (1) Inherently Distinctive Marks and Names 119
         (2) Descriptive or Misdescriptive Marks and Names 120
         (3) Distinctive Product and Business Features 131
      c. Inherently Unsuitable Marks and Names 139
         (1) Deceptive, Immoral, Disparaging or Confusing Marks and Names 140

OUTLINE

Chapter Four. Use of Similar Trademarks and Trade Names—Continued

    (2) Generic Terms 141
    (3) Functional Product and Business Features 146
  3. Assignment, Licensing and Termination of Rights in a Mark or Name ... 151

B. Infringing and Non-infringing Uses 158
  1. Uses Creating a Likelihood of Confusion 161
    a. Proof of Likelihood of Confusion .. 161
    b. Use of Marks and Names on Related But Non-competing Goods, Services or Businesses 166
    c. Use of Marks and Names in Different Geographic Markets 172
    d. Parallel Imports ("Grey Market" Goods) 175
  2. Uses Creating a Likelihood of Dilution 179
  3. Contributory Infringement 184

C. Affirmative Defenses and Remedies 185
  1. Affirmative Defenses 185
  2. Criminal Sanctions and Civil and Administrative Remedies 191
    a. Criminal Sanctions 191
    b. Civil and Administrative Remedies 192

Chapter Five. Product Substitution or Alteration 197

A. Trade Relations Protected 197

OUTLINE

Chapter Five. Product Substitution or Alteration—Continued   Page
B. Actionable and Privileged Substitution or Alteration of Goods 199
   1. Product Substitution 200
   2. Product Alteration 205
C. Affirmative Defenses and Remedies............ 209

PART III. APPROPRIATION OF INTANGIBLE TRADE VALUES

Chapter Six. Appropriation of Publicly Disclosed Trade Values 211
A. Trade Relations and Trade Values Protected 216
   1. Patentable Inventions............................ 216
      a. Subject Matter Protected 217
      b. Obtaining a Patent........................... 221
      c. Transfer and Termination of Patents 223
   2. Copyrightable Literary and Artistic Works 228
      a. Subject Matter Protected 228
      b. Obtaining a Copyright 239
      c. Transfer and Termination of Copyright 243
   3. Mask Works 248
      a. Subject Matter Protected 248
      b. Obtaining Protection 251

OUTLINE

Chapter Six. Appropriation of Publicly Disclosed Trade Values—Continued Page
    4. Other Investments of Intellectual Effort: News, Ephemeral Performances, Publicity 256
B. Actionable and Privileged Appropriation ... 267
    1. Patent Infringement 268
    2. Copyright Infringement and Fair Use 271
    3. Mask Work Infringement and Fair Use 285
    4. Misappropriation 293
C. Affirmative Defenses and Remedies 301

Chapter Seven. Appropriation of Non-publicly Disclosed Trade Values 304
A. Trade Relations and Trade Values Protected 313
    1. Contractual and Confidential Relations 313
    2. Trade Secrets and Ideas 316
B. Actionable and Privileged Appropriation ... 320
    1. Impropriety in the Method of Acquiring a Trade Secret or Idea 321
    2. Unauthorized Use or Disclosure of a Trade Secret or Idea 323
    3. Knowing Use of an Improperly Disclosed Trade Secret or Idea 325
C. Affirmative Defenses and Remedies 327

OUTLINE

PART IV. INJURIOUS PROMOTIONAL AND PRICING PRACTICES

Page

Chapter Eight. Injurious Promotional Practices 331

A. Trade Relations Protected........................... 333
B. Actionable and Privileged Promotional Practices 334
   1. Deceptive Promotional Practices........... 334
      a. Privately Actionable Deceptive Practices... 335
         (1) Defamation 335
         (2) Trade Disparagement 342
         (3) Other Deceptive Advertising and Promotional Practices ... 350
            (a) Common Law Remedies for False Advertising............. 350
            (b) State Deceptive Trade Practices Statutes................... 353
            (c) Federal Statutory Remedies: Section 43(a) of the Lanham Act and RICO .. 354
      b. Public Regulation of Promotional Practices 367
         (1) Federal Trade Commission Regulation of Deceptive Acts or Practices 375
            (a) The Capacity to Deceive.... 375
            (b) Materiality........................... 382

Chapter Eight. Injurious Promotional Practices—Continued

        (2) Federal Trade Commission Regulation of Unfair Acts or Practices and Unfair Methods of Competition 387
        (3) International Trade Commission Regulation of Unfair Methods of Competition in the Import Trade 389
  2. Unfair Promotional Practices 390
    a. Bribery in Commercial Bargaining Relations 391
    b. Consumer–Aimed Promotional Practices 398
        (1) Lotteries, Games and Contests 398
        (2) Giveaways, Premiums and Trading Stamps 400

Chapter Nine. Injurious Pricing Practices 402

A. Trade Relations Protected 406
B. Actionable and Privileged Interference 407
  1. Price Cutting 408
    a. Sales Below Cost 408
    b. Unreasonably Low Prices 411
  2. Price Discrimination 414
    a. § 2(a) Price Discrimination 417
        (1) The Prima Facie Case 417
            (a) Primary Line Injury 421
            (b) Second, Third and Fourth Line Injury 424

OUTLINE

Chapter Nine. Injurious Pricing Practices—Continued

    (2) Defenses to Section 2(a) Price Discrimination 426
        (a) Cost Justification 427
        (b) Changing Conditions.......... 428
        (c) Meeting Competition 428
  b. Unearned Brokerage....................... 431
  c. Discriminatory Promotional Allowances and Services 432
  d. Buyer Liability for Price Discrimination 434
3. Price Discrimination and Predatory Pricing in International Trade 435

INDEX.. 439

TABLE OF CASES

References are to Pages

A.A. Poultry Farms, Inc. v. Rose Acre Farms, Inc., 881 F.2d 1396 (7th Cir.1989), *423*

Abele, In re, 684 F.2d 902 (Cust. & Pat.App.1982), *219*

Abercrombie & Fitch Co. v. Hunting World, Inc., 537 F.2d 4 (2nd Cir.1976), *119*

Abernathy v. Hutchinson, 3 L.J.Ch. 209 (1825), *311*

A. Bourjois & Co. v. Katzel, 260 U.S. 689, 43 S.Ct. 244, 67 L.Ed. 464 (1923), *176*

Adler, Barish, Daniels, Levin and Creskoff v. Epstein, 482 Pa. 416, 393 A.2d 1175 (Pa.1978), *55, 93*

Advance Music Corp. v. American Tobacco Co., 296 N.Y. 79, 70 N.E.2d 401 (N.Y.1946), *14, 60, 61, 343, 350*

A.J. Canfield Co. v. Honickman, 808 F.2d 291 (3rd Cir.1986), *142*

Alfred Dunhill Ltd. v. Interstate Cigar Co., Inc., 499 F.2d 232 (2nd Cir.1974), *364*

ALPO Petfoods, Inc. v. Ralston Purina Co., 913 F.2d 958, 286 U.S.App.D.C. 192 (D.C.Cir.1990), *366*

American Banana Co. v. United Fruit Co., 213 U.S. 347, 29 S.Ct. 511, 53 L.Ed. 826 (1909), *32*

American Cyanamid Co. v. United States Rubber Co., 53 C.C.P.A. 994, 356 F.2d 1008 (Cust. & Pat.App.1966), *163*

American Home Products Corp. v. F.T.C., 695 F.2d 681 (3rd Cir.1982), *378*

American Home Products Corp. v. Johnson and Johnson, 436 F.Supp. 785 (D.C.N.Y.1977), *363*

American–Marietta Co. v. Krigsman, 275 F.2d 287 (2nd Cir.1960), *160*

American Optometric Ass'n v. F.T.C., 626 F.2d 896, 200 U.S.App.D.C. 32 (D.C.Cir.1980), *371*

American Washboard Co. v. Saginaw Mfg. Co., 103 F. 281 (6th Cir.1900), *350*

Amerise, In re, 160 U.S.P.Q. 687 (1969), *129*

Ames, In re, 160 U.S.P.Q. 214 (1968), *139*

Anheuser–Busch Inc. v. Stroh Brewery Co., 750 F.2d 631 (8th Cir.1984), *142*

Anti-Communist World Freedom Congress, Inc., In re, 161 U.S.P.Q. (1969), *140*

TABLE OF CASES

Anti–Monopoly, Inc. v. General Mills Fun Group, Inc., 684 F.2d 1316 (9th Cir.1982), *145*

Apple Computer, Inc. v. Franklin Computer Corp., 714 F.2d 1240 (3rd Cir.1983), *234*

Application of (see name of party)

Arnesen v. Raymond Lee Organization, Inc., 333 F.Supp. 116 (D.C.Cal.1971), *357*

Aronson v. Quick Point Pencil Co., 440 U.S. 257, 99 S.Ct. 1096, 59 L.Ed.2d 296 (1979), *21, 309, 320, 329*

A. S. Rampell, Inc. v. Hyster Co., 165 N.Y.S.2d 475, 144 N.E.2d 371 (N.Y.1957), *90, 91, 93*

Associated Press v. International News Service, 245 F. 244 (2nd Cir.1917), *93*

Associated Press v. United States, 326 U.S. 1, 65 S.Ct. 1416, 89 L.Ed. 2013 (1945), *299*

Aunt Jemima Mills Co. v. Rigney & Co., 247 F. 407 (2nd Cir.1917), *167, 168, 169*

Bajpayee v. Rothermich, 53 Ohio App.2d 117, 372 N.E.2d 817, 7 O.O.3d 86 (Ohio App.1977), *204, 295*

Bally/Midway Mfg. Co. v. United States Intern. Trade Com'n, 714 F.2d 1117 (Fed.Cir.1983), *192*

Baltimore Orioles, Inc. v. Major League Baseball Players Ass'n, 805 F.2d 663 (7th Cir.1986), *264*

Bangor Punta Operations, Inc. v. Universal Marine Co., Ltd., 543 F.2d 1107 (5th Cir.1976), *366*

Beardsley v. Kilmer, 236 N.Y. 80, 140 N.E. 203 (N.Y.1923), *1, 10, 59, 60*

Beatrice Foods Co., Application of, 57 C.C.P.A. 1302, 429 F.2d 466 (Cust. & Pat.App.1970), *174*

Bell & Howell: Mamiya Co. v. Masel Supply Co. Corp., 719 F.2d 42 (2nd Cir.1983), *177*

Berlin v. E. C. Publications, Inc., 329 F.2d 541 (2nd Cir.1964), *283*

Bernard Food Industries, Inc. v. Dietene Co., 415 F.2d 1279 (7th Cir.1969), *362*

Big O Tire Dealers, Inc. v. Goodyear Tire & Rubber Co., 561 F.2d 1365 (10th Cir.1977), *196*

Black & Yates v. Mahogany Ass'n, 129 F.2d 227 (3rd Cir.1941), *347*

Blanchard v. Hill, 2 Alk. 484 (1742), *98, 100*

Board of Trade of City of Chicago v. Dow Jones & Co., Inc., 98 Ill.2d 109, 74 Ill.Dec. 582, 456 N.E.2d 84 (Ill.1983), *298*

TABLE OF CASES

Bohsei Enterprises Co. v. Porteous Fastener Co., 441 F.Supp. 162 (D.C.Cal.1977), *364*

Boise Cascade Corp. v. F.T.C., 837 F.2d 1127, 267 U.S.App.D.C. 124 (D.C.Cir.1988), *424*

Bonito Boats, Inc. v. Thunder Craft Boats, Inc., 489 U.S. 141, 109 S.Ct. 971, 103 L.Ed.2d 118 (1989), *21, 294, 299*

Bose Corp. v. Consumers Union of United States, Inc., 466 U.S. 485, 104 S.Ct. 1949, 80 L.Ed.2d 502 (1984), *345*

Boston Professional Hockey Ass'n, Inc. v. Dallas Cap & Emblem Mfg., Inc., 510 F.2d 1004 (5th Cir.1975), *193, 194, 361, 364*

Branch v. F T C, 141 F.2d 31 (7th Cir.1944), *383, 384*

Brimelow v. Casson, 1 Ch. 302 (1923), *85*

Bristol v. Equitable Life Assur. Soc. of United States, 132 N.Y. 264, 30 N.E. 506 (N.Y.1892), *310, 313*

Brown–Forman Distillery Co. v. Arthur M. Bloch Liquor Importers, 99 F.2d 708 (7th Cir.1938), *164*

Brulotte v. Thys Co., 379 U.S. 29, 85 S.Ct. 176, 13 L.Ed.2d 99 (1964), *19, 225*

Burger King of Fla., Inc. v. Hoots, 403 F.2d 904 (7th Cir.1968), *115, 173*

California Apparel Creators v. Wieder of Cal., 162 F.2d 893 (2nd Cir.1947), *352*

California Retail Liquor Dealers Ass'n v. Midcal Aluminum, Inc., 445 U.S. 97, 100 S.Ct. 937, 63 L.Ed.2d 233 (1980), *406*

Canadian Ingersoll–Rand Co. v. D. Loveman & Sons, Inc., 227 F.Supp. 829, 28 O.O.2d 150 (D.C.Ohio 1964), *397*

Carol Barnhart, Inc. v. Economy Cover Corp., 603 F.Supp. 432 (D.C.N.Y.1985), *238*

Carter Products, Inc. v. Colgate–Palmolive Co., 130 F.Supp. 557 (D.C.Md.1955), *326, 327*

Catalina Inc. v. P. Zwetchkenbaum & Sons, Inc., 107 R.I. 444, 267 A.2d 702 (R.I.1970), *409*

Century 21 Real Estate Corp. v. Nevada Real Estate Advisory Commission, 448 F.Supp. 1237 (D.C.Nev.1978), *108*

Chamberlain v. Columbia Pictures Corp., 186 F.2d 923 (9th Cir.1951), *356*

Champion Spark Plug Co. v. Sanders, 331 U.S. 125, 67 S.Ct. 1136, 91 L.Ed. 1386 (1947), *159, 206*

Chaplin v. Amador, 93 Cal.App. 358, 269 P. 544 (Cal.App. 1 Dist.1928), *294*

Charles of the Ritz Distributors Corp. v. F T C, 143 F.2d 676 (2nd Cir.1944), *376, 377, 383*

TABLE OF CASES

Chemical Corp. of America v. Anheuser-Busch, Inc., 306 F.2d 433 (5th Cir.1962), *181*

Cheney Bros. v. Doris Silk Corp., 35 F.2d 279 (2nd Cir.1929), *257*

Chicago Lock Co. v. Fanberg, 676 F.2d 400 (9th Cir.1982), *322*

Ciba-Geigy Corp. v. Bolar Pharmaceutical Co., Inc., 747 F.2d 844 (3rd Cir.1984), *184*

Cincinnati Bell Foundry Co. v. Dodds, 19 Ohio Weekly Law Bull. 84 (1887), *306*

Cliffdale Associates, Inc., 103 F.T.C. 110 (1984), *377*

Clinton E. Worden & Co. v. California Fig Syrup Co., 187 U.S. 516, 23 S.Ct. 161, 47 L.Ed. 282 (1903), *190*

Clothier Case (Southern v. How), 1656 Poph. 144, *98, 100, 101*

Coca-Cola Co. v. Gemini Rising, Inc., 346 F.Supp. 1183 (D.C.N.Y.1972), *182*

Coleman v. Whisnant, 225 N.C. 494, 35 S.E.2d 647 (N.C.1945), *54*

Colgate & Co., United States v., 250 U.S. 300, 39 S.Ct. 465, 63 L.Ed. 992 (1919), *71*

Colligan v. Activities Club of New York, Ltd., 442 F.2d 686 (2nd Cir.1971), *357*

Columbia Broadcasting System, Inc. v. DeCosta, 377 F.2d 315 (1st Cir.1967), *258*

Columbia Pictures Industries, Inc. v. Professional Real Estate Investors, Inc., 866 F.2d 278 (9th Cir.1989), *276*

Columbia Pictures Industries, Inc. v. Redd Horne, Inc., 749 F.2d 154 (3rd Cir.1984), *275*

Committee on Children's Television, Inc. v. General Foods Corp., 197 Cal.Rptr. 783, 673 P.2d 660 (Cal.1983), *371*

Community for Creative Non-Violence v. Reid, 490 U.S. 730, 109 S.Ct. 2166, 104 L.Ed.2d 811 (1989), *243*

Community of Roquefort v. William Faehndrich, Inc., 303 F.2d 494 (2nd Cir.1962), *130*

Compco Corp. v. Day-Brite Lighting, Inc., 376 U.S. 234, 84 S.Ct. 779, 11 L.Ed.2d 669 (1964), *19, 20, 133, 134, 137, 193, 239, 258, 259, 294, 308, 328, 329*

Conmar Products Corp. v. Universal Slide Fastener Co., 172 F.2d 150 (2nd Cir.1949), *328*

Consumers Union of United States, Inc. v. F. T. C., 691 F.2d 575, 223 U.S.App.D.C. 386 (D.C.Cir.1982), *375*

Consumers Union of United States, Inc. v. Theodore Hamm Brewing Co., 314 F.Supp. 697 (D.C.Conn.1970), *349*

Container Corp. of America, United States v., 393 U.S. 333, 89 S.Ct. 510, 21 L.Ed.2d 526 (1969), *429*

TABLE OF CASES

Continental Distilling Corp. v. Old Charter Distillery Co., 188 F.2d 614, 88 U.S.App.D.C. 73 (D.C.Cir.1950), *151*

Cooper, Application of, 45 C.C.P.A. 923, 254 F.2d 611 (Cust. & Pat.App.1958), *138*

Dallas Cowboys Cheerleaders, Inc. v. Pussycat Cinema, Ltd., 604 F.2d 200 (2nd Cir.1979), *182*

David Crystal, Inc., Application of, 49 C.C.P.A. 775, 296 F.2d 771 (Cust. & Pat.App.1961), *148*

Dawn Donut Co. v. Hart's Food Stores, Inc., 267 F.2d 358 (2nd Cir.1959), *152, 173*

Dawson Chemical Co. v. Rohm and Haas Co., 448 U.S. 176, 100 S.Ct. 2601, 65 L.Ed.2d 696 (1980), *301*

Diamond v. Chakrabarty, 447 U.S. 303, 100 S.Ct. 2204, 65 L.Ed.2d 144 (1980), *219*

Diamond v. Diehr, 450 U.S. 175, 101 S.Ct. 1048, 67 L.Ed.2d 155 (1981), *219*

Diamond Match Co v. Saginaw Match Co, 142 F. 727 (6th Cir.1906), *148*

Dickes v. Fenne, 82 Eng.Rep. 411 (1639), *342*

Dior v. Milton, 2 A.D.2d 878, 156 N.Y.S.2d 996 (N.Y.A.D. 1 Dept.1956), *256, 258*

Drop Dead Co. v. S. C. Johnson & Son, Inc., 326 F.2d 87 (9th Cir.1963), *239*

Dun & Bradstreet, Inc. v. Greenmoss Builders, Inc., 472 U.S. 749, 105 S.Ct. 2939, 86 L.Ed.2d 593 (1985), *339*

DuPont Cellophane Co. v. Waxed Products Co., 85 F.2d 75 (2nd Cir.1936), *202*

Duracell, Inc. v. United States Intern. Trade Com'n, 778 F.2d 1578 (Fed.Cir.1985), *179, 390*

Eastern Air Lines, Inc. v. New York Air Lines, Inc., 559 F.Supp. 1270 (D.C.N.Y.1983), *142*

E. I. Du Pont De Nemours & Co., Application of, 476 F.2d 1357 (Cust. & Pat.App.1973), *171*

E. I. duPont deNemours & Co. v. Christopher, 431 F.2d 1012 (5th Cir.1970), *47, 308, 322, 325*

E. I. Du Pont De Nemours Powder Co. v. Masland, 244 U.S. 100, 37 S.Ct. 575, 61 L.Ed. 1016 (1917), *307*

Electronics Corp. of America v. Honeywell, Inc., 428 F.2d 191 (1st Cir.1970), *351*

Ely–Norris Safe Co. v. Mosler Safe Co., 7 F.2d 603 (2nd Cir.1925), *345, 350*

TABLE OF CASES

Emack v. Kane, 34 F. 46 (C.C.Ill.1888), *347*

Encyclopaedia Britannica Educational Corp. v. Crooks, 447 F.Supp. 243 (D.C.N.Y.1978), *278*

Environmental Tectonics v. W.S. Kirkpatrick, Inc., 847 F.2d 1052 (3rd Cir.1988), *397*

Erie R. Co. v. Tompkins, 304 U.S. 64, 58 S.Ct. 817, 82 L.Ed. 1188 (1938), *258*

Esquire, Inc. v. Esquire Slipper Mfg. Co., 243 F.2d 540 (1st Cir.1957), *183*

Esquire, Inc. v. Ringer, 591 F.2d 796, 192 U.S.App.D.C. 187 (D.C.Cir.1978), *238*

Esso, Inc. v. Standard Oil Co., 98 F.2d 1 (8th Cir.1938), *164*

Evenson v. Spaulding, 150 F. 517 (9th Cir.1907), *67*

Ex parte (see name of party)

Exxon Corp. v. Humble Exploration Co., Inc., 695 F.2d 96 (5th Cir.1983), *152, 359*

Factors Etc., Inc. v. Pro Arts, Inc., 652 F.2d 278 (2nd Cir.1981), *267*

Falls City Industries, Inc. v. Vanco Beverage, Inc., 460 U.S. 428, 103 S.Ct. 1282, 75 L.Ed.2d 174 (1983), *430*

Fashion Originators' Guild v. Federal Trade Com'n, 312 U.S. 457, 312 U.S. 668, 61 S.Ct. 703, 85 L.Ed. 949 (1941), *70*

Federal–Mogul–Bower Bearings, Inc. v. Azoff, 313 F.2d 405 (6th Cir.1963), *358, 359*

Feist Publications, Inc. v. Rural Telephone Service Co., Inc., —— U.S. ——, 111 S.Ct. 1282, 113 L.Ed.2d 358 (1991), *233, 235, 237*

Financial Information, Inc. v. Moody's Investors Service, Inc., 808 F.2d 204 (2nd Cir.1986), *237, 261*

First Comics, Inc. v. World Color Press, Inc., 884 F.2d 1033 (7th Cir.1989), *419*

Fisher v. Star Co., 231 N.Y. 414, 132 N.E. 133 (N.Y.1921), *136*

Fitch v. Kentucky–Tennessee Light & Power Co, for Use and Ben of Tri–City Utilities Co, 136 F.2d 12 (6th Cir.1943), *396*

Florida v. Real Juices, Inc., 330 F.Supp. 428 (D.C.Fla.1971), *357*

Florida ex rel. Broward County v. Eli Lilly & Co., 329 F.Supp. 364 (D.C.Fla.1971), *357*

Folk, In re, 160 U.S.P.Q. 213 (1968), *139*

Follett v. Arbor House Publishing Co., 208 U.S.P.Q. 597 (1980), *362*

Food Fair Stores v. Square Deal Market Co., 206 F.2d 482, 93 U.S.App.D.C. 7 (D.C.Cir.1953), *112*

TABLE OF CASES

Fowler v. Curtis Publishing Co., 182 F.2d 377, 86 U.S.App.D.C. 349 (D.C.Cir.1950), *340*

Franklin Knitting Mills V Fashionit Sweater Mills, 297 F. 247 (D.C.N.Y.1923), *120*

Freeman, Application of, 573 F.2d 1237 (Cust. & Pat.App.1978), *219*

Friedman v. Rogers, 440 U.S. 1, 99 S.Ct. 887, 59 L.Ed.2d 100 (1979), *26, 107*

FTC v. A. E. Staley Mfg. Co., 324 U.S. 746, 65 S.Ct. 971, 89 L.Ed. 1338 (1945), *430*

FTC v. Algoma Lumber Co., 291 U.S. 67, 54 S.Ct. 315, 78 L.Ed. 655 (1934), *383*

F. T. C. v. Colgate–Palmolive Co., 380 U.S. 374, 85 S.Ct. 1035, 13 L.Ed.2d 904 (1965), *387*

F.T.C. v. Henry Broch & Company, 363 U.S. 166, 80 S.Ct. 1158, 4 L.Ed.2d 1124 (1960), *432*

FTC v. Klesner, 280 U.S. 19, 50 S.Ct. 1, 74 L.Ed. 138 (1929), *372*

F. T. C. v. Mary Carter Paint Co., 382 U.S. 46, 86 S.Ct. 219, 15 L.Ed.2d 128 (1965), *384*

FTC v. R. F. Keppel & Bro., 291 U.S. 304, 54 S.Ct. 423, 78 L.Ed. 814 (1934), *387, 399*

F. T. C. v. Sperry & Hutchinson Co., 405 U.S. 233, 92 S.Ct. 898, 31 L.Ed.2d 170 (1972), *299, 388*

Garrett v. Taylor, 97 Eng.Rep. 485 (1621), *45, 49*

Gertz v. Robert Welch, Inc., 418 U.S. 323, 94 S.Ct. 2997, 41 L.Ed.2d 789 (1974), *337, 338, 339, 340, 344, 345*

Gilliam v. American Broadcasting Companies, Inc., 538 F.2d 14 (2nd Cir.1976), *207, 274, 360*

Girl Scouts of the United States of America v. Personality Posters Mfg. Co., 304 F.Supp. 1228 (D.C.N.Y.1969), *182, 360*

Glanzer v. Shepard, 233 N.Y. 236, 135 N.E. 275 (N.Y.1922), *51*

Golden State Linen Service, Inc. v. Vidalin, 69 Cal.App.3d 1, 137 Cal.Rptr. 807 (Cal.App. 1 Dist.1977), *80*

Gold Seal Co. v. Weeks, 129 F.Supp. 928 (D.C.D.C.1955), *128*

Goldstein v. California, 412 U.S. 546, 93 S.Ct. 2303, 37 L.Ed.2d 163 (1973), *20, 137, 229, 259, 297, 300*

Gottschalk v. Benson, 409 U.S. 63, 93 S.Ct. 253, 34 L.Ed.2d 273 (1972), *218*

Grand Rapids Furniture Co. v. Grand Rapids Furniture Co., 127 F.2d 245 (7th Cir.1942), *352*

Great Atlantic & Pacific Tea Co. v. Cream of Wheat Co., 227 F. 46 (2nd Cir.1915), *11, 61*

TABLE OF CASES

Great Atlantic & Pacific Tea Co., Inc. v. F. T. C., 440 U.S. 69, 99 S.Ct. 925, 59 L.Ed.2d 153 (1979), *435*

Gregory v. Duke of Brunswick, 134 Eng.Rep. 816 (1843), *46*

Grillo v. Board of Realtors of Plainfield Area, 91 N.J.Super. 202, 219 A.2d 635 (N.J.Super.Ch.1966), *69*

Guerlain, Inc., United States v., 155 F.Supp. 77 (D.C.N.Y.1957), *177*

Haig & Haig, Limited, Ex parte, 118 U.S.P.Q. 229 (1958), *149*

Hales v. Green Colonial, Inc., 490 F.2d 1015 (8th Cir.1974), *87*

Hamilton Nat. Bank v. Belt, 210 F.2d 706, 93 U.S.App.D.C. 168 (D.C.Cir.1953), *310, 314, 317, 318*

Hampton v. Blair Mfg. Co., 374 F.2d 969 (8th Cir.1967), *329*

Hancock v. American Steel & Wire Co. of New Jersey, 40 C.C.P.A. 931, 203 F.2d 737 (Cust. & Pat.App.1953), *164*

Hannigan v. Sears, Roebuck & Co., 410 F.2d 285 (7th Cir.1969), *89, 90*

Harper & Row Publishers, Inc. v. Nation Enterprises, 471 U.S. 539, 105 S.Ct. 2218, 85 L.Ed.2d 588 (1985), *282*

Harris v. Warren & Phillips, 35 RPC 217 (1918), *203*

Hartford House, Ltd. v. Hallmark Cards, Inc., 846 F.2d 1268 (10th Cir.1988), *132*

Harwood Pharmacal Co. v. National Broadcasting Co., 214 N.Y.S.2d 725, 174 N.E.2d 602 (N.Y.1961), *343*

Heiden v. Ray's Inc., 34 Wis.2d 632, 150 N.W.2d 467 (Wis.1967), *409*

Hershey, In re, 171 U.S.P.Q. (1988), *140*

Hirsch v. S. C. Johnson & Son, Inc., 90 Wis.2d 379, 280 N.W.2d 129 (Wis.1979), *127, 264*

Hisel v. Chrysler Corp., 94 F.Supp. 996 (D.C.Mo.1951), *315*

Hoehling v. Universal City Studios, Inc., 618 F.2d 972 (2nd Cir.1980), *237, 279, 300*

Houston Chronicle Pub Co. v. Martin, 64 S.W.2d 816 (Tex.Civ.App.1933), *344*

Hutchinson Technology Inc., In re, 852 F.2d 552 (Fed.Cir.1988), *126*

Hyatt Corp. v. Hyatt Legal Services, 610 F.Supp. 381 (D.C.Ill.1985), *109, 183*

Imperial Ice Co. v. Rossier, 18 Cal.2d 33, 112 P.2d 631 (Cal.1941), *78, 79*

In re (see name of party)

TABLE OF CASES

International Harvester Co., In re, 104 F.T.C. 949 (1984), *381, 389*

International News Service v. Associated Press, 248 U.S. 215, 39 S.Ct. 68, 63 L.Ed. 211 (1918), *8, 204, 214, 256, 257, 258, 260, 294, 295, 296, 298*

International Order of Job's Daughters v. Lindeburg and Co., 633 F.2d 912 (9th Cir.1980), *132, 194*

International Playtex Corp., In re, 153 U.S.P.Q. 377 (TTAB, 1967), *138*

International Telephone & Telegraph Corp., 104 F.T.C. 280 (1984), *423*

Inwood Laboratories, Inc. v. Ives Laboratories, Inc., 456 U.S. 844, 102 S.Ct. 2182, 72 L.Ed.2d 606 (1982), *148, 184*

Jackson v. Stanfield, 137 Ind. 592, 36 N.E. 345 (Ind.1894), *68, 69*

Jacron Sales Co., Inc. v. Sindorf, 276 Md. 580, 350 A.2d 688 (Md.1976), *339*

Jaillet v. Cashman, 235 N.Y. 511, 139 N.E. 714 (N.Y.1923), *51*

John B. Stetson Co. v. Stephen L. Stetson Co., 14 F.Supp. 74 (D.C.N.Y.1936), *202*

J. Truett Payne Co., Inc. v. Chrysler Motors Corp., 451 U.S. 557, 101 S.Ct. 1923, 68 L.Ed.2d 442 (1981), *424, 433*

Katz v. Kapper, 7 Cal.App.2d 1, 44 P.2d 1060 (Cal.App. 2 Dist.1935), *54, 59, 69*

Keeble v. Hicheringill, 103 Eng.Rep. 1127 (1706), *10, 45*

Kellogg Co. v. National Biscuit Co., 305 U.S. 111, 59 S.Ct. 109, 83 L.Ed. 73 (1938), *141, 143*

Kemart Corp. v. Printing Arts Research Lab., Inc., 269 F.2d 375 (9th Cir.1959), *341, 349*

Kewanee Oil Co. v. Bicron Corp., 416 U.S. 470, 94 S.Ct. 1879, 40 L.Ed.2d 315, 69 O.O.2d 235 (1974), *21, 327*

Kewanee Oil Co. v. Bicron Corp., 478 F.2d 1074 (6th Cir.1973), *308, 309, 329*

Kidd v. Horry, 28 F. 773 (C.C.Pa.1886), *346*

King v. Mister Maestro, Inc., 224 F.Supp. 101 (D.C.N.Y.1963), *240*

King-Seeley Thermos Co. v. Aladdin Industries, Inc., 321 F.2d 577 (2nd Cir.1963), *143*

K Mart Corp. v. Cartier, Inc., 486 U.S. 281, 108 S.Ct. 1811, 100 L.Ed.2d 313 (1988), *178*

TABLE OF CASES

Knights of the Ku Klux Klan v. Strayer, 34 F.2d 432 (3rd Cir.1929), *190*

Kroger Co. v. F. T. C., 438 F.2d 1372 (6th Cir.1971), *435*

L' Aiglon Apparel v. Lana Lobell, Inc., 214 F.2d 649 (3rd Cir.1954), *356, 361*

Landsberg v. Scrabble Crossword Game Players, Inc., 802 F.2d 1193 (9th Cir.1986), *314, 319*

Lear, Inc. v. Adkins, 395 U.S. 653, 89 S.Ct. 1902, 23 L.Ed.2d 610 (1969), *225, 309*

Leigh Furniture and Carpet Co. v. Isom, 657 P.2d 293 (Utah 1982), *14, 44, 58*

Leo Silfen, Inc. v. Cream, 328 N.Y.S.2d 423, 278 N.E.2d 636 (N.Y.1972), *325*

Lever Bros. Co. v. United States, 877 F.2d 101, 278 U.S.App.D.C. 166 (D.C.Cir.1989), *178*

Lever Brothers Company v. United States (D.D.C.1992), *178*

Levi Strauss & Co. v. Blue Bell, Inc., 734 F.2d 409 (9th Cir.1984), *150*

Levi Strauss & Co., In re, 165 U.S.P.Q. 348 (1970), *150*

L. E. Waterman Co. v. Gordon, 72 F.2d 272 (2nd Cir.1934), *167*

L.L. Bean, Inc. v. Drake Publishers, Inc., 811 F.2d 26 (1st Cir.1987), *182*

Loew's Inc. v. CBS, 131 F.Supp. 165 (D.C.Cal.1955), aff'd sub nom. Benny v. Loew's Inc., 239 F.2d 532 (1956) *284*

Lugosi v. Universal Pictures, 160 Cal.Rptr. 323, 603 P.2d 425 (Cal.1979), *266*

Lumley v. Gye, 118 Eng.Rep. 749 (1853), *3, 74, 77, 84, 86, 89*

Maidenform, Inc. v. Munsingwear, Inc., 195 U.S.P.Q. 297 (1977), *122*

Maier Brewing Co. v. Fleischmann Distilling Corp., 390 F.2d 117 (9th Cir.1968), *195*

Manhattan Industries, Inc. v. Sweater Bee by Banff, Ltd., 627 F.2d 628 (2nd Cir.1980), *359*

Marcus v. Rowley, 695 F.2d 1171 (9th Cir.1983), *278, 285*

Marlin Firearms Co. v. Shields, 171 N.Y. 384, 64 N.E. 163 (N.Y.1902), *346*

Martin Luther King, Jr., Center for Social Change, Inc. v. American Heritage Products, Inc., 250 Ga. 135, 296 S.E.2d 697 (Ga.1982), *266*

Mazer v. Stein, 347 U.S. 201, 74 S.Ct. 460, 98 L.Ed. 630 (1954), *238*

TABLE OF CASES

McCormick & Co. v. Manischewitz Co., 206 F.2d 744 (6th Cir.1953), *162*

McGregor–Doniger Inc. v. Drizzle Inc., 599 F.2d 1126 (2nd Cir.1979), *170*

McNary v. Chamberlain, 34 Conn. 384 (Conn.1867), *83, 84*

Mead Data Cent., Inc. v. Toyota Motor Sales, U.S.A., Inc., 875 F.2d 1026 (2nd Cir.1989), *181*

Memphis Development Foundation v. Factors Etc., Inc., 616 F.2d 956 (6th Cir.1980), *266*

Metropolitan Opera Ass'n v. Wagner–Nichols Recorder Corp., 279 A.D. 632, 107 N.Y.S.2d 795 (N.Y.A.D. 1 Dept.1951), *294*

Metropolitan Opera Ass'n v. Wagner–Nichols Recorder Corp., 199 Misc. 786, 101 N.Y.S.2d 483 (N.Y.Sup.1950), *256, 258*

Meyerson v. Hurlbut, 98 F.2d 232 (D.C.Cir.1938), *343*

Midler v. Ford Motor Co., 849 F.2d 460 (9th Cir.1988), *265*

Miller Brewing Co. v. G. Heileman Brewing Co., Inc., 561 F.2d 75 (7th Cir.1977), *141*

Milwaukee Linen Supply Co. v. Ring, 210 Wis. 467, 246 N.W. 567 (Wis.1933), *80*

Minnesota Min. & Mfg. Co. v. Johnson and Johnson, 59 C.C.P.A. 971, 454 F.2d 1179 (Cust. & Pat.App.1972), *120, 122, 123*

Minnesota Mining & Mfg. Co., Ex parte, 92 U.S.P.Q. 74 (1952), *138, 146*

Mirage Editions, Inc. v. Albuquerque A.R.T. Co., 856 F.2d 1341 (9th Cir.1988), *272, 274*

M. Miller Co. v. Central Contra Costa Sanitary Dist., 198 Cal.App.2d 305, 18 Cal.Rptr. 13 (Cal.App. 1 Dist.1961), *51*

Mogen David Wine Corp., Application of, 54 C.C.P.A. 1086, 372 F.2d 539 (Cust. & Pat.App.1967), *149*

Mohawk Maintenance Co., Inc. v. Kessler, 437 N.Y.S.2d 646, 419 N.E.2d 324 (N.Y.1981), *82*

Montgomery v. Thompson, A.C. 217 (1891), *165*

Morseburg v. Balyon, 621 F.2d 972 (9th Cir.1980), *244*

Morton–Norwich Products, Inc., In re, 671 F.2d 1332 (Cust. & Pat.App.1982), *132*

Mosler Safe Co. v. Ely–Norris Safe Co., 273 U.S. 132, 47 S.Ct. 314, 71 L.Ed. 578 (1927), *351*

Motschenbacher v. R. J. Reynolds Tobacco Co., 498 F.2d 821 (9th Cir.1974), *265*

Munn v. Illinois, 94 U.S. 113, 24 L.Ed. 77 (1876), *403*

Murray v. National Broadcasting Co., Inc., 844 F.2d 988 (2nd Cir.1988), *319*

Mutation Mink Breeders Ass'n v. Lou Nierenberg Corp., 23 F.R.D. 155 (D.C.N.Y.1959), *356, 361*

TABLE OF CASES

Nantucket, Inc., In re, 677 F.2d 95 (Cust. & Pat.App.1982), *130*

Nashville Milk Co. v. Carnation Company, 355 U.S. 373, 78 S.Ct. 352, 2 L.Ed.2d 340 (1958), *412*

National Dairy Products Corp., United States v., 372 U.S. 29, 83 S.Ct. 594, 9 L.Ed.2d 561 (1963), *412, 413, 414*

National Petroleum Refiners Ass'n v. F. T. C., 482 F.2d 672, 157 U.S.App.D.C. 83 (D.C.Cir.1973), *372*

National Refining Co. v. Benzo Gas Motor Fuel Co., 20 F.2d 763 (8th Cir.1927), *342, 343*

Near v. Minnesota, 283 U.S. 697, 51 S.Ct. 625, 75 L.Ed. 1357 (1931), *346*

Nebbia v. New York, 291 U.S. 502, 54 S.Ct. 505, 78 L.Ed. 940 (1934), *403, 404*

New York Good Humor, Inc. v. Standard Commercial Body Corporation, 145 Misc. 752, 260 N.Y.S. 167 (N.Y.Sup.1932), *149*

New York Times Co. v. Sullivan, 376 U.S. 254, 84 S.Ct. 710, 11 L.Ed.2d 686 (1964), *337, 338, 340, 344, 345*

Nuodex Products Co., Ex parte, 107 U.S.P.Q. 300 (1966), *149*

NutraSweet Co. v. Stadt Corp., 917 F.2d 1024 (7th Cir.1990), *148*

Orkin Exterminating Co., Inc. v. F.T.C., 849 F.2d 1354 (11th Cir.1988), *388, 389*

Oscar Mayer & Co., Ex parte, 47 U.S.P.Q. 234 (1940), *149*

Owens–Corning Fiberglas Corp., In re, 774 F.2d 1116 (Fed.Cir.1985), *148*

Pacific and Southern Co., Inc. v. Duncan, 744 F.2d 1490 (11th Cir.1984), *283*

Paine, Webber, Jackson & Curtis, Inc. v. Merrill Lynch, Pierce, Fenner & Smith, Inc., 564 F.Supp. 1358 (D.C.Del.1983), *219*

Parker v. Flook, 437 U.S. 584, 98 S.Ct. 2522, 57 L.Ed.2d 451 (1978), *218*

Park 'N Fly, Inc. v. Dollar Park and Fly, Inc., 469 U.S. 189, 105 S.Ct. 658, 83 L.Ed.2d 582 (1985), *187*

Pasley v. Freeman, 100 Eng.Rep. 450 (1789), *49, 50*

Pavesich v. New England Life Ins., 122 Ga. 190, 50 S.E. 68 (Ga.1905), *262, 263*

Peabody v. Norfolk, 98 Mass. 452 (1868), *304, 305, 308, 313*

Perkins v. Standard Oil Co. of Cal., 395 U.S. 642, 89 S.Ct. 1871, 23 L.Ed.2d 599 (1969), *420*

Perma–Maid Co. v. F T C, 121 F.2d 282 (6th Cir.1941), *347*

Perry Manufacturing Co., In re, (1989), *130*

TABLE OF CASES

Pfizer, Inc. [1970 73 Transfer Binder] CCH Trade Reg.Rep. para. 20056 (1972), *378*

Pillsbury–Washburn Flour Mills Co. v. Eagle, 86 F. 608 (7th Cir.1898), *352*

Pittsburgh Athletic Co. v. KQV Broadcasting Co., 24 F.Supp. 490 (D.C.Pa.1938), *295*

Polaroid Corp. v. Polarad Elec. Corp,, 287 F.2d 492 (2nd Cir.1961), *170, 171*

Polaroid Corp. v. Polaraid, Inc., 319 F.2d 830 (7th Cir.1963), *181*

Prestonettes, Inc. v. Coty, 264 U.S. 359, 44 S.Ct. 350, 68 L.Ed. 731 (1924), *159*

Price v. Hal Roach Studios, Inc., 400 F.Supp. 836 (D.C.N.Y.1975), *265*

Radio Corp of America v. Decca Records, 51 F.Supp. 493 (D.C.N.Y.1943), *148*

Rangen, Inc. v. Sterling Nelson & Sons, Inc., 351 F.2d 851 (9th Cir.1965), *396*

Reed, Roberts Associates, Inc. v. Strauman, 386 N.Y.S.2d 677, 353 N.E.2d 590 (N.Y.1976), *80*

Religious Technology Center v. Wollersheim, 796 F.2d 1076 (9th Cir.1986), *316*

Richemond, In re, 131 U.S.P.Q. 441 (1961), *129*

Rickard v. Auto Publisher, Inc., 735 F.2d 450 (11th Cir.1984), *366*

Rivera Watch Corp., Ex parte, 106 U.S.P.Q. 145 (1955), *126*

Roberts v. Sears, Roebuck & Co., 573 F.2d 976 (7th Cir.1978), *91, 225, 309*

Robins Dry Dock & Repair Co. v. Flint, 275 U.S. 303, 48 S.Ct. 134, 72 L.Ed. 290 (1927), *48*

Rosemont Enterprises, Inc. v. Random House, Inc., 366 F.2d 303 (2nd Cir.1966), *282*

Ruckelshaus v. Monsanto Co., 467 U.S. 986, 104 S.Ct. 2862, 81 L.Ed.2d 815 (1984), *306, 307*

Runsdorf, In re, 171 U.S.P.Q. (1971), *140*

Safeway Stores, Inc. v. Oklahoma Retail Grocers Ass'n, 360 U.S. 334, 79 S.Ct. 1196, 3 L.Ed.2d 1280 (1959), *400*

Sambo's Restaurants, Inc. v. Ann Arbor, 663 F.2d 686 (6th Cir.1981), *108*

Saul Steinberg v. Columbia Pictures Industries, Inc., 663 F.Supp. 706 (S.D.N.Y.1987), *279*

Schoolmaster's Case, Y.B.Hen. IV, f, pL. 21 (1410), *3*

TABLE OF CASES

Scientific Mfg. Co. v. FTC, 124 F.2d 640 (3rd Cir.1941), *347*

S. C. Johnson & Son v. Johnson, 175 F.2d 176 (2nd Cir.1949), *169*

S. C. Johnson & Son v. Johnson, 116 F.2d 427 (2nd Cir.1940), *168*

Sears, Roebuck & Co. v. Stiffel Co., 376 U.S. 225, 84 S.Ct. 784, 11 L.Ed.2d 661 (1964), *19, 20, 133, 134, 137, 193, 239, 258, 259, 294, 308, 328, 329*

Seats, Inc., In re, 757 F.2d 274 (Fed.Cir.1985), *142*

Shamhart v. Morrison Cafeteria Co., 159 Fla. 629, 32 So.2d 727 (Fla.1947), *47*

Shellmar Products Co. v. Allen–Qualley Co., 87 F.2d 104 (7th Cir.1936), *328*

Siegel v. Chicken Delight, Inc., 448 F.2d 43 (9th Cir.1971), *156*

Singer Mfg. Co. v. Briley, 207 F.2d 519 (5th Cir.1953), *145*

Singer Mfg. Co. v. June Mfg. Co., 163 U.S. 169, 16 S.Ct. 1002, 41 L.Ed. 118 (1896), *144*

Skil Corp. v. Rockwell Intern. Corp., 375 F.Supp. 777 (D.C.Ill.1974), *363*

Smith v. Chanel, Inc., 402 F.2d 562 (9th Cir.1968), *160*

Smith v. Dravo Corp., 203 F.2d 369 (7th Cir.1953), *314, 318*

Smith v. Snap–On Tools Corp., 833 F.2d 578 (5th Cir.1987), *315*

Societe Comptoir De L'Industrie Cotonniere Etablissements Boussac v. Alexander's Dept. Stores, Inc., 299 F.2d 33 (2nd Cir.1962), *363*

Sony Corp. of America v. Universal City Studios, Inc., 464 U.S. 417, 104 S.Ct. 774, 78 L.Ed.2d 574 (1984), *283*

Southern v. How, 79 Eng.Rep. 1243 (1619), *98*

Standard Paint Co v. Trinidad Asphalt Mfg Co, 220 U.S. 446, 31 S.Ct. 456, 55 L.Ed. 536 (1911), *104*

State of (see name of state)

Stephen Jay Photography, Ltd. v. Olan Mills, Inc., 903 F.2d 988 (4th Cir.1990), *396*

Sterling Brewers, Inc. v. Schenley Industries, Inc., 58 C.C.P.A. 1172, 441 F.2d 675 (Cust. & Pat.App.1971), *152*

Stevenson v. East Ohio Gas Co., 73 N.E.2d 200 (Ohio App.1946), *48*

Sutliff, Inc. v. Donovan Companies, Inc., 727 F.2d 648 (7th Cir.1984), *367*

Syntex Laboratories, Inc. v. Norwich Pharmacal Co., 437 F.2d 566 (2nd Cir.1971), *163*

Tabor v. Hoffman, 118 N.Y. 30, 23 N.E. 12 (N.Y.1889), *307, 308, 318, 321*

TABLE OF CASES

Tarleton v. McGawley, 170 Eng.Rep. 153 (1793), *46*

Taylor Wine Co., Inc. v. Bully Hill Vineyards, Inc., 569 F.2d 731 (2nd Cir.1978), *193*

Testing Systems, Inc. v. Magnaflux Corp., 251 F.Supp. 286 (D.C.Pa.1966), *349*

Texaco, Inc. v. Hasbrouck, 496 U.S. 543, 110 S.Ct. 2535, 110 L.Ed.2d 492 (1990), *425, 427*

Texas & P. Ry. Co. v. Mercer, 127 Tex. 220, 90 S.W.2d 557 (Tex.Com.App.1936), *47*

Thompson Medical Co., Inc. v. F.T.C., 791 F.2d 189, 253 U.S.App.D.C. 18 (D.C.Cir.1986), *379*

Thorn v. Reliance Van Co., Inc., 736 F.2d 929 (3rd Cir.1984), *357*

Trade-Mark Cases, In re, 100 U.S. 82, 25 L.Ed. 550 (1879), *22, 23, 229*

Triangle Publications, Inc. v. Knight-Ridder Newspapers, Inc., 626 F.2d 1171 (5th Cir.1980), *281*

Triangle Publications, Inc. v. Rohrlich, 167 F.2d 969 (2nd Cir.1948), *170*

Truck Equipment Service Co. v. Fruehauf Corp., 536 F.2d 1210 (8th Cir.1976), *193*

Tuttle v. Buck, 107 Minn. 145, 119 N.W. 946 (Minn.1909), *14, 59, 60*

Ultramares Corporation v. Touche, 255 N.Y. 170, 174 N.E. 441 (N.Y.1931), *50*

Union Oil Co. v. Oppen, 501 F.2d 558 (9th Cir.1974), *48*

United States v. ____(see opposing party)

United States Brewers' Ass'n, Inc. v. Nebraska, 192 Neb. 328, 220 N.W.2d 544 (Neb.1974), *65*

United States Golf Ass'n v. St. Andrews Systems, Data-Max, Inc., 749 F.2d 1028 (3rd Cir.1984), *146, 297, 360*

United States Gypsum Co., United States v., 438 U.S. 422, 98 S.Ct. 2864, 57 L.Ed.2d 854 (1978), *430*

United States Healthcare, Inc. v. Blue Cross of Greater Philadelphia, 898 F.2d 914 (3rd Cir.1990), *340, 345*

United Stations of N. J. (United States) v. Kingsley, 99 N.J.Super. 574, 240 A.2d 702 (N.J.Super.Ch.1968), *399*

Universal City Studios, Inc. v. Sony Corp. of America, 429 F.Supp. 407 (D.C.Cal.1977), *364*

University of Georgia Athletic Ass'n v. Laite, 756 F.2d 1535 (11th Cir.1985), *165*

TABLE OF CASES

Van Products Co. v. General Welding & Fabricating Co., 419 Pa. 248, 213 A.2d 769 (Pa.1965), *318*

Vault Corp. v. Quaid Software Ltd., 847 F.2d 255 (5th Cir.1988), *275*

Virginia State Bd. of Pharmacy v. Virginia Citizens Consumer Council, Inc., 425 U.S. 748, 96 S.Ct. 1817, 48 L.Ed.2d 346 (1976), *25, 183, 340, 348, 404*

Wallace Intern. Silversmiths, Inc. v. Godinger Silver Art Co., Inc., 735 F.Supp. 141 (S.D.N.Y.1990), *146*

Walter, Application of, 618 F.2d 758 (Cust. & Pat.App.1980), *219*

Waring v. WDAS Broadcasting Station, 327 Pa. 433, 194 A. 631 (Pa.1937), *256, 258*

Wear-Ever Aluminum, Inc. v. Townecraft Industries, Inc., 75 N.J.Super. 135, 182 A.2d 387 (N.J.Super.Ch.1962), *92*

Weil Ceramics and Glass, Inc. v. Dash, 878 F.2d 659 (3rd Cir.1989), *178*

Weiner King, Inc. v. Wiener King Corp., 615 F.2d 512 (Cust. & Pat.App.1980), *175*

Werts Novelty Co. v. Chandler, 30 F.Supp. 774 (D.C.Mo.1939), *190*

West Pub. Co. v. Mead Data Cent., Inc., 799 F.2d 1219 (8th Cir.1986), *237*

West Pub. Co. v. Mead Data Cent., Inc., 616 F.Supp. 1571 (D.C.Minn.1985), *282*

Wexler v. Greenberg, 399 Pa. 569, 160 A.2d 430 (Pa.1960), *316, 324*

Whelan Associates, Inc. v. Jaslow Dental Laboratory, Inc., 797 F.2d 1222 (3rd Cir.1986), *237*

White v. Mellin, A.C. 154 (1895), *348*

White Tower System v. White Castle System of Eating Houses Corp, 90 F.2d 67 (6th Cir.1937), *149*

William Inglis & Sons Baking Co. v. ITT Continental Baking Co., Inc., 668 F.2d 1014 (9th Cir.1981), *423*

Williams & Wilkins Co. v. United States, 203 Ct.Cl. 74, 487 F.2d 1345 (Ct.Cl.1973), *284*

World of Sleep, Inc. v. La-Z-Boy Chair Co., 756 F.2d 1467 (10th Cir.1985), *433*

Yale Elec. Corp. v. Robertson, 26 F.2d 972 (2nd Cir.1928), *167, 168, 169*

Yameta Co. v. Capitol Records, Inc., 279 F.Supp. 582 (D.C.N.Y.1968), *362*

TABLE OF CASES

Yellow Cab Co. v. Creasman, 185 N.C. 551, 117 S.E. 787 (N.C.1923), *149*

Yovatt v. Winyard, 1 Jac & W. 394 (1820), *311*

Zacchini v. Scripps–Howard Broadcasting Co., 433 U.S. 562, 97 S.Ct. 2849, 53 L.Ed.2d 965 (1977), *26, 263, 264, 300*

Zatarains, Inc. v. Oak Grove Smokehouse, Inc., 698 F.2d 786 (5th Cir.1983), *122*

TABLE OF STATUTES

UNITED STATES

UNITED STATES CONSTITUTION

Art.	This Work Page
I, § 8	211
Amend.	
1	25
	26
	107
	137
	182
	183
	236
	299
	300
	303
	340
	341
5	306
	307
13	96
14	25

UNITED STATES CODE ANNOTATED

7 U.S.C.A.—Agriculture

Sec.	This Work Page
2401 et seq.	220

TABLE OF STATUTES

UNITED STATES CODE ANNOTATED

15 U.S.C.A.—Commerce and Trade

Sec.	This Work Page
1—2	56
13 et seq.	414
13a	411
78 et seq.	398
115	273
1051	116
1051—1127	104
1052(a)	127
	128
	140
1052(c)	127
1052(d)	114
	140
1052(e)	120
	125
	128
1052(f)	121
	124
1057	116
1064	186
1064(c)	141
	145
1064(e)	130
1065	114
	186
1065(4)	157
1114	161
1115—1116	187
1115(b)	187
	189
	190
1117	194
	195
1121a	108
1124	114
	176
	192
1125	114

TABLE OF STATUTES

UNITED STATES CODE ANNOTATED
15 U.S.C.A.—Commerce and Trade

Sec.	This Work Page
1125(a)	208
	354
1126	116
	117
1127	139
	146
	152
	357
	358
1221	64
1331 et seq.	382
1609	188
2801—2841	64

17 U.S.C.A.—Copyrights

Sec.	This Work Page
101 et seq.	213
	230
102	234
106	272
106A	272
108	273
110	276
111	276
116	276
203(a)	311
204(a)	244
205	244
401	241
901 et seq.	214
901(a)(5)	255
901(a)(7)	293
901(a)(8)	293
901(b)	288
902	248
	251
	252

TABLE OF STATUTES

UNITED STATES CODE ANNOTATED
17 U.S.C.A.—Copyrights

Sec.	This Work Page
902 (Cont'd)	253
902(a)	248
902(a)(1)	251
902(a)(2)	252
	253
902(b)	250
902(b)(1)	291
902(b)(2)	291
902(c)	250
904	285
905	285
905(1)	286
	288
905(2)	288
905(3)	288
	289
906(a)	290
	291
906(a)(2)	291
906(b)	289
907	292
908	255
908(a)	255
908(e)	255
909	255
909(a)	293
914(a)	253

18 U.S.C.A.—Crimes and Criminal Procedure

Sec.	This Work Page
1341	367
1343	367
1961—1968	366
2320	113
	191

TABLE OF STATUTES

UNITED STATES CODE ANNOTATED
19 U.S.C.A.—Customs and Duties

Sec.	This Work Page
1202 et seq.	436
1303	438
1317	437
1337	192
	302
	389
	438
1526	176
2411 et seq.	32

35 U.S.C.A.—Patents

Sec.	This Work Page
100	217
102(b)	221
119	223
172	223
261	226
271(a)—(c)	269
271(d)	301
271(e)	271
271(f)	270
271(g)	270

STATUTES AT LARGE

Year	This Work Page
1975, Dec. 12, P.L. 94–415, 89 Stat. 801	405
1980, Dec. 12, P.L. 96–517, 94 Stat. 3015	230
	234

TABLE OF STATUTES

POPULAR NAME ACTS

CLAYTON ACT

Sec.	This Work Page
2	414
	415
	420
2(a)	415
	417
	419
	420
	431
	433
	435
	436
2(a)—(e)	416
2(b)	415
2(c)	395
	396
	397
	415
	431
	432
	433
2(d)	415
	432
	433
2(e)	415
	432
	433
2(f)	416
4	412

COPYRIGHT ACT OF 1976

Sec.	This Work Page
101	243
102	250
	262
102(a)	231

TABLE OF STATUTES

COPYRIGHT ACT OF 1976

Sec.	This Work Page
102(b)	234
	236
	250
	251
	299
103	235
	262
104	242
	252
106	286
107	277
	280
	281
109	274
	275
109(a)	289
109(b)	274
116	246
116A	246
117	234
	275
201(a)	242
201(b)	243
301	19
	261
301(a)	260
	264
301(b)	260
	261
501(a)	302

FEDERAL TRADE COMMISSION ACT

Sec.	This Work Page
2	289
5	368
	369
	370
	383

TABLE OF STATUTES

FEDERAL TRADE COMMISSION ACT

Sec.	This Work Page
5 (Cont'd)	397
	435
12	369
18	372
	373

LANHAM ACT

Sec.	This Work Page
2(a)	127
	128
	140
2(c)	127
2(d)	114
	122
	123
	140
2(e)	120
	122
	123
	125
	128
	141
2(f)	121
	123
14	186
14(3)	141
	144
	145
	157
14(5)	130
	153
15	114
	186
15(4)	157
19	188
23	127
32	161
	178

XLIV

TABLE OF STATUTES

LANHAM ACT

Sec.	This Work Page
33	189
33(b)	187
	189
	190
34	187
34(a)	366
35	187
	194
	195
35(a)	366
36	366
39a	108
42	114
	176
	178
	179
	192
43	114
43(a)	23
	146
	184
	193
	208
	333
	354
	355
	356
	358
	359
	360
	361
	362
	363
	364
	365
	366
	390
44	114
45	105
	127

XLV

TABLE OF STATUTES

LANHAM ACT

Sec.	This Work Page
45 (Cont'd)	146
	358
	359

MODEL STATE TRADEMARK ACT

Sec.	This Work Page
12	179

PATENT ACT

Sec.	This Work Page
271	288
	289

ROBINSON–PATMAN ACT

Sec.	This Work Page
2	434
2(a)	424
	426
	427
	428
	434
2(a)—2(f)	416
2(b)	426
	428
	430
	435
2(c)	434
	435
2(d)	435
2(e)	435
2(f)	434
	435
3	408
	411
	412

TABLE OF STATUTES

ROBINSON–PATMAN ACT

Sec.	This Work Page
3 (Cont'd)	413
	414
	416
	435

SHERMAN ACT

Sec.	This Work Page
2	422
	423

TARIFF ACT

Sec.	This Work Page
303	438
337	179
	192
	302
	303
	389
	390
	438
526	176
	177
	178

TRADE ACT OF 1974

Sec.	This Work Page
301	32

UNIFORM COMMERCIAL CODE

Sec.	This Work Page
1–203	83

TABLE OF STATUTES

STATUTES

WEST'S ANNOTATED CALIFORNIA BUSINESS AND PROFESSIONS CODE

Sec.	This Work Page
16601	81

WEST'S ANNOTATED CALIFORNIA CIVIL CODE

Sec.	This Work Page
990	266
	267

NEW YORK, MCKINNEY'S CIVIL RIGHTS LAW

Sec.	This Work Page
50–51	262
	263

FEDERAL RULES OF CIVIL PROCEDURE

Sec.	This Work Page
52(a)	345

CODE OF FEDERAL REGULATIONS

Tit.	This Work Page
16, § 255.1	385
19, § 133.21	177
37, § 1.14	318
37, § 202.19(e)	312
37, § 202.20(c)(2)(vi)	312
37, § 202.20(c)(2)(vii)	312

TABLE OF STATUTES

FEDERAL REGISTER

Vol.	This Work Page
43, p. 17967	371
43, p. 36973	397
49, p. 31000	379

UNFAIR TRADE PRACTICES
IN A NUTSHELL

Third Edition

*

CHAPTER ONE

INTRODUCTION TO THE LAW OF UNFAIR TRADE PRACTICES

Suppose that a patent medicine manufacturer, incensed by a local newspaper's constant ridicule of its medicine, establishes a rival newspaper with a similar name and tabloid layout, copies the other paper's stories, lures away the other newspaper's employees, advertisers and subscribers with offers of higher wages and lower advertising and subscription rates (all of which it plans to rescind once its purpose is accomplished), and finally succeeds in running its critic out of business. Has the patent medicine manufacturer engaged in any unfair trade practices for which the owners of the defunct newspaper may seek legal redress? Or has the manufacturer merely responded in a permissible way to the newspaper's attack? For that matter, could the defunct newspaper be said to have engaged in an unfair trade practice by constantly ridiculing the medicine and its manufacturer?

This embellished statement of the facts in *Beardsley v. Kilmer* (1923) illustrates the principal topics that will be covered in this book—namely, interference with prospective and existing contractual relations (Part I), product, service and business identification (Part II), appropriation of intangible trade values (Part III) and injurious promotional and pricing practices (Part IV).

The body of law which deals with these subjects is drawn from a variety of sources. So diverse are these sources that at first glance the law of unfair trade practices appears not to be a coherent body of law at all, but rather a patchwork of miscellaneous legal materials having as much in common with other bodies of law as with each other.

A. SOURCES OF THE LAW OF UNFAIR TRADE PRACTICES

1. COMMON–LAW SOURCES

The law of unfair trade practices is of both common-law (i.e., judicial) and statutory origin. The common law of unfair trade practices—variously known as commercial tort law or the common law of unfair competition—affords businesses a private judicial remedy for various types of interference with trade relations. As such, it is but a part of a larger body of tort law concerned with protecting advantageous relations in general from harm.

The common law of unfair trade practices developed piecemeal. Early English common law was at first wholly preoccupied with maintaining the physical security of persons and property and did not protect trade or other relations as such or provide remedies for purely pecuniary harm. Parties to a trade relation could only claim protection from direct physical injuries and threats of same to their persons or direct trespasses to their property. In the seminal *Schoolmaster's Case* [1410] for example, two schoolmasters were held to have no cause of action for nuisance when a third schoolmaster opened a new school in competition with the plaintiffs and apparently attracted students at the expense of plaintiffs by cutting fees. While the case has subsequently been cited as having established a common-law privilege of competition, it is probably equally accurately viewed as a simple judicial refusal to consider claims of pecuniary harm in the absence of some direct or indirect physical injury.

Gradually, just as the law of contracts emerged to prevent parties to trade and other advantageous relations from being economically harmed by the breach of promises made by the other party to the relation, so there emerged a body of tort law which protected parties to trade and other advantageous relations from economically injurious interference by third parties. This body of tort law may be divided into that which developed in order to protect advantageous relations generally and that which developed in order to protect trade relations as such.

a. Tortious Interference With Advantageous Relations Generally

Relational interests were first protected through the simple expedient of expanding the scope of protection afforded persons and property. The first step in that expansion was the law of nuisance, which protected persons and property from direct and indirect physical interference causing only pecuniary harm.

Just as the law of torts protected persons and property from direct and indirect physical interference, so it protected them from various forms of injurious speech. In addition to protecting persons from threats and verbal harassment, the courts also provided remedies for deception and falsehood. The courts early developed two distinct forms of protection against such misconduct. They protected persons who were deceived to their physical or economic detriment and they protected persons who were likely to suffer economic harm as a result of defamatory or disparaging statements made to others.

In addition to the foregoing prohibitions against specific types of physical and verbal interference, the courts in the nineteenth century became concerned with protecting contractual relations in particular from virtually any active intentional interference and with protecting advantageous relations in general from certain specified non-physical and non-deceptive interference. Out of this two-fold concern grew, on the one hand, a general prohibition against interference with contractual or confidential relations, and, on the other, a general prohibition against coercion, conspiracy and invasion of privacy.

The English and American courts came to view contractual relations of all kinds as a kind of property, any intentional interference with which was prohibited as "malicious," even where there were sound commercial reasons for the interference. Equity courts in the nineteenth century became particularly concerned with protecting relationships of trust or confidence and preventing the unauthorized use or disclosure of any writings or secrets which were confidentially disclosed in the course of such relations. Out of such grants of equitable relief grew the common law of copyright and trade secrets.

In the twentieth century, American courts for the first time recognized the tort of invasion of privacy. Included under that heading are both intrusive invasions of privacy, such as eavesdropping, wiretapping and other forms of covert surveillance, and invasions by publication of certain injurious or privileged information, including the unauthorized use of another's name or likeness for a commercial purpose.

b. Unfair Competition

Beyond the protection afforded advantageous relations generally, English and American courts also concerned themselves with the protection of trade relations specifically. Thus emerged what has come to be called the law of unfair competition.

The term "unfair competition" first came into use, not to describe any of the previously mentioned types of misconduct—which, after all, could be engaged in by non-commercial as well as commercial parties—but in a number of early cases involving attempts by one merchant to palm off inferior goods as those of another more reputable merchant by making deceptive use of the other merchant's trademark.

(1) Palming Off and Trademark Infringement

Although the earliest form of palming off consisted of the deceptive use of another merchant's mark, the courts soon realized that palming off could be accomplished by other deceptive means as well, such as the deceptive substitution or alteration of goods requested by a customer. At the same time, certain particularly distinctive trademarks, termed technical trademarks, came to be thought of as a form of intangible property, protected by equity courts against infringement, whether or not there was any fraudulent intent on the part of a subsequent user of the mark or any actual diversion of a merchant's customers. Consequently, the tort of trademark infringement came to be distinguished from the tort of palming off (or unfair competition as it came to be called in the United States). Palming off and unfair competition came to be associated primarily with the deceptive substitution or alteration of goods and the deceptive imitation of product and business features whose identifying function was more or less secondary to some other commercial function.

Actually, the term "unfair competition" is an unfortunate one, for it inaccurately implies that palming off necessarily consists of interference by a competitor. In a stratified distributive chain, however, palming off claims more often than not are brought by manufacturers seeking to prevent retailers or wholesalers, whether in competition with the manufacturer's customers or not, from injuring the manufacturer's consumer relations by palming off inferior quality goods as those of the manufacturer.

Inaccurate though it is, the term "unfair competition" has nevertheless become firmly entrenched in the American legal lexicon. Indeed, in the twentieth century, the law of unfair competition has expanded well beyond the older nominate torts of trademark infringement and palming off. Some courts, for example, have applied the term to commercial instances of interference with contractual relations and trade disparagement. Still more courts have applied the term to the distinctly twentieth century commercial tort of misappropriation and the earlier developed but more amorphous tort of malicious competition.

(2) Misappropriation

The tort of misappropriation originated in *International News Service v. Associated Press* (1918). Representing the culmination of an era in which the Supreme Court fashioned general principles of common law for use in federal diversity-of-citizenship cases, the *INS* decision held that one news service engaged in unfair competition when it copied or paraphrased another service's uncopyrighted stories as they were published on the east coast of the United States and then used those stories to compete with the other service on the west coast.

The Court in *INS* characterized the defendant's misconduct as the converse of palming off: "Instead of selling its own goods as those of the complainant, it substituted misappropriation in place of misrepresentation, and sells complainant's goods as its own." While recognizing that uncopyrighted news matter could not be owned in any absolute sense after its first publication, the Court concluded that, because it could not be gathered without a considerable investment of labor, skill and money, it was to be regarded as quasi-property. The Court went on to define the tort of misappropriation as the diversion of profits from those who have earned them to those who have not—or more poetically as attempting to reap where one has not sown, thereby appropriating the harvest of those who have sown.

The principal distinguishing characteristic of the type of misappropriation recognized in the INS case is that it is not concerned with protecting contractual or confidential relations to which the misappropriator is a party; nor is it concerned with preventing public confusion as to the identity of goods or public disclosure of non-public information. The wrong is simply the appropriation of the fruits of another's investment of money, time and intellectual effort. The nominate tort of misappropriation may thus be viewed as an expansion of the concept underlying the older tort of conversion. It would be indistinguishable from that tort were it not for the fact that conversion was initially limited to the appropriation of chattels, a tangible form of property whose rules of ownership are well-settled. Misappropriation, by contrast, involves the appropriation of intangible values whose capacity for ownership is still in dispute. Indeed, as time has worn on, the dispute has sharpened as the highly individualistic labor theory of property implicit in the law of misappropriation has given way to a social utility theory, which would grant or deny a private right to the exclusive use of an intangible value only after weighing the extent to which the grant or denial of such a right will redound to the benefit of the public as a whole.

(3) Malicious Competition

Having extended the concept of unfair competition beyond trademark infringement and palming off to the tort of misappropriation (and to a lesser extent to the torts of trade disparagement and interference with contractual relations), the courts ultimately came to apply the term as well to commercial instances of pecuniary interference constituting a private or public nuisance. The law of nuisance, in the meantime, had begun condemning not only threats or physical violence, but virtually any purely malicious or predatory conduct—i.e., otherwise lawful conduct undertaken purely for the purpose of injuring another.

The classic example of malicious nuisance is to be found in cases prohibiting the erection or ordering the removal of a residential "spite" fence, whose only purpose is to block another's light and air, but the principle has commercial applications as well. In *Keeble v. Hickeringill* (1706), for example, where the commercial trapper of wild fowl was held to have a cause of action against a person who discharged guns nearby, the court emphasized that the guns were discharged "maliciously"—by which it apparently meant purely for the purpose of scaring away the wild fowl. The court indicated in dictum that had the defendant set up his own decoys for the purpose of competing with the plaintiff, no action would lie. (We are left to wonder what the court would have done had the gun been being used to hunt rather than scare the wildfowl).

Because of the public interest in encouraging competition, the courts have been reluctant to condemn competitive conduct which is undertaken partly for legitimate business reasons and partly for vindictive, or spiteful ones. See, e.g., *Beardsley v. Kilmer* (1923) (holding a patent medicine manufacturer's successful effort to run out of business a newspaper critical of its medicine not to be actionable). Consequently, they have held that, in order to be actionable, otherwise lawful commercial activity must have been undertaken solely, or at least primarily, for a malicious or predatory purpose. The normal commercial activity of a single business operating under competitive conditions will thus be actionable only in the relatively rare case where the business can be shown to have been operated purely for the purpose of causing economic harm to another business and with the intention of terminating the business after that purpose is accomplished. Where a single business dominates a market or a group of businesses act in concert, on the other hand, actionable predatory misconduct will more readily be found.

In at least one situation, even purely malicious commercial conduct may be privileged. The simple refusal by one person or business to deal with another person or business has been held not to be actionable, even though the refusal is motivated solely by whim, caprice, prejudice or malice. See *Great Atlantic & Pacific Tea Co. v. Cream of Wheat Co.* (1915). The interest in individual freedom is deemed to outweigh the interest in preventing economic injury—at least where competitive conditions prevail and no concerted group refusal to deal (i.e. group boycott) or violation of anti-discrimination laws is involved.

c. Prima Facie Tort

From the foregoing catalogue of nominate torts, some courts and commentators have extrapolated a broader principle—namely that any intentional infliction of injury requires justification in order for legal liability to be avoided. Termed "prima facie tort," this principle is viewed as synthesizing the various branches of the law of unfair competition and, indeed, the entire body of nominate intentional torts, just as negligence principles have synthesized the law governing accidental infliction of injury.

Under the prima facie tort theory, the law of intentional torts, like the law of negligence, is viewed as involving a balancing of the utility of injurious conduct against the utility of the interest invaded. In weighing the utility of injurious conduct, malicious conduct is normally entitled to no weight whatsoever. Thus, the intentional infliction of pecuniary harm for a purely spiteful purpose is generally unprivileged, even though, absent malice, the injurious commercial conduct itself would be perfectly justifiable.

Likewise, the use of improper means, even for the otherwise legitimate purpose of commercial gain, cannot be justified. Improper means include not only those which threaten the physical security of persons or property but also those which tend to subvert competition and bargaining on the merits. Hence, the special opprobrium which early attached to palming off, defamation and disparagement. Such conduct is of no more social value than purely spiteful conduct.

Even the use of otherwise legitimate commercial means for legitimate commercial ends may not be justified if the interest invaded is sufficiently great. Not only the security of person and property but the security of certain socially useful relations, such as contractual and fiduciary relations, have been held to be entitled to greater weight than the freedom to compete.

Where interests in the security of persons, property or those relations deemed necessary to society are not at stake, the common law views non-deceptive but economically injurious commercial conduct, such as price cutting, hard bargaining or simple refusals to deal with another business, to be privileged conduct on the part of a single non-monopolistic business. Even a purely malicious refusal to deal with another is likely to be privileged, because the interest in being free to choose one's business associates is deemed to outweigh the pecuniary harm done. On the other hand, even a non-malicious refusal to deal may become actionable if engaged in by a single business having market dominance or a group of businesses acting in concert, because there is less social interest and greater social danger in permitting such conduct.

While the prima facie tort theory has value as a synthesizing principle, courts have generally been reluctant to embrace it. One court has criticized the prima facie tort theory because it puts the burden on the defendant to justify his conduct and thus "requires too little of the plaintiff." *Leigh Furniture & Carpet Company v. Isom* (1982). See also *Tuttle v. Buck* (1909) (dissenting opinion). The few jurisdictions which have expressly adopted the principle have tended to apply it only in cases where the trade practice involved falls squarely within or just short of the traditional definition of some nominate tort. In the leading case of *Advance Music Corp. v. American Tobacco Co.* (1946), for example, the court held that the capricious omission of plaintiff's songs from defendant's radio program called "Your Hit Parade" amounted to prima facie tort, given the lack of any legitimate commercial justification for omitting the songs. Arguably, however, the intentional or reckless omission of plaintiff's "hits" from a show billing itself as "Your Hit Parade" could just as easily have been viewed as a novel type of disparagement of plaintiff's product, given the false implication created by the defendant that plaintiff's songs were not hits. In fact, the case was first brought as a disparagement case, but because of the strict pleading requirements with respect to damages (see Chap. 8 infra) had been dismissed.

Notwithstanding the limited judicial use of the prima facie tort principle in deciding specific cases, it does serve to remove the nominate intentional torts from their definitional strait jackets and expose an underlying unity in the common law of unfair trade practices. It also serves to expose two assumptions which were central to the development of a private judge-made law of unfair trade practices but which are increasingly being called into question. First is the assumption that the courts in the context of private litigation can adequately balance the public interest in maintaining both freedom and stability of trade relations. Second is the assumption that the balance struck by the courts can adequately be expressed in conventional private remedies where unfair bargaining or competitive practices are found. The emerging public law of domestic and international trade regulation, including a rapidly developing statutory and administrative law of unfair trade practices, challenges both assumptions, thereby creating a point of tension between the common law of unfair competition and the statutory law of trade regulation.

2. STATUTORY, CONSTITUTIONAL AND TREATY SOURCES

The statutory law of unfair trade practices not only supplements the private remedies of the common law but also provides for public (i.e., government) regulation of trade practices. As such, it is but a part of the larger statutory and administrative law of trade regulation, having a particularly close connection and at points actually merging with the law of antitrust and consumer protection. To complicate matters further, some of the statutory and judge-made law of unfair trade practices, namely the law of trademarks and trade secrets, is frequently described, together with the federal statutory law of patents and copyrights, as comprising the law of intellectual property.

The statutory law of unfair trade practices (and trade regulation generally) developed as a result of perceived inadequacies in the common law of unfair competition. The common law, for example, proved totally unequal to the task of balancing the competing interests of business and labor in labor disputes. As a result, federal statutory labor relations law has largely pre-empted the field.

Likewise, the common-law courts (including federal courts in diversity-of-citizenship cases) have all too often simply assumed that any copying of a product or a valuable business idea or scheme which has cost another business time, labor and money to produce, constitutes a misappropriation. They have thus endowed the copied product, idea or scheme with the legal attributes of intangible property without ever having balanced the utility of granting such a right against the cost to the competitive process of denying others free use of the product, idea or scheme. That reflexive judicial response to the problem of commercial copying has drawn into question the fitness of the matter for ad hoc judicial resolution, particularly in light of the existence of federal statutory patent and copyright protection.

If the common-law courts have on occasion been guilty of providing a legal remedy for the "harm" of hard bargaining or competition, they have also failed to provide adequate legal remedies for conduct which manifestly undermines the bargaining or the competitive process but causes no easily discernible private injury. At one time, for example, courts flatly stated that in the absence of evidence of palming off or commercial disparagement (i.e., deception which specifically identified its commercial victim), businesses had no remedy for a competitor's consumer-aimed false advertising. A few courts have held a cause of action to exist in the unusual case where one business can be shown to divert the customers of another business by making false claims about its own product. In general, however, the common law has been unable to provide an effective remedy for false advertising which does not identify its commercial victim—for the understandable reason that the practice is often more a public than a private wrong.

Although the most direct method of curing defects in state judge-made law is through state legislation, the latter has not always proved adequate to the task. At best, state legislative law can only deal effectively with trade practices which are essentially local in scope. At worst, state legislative prescriptions for curing the inadequacies of the common law have proved to be more harmful to the health of the competitive process than the common law itself. Some state trade regulation has unfortunately appeared to be concerned primarily with protecting vested and politically powerful local commercial interests from the "harm" of competition. State legislative modification of the common law of unfair competition has thus generated a second point of potential tension in the law of unfair trade practices—namely between state and federal trade regulation.

a. Federal Trade Regulation

The power of Congress to regulate trade relations stems from two distinct constitutional sources. The patent and copyright clause gives Congress power to "promote the progress of Science and useful Arts by reserving for limited times to Authors and Inventors the exclusive right to their respective Writings and Discoveries." Within the limits placed by the constitutional language, this grant of power explicitly authorizes federal creation of intangible property rights. Quite apart from that power, Congress is authorized to regulate interstate and foreign commerce, a grant of power which has been broadly construed but nevertheless does not extend to purely local activity which does not affect interstate commerce.

The power of Congress and the courts to invalidate state law in conflict with federal statutes and the Constitution derives from the supremacy clause, which declares the federal Constitution, treaties and statutes enacted pursuant thereto to be the supreme law of the land. That declaration not only authorizes Congress expressly to preempt state law but also empowers the courts (and ultimately the Supreme Court) to decide whether state law—judge-made or legislative—conflicts with the federal Constitution, treaties or statutes.

(1) Preemptive Federal Legislation: Patent, Copyright, and Labor Law

Federal legislation regulating trade relations has been both preemptive of and concurrent with state regulation. Section 301 of the Copyright Act of 1976, for example, expressly preempts state law that grants exclusive rights equivalent to those specified in the Act to fixed works of authorship that come within the various categories of copyrightable subject matter specified in the Act. Before 1976, federal copyright law had merely supplemented the common law of copyrights by extending the right to prohibit unauthorized copying to published works, just as the common law had long protected unpublished works.

In addition to this express congressional preemption of the field of copyright law, the Supreme Court has had a number of occasions to consider the extent to which states can extend the scope of federal patent or copyright protection or protect writings and discoveries which do not qualify for patent or copyright protection. In *Brulotte v. Thys Co.* (1964), for example, the Court held that states may not enforce a patent license provision which attempts to extend the payment of royalties beyond the seventeen year term of the patent. Likewise, in *Sears, Roebuck and Co. v. Stiffel Co.* and *Compco Corp. v. Day-brite Lighting, Inc.* (1964)

(known collectively as *Sears–Compco*), the Court held that because of the federal patent laws a state may not through its unfair competition law prohibit the copying of an unpatented and uncopyrighted article or award damages for such copying. In both cases lower courts had granted relief against the copying of articles whose patents had been declared invalid for want of the degree of invention required by federal patent law. The Court concluded that to forbid copying would interfere with federal policy found in the patent and copyright clause of the Constitution and the implementing federal statutes, of allowing free copying of whatever the federal patent and copyright laws leave in the public domain.

Subsequent to *Sears–Compco,* but prior to the time Congress expressly preempted the field of copyright, the Court, in *Goldstein v. California* (1973), had occasion to consider the effect of federal copyright law on a state criminal statute prohibiting record piracy. The Court upheld the state statute, distinguishing *Sears–Compco* as having involved the federal patent statute, which contained a set of standards indicating not only what Congress wished to protect but what it wished to remain in the public domain. For state law to prevent the copying of articles which federal patent law would leave in the public domain would disturb the balance Congress had drawn. The 1909 federal copyright statute, on the other hand, reflected no congressional balancing with respect to sound recordings, but had merely left the area unattended. Thus, the states remained free to act.

In *Kewanee Oil Co. v. Bicron Corp.* (1974), the Court held that state trade secret law does not undermine federal patent policy, even where protection is sought for trade secrets which are clearly patentable, and thus no conflict requiring preemption exists. Similarly, in *Aronson v. Quick Point Pencil Co.* (1979), the Court held that federal patent law did not preempt state contract law so as to preclude enforcement of a contract to pay royalties to a patent applicant for as long as the contracting party sold articles embodying the putative invention, even after a denial of the patent application. While *Kewanee* and *Aronson* appeared to tilt away from further judicial preemption in favor of continued state regulation, the Court in *Bonito Boats, Inc. v. Thunder Craft Boats, Inc.* (1989), again preempted state law, holding that a Florida statute prohibiting the unauthorized use of direct molding to duplicate for the purpose of sale any manufactured boat hull made by another conflicted with, and was thus preempted by, federal patent law.

Congressional exercise of its authority over interstate and foreign commerce, like its exercise of the authority to grant patent and copyright protection, has been both exclusive of and concurrent with state regulation. Federal labor law, for example, has been held to have preempted state law governing peaceful labor activity which might formerly have been treated as tortious interference with employment and commercial contracts. The states are only free to enjoin picketing marked by violence or physical intimidation. By contrast, although Congress has enacted both trademark and antitrust legislation, the states also remain largely free to regulate in these areas.

(2) Non-preemptive Federal Legislation: Trademark and Antitrust Law

In contrast to federal patent, copyright and labor legislation, federal trademark law—most recently embodied in the Lanham Act—manifests an overall Congressional intent merely to supplement state trademark law, subject only to specific preemptive exceptions. That limited legislative intent was mandated to some extent by the Supreme Court's decision in the *Trademark Cases* (1879), holding unconstitutional a predecessor to the Lanham Act which failed to evidence any intent to regulate only the interstate or foreign use of trademarks.

The Court in the *Trademark Cases* ruled that trademarks could not be considered a discovery or writing within the meaning of the patent and copyright clause because, at least where a mark consisted of a common word or symbol, as it did in this case, it lacked sufficient novelty, invention or work of the brain. Thus, the regulation of trademarks was beyond congressional patent and copyright power. While recognizing that a trademark might function as a useful and valuable aid or instrument of commerce, the Court noted that Congress nowhere purported to regulate only interstate or foreign commerce and thus exceeded its constitutional authority under the commerce clause.

Although the test for what constitutes interstate commerce has broadened considerably since the Court decided the *Trademark Cases,* federal authority nevertheless does not extend to purely local uses of marks and names.

Notwithstanding these limits on federal trademark protection power, the Lanham Act nevertheless provides an important supplement to the common law by establishing a system of federal registration. Registration is not mandatory but is encouraged through incentives which offer businesses engaged in interstate or foreign commerce significant protection beyond that provided by state trademark law. Quite apart from the registration provisions of the Lanham Act, section 43(a) of the Act provides a statutory cause of action for that form of false advertising which the common law has largely failed to reach—namely, false or misleading representations in commerce that do not amount to palming off or disparagement.

Federal antitrust law, like federal trademark law, is designed for the most part to run concurrently with state law. Like the Lanham Act, the antitrust laws may provide commercial parties with public and private remedies which are not available at common law. While the Sherman

Act's prohibition of joint efforts to restrain trade and unilateral abuse of market power and the Clayton Act's prohibition of certain anticompetitive acts focus exclusively on unreasonable restraints on trade, certain other antitrust laws, notably the Federal Trade Commission Act and the Robinson–Patman Act, are arguably as concerned with prohibiting unfair diversions of trade as they are with prohibiting unreasonable restraints as such.

The Federal Trade Commission Act, as amended, gives the FTC broad authority over "unfair methods of competition in or affecting commerce and unfair or deceptive acts or practices in or affecting commerce"—which includes broad power to protect consumers as well as commercial parties from unfair trade practices. The FTC has exercised its authority by prohibiting a wide variety of trade practices for which there may be no effective private remedy. Similarly, the Robinson–Patman Act's prohibitions against price discrimination define a body of unfair trade practices largely beyond the reach of the common law.

(3) Constitutional Limits on State and Federal Trade Regulation

Quite apart from the question of expressed or implied legislative preemption of state law, the federal courts have long asserted an autonomous power to invalidate state and federal law which is in conflict with the federal Constitution itself. For a time the Supreme Court transformed the due process clause of the Fourteenth Amendment into a formidable weapon against state attempts to regulate commerce, by declaring its power to review not merely the fairness of the process by which states deprive persons of life, liberty and property, but the fairness of the deprivation as such. This standard of review, known as substantive due process review, was used to strike down state economic regulation and further a judicially developed national policy of unfettered economic development.

Although ultimately abandoned by the Court as an unworkable standard of review for state trade legislation, substantive due process appears to have a constitutional successor in the First Amendment to the Constitution. While the Court for a time seemed to draw a distinction between commercial and non-commercial speech in First Amendment cases, it has more recently held that truthful advertising no less than other forms of expression is entitled to constitutional protection. See, e.g., *Virginia State Board of Pharmacy v. Virginia Citizens Consumer Council, Inc.* (1976) (holding that a state cannot prevent the truthful advertising of prescription drug prices under the guise of protecting the public from unscrupulous price cutters).

At the same time, the Court appears mindful of a countervailing constitutional interest, implicit in the federal system itself, in allowing states to regulate their own commercial affairs. Just as it has refused to preempt state legislation prohibiting record piracy and the common law of trade secrets, so the Court has held there to be no First Amendment immunity for a television station charged with misappropriating a performer's human cannonball act by videotaping the entire act and broadcasting it on a television news program, *Zacchini v. Scripps–Howard Broadcasting Co.* (1977), nor any First Amendment violation in a state statute prohibiting the practice of optometry under a trade name. *Friedman v. Rogers* (1979). Thus, while some state law regulating trade relations may have been preempted or invalidated because of conflicts with federal statutory or constitutional policy, a far more voluminous body of non-conflicting state trade regulation continues in force, supplementing both the common law of unfair competition and federal statutory and administrative trade regulation.

b. State Trade Regulation

Much of the state statutory law of trade regulation is patterned after, analogous to or specifically incorporates federal statutory law or administrative trade regulation rules, and thus gives federal policy a local application. In some significant respects, however, state statutory law protects trade relations in ways unknown either to the common law or to federal statutory law. Two of the most prominent examples are state statutes protecting distinctive trademarks from "dilution" (i.e., non-deceptive imitation) and state sales-below-cost statutes. Anti-dilution statutes specifically recognize and seek to protect the advertising value of particularly distinctive trade symbols by prohibiting other businesses from using the same or a similar mark even though it creates no confusion with respect to the goods or services but merely dilutes the impact of the original symbol. Sales-below-cost statutes purport to supplement (but may in fact subvert) the federal antitrust laws by prohibiting pricing practices which fall short of an antitrust violation.

c. International Trade Regulation

Beyond the purely domestic matter of allocating regulatory power among the various branches of federal and state government is the increasingly important matter of regulating international trade practices. While the Constitution squarely places this responsibility on the shoulders of the federal government and declares that treaties as well as federal statutes are a part of the supreme law of the land, difficult questions have arisen with respect to the application of federal law to extraterritorial commercial activity.

The United States has entered into a number of international agreements, some of whose provisions are self-executing (and thus, according to the supremacy clause, a part of the supreme law of the land), while other provisions are not self-executing and thus require domestic enabling legislation before they become law.

(1) International Agreements

The United States belongs to the International Union for the Protection of Industrial Property (the Paris Union), which was established by the Paris Convention in 1883. This convention is a multilateral treaty concerned with the international protection of patents and trademarks and the prevention of unfair competition in international trade. Some provisions of the convention are regarded as self-executing while other provisions require implementing legislation by each member country. Some of the subsequent modifications of the Paris Convention have been accepted by the United States while others have not. The principal objective of the Paris Convention is to ensure that in each of the member countries the citizens of all other member countries as well as all persons domiciled or having business establishments in the member countries will be entitled to the same protection of their patents and trademarks as citizens of that country.

The United States has ratified the Patent Cooperation Treaty, which came into force in 1978 and establishes procedures which facilitate the filing of parallel patents in signatory countries. The United States is also a party to the Universal Copyright Convention of 1954 and a number of similar multilateral and bilateral treaties concerned with the international protection of copyrights. As with the Paris Convention, the objective of the Universal Convention is "national" (i.e. non-discriminatory) treatment. In 1988, the United States adhered to the older Berne Convention of 1886, which, as most recently revised in Brussels in 1948, generally requires member countries to provide, without requiring any prerequisite formalities, a very high level of copyright protection, including the protection of an author's *droit moral* (i.e., the moral right to have a work attributed to him in form in which he created it).

Finally, the United States is a signatory to the General Agreement on Tariffs and Trade (GATT), which lays down rules for the conduct of international trade. This agreement, in addition to providing a mechanism for reciprocal lowering of tariffs and other trade barriers, provides for the regulation of discriminatory pricing practices and other international unfair trade practices. As with the Paris Convention and other treaties, GATT has required the enactment of implementing trade legislation.

(2) U.S. Foreign Trade Legislation

Pursuant both to the foregoing treaties and to its own power to regulate foreign commerce, Congress has enacted a number of statutes specifically regulating international trade practices. This legislation may be divided into that concerned with regulating the *import* trade and that concerned with regulating the *export* trade. The purpose of each type of legislation is quite different.

Import trade legislation is designed to put foreign importers on an equal footing with domestic enterprise, while protecting domestic enterprises from the unfair trade practices of importers. Import trade legislation includes certain provisions in the Lanham Act which provide for the registration of foreign trademarks and the protection of domestically owned trademarks against infringement by the trademarks on imported goods; certain provisions of the Tariff Act of 1930, which, as amended by the Trade Act of 1974, the Trade Agreements Act of 1979, the Trade and Tariff Act of 1984, and the Omnibus Trade and Competitiveness Act of 1988, prohibits such unfair methods of competition as patent, copyright, trademark and tradename infringement, passing off, trade secret misappropriation, false advertising, dumping (i.e., a form of international price discrimination) and other predatory pricing or otherwise anticompetitive practices; and certain other enactments which also apply U.S. antitrust law to foreign importers.

Export trade legislation is designed to protect domestic exporters from both foreign government discrimination and the unfair trade practices of other domestic exporters. Export trade legislation includes certain other provisions of the Tariff Act of 1930, as amended by the Trade Act of 1974, providing for government retaliation against the import trade of any country which discriminates against U.S. exporters; provisions of the Robinson–Patman Act prohibiting price discrimination in the form of false brokerage or promotional payments or allowances or commercial bribery in U.S. commerce; a provision of the Webb–Pomerene Act which exempts certain trading associations from the reach of domestic anti-trust laws but gives the Federal Trade Commission explicit authority to prohibit unfair methods of competition in the export trade; the newer Export Trading Company Act of 1982, which provides qualified antitrust immunity for export activities certified by the Department of Commerce and expressly provides that the Sherman Act does not apply to restraints in the export trade unless the conduct has a direct, substantial, and reasonably foreseeable effect on the import or domestic commerce of the U.S.; the Foreign Corrupt Practices Act, which prohibits bribery of foreign government officials; and the 1974 Trade Act, as amended most recently by the 1988 Omnibus Trade and Competitiveness Act, which directs the U.S. Trade Representative to identify and impose sanctions on countries that give inadequate or ineffective intellectual property protection to U.S. Nationals. The amended 1974 Act also establishes a Generalized System of Preferences, and authorizes the President, in determining which developing countries are entitled to relief from the imposition of import duties, to take into account the protection provided intellectual property in those countries.

In addition to the foregoing legislation, which explicitly regulates international trade, the courts have had to consider whether and to what extent domestic trade regulation may be applied to the extraterritorial conduct of domestic and foreign companies. That question was seemingly given a restrictive answer in *American Banana Co. v. United Fruit Co.* (1909), when the Supreme Court, affirming the dismissal of an antitrust complaint alleging that the defendants induced the Costa Rican government to seize plaintiff's rubber plantation and arrange a sale of the plantation to the defendant, held that the Sherman Act did not apply to actions occurring outside the United States that were lawful in the country in which they were performed. The *American Banana* decision has subsequently been viewed, however, as having dealt only with the narrower issue of applying U.S. law to extraterritorial conduct in which there is a heavy foreign government involvement. In general, the courts today hold that so long as foreign government involvement is sufficiently limited, U.S. law will apply to extraterritorial conduct which has an effect on U.S. foreign or domestic commerce. Conversely, where foreign government involvement in foreign trade activity is sufficiently great, interested persons and industries in the U.S. may, under section 301 of the Trade Act of 1974, as amended by the Trade and Tariff Act of 1984, and the Omnibus Trade and Competitiveness Act of 1988, 19 U.S.C.A. § 2411 et seq., petition the U.S. Trade Representative to investigate and recommend intervention by the U.S. Government through formal dispute resolution processes, such as those provided by GATT, that are only available, as a matter of international law, to sovereign states.

B. OBJECTIVES OF THE LAW OF UNFAIR TRADE PRACTICES

If it is useful to speak of a law of unfair trade practices at all, it must thus be described as a creature not merely of the judicial and legislative branches of state and federal government, but of the Constitution which binds those governments together and the international agreements that govern relations with other nations. The very diversity of the sources of the law of unfair trade practices compels a consideration of its underlying objectives.

The law of unfair trade practices seeks to protect the trade relations of businesses from undue interference by other businesses, while at the same time promoting bargaining and competition among businesses. The interest in protecting trade relations, as we shall see, is in constant tension with the interest in promoting bargaining and competition. A useful approach to the study of the law of unfair trade practices, accordingly, is first to identify the particular trade relations and broader relational interests which are the subject of legal protection and then to distinguish those forms of interference which are prohibited as unfair from those which are privileged as legitimate bargaining or competitive practices.

1. TRADE RELATIONS AND RELATIONAL INTERESTS PROTECTED

The trade relations of a business may be divided into its internal (employment and owner) relations and its external (commercial and consumer) relations. The employment relations of a business include its management and labor relations. Where a business is co-owned and not a sole proprietorship, its owner relations will consist of either partner or shareholder relations. Commercial relations of a business consist of its relations with other businesses, including both its vertical (or bargaining) relations with customers and suppliers and its horizontal relations with businesses at the same level in the distributive chain, in such enterprises as joint ventures and trade associations. Consumer relations include not only the individual customer relations of a retail business but also the more general public relations that retailers and non-retailers alike seek to establish and maintain for themselves and their product or service through advertising and related promotional activity. Where such activity stimulates commercial as well as consumer relations, the public relations of a business are more accurately viewed as a distinct type of trade relation, rather than as a particular species of the consumer relation.

With the exception of public relations, businesses may embody any or all of their trade relations in express or implied contracts. Whether a going business reduces particular trade relations to enforceable contracts or not, however, its trade relations, including its public relations, constitute a valuable albeit intangible business asset known as "good will."

Good will is generally defined as the expectation of future patronage. One court has called it what makes tomorrow's business more than an accident. Good will derives from the good reputation or distinctive identity of the business or its product or service. A distinctive identity, in turn, may be created and maintained by use of identifying trademarks, trade names and trade dress.

Good will is not the only intangible asset which adds to the value of a business. In the course of employment or commercial relations, for example, a business may receive, develop or disclose ideas, information, writings or other products of intellectual effort, whose value depends either on maintaining their secrecy while being exploited or on obtaining an exclusive legal right to exploit them publicly.

In all types of trade relations, businesses have two distinct relational interests: First is an interest in pursuing purely prospective trade relations, including those trade relations being sought or already established by other businesses. Second is an interest in creating a degree of stability in those trade relations which are successfully established and fending off attempts by other businesses to divert them. New businesses or businesses expanding in a horizontal or vertical direction have a particular interest in being free to pursue trade relations, while those established businesses whose share of a given market or position in the distributive chain has become more or less static have a particular interest in maintaining the stability of trade relations. Pursuit of either of these interests, of course, is likely to interfere with the prospective or existing trade relations of some other business. The aim of the law of unfair trade practices is to distinguish those forms of interference that are actionable wrongs from those that are privileged.

2. ACTIONABLE AND PRIVILEGED INTERFERENCE WITH TRADE RELATIONS

Interference with the relational interests of another must be distinguished from interference with the physical security of another's person or property. While physical and relational interference may occur simultaneously, physical interference involves only the party inflicting and the party suffering some form of physical harm. Relational interference, on the other hand, necessarily involves three parties (i.e., the two parties to the relation and the party interfering with it) and some form of purely pecuniary harm to one or both parties to the relation.

Not every infliction of pecuniary harm is unlawful. In fact the general rule is to the contrary. Businesses are privileged to pursue trade relations and attempt to prevent their diversion, even to the point of knowingly inflicting pecuniary harm on other businesses. As Mr. Justice Holmes has remarked, "a man has a right to set up a shop in a small village which can support but one of a kind, although he expects and intends to ruin a deserving widow who is established there already." Holmes, Privilege, Malice and Intent, 8 Harv. L.Rev. 1, 117, 120–21 (1894). Obviously, the deserving widow has a right to retaliate in kind, if she can, by lowering prices or otherwise rallying the small village to her cause.

The implicit assumption running throughout the law of unfair trade practices, in other words, is that bargaining and competition among businesses, although economically injurious to those individual businesses which inevitably lose out in the struggle, nevertheless serves the larger public interest by promoting lower prices and higher quality goods and services than either a privately or a publicly controlled economy. Only where economically injurious commercial conduct also injures some other private interest, such as the physical security of person or property, or threatens the larger public interest in the security and effectiveness of the bargaining and competitive processes as a whole, does the law step in and prohibit the injurious conduct as unfair.

C. A SUGGESTED APPROACH: THE LAW OF UNFAIR TRADE PRACTICES IN FUNCTIONAL CONTEXT

The list of trade practices deemed to threaten the security of the bargaining and competitive processes has developed over time, influenced not only by changing socio-economic conditions but also by changing (and sometimes conflicting) judicial, legislative and administrative perceptions of the proper balance to be drawn between the competing interests in trade freedom and trade stability. In order to answer the substantive question of what makes a given trade practice unfair, therefore, it is necessary to consider the antecedent question of who among the courts, legislatures and executive or administrative branches of state and federal government is best able (1) to decide what trade practices at a given level in the distributive chain are fair or unfair and (2) to provide the most effective remedy for those practices which are determined to be unfair. Both questions will be discussed as succeeding parts of this book consider the law of unfair trade practices in functional context—namely as it relates to each phase of the effort by businesses at various levels in the distributive chain to establish and maintain advantageous trade relations.

An appropriate order of study is to begin by examining those trade relations capable of being reduced to contract and the largely judge-made law which applies to them; then to examine the mixture of judge-made and statutory law governing public and confidential trade relations of businesses; and finally to examine the largely statutory law governing promotional and pricing practices. That progression not only has the advantage of presenting the law of unfair trade practices in roughly the order of its historical development, moving as it does from the private remedies of the common law to the public remedies provided by the statutory and administrative law of trade regulation, but also approximates the order in which an individual business will seek to establish its various trade relations.

PART I

INTERFERENCE WITH PROSPECTIVE AND EXISTING CONTRACTUAL RELATIONS

CHAPTER TWO

INTERFERENCE WITH PRECONTRACTUAL AND NON–CONTRACTUAL RELATIONS

A business can hardly go into business without establishing trade relations with individual employees, suppliers and customers. While some of these relations become "established" only in the sense that there is an expectation that relations will continue, all are capable and some may in fact become embodied in legally enforceable contracts.

Whether reduced to contract or not, trade relations capable of being embodied in a contract have long been protected against interference. The common law courts from an early date protected merchants from actual or threatened physical violence. From an equally early date the courts became concerned with preventing interference with master-servant relations and consequently began providing a civil remedy for any attempt, whether or not physical violence or threats were employed, to lure away the servants of another. From these antecedents the common law has subsequently developed in two directions.

One line of cases, expanding on the common law's protection of merchants and others from direct or indirect physical injury, has come to protect trade and other advantageous relations, whether reduced to contract or not, from interference falling short of actual or threatened physical violence. The other line of cases, expanding on the law's early protection of the master-servant relation, has come to protect existing contractual relations from interference that would be wholly unobjectionable in the absence of a contract.

Much of this common law remains intact notwithstanding subsequent state and federal legislation. Federal and state statutes have generally concerned themselves with specific problems, such as the prevention of misrepresentation in investment transactions and the prevention of monopoly or group interference with trade relations. Today, federal and state securities laws largely govern shareholder relations, while federal labor law and state and federal antitrust laws largely govern group interference with trade relations. The common law is nevertheless used as a supplement to federal labor law in the prevention of violent labor union activity and as an alternative to statutory securities and antitrust law in the prevention of deception, monopoly and concerted group interference. Individual interference with trade relations, moreover, is still largely a matter regulated by state common law.

This chapter will deal with the line of common-law cases which define what constitutes actionable interference with precontractual and noncontractual relations, while Chapter 3 will deal with the line of cases which defines what constitutes actionable interference with trade relations which have been reduced to contract. Consistent with the approach suggested in Chapter 1, we will first identify the particular trade relations and the broader relational interests which are the subject of protection and then distinguish those forms of interference which are actionable from those which are privileged.

A. TRADE RELATIONS AND RELATIONAL INTERESTS PROTECTED

The trade relations whose protection is the subject of this chapter and the next include all of those trade relations which are capable of being embodied in a contract. Thus, protection extends to owner, employment, commercial and face-to-face consumer relations—all types of trade relations, in short, except the public relations of a business.

The specific focus of this chapter is on those trade relations which, although capable of being embodied in a contract, have not in fact been reduced to contract. This includes both purely prospective (or pre-contractual) relations and existing but non-contractual relations.

The principal relational interest protected by the body of law we will be examining is trade freedom—specifically the freedom of a business to pursue prospective trade relations, including relations with the employees and customers of other businesses, without undue interference from those businesses. Because this body of law also protects existing non-contractual trade relations from the same sort of interference, however, it can also be said to promote trade stability.

B. ACTIONABLE AND PRIVILEGED INTERFERENCE

The common law of unfair trade practices began, as we have seen, by delineating various types of actionable interference with advantageous relations. Applied to business conduct, these nominate torts amounted to a catalogue of improper business methods. Later, the courts began to prohibit certain otherwise unobjectionable interference with advantageous relations where the purpose behind the interference was purely malicious or predatory (i.e., designed solely to injure). Applied to business conduct, this became a prohibition against certain improper business objectives.

Implicit in these specific common-law prohibitions is the notion that one party's interference with the pre-contractual relations of another is presumptively lawful and must be shown to have been accomplished by improper means or for improper ends to be actionable. See, e.g., *Leigh Furniture & Carpet Company v. Isom* (1982) (In order to recover damages, the plaintiff must prove (1) that the defendant intentionally interfered with plaintiff's existing or potential economic relations, (2) for an improper purpose or by improper means, (3) causing injury to the plaintiff). The same presumption does not apply, however, to concerted group interference with the trade relations of another (or, as we shall see in Chapter 3, with a single party's interference with another's contractual relations). Here, interference is presumptively unlawful and must be justified if liability is to be avoided.

The remainder of this chapter will examine what constitutes improper business methods; what constitutes improper business objectives; and what constitutes improper concerted group conduct.

1. IMPROPER BUSINESS METHODS

In Chapter 1 we saw that improper business methods include physical interference, injurious speech and coercive conduct. Such interference generally must be shown to have been intentional in order for purely pecuniary harm to be actionable. Even where such interference is intentional, a number of defenses may be raised to defeat liability.

a. Physical Interference

The common law from an early date protected merchants and others from direct physical injury to their persons or property. In time the courts also began to entertain claims for pecuniary harm resulting from direct injury to or detention of the merchant's person or property. That simple extension of the common law was profound, for at that point the common law departed from its narrow concern with protecting the physical security of persons and property and began to concern itself, albeit unconsciously, with relational security as well.

With the development of the law of private and public nuisance, the law courts began to award damages and the equity courts injunctions to protect persons and property against indirect physical interference, including physical interference causing only pecuniary harm. Private nuisance may be defined as indirect interference with the peaceful use and enjoyment of land, including the commercial use of land. In *Garrett v. Taylor* (1621), for example, threats and acts of violence aimed at the workmen and customers of a free mason were deemed to impair the latter's lease on a stone pit. Similarly, in *Keeble v. Hickeringill* (1706), the malicious discharge of firearms so as to frighten away wild fowl being decoyed by another for commercial purposes was in effect held to interfere with the decoyer's peaceful use and enjoyment of the pond on which he floated his decoys.

The law of public nuisance extended legal protection beyond unreasonable interference with the use and enjoyment of land and proscribed virtually any conduct, including purely verbal conduct, which substantially interfered with the exercise of rights common to members of the general public. Originally simply a low order crime designed to protect the public health, safety and convenience, public nuisance came to be recognized as privately actionable where an individual could show particular harm above and beyond that suffered by the general public. Thus, commercial users of public highways and waterways might well have a cause of action for economic losses suffered as a result of obstructions, pollution or other forms of interference. In *Tarleton v. McGawley* (1793), for example, the firing on the canoes of African natives with whom a slave trader sought to do business was in effect held to be an interference with the right held in common with members of the public—namely, the right to use navigable waterways for trade. Similarly, in *Gregory v. Duke of Brunswick* (1843), the defendant was held liable for conspiring to prevent the plaintiff, an actor, from performing, by hiring persons to hoot, hiss, yell and groan during plaintiff's performances.

Physical interference need not be malicious in order to be actionable. Any intentional and unreasonable physical interference with another, whether direct or indirect, will be actionable even though only pecuniary harm results. Thus a cafeteria whose customers form lines blocking entrances of an adjoining drugstore has been held to have created a nuisance, *Shamhart v. Morrison Cafeteria Co.* (1947), as has a railroad which without authorization blocked a highway, thereby damaging a nearby milk and vegetable business which was unable to get its produce to town. *Texas & Pacific Railway Co. v. Mercer* (1936).

Along somewhat similar lines, the taking of aerial photographs of an unfinished chemical plant in order to discover a secret manufacturing process has been held to constitute an improper means of discovering the secret. *E.I. duPont de Nemours & Co. v. Christopher* (1970). In countless other cases in which bona fide business operations are known to interfere with other businesses, courts have enjoined interference found to be unreasonable, and where the extent of past pecuniary injury can be established with sufficient certainty, have awarded compensatory damages as well. The absence of malice merely bars the award of punitive damages.

As a general rule, however, no cause of action lies against one who merely negligently prevents a stranger from obtaining a prospective pecuniary advantage. Recovery of damages for negligent infliction of pecuniary loss is for the most part limited to those cases in which the interference causes physical as well as pecuniary harm or arises in the course of a "special relationship" (e.g., a contractual, professional or fiduciary relationship) between the parties. Where negligent interference causes only pecuniary harm and no special relation exists, the courts have generally denied recovery of damages on the theory that economic losses are unforeseeable, too remote or out of proportion to the defendant's fault. Thus, negligently causing a fire which does no physical damage to others but interrupts the trade of a neighboring business, thereby throwing an employee out of work, does not give rise to an action for lost wages. *Stevenson v. East Ohio Gas Co.* (1946). Nor does negligently damaging a propeller of a vessel owned by one party but chartered to another give rise to an action for pecuniary loss suffered by the charterer as a result of the delay in the ship's return to service. *Robins Dry Dock & Repair Co. v. Flint* (1927).

In *Union Oil Co. v. Oppen* (1974), a court did allow commercial fishermen a cause of action against an oil company for loss of business resulting from a negligently caused oil spill. The court nevertheless appears to have limited the action for pecuniary injury to circumstances in which a defendant has special reason to anticipate that a limited class of persons conducting a business in close proximity with defendant's own would be particularly vulnerable to economic injury as a result of defendant's negligence. In the absence of such special circumstances, the action for purely pecuniary loss resulting from indirect interference with the business of a stranger remains limited to instances of intentional misconduct.

b. Injurious Speech: Deceit, Defamation, Disparagement

The common law protects businesses from various forms of economically injurious speech. The earliest type of protection was against threats or verbal harassment aimed at employees or customers of a business. See *Garrett v. Taylor,* supra. The common law also came to provide two distinct forms of protection against deception and falsehood—namely, protection for persons who are misled by another's misrepresentations and protection for persons who suffer pecuniary harm as a result of misrepresentations made to others.

At first, the common law action for deceit was thought to be limited to the intentional acts of persons in a contractual relation with each other. Later cases, protecting persons from the deceit of non-contractual parties as well, have been called the parent of the modern tort of deceit. In *Pasley v. Freeman* (1789), an action for intentional and negligent misrepresentation was for the first time held a lie in favor of a merchant against a person who had not had any dealings with the merchant other than to induce the merchant to enter into trade relations with and extend credit to a third party whom the person described as one "safely to be trusted and given credit." After *Pasley,* it was clear that the tort action for deceit did not depend on the existence of a contractual relation between the party who deceived and the party who was injured and that the tort of deceit was independent of the law of contracts.

Even after *Pasley,* however, the existence of an express or implied contractual relation between the party making a misrepresentation and the party injured has continued to have importance in two situations—namely in actions for deceptive non-disclosure and actions for negligent misrepresentation. Except where two parties are in a fiduciary relation or one party holds himself out as having special knowledge not available to the other, the courts have generally refused to impose liability for a mere nondisclosure of information, at least where the injury is purely pecuniary. Similarly, courts have generally limited liability for economically injurious negligent misrepresentations which cause no physical injury to situations where the parties are in a special relation (i.e., contractual, professional or fiduciary), giving the one the right to rely upon the other for information.

In the absence of physical injury or a special relation, liability is thus limited to intentional or reckless misrepresentations. In *Ultramares Corp. v. Touche, Niven & Co.* (1931), for example, the court held that accountants who certified a corporation's balance sheet, knowing it would be used by the corporation in some unspecified financial dealings, could be held liable for deceit (i.e., intentional or reckless misrepresentation) but not for mere negligence where a lender relied on the balance sheet to its economic detriment. Similarly, the spectre of potentially unlimited liability for economic losses suffered as a result of inadvertent misrepresentations has led courts to limit the negligence liability of those who provide stock ticker services. See *Jaillet v. Cashman* (1923) (stock ticker service held not liable to customers of brokers receiving the service, for erroneously reporting that U.S. Supreme Court had held that stock dividends constituted taxable income).

In a few instances courts have extended liability for negligent misrepresentation to persons who in the course of their business, profession or employment provide information to persons with whom they have no contract—namely where they have special reason to anticipate that the person provided with the information or a limited number of third persons will rely on the information. Thus, in *Glanzer v. Shepard* (1922) a public weigher hired by a seller of beans was held liable to the buyer of the beans for negligently certifying the weight of the beans. Similarly, in *M. Miller Co. v. Central Contra Costa Sanitary District* (1961), an engineering company hired to prepare a soil report knowing it would be made available to and be relied upon by bidders for work on a sewer system, was held liable when the successful bidder suffered economic injury as a result of the engineering company's negligent misrepresentations.

For the most part, however, courts have required either a special relationship between the parties or a knowing or reckless misrepresentation. Thus, as with indirect physical interference causing pecuniary harm to the trade relations of a stranger, interference by means of deceptive speech remains largely an intentional tort.*

Just as the common law protected persons who were deceived, so it protected persons threatened with pecuniary harm resulting from falsehoods aimed at others. The law of defamation, which protects as an incident of personality one's reputation in the community, was from the first particularly solicitous of the reputation of merchants and tradespeople, perceiving the danger of harm for defamatory remarks about another's trade or business to be sufficiently clear as to obviate the need for proof of actual pecuniary harm. At the same time the courts recognized, as an incident of the ownership of real, personal or intangible property, the right to be free from false statements casting aspersions on one's title to the property (slander of title) or the quality of the property. Gradually, liability was extended to any injurious statement maliciously made about another's business. That form of injurious falsehood came to be referred to as trade disparagement.

* The federal law of securities regulation has, of course, modified the common law with regard to representations made in connection with various types of investment security transactions. In many instances, federal law imposes strict liability for misleading statements. See generally *D. Ratner, Securities Regulation in a Nutshell* (1988).

Just as it is unlawful to defame a merchant or disparage his title to property or the quality of his merchandise, so it became unlawful to palm off inferior quality goods as those of another, more reputable merchant. Together, these three prohibitions contain the seed of much of the modern common law of unfair competition, which protects the public relations as well as the prospective contractual relations of businesses. For that reason, the common law's protection of those likely to be economically injured by communications made to third persons will be deferred for consideration in Parts II and IV.

c. Coercive and Other Improper Conduct

While English and American courts in the nineteenth century recognized the need to protect express or implied contractual relations, even to the point of tolerating a degree of economic heavy handedness in arms-length transactions, the American courts in particular became equally concerned with preventing the coercive use of superior bargaining power in the formation, modification, termination or refusal to enter into contractual relations, particularly where that superior bargaining power was the result of market dominance by a single business or concerted conduct by a group of businesses. Hence, the law's condemnation of coerced and otherwise unconscionable contracts, contracts in restraint of trade and oppressive group conduct, particularly group boycotts and other combinations and conspiracies in restraint of trade.

Not every form of economic coercion is actionable. Indeed, because of the common law's countervailing concern with protecting each individual's effort to derive maximum economic advantage from bargaining and competition, the presumption is to the contrary. Thus, in *Katz v. Kapper* (1935), the court dismissed the complaint of a wholesale fish dealer who alleged that a rival wholesaler, after threatening plaintiff's customers with ruin if they continued to purchase fish from plaintiff and promising them substantial reductions in price if they purchased fish from defendant, did in fact open a retail store which sold fish for less than their wholesale price, causing a considerable number of plaintiff's customers to begin making their wholesale purchases from defendant. The court held that it was not unlawful to threaten to do that which could lawfully be done. Because defendant was free to compete with plaintiff's customers, he was therefore free to threaten them with competition, even though the purpose was to coerce them into trading with defendant.

Only where coercion is exerted by means or for ends which are themselves improper does the law step in and provide a remedy. We have already seen that improper means can consist of direct or indirect physical interference or deceptive or otherwise injurious speech. Other clearly improper means include initiating groundless litigation or violating an established standard of a trade or profession, or bribery of employees. See, e.g., *Coleman v. Whisnant* (1945) (alleged threats of groundless litigation). *Adler, Barish, Daniels, Levin & Creskoff v. Epstein* (1978) (Former associate in law firm held to have improperly interfered with law firm's client relations by improperly soliciting clients while still in firm's employment). For bribery of employees, see Chapter 8 infra. Cases holding coercion actionable in the absence of such conduct have generally involved the coercive use of a gross inequality of bargaining power or an abuse of a less than arm's length business relation between the parties, and have often involved the pursuit of an improper business objective as well. In order to understand what might constitute actionable coercion where the means employed do not constitute improper physical interference or deceptive speech, it is thus necessary to consider the larger question of what constitutes an improper business objective.

2. IMPROPER BUSINESS OBJECTIVES

Although a business is generally privileged to knowingly inflict pecuniary harm on another business, some reasons for doing so are impermissible. A business may not seek to restrain or destroy competitive conditions in the market place. Nor may it actively inflict pecuniary harm for an entirely malicious purpose. Where pecuniary injury is not the result of affirmative business conduct, but rather a malicious refusal to deal with another business, it is more difficult to state a general rule.

a. Anticompetitive Conduct

A primary example of an improper business objective is the objective of restraining or destroying competitive conditions in the market place. The common law has long condemned the misuse of market dominance and contracts, combinations and conspiracies in restraint of trade. As those prohibitions suggest, anticompetitive conduct generally involves not only an improper business objective but also some type of misuse of market dominance or concerted group conduct.

The common-law prohibition against anticompetitive conduct has largely been superceded by the federal and state antitrust statutes. The Sherman Antitrust Act, 15 U.S.C.A. §§ 1–2, broadly prohibits (1) contracts, combinations and conspiracies in restraint of interstate or foreign trade and (2) monopolization, attempts to monopolize or combinations or conspiracies to monopolize any part of interstate or foreign trade. In an attempt to give these broad legislative prohibitions a more precise content, the courts have identified certain types of conduct as so inimical to the competitive process and lacking in legitimate purpose that they are never justified and therefore *per se* unlawful, without regard to the purpose or effect of the conduct. *Per se* violations of the Sherman Act include horizontal and vertical price-fixing, horizontal division of markets, group boycotts and at least some instances of tying of the sale of one product to the purchase of another unwanted product. The lawfulness of all other restraints on trade is governed by a rule of reason, which requires the courts to determine whether the practice merely regulates and perhaps thereby promotes competition or whether it tends to suppress or destroy competition.

The Clayton Act and the Federal Trade Commission Act constitute a two-pronged effort to supplement the Sherman Act. The aim of both is to nip anticompetitive practices in the bud, before they blossom into an actual lessening of competition or monopolization. The Clayton Act, as amended by the Robinson–Patman Act, prohibits four specific types of misconduct—namely (1) price discrimination and sales at unreasonably low prices, (2) exclusive dealing and tying arrangements, (3) anticompetitive mergers and acquisitions and (4) interlocking directorates. The FTC Act broadly prohibits conduct violative of the spirit if not the letter of the antitrust laws as well as any other business conduct which is deceptive or otherwise unfair to consumers or other businesses. (See Chapters 8–9 infra.) For application of U.S. antitrust law to extraterritorial conduct, particularly conduct involving a foreign government, see p. 32 supra.

b. Malicious or Predatory Conduct

Just as activity undertaken for an anticompetitive purpose is improper, so too is activity undertaken for a malicious or otherwise unjustified noncompetitive purpose. Although the question of whether ill motive will render otherwise lawful conduct unlawful was at one time hotly debated, the controversy seems to have dissipated with judicial recognition that a distinction must be drawn between cases in which the motive is either purely or primarily malicious and those in which a malicious motive merely accompanies a legitimate one. Because of the importance attached to encouraging bargaining and competition, the courts have been reluctant to condemn conduct which is undertaken partly for legitimate business reasons and partly for vindictive or spiteful ones. Consequently, they have held that, in order to be actionable, otherwise lawful business activity must be shown to have been undertaken solely or at least primarily for the purpose of causing economic loss to another. Cf. *Leigh Furniture & Carpet Co. v. Isom* (1982) (deliberate breach of contract for the purpose of ruining another's business held to be tortious).

Needless to say, the courts have found it necessary to create guidelines for pleading and proof in such cases. Otherwise, the cause of action for predatory conduct could very quickly degenerate into an action for injury resulting from bargaining or competition itself.

Vindictive statements may be evidence of malice but do not exclude the possibility of an accompanying legitimate commercial motive. Likewise, selling below cost or operating a business at a loss may be evidence of a malicious motive, but neither is conclusive on the matter, for such tactics might just as likely be utilized for legitimate competitive purposes. Pure malice is conclusively established only where it is shown that a person is essentially acting out of "disinterested malevolence." Such would be the case, for example, where one business can be shown to have engaged in purely specious competition, with the intention of going out of business after destroying another's business. It might also be the case where one business gratuitously injures a business with whom it is *not* in a competitive or bargaining relation.

Where a competitive justification is clear on the face of the plaintiff's pleading, the complaint will be summarily dismissed. Such was the case in *Katz v. Kapper*, supra, where the defendant wholesale fish dealer was concededly a competitor of the plaintiff and was not charged with using any improper means or market dominance to lure away plaintiff's customers. A similar result was reached in *Beardsley v. Kilmer* (1923), where the defendant went into the newspaper business in response to the plaintiff's published attacks on his business and remained in the newspaper business after driving the plaintiff out of it.

What constitutes a sufficient allegation of malicious competition, on the other hand, is more difficult to say. In *Tuttle v. Buck* (1909), for example, a barber's complaint was allowed to stand against a banker who was allegedly attempting, for the sole design of injuring the barber and not for any legitimate interest of his own, to drive the barber out of business by circulating "false and malicious reports and accusations" (apparently not amounting to slander), by inducing customers, through "threats of his personal displeasure" not to patronize the barber, and finally by setting up a rival barber who was paid a full salary and provided a shop rent free. The banker's justification for going into an unrelated business was not so clear on the face of the complaint as had been the case in *Beardsley* and the banker was running the business at a loss. Significantly, the complaint in *Tuttle* made veiled allusions not only to the banker's use of false and malicious reports and accusations but also to a possible abuse of the banker's "great wealth and prominence" in the community. If the allegations in *Tuttle* did not present a case of clearly improper competitive methods or a purely malicious purpose, neither did they indisputably establish that the banker's methods were proper and his motives were commercial. Because the banker's conduct and motives were left open to question by the barber's complaint, the court required the banker to answer the complaint and justify his conduct, though the judges writing the opinion for the majority still found plaintiff's allegations to be insufficient.

In some circumstances, business activity will be held to lack justification even in the absence of subjective malice. In *Advance Music Corp. v. American Tobacco Co.* (1946), for example, the court held that the capricious omission of plaintiff's songs from defendant's radio program called "Your Hit Parade" amounted to prima facie tort, given the lack of any commercial justification for omitting the songs. The plaintiff's complaint contained no allegation of malice, but merely claimed in one count that the defendant was acting "wantonly [i.e. recklessly] and without good faith" and in the other that he was acting "with intent to injure the plaintiff." As we have seen, however, the defendant's conduct in *Advance Music* was arguably an improper business method (i.e. a disparagement of plaintiff's songs), as well as having no apparent justification, given the absence of competition between the parties.

c. Refusals to Deal With Another Business

If injurious commercial activity will sometimes be held to lack justification even in the absence of subjective malice, certain conduct causing economic harm will be held privileged even though it springs from the basest of motives. A simple refusal to deal with another person, for example, has long been held not to be actionable at common law even though the refusal is motivated solely by spite, prejudice, whim or caprice. While the conduct itself lacks justification, it has been described as an aspect of one's constitutionally protected liberty. See *Great Atlantic & Pacific Tea Co. v. Cream of Wheat Co.* (1916).

Economic liberty, of course, is not the only value protected by the Constitution. The judicial and legislative branches of government have become increasingly concerned with promoting equality of economic opportunity and legal control of economic power. It is thus somewhat misleading to speak of refusals to deal as constitutionally protected conduct. The real reason that such refusals are treated as an exception to the rule that purely malicious conduct is unjustified appears to be that under normal competitive conditions, where alternative sources of goods, services, labor and employment are readily available, such refusals are unlikely as a practical matter to result in serious economic injury to others or undue advantage to individual businesses which withhold custom. Significantly, the common law has long restricted the right of public utilities or those engaged in other public callings whose importance dictates the law's recognition and regulation of monopolies or quasi-monopolies, to refuse to deal with a member of the public.

A number of statutes have placed still other limitations on the right to refuse to deal with others in the market place. Just as the common law has limited the right of public utilities to refuse to deal with members of the public, so the federal antitrust laws have limited the right to refuse to deal with others where the refusal is a part of an attempt to monopolize or a combination in restraint of trade. Various civil rights statutes have limited the right to refuse to deal with persons on account of their race, religion, sex or national origin. Federal labor law limits the right of businesses to refuse to deal with unions or employees who belong to unions. Federal statutes have also limited the right of food processors and others to refuse to deal with farmers who belong to agricultural associations.

Two recent federal statutes and a number of similar state statutes purport to limit the circumstances in which a franchisor can terminate its contractual relations with a franchisee.

Franchising is a relatively new method of distributing goods and services. As a distribution system, it falls midway between a company-owned (i.e., vertically integrated) distribution system and the traditional three-tiered (i.e., manufacturer-wholesaler-retailer) distribution system. Franchise operations may be divided into three distinct types: (1) Manufacturing franchises, by which the franchisor exploits a trade secret or other business idea by licensing others to manufacture and distribute a product; (2) distributing franchises, by which the franchisor distributes its trademarked products, such as automobiles and associated auto and petroleum products, through facilities owned or operated by others; and (3) style-of-business franchises, by which the franchisor who has developed the commercial (i.e., advertising) value of a trademark and an associated style of business, licenses their use to others who agree to operate a retail outlet for a product (such as fast foods) or a service (such as dancing instruction or insect extermination) in accordance with standards set by the franchisor.

In theory at least both the franchisor and the franchisee benefit from the arrangement. The franchisor is able to maintain a large number of sources or outlets for its product or service without having to invest its own capital in them, while the franchisee is able to operate an independent business, but with the technical and advertising assistance of the franchisor. In reality, many franchise relationships, particularly distribution and style-of-business franchises, are marked by such a vast inequality of bargaining power that the franchisee is actually little more than a terminable-at-will employee with a substantial investment in the business.

Because franchise relations may be marked by such an inequality of bargaining power, a franchisor's decision to terminate the relation may destroy the franchisee's business. Accordingly, the Automobile Dealers' Franchise Act, (ADFA) 15 U.S.C.A. § 1221 permits an auto dealer to bring an action in federal court to prevent a franchisor who is not acting "in good faith and without coercion" from terminating the franchise relationship. Likewise, the Federal Petroleum Marketing Practices Act, (FPMPA) 15 U.S.C.A. §§ 2801–2841, strictly limits the permissible reasons for terminating the franchise of a motor fuel distributor or dealer and specifies certain procedures for terminating a franchise. The FPMPA expressly preempts state statutes which conflict with its provisions. While the ADFA contains no such provision, a number of state statutes extending protection of franchisees beyond that provided automobile dealers under the ADFA have been held to be unconstitutional. See e.g. *U.S. Brewers' Association v. Nebraska* (1974) (declaring a Nebraska statute regulating the termination of liquor distributors to be unconstitutional).

While an unconditioned refusal by a business to deal with another business or a prospective employee is privileged if it falls outside the foregoing common-law or statutory prohibitions, the same is not true of a conditioned refusal to deal with another. A conditioned refusal to deal amounts to a threat and is improper if the objective sought is improper. Thus, use of a conditioned refusal to deal in order to induce another to breach a contract may constitute an actionable interference with contractual relations. Even in the absence of an actual breach of contract, the use of a conditioned refusal to deal with another in order to induce the modification of a contract might well be condemned where it involves the use of superior bargaining power. (See Chapter 3 infra.) Finally, a refusal to deal with another, whether conditioned or unconditioned, may be actionable if it is a product of concerted group conduct.

3. CONCERTED GROUP CONDUCT

If individual interference with the trade relations of another is presumptively privileged and must be shown to have been accomplished through improper means or for improper ends in order to be actionable, group interference with the trade relations of another is presumptively unlawful and must be justified if liability is to be avoided. This general prohibition extends to concerted group refusals to deal (i.e., group boycotts). The reason for this difference in attitude toward individual and concerted group interference with the trade relations of another is that group interference may well close off alternative sources of goods, services, labor and employment and thus result in both serious economic injury to those from whom custom is withheld and undue economic advantage to those businesses which act in concert.

The presumption against the legality of economically injurious concerted group conduct is embodied not only in the common-law action for civil conspiracy but in the federal antitrust laws, which draw a sharp distinction between the acts of a single business (which are illegal under the antitrust laws only if they constitute an attempt to monopolize any part of trade or commerce) and concerted acts (which are illegal under the antitrust laws wherever they constitute an unreasonable restraint of trade).

Most litigation concerning concerted commercial conduct has occurred under federal or state antitrust law, due to the general availability of treble damages. The common law tort of civil conspiracy is only resorted to where antitrust law does not apply or provide any remedial advantages. As a result, most of the common-law conspiracy cases either predate federal and state antitrust laws or rely heavily on cases decided under those acts.

As with individual interference with the trade relations of others, those who act in concert will be held liable for civil conspiracy only where they use improper means or pursue improper ends. Needless to say, any interference which would be improper for an individual will be improper when engaged in by a group. The only question unique to civil conspiracy cases is whether conduct which is lawful for an individual can become unlawful solely because it is engaged in by a group of persons.

In practice, a finding of improper group conduct often simply serves as a shorthand way of condemning a whole series of group practices any one of which would have been improper even had it been the act of an individual business. In *Evenson v. Spaulding* (1907), for example, the court affirmed the issuance of an injunction forbidding an association of businesses from continuing a program of systematic interference with a peddler's buggies and wagons. Agents of the association dogged the steps of the peddler, accosted customers and advised them not to buy, even though they themselves had no goods to offer, and on occasion even carried arms and arranged to be deputized in order to enforce laws which were no longer valid. While there may have been some isolated aspects of this course of conduct which would not have been tortious had it been the act of an individual competitor, the course of conduct as a whole was unlawful not merely because it involved group conduct but because it involved systematic group harassment using a host of improper means for a purpose which must have been either to restrain competition or simply to destroy another's business.

There are occasions, however, where group conduct is condemned solely because it is group conduct. A primary example is the prohibition against concerted group refusals to deal (i.e., group boycotts). Although an individual business is often privileged, as we have seen, to refuse to deal with other businesses even for purely vindictive and malicious reasons, a group refusal to deal with a business will in all likelihood be branded an illegal boycott unless an adequate justification for the group conduct can be raised. Justifying a group boycott, moreover, has proved to be very difficult indeed. This is particularly true where the boycott is a "secondary" boycott—i.e., a conditioned refusal to deal with one business because of its relations with another business.

For example, in *Jackson v. Stanfield* (1894), which was a common law conspiracy case, the court found an element of coercion and intimidation in a lumber retailers association rule which provided for the boycott of wholesalers or manufacturers who sold directly to consumers or supplied lumber to non-retailers who did. The association circulated the names of offending businesses and penalized members who violated the rule. The court observed that "it is not a mere passive, let-alone policy ... that creates liability but the threats and intimidation shown in the complaint." As we have seen, similar threats and intimidation were found to be lawful where a single wholesale fish dealer threatened retailers with ruin if they continued purchasing from a rival. See *Katz v. Kapper,* supra. *Katz* and *Jackson* suggest that although an individual business (at least one which is not shown to dominate the market) may be privileged to use threats, including a conditioned refusal to deal, in order to induce another business to terminate relations with a third party, a combination of businesses is not similarly privileged.

Further evidence that what is lawful for an individual business may not be lawful for an association of businesses is to be found in such cases as *Grillo v. Board of Realtors of Plainfield Area* (1966), in which an unconditioned group refusal to deal—i.e., a boycott lacking any elements of coercion or intimidation—was found to be unlawful as a matter of common law because it constituted an unreasonable restraint on trade. In *Grillo,* a real estate broker excluded from membership in a local real estate board—apparently in part because of his race—claimed that a multiple listing service operated exclusively for the members of the board created an unlawful restraint on trade. The court, noting that the action of a combination of businesses is unreasonable if its operation tends to prevent competition, raise prices or create a monopoly and cannot be justified under the circumstances, found no such justification for the multiple listing service and declared it to be unlawful, even though there was concededly no evidence that the board, in carrying out its restrictive practices, was motivated by any desire to injure the plaintiff. The justification offered by the board was that the restrictive practices were necessary to establish and improve the professional standards of its membership. The court found the justification inadequate in view of a comprehensive statutory scheme for the licensing of real estate brokers.

Other privately administered policing schemes have met a similar fate even where comprehensive public regulation was admittedly lacking. In *Fashion Originators' Guild of America, Inc. v. Federal Trade Commission* (1941), for example, the Supreme Court held that, notwithstanding a number of common-law cases which had held design piracy to be tortious misconduct, an association of dress designers and manufacturers violated the federal antitrust laws when they conditioned sales to buyers on an agreement not to deal with design pirates. (For more on design piracy, see Chapter 6, infra.) Where privately administered policing schemes have been upheld, the typical scheme not only utilizes objective standards and fair policing procedures, but also lacks any elements of an explicit group boycott. An individual member's decision not to deal with a business subjected to the policing effort may be based on the policing association's announcement of its findings but may not be the result of any "concerted" action by the association.

One early antitrust case illustrates the potential difficulty in deciding when conduct is concerted and when it is unilateral. In *United States v. Colgate & Co.* (1919), a case in which Colgate was charged with attempting to maintain retail prices of its products by refusing to deal with wholesale and retail price cutters, the Court affirmed the dismissal of the indictment, holding that just as a business was free to exercise its independent discretion as to the parties with whom it would deal, so it could announce in advance the circumstances under which it would refuse to sell. Unilateral decisions by others to comply with those conditions would not amount to concerted action. Although *Colgate* is of questionable authority as an antitrust precedent, it may well reflect the common law view as to the dividing line between unilateral and concerted conduct. (For more on price cutting, see Chapter 9, infra.)

Notwithstanding the general prohibition against concerted commercial conduct, one explicit form of boycott is privileged—at least so long as no improper means are utilized. This is a group boycott undertaken not for commercial purposes at all but for political, religious or social purposes. Obviously, the courts will be alert to detect sham purposes when a "non-commercial" boycott is sponsored by competitors of the business being injured. But presumably a group of businesses could agree to refuse to deal with a business which itself engaged in illegal activities, such as pornography, prostitution or gambling. Whether a combination of businesses could use economic coercion to induce another business to refuse to deal with a competitor whose conduct was found to be politically or morally objectionable remains considerably in doubt.

C. AFFIRMATIVE DEFENSES AND REMEDIES

In actions alleging interference with pre-contractual and non-contractual relations, the principle affirmative defenses, in addition to the various justifications or privileges already mentioned, are that the action is barred by the statute of limitations or that plaintiff's laches (i.e., delay) in bringing the suit or unclean hands in the matter in controversy should limit or bar the grant of relief. Where no affirmative defense has been established, the available remedies include damages, restitution and injunctive relief. Where the extent of past pecuniary injury can be established with sufficient certainty, compensatory damages may be recovered. Where the interference was malicious, either punitive damages or restitution of the defendant's profits may be allowed. Where an award of monetary relief will not adequately protect the plaintiff, injunctive relief may be granted.

CHAPTER THREE
INTERFERENCE WITH CONTRACTUAL RELATIONS

Just as the common law protects pre-contractual and non-contractual relations from specified types of interference, so it protects contractual relations from virtually any form of intentional interference. Although English common law early provided a remedy for interference with master-servant relations, the modern origin of the tort of interference with contractual relations is *Lumley v. Gye* (1853). In that case, the manager of an opera company was held liable for having induced a noted singer to breach her contract to sing exclusively with the plaintiff's rival opera company for a particular season.

The *Lumley* case is important for a number of reasons. First, the court conceded that the singer was not a servant of the plaintiff. In granting protection to a service contract, the court expanded the common law's protection of contractual relations beyond master-servant relations and thus laid the foundation for protecting contractual relations of all kinds. Second, while much was made of the defendant's supposed "malice" the court nowhere cited specific evidence of malicious conduct. No mention was made of the use of any improper means, such as coercion, intimidation or deceit, to induce the singer to breach her contract; it appears that she voluntarily breached. It also appears that the defendant had sound commercial reasons for wanting to employ her. The "malice" found in this case apparently amounted to nothing more than the defendant's intentional offer of an inducement to the singer to breach her contract. *Lumley* may thus be said to protect contractual relations even from bona fide competitive interference. Finally, it is to be noted that the contractual provision the defendant induced the singer to breach was an exclusive dealing provision which itself tended to restrain trade. In granting protection to such a contract, the court thus intimated that even certain contracts which restrain trade may be protected against competitive interference.

Judicial decisions since *Lumley v. Gye* have simply refined the basic conclusions reached in that case with respect to (1) what contractual relations are protected and (2) what interference with those relations is actionable.

A. CONTRACTUAL RELATIONS PROTECTED

As we have seen, trade relations capable of being embodied in a contract include the owner, employment and commercial relations of any business and the individual consumer relations of a retail business. Because the principal threat of economic harm to partner, shareholder and consumer relations comes from conduct which is likely to be tortious even in the absence of a contract, the principal focus of this chapter will be on employment and commercial contracts.

As with employment relations themselves, employment contracts may consist of both management and labor contracts. Similarly, commercial contracts include contracts between parties at the same and at different levels in the chain of distribution of goods and services. Contracts among businesses of the same general type are likely to involve joint ventures, trade association activities or the sale of business assets, including intangible assets such as business good will or intellectual property. Contracts between businesses of different types or at different levels of the distributive chain are likely to involve financial transactions, the sale or lease of business premises or goods, the sale or licensing of some form of intellectual property, the performance of services, or some combination of all of these—as is the case, for example, in franchise operations.

Contracts of all types may range from elaborate written contracts to contracts whose terms are entirely implied from a course of dealing between the parties. Contracts may remain in force for a definite or indefinite term or may be terminable at the will of one or both parties. They may also contain post-contractual covenants, such as warranties of title or merchantability and covenants not to compete or disclose confidential information. Contracts which by their terms cannot be performed within one year, or involve the sale or mortgaging of real property or the authorization or employment of a real estate agent or broker or the sale of goods priced at $500 or more or claims in an amount or value of more than $5,000 must satisfy the statute of frauds and may be voidable if not expressed in writing.

Today, virtually any contract, whether express or implied, term or terminable at will, enforceable or unenforceable, qualifies for protection against interference. The willingness of courts to imply terms where none are expressed, to prevent interference with contracts which may be terminable at the will of the parties and to protect contractual relations where the contract itself is unenforceable indicates that the interest being protected is not merely the contractual interest in the performance of promises but a larger commercial interest in the stability of existing advantageous relations.

1. EXPRESS CONTRACTS: TERM, TERMINABLE AT WILL, AND UNENFORCEABLE CONTRACTS

Most courts have held that a contract terminable at the will of the parties, no less than a term contract, is protected against interference, even though technically one cannot induce a "breach" of such a contract. Some courts have likewise held that contracts, such as those unenforceable under the Statute of Frauds, are nevertheless protected against interference by third parties, at least where both parties would have performed but for defendant's interference. The theory in such cases is apparently that the trade relation is of value even if the contract itself cannot be enforced. When it comes to determining what constitutes actionable interference with such contracts, however, we shall see that courts treat such contracts much as they do pre-contractual or non-contractual trade relations.

Unenforceable contracts are not only to be distinguished from enforceable contracts but also from contracts which are considered altogether void because illegal or contrary to public policy. Void contracts, courts agree, are entitled to no protection whatsoever. Thus, usurious or gambling contracts are unprotected, as are those which unreasonably restrain trade.

As *Lumley v. Gye* illustrates, actions for interference with contractual relations often involve contractual terms, such as exclusive dealing provisions and covenants not to compete, which tend to restrain trade. Whether such provisions are enforceable and thus protected against interference or void and thus unprotected depends on whether they are found to be reasonable or unreasonable restraints on trade.

Contracts by their very nature place restraints on trade, but they are so useful in bringing order and stability to existing trade relations that the restraint is generally deemed reasonable. A closer question is presented by exclusive dealing contracts and post-contractual covenants not to compete.

Today the validity of exclusive dealing contracts is generally determined by reference to federal or state antitrust laws. The validity of covenants not to compete, by contrast, may well be determined in the context of a common-law tort claim for interference with the contract. See, e.g., *Imperial Ice Co. v. Rossier* (1941) (holding valid the claim of an owner of an ice distributing business who brought a common-law action against another ice distributor for inducing a former owner of the plaintiff's business to breach a covenant not to engage in the business of selling or distributing ice in a given city "so long as the purchasers, or anyone deriving title to the goodwill of said business from said purchasers, shall be engaged in a like business therein"). Covenants not to compete often accompany contracts for the sale of a business and contracts of employment. Purchasers of a business and employers are likely to insist on such covenants as a means of protecting their business good will from subsequent appropriation by the other party to the contract. Express noncompetition covenants which are ancillary to a valid employment or commercial contract and necessary to protect one of the contracting parties will generally be upheld if the covenant is reasonable in scope—i.e., is not more extensive in time or space than is necessary to protect the party insisting on the covenant nor so extensive as to be oppressive to the covenanting party or inimical to the public interest.

Determinations as to the reasonableness of the temporal and territorial coverage of covenants not to compete will necessarily vary with the subject matter of the contract. A citywide territorial restriction on the right to compete may be reasonable for the protection of the owner of a large retail business but too broad for the protection of the owner of a neighborhood barber shop. A two year temporal restriction on competition may be reasonably necessary to protect the owner of a purely commercial enterprise having many competitors and producing goods or services which are in plentiful supply but unreasonable as applied to the purchase of a medical practice at a time when doctors are in short supply.

While generalizations about the reasonableness of covenants not to compete are thus difficult, it may be noted that courts view contractual restrictions on former employees more suspiciously than they do restrictions on former owners of a business. In contracts for the sale of a business, where it is clear that a transfer of good will is intended, covenants not to compete are generally presumed to be valid. A majority of courts have held, for example, that the mere fact that a seller's covenant not to compete contains no time limit does not render the covenant per se unreasonable. Cf. *Imperial Ice Co. v. Rossier,* supra (allowing an ice distributor to bring an action against another ice distributor for interference with a covenant to compete, even though the covenant ran for an indefinite term).

Limitations on an employee's freedom after termination of employment, on the other hand, are much more difficult to justify. Courts will generally only enforce an employee's express covenant not to compete in two situations: (1) where the employee had close personal relations with a significant number of the employer's customers or (2) where the employee had access to confidential customer information or other trade secrets of the employer. See e.g., *Reed, Roberts Associates v. Strauman* (1976) (refusing to enforce a covenant not to compete where former employee did not have close relations with particular customers and was not privy to any trade secrets). Only in these two situations is the employee deemed to be in a position to divert a significant portion of the employer's good will or other intangible business assets. Even then the courts will refuse to enforce an employee's covenant not to compete (as opposed to a simple covenant not to disclose trade secrets) if it lacks definite temporal and territorial limits or imposes an undue hardship on the former employee. In *Milwaukee Linen Supply Co. v. Ring* (1933), for example, a covenant not to call on customers of a linen supply business or otherwise compete within a given metropolitan area for two years was held invalid, as applied to a discharged route manager whose partial physical disability and physical appearance reduced his ability to procure employment elsewhere, notwithstanding the covenant's similarity to an employment contract which had previously been held reasonable as applied to a route driver who had a closer relation with more customers of a laundry than did the route manager of the defendant's linen supply business.

In addition to these common law limitations on employee covenants not to compete, most states have antitrust statutes which provide that every contract which restrains one from engaging in a lawful profession, trade or business is to that extent void. The courts in some of these states have held that employee covenants not to compete or work for a competitor are void and unenforceable, whether reasonable or not. See, e.g., *Golden State Linen Service v. Vidalin* (1977) (so construing Cal. Bus. and Prof.Code § 16601). In most jurisdictions having such a statute, however, either the courts or the legislatures have created a narrow class of exceptions to the void per se rule. In some, statutes set out the maximum permissible temporal and territorial restrictions, while in others, the courts have construed the statute as excepting such contractual provisions as employee promises not to solicit former customers.

2. IMPLIED CONTRACTS AND THE OBLIGATION OF FAIR DEALING

Even in the absence of an express contract, the courts are likely to imply certain contractual terms from the mere fact that a trade relation exists. For example, when parties bargain for the sale of a business the courts will imply from the bargaining relationship itself a covenant on the part of the prospective buyer not to disclose or exploit information disclosed in confidence, should the sale not go through, and a covenant on the part of the seller not to interfere with the good will of the business by soliciting former customers after a sale of the business is consummated. See e.g. *Mohawk Maintenance Co. v. Kessler* (1981) (holding that the right acquired by the purchaser of the good will of a business by virtue of the implied covenant to refrain from soliciting customers must logically be regarded as a permanent one that is not subject to divestiture upon the passage of a reasonable amount of time). The implied covenant of a seller not to derogate the value of good will sold is nevertheless narrower than an express covenant not to compete. It does not prevent the vendor of a business from engaging in a competing business, but merely prevents the direct solicitation of patrons of the business sold. While the courts will not imply an analogous obligation on the part of a former employee not to solicit the former employer's customers, they will imply both a duty on the part of the employee to remain loyal to the employer during the course of employment and a covenant on the part of the employee not to use or disclose a former employer's trade secrets—including confidential customer lists—after that employment has terminated.

Terms are often implied without reference to whether there was actually a tacit meeting of the minds on them. In reality, the implied term merely serves as a device by which the court or legislature imposes an obligation of good faith and fair dealing on the parties to a trade relation. See, e.g., U.C.C. § 1–203 (imposing an obligation of "good faith" on parties to contracts governed by the U.C.C.). One who induces a party to breach such an implied obligation, however, no less than one who induces a party to breach an express contractual provision, can be held liable for or enjoined from interfering with the contractual relation.

B. ACTIONABLE AND PRIVILEGED INTERFERENCE

Not every interference with contractual relations is necessarily actionable. Nor must every interference necessarily result in a breach of contract in order to be actionable. Interference which is wrongful quite apart from its effect on the contractual relation is, of course, clearly actionable, whether or not an actual breach of contract results. In *McNary v. Chamberlain* (1867), for example, the court found an actionable interference where the defendant intentionally damaged a road that plaintiff was under contract to repair. Even though the plaintiff did not own the road on which the defendant trespassed and even though the trespass did not produce a breach of contract, it made the plaintiff's performance of the contract more costly. Had the plaintiff been unable to perform the contract, then the owner of the road would have had a cause of action not only for the physical consequences of the trespass but also for interference with the contractual relation.

The principles on which the *McNary* case was based were well established long before *Lumley v. Gye*. See Chapter 2 supra. The *Lumley* case is important, however, for having established that interference with a contract need not be independently wrongful in order to be actionable. It is sufficient that one "maliciously" induce the breach of a contract.

1. INDUCING BREACH OF CONTRACT

Where a contract is for a definite term, as in *Lumley,* "malice" may amount to no more than knowing of the contract at the time the inducement is offered. Where the contract is voidable or terminable at the will of the parties and thus capable of non-performance or termination without actionable breach, on the other hand, the party complaining of "malicious" interference will generally be required to show that the interference is accomplished by improper (i.e., deceptive or coercive) means or for an improper (i.e., anticompetitive or predatory) purpose.

Because "malice" is a term of such variable meaning, some courts, influenced no doubt by the prima facie tort theory, have abandoned the concept of malice altogether and speak rather of justifiable and unjustifiable interference. Where the interest in contractual stability is strong (as with valid term contracts), even interference for bona fide business reasons is unjustified and thus actionable. The freedom to pursue trade relations in that instance has less (or at least no more) social utility than the stability of trade relations. In order to justify interfering with such contractual relations, the interference must be in defense of an interest with greater countervailing social utility than contractual stability. In *Brimelow v. Casson* (1923), for example, where the manager of the "Wu Tut Tut Review" so seriously underpaid the women in his chorus line that they were forced to ply an older and less honorable trade, an official of an actors' association was held justified in prevailing on theatres to cancel contracts unless higher wages were paid. The interference was considered justified because it was in defense of public health, safety and good morals. Implicit in *Brimelow* is the same assumption which underlies modern labor law, namely that improving working conditions is of sufficient social importance to justify peaceful concerted activity to that end, even though the effect is to interfere with employment and commercial contracts.

As the interest in contractual stability becomes more attenuated (as with voidable contracts and contracts terminable at will), the freedom to interfere is correspondingly greater and includes the freedom to interfere for bona fide business reasons.

In order for interference with such relations to be actionable, it must be shown that the interference was either undertaken for other than bona fide business reasons or that improper means were employed.

While the requirement of malice has thus either been fictionalized to some extent or altogether displaced by a balancing approach to the question of what intentional interference with contractual relations is actionable and what is privileged, courts have generally refused to extend liability beyond intentional or reckless interference to purely negligent interference with contractual relations. That refusal reflects a broad judicial concern with containing tort liability within definite borders and a corresponding reluctance to extend liability for negligence beyond conduct causing physical injury to person or property. As with most general rules of law, however, the rule limiting actions for interference with contractual relations to intentional misconduct is subject to a number of exceptions designed to avoid unjust results.

The general rule denying liability for negligent interference of contractual relations is most useful in pure inducement cases similar to *Lumley v. Gye*. To impose a duty of care on a business to avoid inducing another party to breach an existing contract would unduly burden the former's freedom to contract. Moreover, it would render a purely negligent actor responsible for what is likely to be an intentional breach of the contract by the induced party—a party whom the law of contracts in any event will hold strictly liable for the breach. The only argument in favor of imposing a duty of care on the negligent inducer would be to ensure that the plaintiff is compensated in the narrow event that the breaching party turns out to lack attachable assets—an eventuality which the contracting party could guard against in advance by obtaining some form of security.

Different considerations apply where the interference complained of creates an unreasonable risk of harm to the person or property of one of the contracting parties and does in fact result in such injuries. Both of the parties to the contractual relation may be blameless and their contractual relation perfectly foreseeable to the interfering party. If both conditions are met, the interfering party would in any event be liable for any physical injuries caused. It is thus not surprising that courts have allowed recovery of pecuniary loss resulting from negligent interference with contractual relations where it accompanies a negligent infliction of injury to the plaintiff's person or property. One court has even awarded consequential damages for economic loss where the underlying basis for liability for the physical injury was strict liability rather than negligence. See *Hales v. Green Colonial, Inc.* (1974).

In one limited circumstance, the courts have gone so far as to allow one party to a contract to recover pecuniary damages for the negligent infliction of physical injury to the *other* party to the contract. No doubt influenced by the historical origins of the tort of interference with contractual relations, the courts have allowed a master to recover for the loss of services resulting from negligent injury of a servant whose services are personal or unique.

In addition to the question of the requisite culpability required, the courts have struggled over what constitutes an "inducement" to breach a contract. Doubtlessly discomfitted by the fact that the injury in inducement cases is ultimately the result of the intervening intentional acts of the breaching party, the courts have insisted that the inducement be sufficiently overt to justify treating it as a concurring cause of the injury. Thus, it is not enough that one simply enter into trade relations with a party who has breached a contract, or that one hold out to the general public attractive terms, knowing that another party will be motivated to breach an existing contract, or even that one enter into a trade relation with another knowing that it will be impossible for the other party to perform a preexisting contract as a result. It must be shown that the defendant has actively and affirmatively induced a party to a contractual relation to breach that contract.

2. COERCING MODIFICATION OF CONTRACTS AND ABUSE OF TRUST OR CONFIDENCE

Although an inducement to breach a contract must be affirmative and active to be actionable, cases both before and after *Lumley v. Gye* demonstrate that the cause of action for interfering with contractual relations is not limited to such inducements and that neither an inducement nor a resulting breach are absolute prerequisites to bringing suit. As we have seen, interference by such means as physical interference or deception was considered actionable even before *Lumley v. Gye,* whether or not a contractual relation was involved or a breach of contract resulted. See Chapter 2 supra. Cases following *Lumley* have extended the cause of action for interference with contracts to cases involving coerced modification of contracts, abuse of relationships of trust or confidence and concerted group interference with contractual relations.

In *Hannigan v. Sears, Roebuck and Co.* (1969), for example, the court held that a retailer had actionably interfered with a distributor's contractual relations when the retailer used economic coercion to force modification of a contract between the distributor and a metal building manufacturer who sold most of its output directly to the retailer. The distributor had conceived an idea for a metal outdoor locker and arranged to purchase the manufacturer's entire output of the lockers. Rather than purchase the lockers from the distributor, the retailer used its economic power to coerce the manufacturer to sell the lockers directly to it and pay the distributor a commission which was much smaller than the distributor's ordinary markup on the lockers. The court in *Hannigan* concluded that in this case, at least, coercing modification of a contract was the functional equivalent of inducing a breach of contract. It may be noted that the retailer's conduct in forcing a price concession could have amounted to an antitrust violation (i.e. inducing price discrimination, see Chapter 9) and, in any event, involved exploiting an inequality of bargaining power.

The common law's disapproval of efforts to take advantage of an inequality of bargaining power or a relationship of trust or confidence likewise goes a long way toward explaining its protection of contractual relations that are terminable at the will of the parties. In *A.S. Rampel, Inc. v. Hyster Co.* (1957), for example, the court held that a dealer-distributor had a cause of action against its manufacturer and one of its own salesmen for interfering with the employment relations of the dealer-distributor by allegedly fomenting dissension in the latter's sales force and luring away a number of members of the sales force prior to terminating relations with the dealer-distributor. In sustaining the dealer-distributor's complaint against the manufacturer, the court emphasized that it was not dealing with competition among economic equals, but rather with a manufacturer-distributor arrangement, which is generally recognized as involving an inequality of bargaining power and which, in this instance at least, also involved a relationship of trust and confidence, given allegations that the dealer-distributor was required to make extensive disclosures of customer lists and other information to the manufacturer. Similarly, the court concluded that a cause of action had been made out against the defendant salesman who, while still an employee of the dealer-distributor and bound by a duty of fidelity, allegedly induced the manufacturer to terminate the distributorship agreement, negotiated for a competing dealership and induced several other salesmen to terminate their employment with the dealer-distributor. The *Rampel* case is particularly important because it illustrates the principal common-law theories on which franchisees have been able to base a claim for relief from the coercive or oppressive conduct of franchisors. See also *Roberts v. Sears, Roebuck & Co.* (1978) (upholding a jury verdict awarding profits and damages against an employer who was found to have engaged in fraud, breach of a confidential relationship, and negligent misrepresentation in procuring an assignment of an employee's patent rights in a new type of socket wrench invented during the employee's off-duty hours).

3. CONCERTED GROUP INTERFERENCE WITH CONTRACTUAL RELATIONS

The likelihood that economic coercion or oppression will be held to constitute actionable interference with contractual relations even in the absence of a breach of contract is greater still in cases involving concerted group conduct. Although a number of courts have stoutly insisted that an organized group is entitled to do whatever an individual may do, other courts, cognizant of the greater potential for coercion or oppression in concerted group conduct and influenced no doubt by the common law's disdain for contracts and conspiracies in restraint of trade, have held that group conduct may be actionable even though it would have been privileged had it been the conduct of an individual.

Concern over concerted group conduct largely explains the judicial willingness to protect contractual relations that are terminable at the will of the parties. In *Wear-ever Aluminum, Inc., v. Towncraft Industries, Inc.* (1962), for example, the court held that one cooking utensil manufacturer had actionably interfered with the contractual relations of a competitor when it hired away approximately 35 members of the competitor's sales force, all of whose contracts of employment were terminable at will. As a result of the mass exodus, the plaintiff's sales effort was virtually destroyed.

While the court in *Wear-ever* stretched to find elements of deception in a meeting between the defendant and a group from plaintiff's sales force, it is apparent that liability rested principally on the crippling effect of the mass exodus organized by the defendant and on the defendant's capture, not merely of individual members of plaintiff's sales organization, but of the benefits of plaintiff's training and organization investment. The latter basis for imposing liability amounts to a conclusion that the defendant misappropriated plaintiff's sales organization. (For more on misappropriation, see Chapters 6–7 infra.) In part, however, defendant's wrong consisted of organizing a group plan designed to injure plaintiff. It should be noted that a similar claim of concerted interference on the part of the manufacturer and the salesman of the dealer-distributor in *A.S. Rampel v. Hyster Co.,* supra, was allowed to stand along with the counts alleging that the manufacturer and salesman both abused relationships of trust and confidence.

4. OTHER IMPROPER INTERFERENCE

Any conduct, such as bribery of another's employees or violating an established standard of a trade or profession, which would be improper even in the absence of any contract, will also be improper where it interferes with an existing contractual relation. See *Associated Press v. International News Service* (1917) (bribing a telegraph editor to leak news to non-member of wire service); *Adler, Barish, Daniels, Levin and Creskoff v. Epstein* (1978) (former associate in law firm held to have improperly interfered with law firm's existing client relations by improperly soliciting clients while still in firm's employment). See generally Chapter 2 supra.

C. AFFIRMATIVE DEFENSES AND REMEDIES

The principal affirmative defenses that may be raised to an action for interference with contractual relations are: (1) that the contract is void or (2) that the interference is justified. As we have seen, contracts are void if they are illegal or contrary to public policy, while interference may be justified if it has as its purpose the defense of public health, safety and morals.

The remedies available for an actionable interference with contractual relations include damages, restitution and injunctive relief. Frequently an award of damages will be sufficient to make the plaintiff whole. Indeed, where the interference consists of inducing another to breach a contract, the plaintiff may have a contract claim for damages against the breacher as well as a tort claim for damages against the inducer. In order to prevent double recovery, while providing adequate compensation to the plaintiff, courts generally allow a plaintiff to pursue both claims but prohibit the recovery of the same damages twice. If the contract cannot be enforced against the breacher, the plaintiff may look to the party inducing the breach for all of his damages.

The plaintiff may recover general contract damages (i.e., the plaintiff's reasonable expectation of profit under the contract) from either the breacher or the inducer and may also recover any special damages flowing from the breach, so long as such damages can be proved with sufficient certainty and are not too remote. The rules governing the remoteness of special damages, however, will differ significantly in the contract and the tort action. Special damages for contract breach are limited to those within the contemplation of the parties when the contract was entered into. The award of special damages in tort actions has been more generous, particularly in cases of intentional misconduct. Thus, although the recovery of special damages from the breacher may be limited by the contract rule of remoteness, the recovery of special damages from one who induced a breach is generally held to be governed by the tort rule. Likewise, while punitive damages are not generally available in contract actions, they may be awarded in intentional tort actions. Finally, an award of restitution (i.e., defendant's profits) is more likely in a tort action than in a contract action. A plaintiff's monetary claim against a party who induces a breach may thus be considerably higher than his claim against the contract breacher.

If money relief will not provide an adequate remedy for the interference, injunctive relief may be available. Although an employee may not be compelled to specifically perform an employment contract, since this would constitute involuntary servitude in violation of the Thirteenth Amendment of the Constitution, other contracts may be specifically enforced. In an appropriate case, moreover, a former employee can be enjoined from going to work for a competitor and the competitor enjoined from accepting the services of the former employee.

PART II
PRODUCT, SERVICE AND BUSINESS MISIDENTIFICATION

CHAPTER FOUR
USE OF SIMILAR TRADEMARKS AND TRADE NAMES

In today's increasingly complex and impersonal economy, it is not enough that a business be free to enter into individual trade relations with particular employees, suppliers and customers and enjoy a degree of stability in such relations once they are established. Businesses must normally invest considerable time, money, and intellectual labor in the effort to establish an identity for their product, service or business so that the public at large will become and remain aware of them amid the din of the marketplace. Even if a business does not engage in a deliberate effort to develop distinctive marks and names to identify itself or its product or service it has an interest in preventing other businesses from diverting its trade by confusing the public as to the identity of their own product, service or business.

The law protecting the identity of products, services and businesses began as little more than an off-shoot of the common law of deceit. In an unreported sixteenth century case, known only as the *Clothier Case,* the English Court of Common Pleas apparently found a cause of action to exist where one clothier deceptively used the mark of another clothier on his own ill-made cloth. In the later cases which mention it, the *Clothier Case* is variously described as having been brought by a purchaser who had been deceived by the use of the mark on the ill-made cloth and by the clothier whose mark was deceptively used. See, e.g., *Southern v. How* (1619) (describing the case as having been brought by the clothier). The purchaser's action, of course, would be one for deceit. The clothier's claim, on the other hand, would be one for diversion of trade and injury to his reputation and that of his cloth. Whatever the actual state of affairs, the *Clothier Case* was subsequently cited as authority for the proposition that the attempt to palm off one's goods as those of another merchant is an actionable commercial tort. See, e.g., *Blanchard v. Hill* (1742).

From that beginning, the law governing the identification of products, services and businesses developed in two different directions. One branch of the law focused on those types of trademark and trade name infringements which did not necessarily involve conscious palming off. Another branch of the law focused on forms of palming off which did not necessarily involve the deceptive use of another's trademark or trade name. Accordingly, the present chapter will be concerned with actionable and privileged interference with distinctive trade symbols, while Chapter 5 will be concerned with other forms of palming off.

A. TRADE RELATIONS AND TRADE SYMBOLS PROTECTED

The trade relations whose protection is the subject of this chapter and the next are basically the public relations, or good will, of a product, service or business. The specific concern of this chapter is with those forms of good will which become embodied in two types of distinctive trade symbols—namely, trademarks and trade names.

1. MARKS AND NAMES PROTECTED

Merchants have used distinctive marks to identify their goods for centuries. Some of these marks functioned—much like the modern-day cattle brand—to indicate ownership of goods. Other marks, however, (or even obsolete ownership marks, for that matter) merely served to identify the origin of goods. The latter type of mark, precursor of the modern-day trademark, was first used by individual artisans at the insistence of powerful (and monopolistic) trade guilds, as a police mark to aid in the identification of foreign (i.e., non-member) goods and shoddily crafted member goods.

In time, marks used on certain durable goods, such as cutlery or cloth, which were frequently transported to distant trade fairs before being sold, became sufficiently well-established to function more as an asset—symbolizing the good will that a product had built up—than as a liability for the producer. In general, however, the value of trademarks as symbols of good will remained limited so long as producer and consumer were in close contact. Only after the Industrial Revolution stratified and depersonalized the marketplace were identifying trade symbols transformed into assets for businesses generally.

No sooner had the trademark begun to emerge as a business asset than did unscrupulous merchants, such as the one involved in the *Clothier Case,* attempt to steal the asset and the good will it symbolized, by using the mark of a reputable merchant to palm off inferior quality goods. Hence, the early recognition of a common-law cause of action for palming off.

The first reported trademark case after the spate of references to the *Clothier Case* confirmed that trademark infringement required a showing of some form of deception. In *Blanchard v. Hill* (1742), a cardmaker sought to enjoin another cardmaker from using the mogul stamp on his cards. The court, in denying the request for injunctive relief, distinguished the *Clothier Case* and stated that it was not the single act of making use of the mark that was sufficient to maintain the action but "doing it with a fraudulent design, to put off bad cloths by this means, or to draw away customers from the other clothier."

As the Industrial Revolution progressed, however, the courts began to focus less on the defendant's deceptive conduct and more on the plaintiff's rights in the trade symbol. Thus, what began as an off-shoot of the law of deceit has emerged somewhat uncertainly as a branch of the law of intellectual property. In the course of that transformation, the terms "trademark" and "trade name" took on two distinct meanings—an older, common-law meaning and a more modern statutory meaning.

a. Common-Law Trademarks and Trade Names

The common-law courts drew a distinction between technical trademarks and trade names. Technical trademarks were defined as any fanciful, arbitrary, unique, distinctive and non-descriptive mark, word, letter, number, design or picture denominating and affixed to goods—those trade symbols, in short, which were inherently distinctive and identified a product. One could obtain rights in a technical trademark merely by adopting a mark or word and using it as a trademark. Rights in the trademark could thereafter be vindicated in suits for trademark infringement.

Words which were descriptive of a product, service or business or were names of persons, partnerships, corporations or a particular geographic location, on the other hand, were classified by the courts as trade names, in recognition of their common use in commercial discourse. A trade name could only be protected in actions for palming off (or unfair competition as the tort came to be called in the United States) where the name could be shown to have acquired a "secondary meaning"— that is, had come to be thought of by the public, not primarily as a descriptive word or a common name for a person, business or geographic location, but as a designation for the goods, services or business of a particular merchant. The courts eventually granted analogous common-law protection for product features, packaging, or other forms of trade dress, and literary or artistic titles and characterizations which had acquired a secondary meaning—though it hardly seemed appropriate to speak of such features as trade *names.*

For a time the courts not only distinguished the manner by which rights in technical trademarks and trade names were acquired, but also the scope of protection to which trademarks and trade names were entitled and the rationale for that protection. A few courts, for example, went to the extreme of enjoining substantial copying of technical trademarks not only in the absence of any evidence of intent to deceive but also in the absence of any evidence that the public would likely be deceived as to the origin of the goods. Thus, the harm being protected against was no longer the deceptive diversion of customers at all but rather the misappropriation of the trade symbol itself. Even though most courts continued to insist on at least some evidence of a likelihood of consumer confusion as to the origin of goods, they tended to resolve doubts as to the likelihood of confusion in favor of the plaintiff.

On the other hand, because trade names consisted of words commonly used in commercial discourse, courts were reluctant to find unfair competition in the use of another's trade name or trade dress, even for purposes of granting injunctive relief, unless there was sufficient evidence of actual public confusion over the origin of goods to give rise to a strong inference of the defendant's deceptive intent and an actual diversion of plaintiff's trade. The grant of injunctive relief in such cases was normally much more limited in scope than that granted in suits for technical trademark infringement. The courts tended to view the plaintiff's trade, and not his trade name or trade dress, as the value to be protected and for that reason they generally limited injunctive relief to requiring additional identifying words to eliminate the confusion.

While some courts still use the terms "trademark" and "trade name," in their common-law sense, the substantive importance of the distinction between technical trademarks and trade names has gradually disappeared as the courts have increasingly tended to grant the same degree of protection to technical trademarks and those trade names which have acquired a secondary meaning. A showing of some likelihood of public confusion as to the identity of goods or services has increasingly tended to be treated as both a necessary and a sufficient condition for establishing an infringement, while fraudulent intent is relevant only in determining the appropriateness of ordering an accounting of defendant's profits or awarding plaintiff compensatory or punitive damages. Accordingly, a number of courts have ceased using the terms "trademark" and "trade name" in their common-law sense and have begun using them as they are defined in the Lanham Act and state registration statutes modeled on the Lanham Act.

b. Statutory Trademarks, Service Marks and Trade Names

The common-law distinction between technical trademarks and trade names was initially carried over into federal trademark law when the Supreme Court in *Standard Paint Co. v. Trinidad Asphalt Manufacturing Co.* (1911), construed the Trademark Act of 1905 so as to limit federal registration under that Act to common-law technical trademarks. The enactment of the Lanham Trademark Act of 1946, 15 U.S.C.A. §§ 1051–1127, and similar state registration statutes, on the other hand, have brought about a redefinition of the terms "trademark" and "trade name." Section 45 of the Lanham Act, for example, defines a trademark as any word, name, symbol, or device or any combination thereof adopted and used by a manufacturer or merchant to identify his *goods* and a trade name as any name used by manufacturers, industrialists, merchants, agriculturalists and others to identify their *businesses, vocations* or *occupations*. Under the Lanham Act, a trademark of either inherent or acquired distinctiveness may be federally registered. Trade names, on the other hand, are not federally registrable.

To fill a gap created by the foregoing redefinition of terms, the Lanham Act specifically provides for the registration of "service marks"—that is, marks used in the sale or advertising of services. Under the Lanham Act, trademarks and service marks may be of virtually any format, whether *verbal* (i.e., words, names, numbers, slogans, titles and character names) or *audio-visual* (i.e., symbols, pictures, designs, devices, or distinctive sounds, product configurations, trade dress, advertising formats and artistic characterizations).

The Lanham Act also provides for the registration of two specialized types of trade or service marks, both of which designate a particular relation between the user of a mark and the organization which actually owns the mark. A "certification mark" is used to certify that goods or services of someone other than the owner of the mark come from a particular region or other origin, possess particular characteristics in the material, mode of manufacture, quality, accuracy of the goods or service or were the product of the labor of members of a union or other organization. A "collective mark" is a trademark or service mark used by members of a cooperative, association or other collective group or organization, including marks used to indicate membership in the group.

The reason why marks of all sorts are federally registrable but business names are not is due to the different functions played by marks and trade names. Trademarks and service marks are generally used by manufacturers and franchisors to "reach over the shoulder" of retailers and franchisees, enabling the manufacturer and franchisor to establish the identity of the product or service in the mind of the consumer independently of the efforts of retailers or franchisees. Indeed, with the increasing depersonalization of consumer relations and the proliferation of franchising, the function of trade marks and service marks has gradually shifted from that of identifying a single known source of goods or services to that of assuring a uniform quality in goods or services originating from a single unknown source or a number of different sources, known or unknown.

With that shift in the function served by trademarks and service marks, it has been but a short further step for businesses to begin using trademarks purely as an advertising device to *create* goodwill for new products and services. An established business, for example, may create a family of marks or an all-purpose "house" mark in order to associate new products or services with the reputation of an established product or service or the business itself. Likewise, a new business may create marks with a sufficiently powerful advertising image that they create instant consumer demand for a wholly new product or service.

These uses of trademarks and service marks are generally national or international in scope and are thus an appropriate subject for federal regulation—though continued state protection of such marks is by no means excluded. Marks which incorporate the tradename of a business are fully protectible as trademarks or service marks. The misleading use of other business names (as well as other forms of palming off, such as deceptive product substitution and alteration), on the other hand, is more likely to involve purely localized conduct on the part of distributors and retailers and is thus a more appropriate subject for state common-law or statutory regulation.

So long as there is no conflict with federal law, states have considerable latitude in how they choose to regulate the local use of marks and names. In *Friedman v. Rogers* (1979), for example, the Supreme Court found no First Amendment violation in a state statute prohibiting the practice of optometry under a trade name, noting that the ill-defined association of tradenames with price and quality information can be manipulated by users of trade names, creating a significant possibility that trade names will be used to mislead the public, while restrictions on the use of trade names will have only the most incidental effect on the contents of the commercial speech of optometrists. But see *Sambo's Restaurants Inc. v. Ann Arbor* (1981) (holding that a restaurant had a constitutional right to use the name "Sambo's" and that a city's refusal to permit the erection of a "Sambo's" sign because it connoted a racial stereotype violates the First Amendment). See also Lanham Act § 39a, 15 U.S.C.A. § 1121a, enacted in 1984 to legislatively overrule *Century 21 Real Estate Corp. v. Nevada Real Estate Advisory Commission* (1978), which had held that the Lanham Trademark Act did not preempt a state regulation requiring licensed Century 21 real estate brokers to modify federally registered trademarked logos so that 50 percent rather than 20 percent of the surface area of any advertisement would display the name of the local franchisee. The new section 39a prohibits states or other political subdivisions from requiring the alteration of a federally registered mark or requiring the display of any additional mark in a manner differing from the certificate of registration.

State statutory trademark law offers protection not available under either common law or federal law. While the Lanham Act is limited to eliminating confusion in commerce, for example, state trademark statutes also protect against the nondeceptive dilution of the advertising impact of particularly distinctive trade symbols. But cf. *Hyatt Corporation v. Hyatt Legal Services* (1985) (holding there to be a conflict between an interpretation of a state anti-dilution law, allowing for a nationwide injunction, and the Commerce Clause of the U.S. Constitution.)

c. A Note on Nomenclature

Given the difference between the common-law and statutory definitions of the terms "trademark" and "trade name," it is necessary to specify a uniform system of nomenclature. Hereafter, the terms will be used in their modern sense unless otherwise specified. The term "mark" will normally refer to trademarks, service marks, certification marks and collective marks as defined in the Lanham Act. The terms "trademark" and "service mark" will also be used in their modern sense, as defined by the Lanham Act, and when used together, will impliedly refer to certification and collective marks as well since, as we have seen, these marks are simply specialized types of trade or service marks. The term "trade name" will normally refer exclusively to business names. The phrase "mark or name" will be used as a shorthand way of referring to trademarks, service marks and trade names.

2. ACQUIRING RIGHTS IN A MARK OR NAME

The process by which a business acquires common-law rights in a mark or name and prevents others from interfering with those rights is essentially a unitary one. A business merely adopts a trade symbol, begins using it to identify goods, services or the business, and brings infringement proceedings against any subsequent users of the same or a similar mark or name.

The process by which one acquires and vindicates federal (or state) statutory rights in a mark, on the other hand, is a bifurcated one. To obtain federal protection, for example, a business must register its mark with the Patent and Trademark Office (PTO) of the U.S. Department of Commerce. Only after a mark is registered may a business bring federal statutory infringement proceedings.

In 1988, Congress amended the Lanham Act to allow a pre-use application for registration by a person having a bona fide intention to use the mark in commerce. Prior to that amendment, applicants had to establish, as a condition for federal registration, that they had actually used the mark in commerce.

The PTO maintains two registers. Marks intended for use or actually used in commerce or registered in certain foreign countries and having sufficient inherent or acquired distinctiveness to identify and distinguish goods or services may be registered on the Principal Register. Marks which are merely capable of identifying and distinguishing goods or services may be registered on the Supplemental Register. Only registration on the Principal Register provides the registrant with any federal trademark protection. Supplemental registration merely enables a U.S. national to obtain protection abroad under trademark systems which permit registration without proof of actual use or secondary meaning but require foreign marks to be registered at home as a condition for local registration.

The registration process may take the form of an *ex parte* examination by a PTO trademark examiner, with a right of administrative appeal to the PTO's Trademark Trial and Appeal Board (TTAB), or it may take the form of an *inter partes* (i.e., contested) proceeding conducted before the TTAB in its trial capacity. (Before 1958, incidentally, *inter partes* proceedings and appeals of *ex parte* proceedings were heard by the Commissioner of Patents or his designate. With the establishment of the TTAB, appeals to the Commissioner in his supervisory capacity are reserved for unusual circumstances.)

Any person likely to be commercially damaged by registration of a mark may file an opposition to registration or, if the mark has already been registered, a petition to cancel the registration. Final administrative decisions regarding registration may be judicially reviewed in one of two ways: (1) by appealing directly to the Court of Appeals for the Federal Circuit (CAFC), (a court created in 1982 to assume jurisdiction of the old Court of Customs and Patent Appeals (CCPA) and Court of Claims) which essentially reviews the closed administrative record of proceedings before the PTO, much as an appellate court reviews the record of a trial court; or (2) by filing a civil action in a federal district court for de novo proceedings in which one can litigate infringement claims and introduce new evidence with respect to issues raised in PTO registration proceedings. Federal district court proceedings may be appealed to the federal courts of appeals.

Although federal district court proceedings technically constitute de novo trial proceedings in which parties may present new evidence, review of PTO proceedings is limited to those issues raised before the PTO. The standard of review for PTO findings has been variously stated, but in general the courts appear reluctant to reverse administrative findings unless they are "clearly erroneous" or the district court, confronted with new evidence, has a "thorough conviction" to the contrary.

Federal registration confers a number of benefits. At common law, for example, priority in the use of a mark or name gives priority of right only in those markets in which the mark or name is actually being used or into which expansion is probable. See, e.g., *Food Fair Stores, Inc. v. Square*

Deal Market (1953) (holding that a local supermarket's priority of use of the name "Food Fair" in the District of Columbia gives it, rather than an east coast supermarket chain originally founded in Baltimore, priority in the entire Washington D.C. metropolitan area). Federal registration on the Principal Register, on the other hand, constitutes nationwide constructive notice and thus confers nationwide protection for marks which would otherwise be only locally protected. Registration on the Principal Register also constitutes prima facie evidence, in any subsequent proceedings, of the registrant's exclusive right to use the mark in commerce. After five years that prima facie right can become incontestable, upon compliance with certain formalities and subject to certain specified limitations. Federal courts have jurisdiction, without regard to the amount in controversy, over infringement actions involving federally registered marks. The registrant has the right to *ex parte* seizure of goods bearing a counterfeit mark, which the Act defines as "a spurious designation that is identical with or substantially indistinguishable from a registered mark." The registrant also has the right to treble damages and attorney's fees against an intentional user of a counterfeit mark, absent extenuating circumstances. In addition, there are severe criminal penalties for the use of counterfeit marks. See 18 U.S.C.A. § 2320. Finally, registration on the Principal Register gives the registrant the right to have the Bureau of Customs exclude imports bearing marks that would infringe the registered mark.

While one may not federally register a trade name, the Lanham Act does provide trade names with certain other forms of protection. If a trade name is used to identify goods or services as well as a business, it can be registered as a trade or service mark. The owner of a trade name may also oppose the registration of a confusingly similar mark, section 2(d), 15 U.S.C.A. § 1052(d); may prevent a federally registered mark from becoming incontestable, section 15, 15 U.S.C.A. § 1065; may prevent importation of articles which copy or simulate the name, section 42, 15 U.S.C.A. § 1124; and may utilize section 43 of the Lanham Act, 15 U.S.C.A. § 1125, which creates a federal civil cause of action against anyone who uses in commerce a false designation of origin or a false or misleading description or representation of facts. See Chapter 8 infra. Section 44 of the Lanham Act provides explicit protection for trade names of nationals of countries with which the U.S. has entered into treaties for the protection of marks and names.

State statutes providing for registration of marks are generally patterned after the U.S. Trademark Association's Model State Trademark Bill, which is, in turn, patterned in large part on the Lanham Act. Registration under these statutes is available for marks which are not eligible for federal registration due to their non-use in interstate or foreign commerce. In most states trade names may not be registered.

In contrast to federal registration, state registration confers few advantages over common-law protection. See, e.g., *Burger King of Florida, Inc. v. Hoots* (1968) (holding that registration under Illinois Trade Mark Act did not give more protection than was available under common law and could not enlarge the common law so as to prohibit statewide use of a federally registered mark). Indeed, the most important feature of the Model Bill is the protection it provides against "dilution," and that protection is available to both registered and unregistered marks and to trade names as well.

While the procedures for obtaining common-law and statutory protection are different, the substantive prerequisites for obtaining protection are quite similar. For a business to establish and maintain common-law rights in a mark or name, the mark or name must (1) be in actual use in association with goods, services or a business, (2) possess sufficient inherent or acquired distinctiveness to succeed in identifying the goods, services or business, and (3) be otherwise suitable for use as a trade mark, service mark or trade name. For federal registration, only the first requirement is different. A mark must either be intended for use or in actual use in U.S. commerce or be registered in a country which is a party to any trademark convention or treaty to which the U.S. is also a party.

a. Actual Use/Intended Use/Foreign Registration

Actual and continuous use of a mark or name to identify goods, services or a business is a necessary condition for acquiring and maintaining common-law rights in the mark or name. Priority of such use determines who has priority of rights—even for those common-law marks which qualify for federal registration. Priority among federally registered marks which are also protected at common law is not separately governed by first interstate use or a race to the Patent and Trademark Office but, as with purely common-law trademarks and trade names, by the initial race to the marketplace.

The extent and duration of use of a mark or name need not be great, so long as the mark or name is used in this country by a going business whose sales are more than token or sporadic. The Trademark Revision Act of 1988 amended the Lanham Act to make clear that "use in commerce" means the bona fide use of a mark in the ordinary course of trade and not merely a token use to reserve a right in the mark. 15 U.S.C.A. § 1126.

If a mark has not been used in U.S. commerce, it may nevertheless be federally registered if: 1) There is a bona fide intent to use the mark in U.S. commerce, in which case the filing date will constitute a constructive use date, 15 U.S.C.A. §§ 1051, 1057, or 2) registration is based on a foreign registration by a person whose country of origin is a party to an international convention relating to marks, to which the U.S. is also a party, in which case the foreign filing date will be treated as a constructive U.S. filing for purposes of determining priority. 15 U.S.C.A. § 1126. Under the provisions for pre-use application for federal registration, the applicant has six months in which to file a verified statement of use in commerce, which maybe extended for successive six month periods aggregating not more than 24 months. Applicants for federal registration based on a qualifying foreign registration may obtain registration without proof of actual use in U.S. commerce or anywhere else in the world. The latter provision implements Article 4 of the International Convention for the Protection of Industrial Property (the Paris Convention) and a number of similar treaties to which the U.S. is a signatory.

Just as a foreign trademark may be federally registered even though it has not been used in the United States or elsewhere, so a domestic mark which is capable of distinguishing goods or services but has not actually been used in the United States or acquired a secondary meaning, may be federally registered for the limited purpose of qualifying the mark for registration in foreign countries. These marks, as we have seen, are registered on the Supplemental Register, whereas foreign marks actually used in commerce or registered in a foreign country are registered on the Principal Register. Supplemental registration, it will be recalled, confers no domestic rights but merely enables a U.S.

national to obtain trademark rights in a foreign country. Principal registration, on the other hand, affords the registrant the full panoply of federal protection.

In order to register any mark—foreign or domestic—on the Principal Register, however, the mark or name must possess sufficient inherent or acquired distinctiveness to succeed in identifying a specific product, service or business and must be otherwise suitable for use as a mark or name. Similar requirements must be met in order to obtain common-law protection for a mark or name.

Where a mark or name has acquired distinctiveness (i.e. secondary meaning), priority of secondary meaning rather than priority of use determines the priority of rights in the mark or name. If a mark or name is inherently unsuitable for use as a product, service or business identifier, the mark or name will be denied protection even if it has acquired secondary meaning. It is to these two requirements—inherent or acquired distinctiveness and suitability for use as a mark or name—that we now turn.

b. Inherent and Acquired Distinctiveness

Marks and names are not all of the same degree of distinctiveness. They may be viewed, rather, as falling along a spectrum of distinctiveness, ranging from inherently distinctive marks and names, which include fanciful, arbitrary or suggestive marks and names, and merely descriptive marks and names that must acquire distinctiveness in order to be legally protected, to those which are inherently unsuitable for use as a mark or name because they are either a generic term, a functional product feature or deceptive. See *Abercrombie & Fitch Co. v. Hunting World, Inc.* (1976) (arranging marks in ascending order of strength into the categories (1) generic, (2) descriptive, (3) suggestive, and (4) arbitrary or fanciful).

(1) Inherently Distinctive Marks and Names

Inherently distinctive marks (known at common law as "technical trademarks") and inherently distinctive trade names are those marks and names which are either *fanciful* (i.e., expressly created for the purpose of identifying a product, service or business) or *arbitrary* (i.e., in common usage but used in a new and arbitrary way in order to identify a product, service or business). Businesses may obtain common-law protection for inherently distinctive marks and names and federally register inherently distinctive marks immediately upon adoption and the requisite intended or actual use or foreign registration. Businesses frequently choose, however, to use a descriptive word or name or a distinctive product or business feature to identify their product, service or business. To obtain protection for marks and names of either sort, proof of secondary meaning has traditionally been required.

Federal registration under the 1905 Act, as we have seen, was only available for "technical" (i.e., inherently distinctive) trademarks. In applying the Act, however, the lower federal courts often strained to avoid classifying marks as descriptive (and hence not federally registrable) and thus developed a third category of inherently distinctive marks which was subsequently recognized by implication in the Lanham Act—namely marks which are suggestive as opposed to descriptive. Suggestive marks were said to shed some light on the characteristics of a product but only by way of suggestion. Under section 2(e) of the Lanham Act, 15 U.S.C.A. § 1052(e), only those marks which are "merely descriptive" are to be denied registration in the absence of proof that they have become distinctive of the applicant's goods. Thus, whereas in *Franklin Knitting Mills, Inc. v. Fashionit Sweater Mills, Inc.* (1923), "Fashion Knit" was classified as descriptive of knitted sweaters and thus not entitled to registration under the 1905 Act, the term "Skinvisible" was held in *Minnesota Mining and Manufacturing Co. v. Johnson & Johnson* (1972) to be suggestive rather than "merely descriptive" of transparent adhesive bandage tape and thus registrable under the Lanham Act without proof of secondary meaning.

(2) Descriptive or Misdescriptive Marks and Names

Today, federal as well as common-law protection is available for descriptive marks. The distinction between suggestive and descriptive marks remains important, however, for it marks the dividing line on the spectrum of distinctiveness between inherently distinctive marks and names and those which must be shown to have become distinctive. On the one side, inherently distinctive marks and names, including suggestive marks and names, are entitled to legal protection merely upon a showing that they are being used to identify goods, services or a business. On the other side, descriptive marks and names are only entitled to protection upon a showing that they have acquired a "secondary meaning"—that is, an association in the mind of the consuming public with a particular company or its product or service.

The term "secondary meaning" is somewhat misleading. The secondary meaning of the mark or name is secondary only in the sense that it is a new meaning given to a mark or name with an older "primary" meaning. In order for a descriptive mark or name to be protected as a trademark, service mark or trade name, its new or "secondary" meaning must in fact be the meaning the public usually attaches to the mark or name. In that sense, secondary meaning is not secondary at all, but the primary significance which the public attaches to the mark or name. Because of the inherent ambiguity in the term "secondary meaning," section 2(f) of the Lanham Act simply requires that a descriptive mark "become distinctive" of the applicant's goods in commerce in order to be registered. 15 U.S.C.A. § 1052(f).

In many cases the line between suggestive and descriptive marks and names is difficult to draw. The standard test used by the courts is whether the mark "requires imagination, thought and perception to reach a conclusion as to the nature of the product or service." Compare *Maidenform, Inc. v. Munsingwear, Inc.* (1977) (slogan "Underneath It All" as applied to ladies' undergarment apparel held to require such an exercise of imagination) with *Zatarains, Inc. v. Oak Grove Smokehouse, Inc.* (1983) ("Fish–Fri" and "Chick–Fri") as applied to batter mixes used to fry food held to require no such exercise of imagination). A second approach is to consider the burden which a grant of immediate protection will place on others attempting to describe their own goods, services or business. The secondary meaning requirement, in other words, should be viewed as protecting the public's right to use common descriptive words and symbols.

Some judges and commentators have expressed the view that section 2(d) of the Lanham Act (which prohibits the registration of a mark which so resembles another previously used mark or name as to be likely to cause confusion, mistake or deception) protects the private property in a previously used trademark or trade name with a wider moat or higher fence than is required by section 2(e) to be built around publicly owned descriptive words or phrases. See, e.g., *Minnesota Mining & Manufacturing Co. v. Johnson and Johnson* (1972) (opinion of Rich, J.). A majority of the CCPA, however, takes the view that an opposer's right under section 2(e) to protect his and the public's interest in using the allegedly descriptive term is no weaker than the right under section 2(d) to protect a private property interest in a previously used mark or name. See *Minnesota Mining & Mfg. Co.,* supra (opinions of Baldwin, J., Almond, J., and Lane, J.). The only difference is that a PTO refusal to register a descriptive mark amounts merely to a finding that federal registration is premature in the absence of evidence of secondary meaning, whereas a refusal to register a mark because of its confusing similarity with a previously used mark or name amounts to a finding that registration is altogether inappropriate so long as the likelihood of confusion continues to exist.

Because secondary meaning is essentially a question of fact it must be established by the party seeking protection of the mark or name, through either direct or circumstantial evidence. The most comprehensive (and expensive) form of direct evidence is a properly designed and conducted consumer survey. Expert testimony or even the testimony of random purchasers, however, may suffice. Secondary meaning may even be established by circumstantial evidence, such as proof of the amount expended on promoting the mark or name in advertising and the duration of use of the mark or name, from which buyer association may be inferred. Section 2(f) of the Lanham Act goes one step further by specifically providing that proof of substantially exclusive and continuous use of a mark for five years prior to an application for registration on the Principal Register may be accepted by the Patent and Trademark Office as prima facie evidence that a mark has become distinctive and therefore registrable. See 15 U.S.C.A. § 1052(f).

Geographically descriptive marks are distinguishable from other descriptive marks only insofar as the Lanham Act is attempting to draw a meaningful distinction between marks which are "merely" descriptive and those which are "primarily" geographically descriptive. The difference in terminology suggests that marks are descriptive only if they perform no other function, while marks are geographically descriptive if their primary (but not necessarily sole) function is to describe geographically.

Even if a term is primarily geographically descriptive and has not come to identify a particular producer of goods, businesses from a locale generally known for high quality goods may have a cause of action for false advertising against a business that falsely represents its goods as coming from that locale. (See Chapter 8, infra.)

Included within the category of descriptive marks and names are not only those terms which describe a specific characteristic, component or geographic origin or locale of goods, services or businesses but also those terms which describe the intended use or users or merely ascribe merit to or promise a pleasurable result from the product, service or business. Personal names are likewise treated as lacking sufficient inherent distinctiveness to identify a product, service or business and thus must be shown to have acquired a secondary meaning in order to be protected as a trade mark, service mark or trade name.

Because personal names may be used by more than one person, the use of a personal name in connection with a product, service or business merely serves to indicate that a person by that name happens to be associated with the product, service or business and not to indicate that all products, services or businesses identified by a personal name are necessarily associated with a single person by that name. Accordingly, the common law will not protect a personal name as a trademark in the absence of proof of secondary meaning. Similarly, under § 2(e) of the Lanham Act, 15 U.S.C.A. § 1052(e), a name which is "primarily merely a surname" will be denied registration on the Principal Register in the absence of proof that it has become distinctive. Although the applicant has the burden of establishing that a surname has acquired a secondary meaning, the PTO has the initial burden of proving that a word is in fact "primarily merely" a surname.

While the statutory language itself sheds no light on how a name can be both "primarily" and "merely" a surname, the PTO and CCPA have agreed that the test to be applied in the registration of names is whether the primary significance of the word to the purchasing public is merely that of a surname. See e.g., *Ex parte Rivera Watch Corp.* (1955) (holding that the average member of the consuming public would not consider "Rivera" to be merely a surname). Although each case must ultimately be decided on its own facts, some guidelines have emerged. Adding a first name to a surname or merely hyphenating two surnames, for example, may be enough to allow registration without proof of secondary meaning, though merely adding initials to a surname apparently is not. Only when a surname predominates, in other words, will a mark be deemed lacking in inherent distinctiveness and thus in need of proof of secondary meaning for federal registration. See, e.g. *In re Hutchinson Technology, Inc.* (1988), in which the CAFC held that, notwithstanding the PTO examiner's citation to telephone directories containing over 200 persons with the surname "Hutchinson", and the examiner's conclusion that the term "technology" was merely descriptive and added nothing to the mark, the mark "Hutchinson Technology," as applied to the goods of a business located in Hutchinson, Minnesota, was not primarily merely a surname and the PTO's refusal to register was in error.

Historical names, such as "George Washington" may be used as a trademark, service mark or trade name without proof of secondary meaning so long as they do not disparage or falsely suggest a connection with a living or deceased person. See

Lanham Act, section 2(a), 15 U.S.C.A. § 1052(a). The rationale for treating historical names as inherently distinctive is apparently that such names will be understood to be functioning as a trademark, service mark or trade name when used in association with goods, services or a business.

Unauthorized use of names, portraits or signatures of living persons and deceased presidents whose spouses are still living, on the other hand, will be denied federal registration, see Lanham Act, section 2(c), 15 U.S.C.A. § 1052(c) and may be held to constitute a common-law invasion of privacy as well. See, e.g., *Hirsch v. S.C. Johnson & Son, Inc.* (1979) (holding that use of the term "Crazylegs" on a moisturizing shaving gel for women constituted an actionable appropriation of a well known athlete's nickname as well as an infringement of the athlete's common-law trade name). See generally Chapter 6, infra.

Although the Lanham Act explicitly mentions slogans only in section 23's definition of a mark entitled to be registered on the Supplemental Register and in section 45's definition of a service mark, the courts have held that even rather lengthy slogans may also be registered on the Principal Register as trademarks. If the slogan is sufficiently imaginative (e.g., contains a double entendre), it is registrable without proof of distinctiveness. Purely laudatory or descriptive slogans, on the other hand, will require such proof.

Likewise treated as descriptive are a class of marks and names which do not describe but rather *misdescribe* a product, service or business in a nonobvious but harmless way. Under section 2(e) of the Lanham Act, marks of this sort are termed "deceptively misdescriptive" marks. See 15 U.S.C.A. § 1052(e). They are to be distinguished from "deceptive" marks, which are deemed wholly unsuitable for use as a mark and thus not federally registrable. See Lanham Act, section 2(a), 15 U.S.C.A. § 1052(a). Deceptively misdescriptive marks, by contrast, may be registered if they have a secondary meaning. The trademark "Glass Wax," for example, does not accurately describe but actually deceptively misdescribes the product it identifies—a metal and glass cleaner which contains little or no wax. When federal registration was sought for "Glass Wax," the PTO found the mark to be deceptive and refused to register it. On appeal the court, while finding no evidence that consumers would have felt deceived if informed the product contained no wax, nevertheless upheld the PTO's denial of registration, not because the mark was deceptive but because, as a deceptively misdescriptive mark, it had not been shown to have acquired a secondary meaning. *Gold Seal Co. v. Weeks* (1955). The mark was later registered on the basis of its having presumptively acquired secondary meaning as a result of exclusive and continuous use for a period of five years.

The reason a deceptively misdescriptive mark is entitled to any protection at all is that, while it misdescribes the product it identifies, it does so in a way that does not affect a consumer's decision or preference and is thus not materially deceptive. Unlike an obviously misdescriptive (and hence arbitrary) mark, however, a deceptively misdescriptive mark does *appear* to describe a product or service. Thus, it is no more distinctive than an accurate description and must be shown to have acquired a secondary meaning before it can be protected or registered.

A similar distinction can be drawn between arbitrary, deceptively misdescriptive and deceptive geographic terms. Use of the term "North Pole" to identify ice cream, for example, is an arbitrary or suggestive use of a geographic term and will be protected without proof of secondary meaning. Use of the phrase "Maid in Paris" as a designation for perfumes not made in Paris, on the other hand, has been held to be deceptive, given a discernible consumer preference for Parisian perfumes, and is thus not entitled to federal registration under any circumstances. *In re Richemond* (1961). Falling between these two extremes is the term "Italian Maide" which as used on canned vegetables has been held not to be so obviously misdescriptive as to constitute an arbitrary use of a geographic term, nor so deceptive, in the absence of proof of a discernible consumer preference for Italian vegetables, as to be beyond all legal protection. *In re Amerise* (1969). Accordingly, the term was classified as a "primarily geographically deceptively misdescriptive" mark for which secondary meaning was required in order to obtain federal registration. Compare *In re Perry Manufacturing Co.* (1989) (holding that because New York is the home of a thriving garment industry and a hub of fashion, the mark "Perry New York" as applied to clothing manufactured in North Carolina is deceptive and thus unregistrable) with *In re Nantucket, Inc.* (1982) (holding that because there was no indication that the public would expect men's shirts to come from Nantucket Island, registration could not be denied on the ground the mark "Nantucket" is primarily geographically deceptively misdescriptive).

A descriptive geographic term may also be used as a certification mark, in which case it may be registered without proof of secondary meaning. See, e.g., *Community of Roquefort v. William Faehndrich, Inc.* (1962) (holding the term "Roquefort" to have been validly registered, without proof of secondary meaning, as a certification mark for cheeses processed in the community of Roquefort, France, according to traditional methods). Certification marks may be cancelled, however, if they do not continue to meet the Lanham Act's strict standards for a certification mark. Section 14(5) of the Act, 15 U.S.C.A. § 1064(5), allows a private person who believes he will be damaged by the registration of a certification mark to petition for cancellation of the mark if the registrant (1) does not control or is not able legitimately to exercise control over the mark, (2) engages in the production or marketing of any goods or services to which the certification mark is applied, (3) permits the use of the certification mark for purposes other than to certify or (4) discriminately refuses to certify or continue to certify the goods or services of any person who maintains the standards or conditions the mark certifies.

(3) Distinctive Product and Business Features

A final class of trade symbols for which proof of secondary meaning is required are those composed of distinctive product or business features, such as distinctive product designs, packaging, service uniforms, vehicles, business premises, literary or artistic titles or characters or a host of other similar features. Because distinctive product and business features did not fit comfortably under the common law's definition of technical trademarks and trade names, the courts tended to treat the protection of distinctive product and business features as a distinct branch of the law of unfair competition, separate from the common law of trademarks and trade names. The PTO and the federal courts, for their part, were initially slow to grant federal trademark protection for such features, but have increasingly followed the lead provided by the common law of unfair competition. At the same time, federal patent and copyright law have placed certain limitations on common-law protection of distinctive product and business features.

The test generally used to distinguish those product and business features that may serve as a protectible mark from those that may not is that of "functionality." See generally *In re Morton–Norwich Products, Inc.* (1982). A feature may be described as functional not only where it contributes in some utilitarian way but also where it contributes in some aesthetic way to the value of a product. A red heart-shaped box, for example, is as much a functional feature for Valentine's Day candy as a particular shape is for a wrench. See also *International Order of Job's Daughters v. Lindeburg & Co.* (1980) (holding that use of the insignia of a fraternal organization on jewelry constituted a functional aesthetic component of the jewelry, not a trademark). But see *In re Morton–Norwich, Products, Inc.* (1982) (holding that the shape of a plastic spray bottle container that was also the subject of a design patent was not *de jure* functional). A feature is non-functional only if, when it is changed or omitted, the value of the goods themselves (apart from any value gained by association with a particular producer) is not substantially reduced. However, a combination of features may be nonfunctional even though elements of the combination are functional. See *Hartford House, Ltd. v. Hallmark Cards, Inc.* (1988) (holding that the overall appearance of plaintiff's line of greeting cards constituted nonfunctional, inherently distinctive trade dress protectible under section 43(a) of the Lanham Act and that defendant's competing line of cards was confusingly similar).

While many common-law courts recognized the need and attempted to achieve a balance between the interest in protecting the public from deception and the interest in allowing the duplication of unpatented and uncopyrighted features of a product, many other courts, influenced by the emerging tort of misappropriation (see Chapter 6, infra) were less willing to protect the interest in free copying.

Because of the tendency of some courts to provide relief against copying per se rather than against deceptive copying, the Supreme Court of the United States eventually found it necessary to consider whether there was a conflict between federal patent law and state unfair competition law when the latter imposes liability for or prohibits the copying of an article which is protected by neither a federal patent nor a copyright. See *Sears, Roebuck & Co. v. Stiffel Corp.* (1964) and *Compco Corp. v. Day–Brite Lighting, Inc.* (1964), discussed in Chapter 1, supra, where the Court found such a conflict to exist.

As sweeping as the *Sears–Compco* decisions initially appeared to be, they in fact left considerable room for continued state protection of distinctive product features. The Court noted by way of dictum, for example, that just as a state "may protect businesses in the use of their trademarks, labels or distinctive dress in the packaging of goods," so it "may, in appropriate circumstances, require that goods, whether patented or unpatented, be labeled or that other precautionary steps be taken to prevent customers from being misled as to the source of goods and may impose liability on those who violate such requirements." From that dictum it appears clear that, whatever effect *Sears–Compco* may have had on the common law of misappropriation (see Chapter 6, infra), it merely places *remedial* limitations on the power of states to prevent palming off, and does not altogether abolish state power to protect distinctive product features.

The foregoing dictum also suggests that a distinction can be drawn between preventing the copying of a product and preventing copying of the container or packaging in which the product is marketed. A state is arguably free not only to require that a product be labeled but also to prohibit the copying of a container or packaging whose use would be misleading. If a packaging or container feature is capable of being patented or copyrighted, however, *Sears–Compco* would appear to limit the power of states to prohibit the copying of that feature just as it limits the power of states to prohibit copying of the product itself.

The *Sears–Compco* cases also left open the possibility that states may protect distinctive product and packaging features where such protection does not in fact conflict with federal law. Determining whether there is a conflict between federal and state law requires an examination not only of the policy being furthered by state law but also the policy underlying the particular federal statute in question. Although the 1976 Copyright Act expressly preempted state law which seeks to grant rights equivalent to copyright in works capable of federal copyright protection, for example, it expressly permitted state protection with respect to (1) subject matter not covered by the Act or (2) the extension of rights not equivalent to those created by the Act. See Chapter 6, infra.

An illustration of the distinction between subject matter not covered by federal copyright law and rights not equivalent to federal copyright is to be found in that branch of the common law of unfair competition which protects literary or artistic titles and characters. Titles and characters have long received the same protection as other distinctive product features. They are to literary and artistic products what color and design are to products generally. Literary or artistic characters may be entitled to a measure of federal copyright protection, either independently or as a part of a larger copyrightable work, but a copyright on a particular work does not include an exclusive right to the title of the work.

While there is no constitutional prohibition against federal copyright protection for literary titles, nor for that matter any expressly prohibitory language in the federal copyright law itself, the courts interpreted the 1909 Copyright Act as not extending to literary titles and Congress, by its silence on the matter in the 1976 Copyright Act, has apparently approved that construction. Consequently, states remain free and under their common law of unfair competition have in fact provided legal protection for literary and artistic titles.

For the most part, the protection provided has simply been a species of the common-law prohibition against palming off and thus constitutes a right not equivalent to those created by the federal copyright act. Because literary and artistic titles are not copyrightable subject matter, however, states are free, if they so choose, to protect them against copying per se, just as they are free to prevent dilution of distinctive trademarks and tradenames.

Literary and artistic characters, like literary and artistic titles, have been found to be qualified for common-law protection as distinctive identifying features of a literary or artistic work. For example, just as Bud Fisher was able to federally register the title of his cartoon strip "Mutt and Jeff," so he was able to obtain protection for the cartoon characters themselves, upon showing that both the title and the characters had acquired a secondary meaning, denoting the cartoons of Bud Fisher. See *Fisher v. Star Co.* (1921).

In contrast to literary and artistic titles, however, literary and artistic characters may be entitled to federal copyright protection. Cartoon characters in particular are clearly entitled to such protection. If rendered in three dimensional form, cartoon characters may even be entitled to design patent protection. (See Chapter 6, infra.) Copyrightable or patentable characters may nevertheless be protected under the common law of unfair competition against deceptive imitation so long as the state protection against deception does not grant a right equivalent to copyright. States may thus require labelling, even if they may not prohibit copying. As with product features generally, federal patent and copyright law merely limit the remedies which a state may make available to prevent deception.

A final possibility left open by *Sears–Compco* is that of obtaining *federal* trademark protection for distinctive product and business features. While for a time some lower courts viewed *Sears–Compco* as having held that the patent and copyright clause of the Constitution placed constitutional limits on the power of any government—federal or state—to prevent the simulation of unpatented articles, the prevailing view, adopted by the Supreme Court itself in *Goldstein v. California* (1973), is that *Sears–Compco* is merely to be read as having held that, because of the supremacy clause of the Constitution, federal patent law preempts state unfair competition law where there is a conflict between the two. Thus, the federal government remains free to prohibit or otherwise regulate product and business imitation—at least so long as such regulation is within its constitutional powers to grant patents and copyrights or regulate commerce and does not conflict with other constitutional provisions, such as the First Amendment.

Not surprisingly, businesses have increasingly resorted to federal trademark law to obtain protection of distinctive product and business features.

For a time, the PTO simply refused to grant registration on the Principal Register for any distinctive product configurations or containers. See, e.g., *Ex parte Minnesota Mining & Mfg. Co.* (1952) (holding the sleigh shaped dispenser for "Scotch Brand Cellophane Tape" not to be a "device" within the Lanham Act's definition of a trademark). Even today the PTO will ordinarily require proof of secondary meaning before registering product configurations, packaging shapes or colors on the Principal Register and will altogether deny federal registration for "functional" product or packaging features—even where such features have acquired a secondary meaning. Where a container configuration or some other form of trade dress obviously serves only to identify the source of the product or service, on the other hand, proof of secondary meaning is apparently unnecessary for federal protection. See e.g., *In re International Playtex Corp.* (TTAB, 1967) (permitting an ice cream cone shaped container for holding baby pants to be registered on the Principal Register without proof of secondary meaning).

The PTO was also slow to permit registration of literary or artistic titles. Regardless of the arbitrary or fanciful nature of the title of a single book, drama, movie, record, song or radio or television program, it must be shown to have acquired secondary meaning (i.e., an established association with the particular work) in order to be federally registrable as a trademark or service mark. See, e.g., *Application of Cooper* (1958) (affirming PTO refusal to register "Teeny-big" as a trademark for a book for children and holding that in the absence of proof of secondary meaning, the title was to be treated as descriptive or generic).

The CCPA has indicated a greater willingness to order the registration of literary or artistic *series* titles without proof of secondary meaning, inasmuch as the name for a series serves a more obvious trademark or service mark function by indicating that each unit in the series comes from the same source. For similar reasons, the PTO has permitted registration of a fictitious name of a performer and the name of a musical group as service marks identifying the entertainment services rendered. See, e.g., *In re Folk* (1968) (allowing a radio and television story teller to register "The Lollipop Princess"); *In re Ames* (1968) (allowing a band to register "Neal Ford and the Fanatics"). Section 15 of the Lanham Act specifically provides for service mark registration of titles, character names and other distinctive features of radio or television programs. See 15 U.S.C.A. § 1127.

c. Inherently Unsuitable Marks and Names

Marks and names requiring proof of secondary meaning are to be distinguished not only from inherently distinctive marks and names but also from those words, symbols, designs and devices which are deemed wholly unsuitable for use as a trademark, service mark or trade name. A mark or name may be deemed unsuitable either because it is deceptive, immoral, disparaging or confusing or because it constitutes a generic term or a functional product or business feature.

(1) Deceptive, Immoral, Disparaging or Confusing Marks and Names

Section 2(a) of the Lanham Act, 15 U.S.C.A. § 1052(a) authorizes the PTO to refuse registration of marks which consist of deceptive, immoral or scandalous matter or matter which may disparage or falsely suggest a connection with persons living or dead, institutions, beliefs or national symbols, or bring them into contempt or disrepute. See e.g. *In re Anti–Communist World Freedom Congress, Inc.* (1969) (refusing to register a mark composed of a hammer and sickle with a big cross through it as tending to disparage a national symbol of the then Soviet Union); *In re Runsdorf* (1971) (refusing to register "Bubby Trap" as a mark for brassieres on the ground that it would be offensive to a segment of the public's sense of propriety or morality). But see *In re Hershey* (1988) (holding that "BIG PECKER BRAND" as applied to T-shirts is not scandalous). As we have seen, a mark or name may also be deemed unsuitable because it so resembles another previously used mark or name as to be likely to cause confusion, mistake or deception. See Lanham Act § 2(d), 15 U.S.C.A. § 1052(d).

(2) Generic Terms

A mark or name may also be deemed unsuitable because it consists of a generic term. Section 14(3) of the Lanham Act, 15 U.S.C.A. § 1064(3), originally referred somewhat confusingly to this type of term as a "common descriptive name," which is not to be confused with section 2(e)'s reference to "merely descriptive" or "primarily geographically descriptive" terms. The Trademark Revision Act of 1988 eliminated the confusion by amending section 14(3), changing the term "common descriptive name" to "generic name." Generic terms are to be distinguished from descriptive terms. Descriptive terms, as we have seen, are those adjectives or adverbs commonly used to describe a product, service or business. They are capable of acquiring a secondary meaning and receiving protection as trade marks, service marks or trade names even though they continue (albeit in a subsidiary sense) to perform their descriptive function. Generic terms, on the other hand, are nouns which function as names for whole classes of products, services or businesses and are consequently deemed wholly unsuitable for use as a mark or name.

A descriptive term can become a part of a larger generic term and thus become altogether unsuitable for use as a mark. See, e.g., *Kellogg Co. v. National Biscuit Co.* (1938) ("Shredded Wheat" held to be generic rather than descriptive); *Miller Brewing Company v. G. Heileman Brewing Compa-*

ny, Inc. (1977) ("light" and its phonetic equivalent, "Lite" held to be a generic or common descriptive term as applied to beer); *A.J. Canfield Co. v. Honickman* (1986) ("chocolate fudge" held to be generic rather than descriptive, as applied to diet soda, in large part because of the inability of competitors to communicate to the public that their product possessed a particular functional flavor characteristic without using the term). But see *Anheuser–Busch, Inc. v. The Stroh Brewery Company* (1984) ("LA" held to be suggestive rather than generic as applied to low alcohol beer). Cf. *In re Seats* (1985) ("Seats" held not generic as applied to ticket reservation service); but see *Eastern Air Lines, Inc. v. New York Airlines* (1983) (The fact that "shuttle" may have taken on specialized meaning, denoting plaintiff's air services, does not of itself deprive the term of its principal, generic or descriptive meaning). Geographic terms may likewise become part of a generic name, such as "french fries", "english horns" or "danish pastries," and thus be wholly incapable of obtaining trademark protection.

Whereas descriptive terms only secondarily acquire trademark, service mark or trade name significance, generic terms often originate as inherently distinctive (i.e., technical) trademarks and only secondarily acquire a generic meaning. Over the past century alone the English language has been enriched with such words as "aspirin," "cellophane," "escalator," "thermos," "trampoline," and "yo-yo," all of which were originally coined by a manufacturer as a trademark for a new product.

Because the products had no established name, the consuming public promptly began using their trademarks as generic terms and the manufacturers ultimately lost or retained only limited rights in the trademark. Compare *Kellogg Co. v. National Biscuit Co.* (1938) (trademark rights to "Shredded Wheat" lost) with *King–Seeley Thermos Co. v. Aladdin Industries, Inc.* (1963) (trademark rights in "Thermos" limited to exclusive right to use the word with its first letter capitalized).

Although this process of "genericide" is frequently the result of a failure to take adequate steps to protect one's rights in a particularly distinctive mark or name, and thus amounts to abandonment of the trade symbol, genericide may occur even though the user of the trade symbol exercises due diligence in an effort to prevent genericide. In *King–Seeley Thermos Co. v. Aladdin Industries* (1963), for example, the court expressed doubt that the loss of distinctiveness of the registered trademark "Thermos" was the result of some failure on the registrant's part, but nevertheless found that "thermos" had become largely understood as a generic term for vacuum bottles and, accordingly, limited the plaintiff's exclusive right in the term to the right to use it with its first letter capitalized.

Genericide may also prevent a descriptive term from acquiring a secondary meaning. In *Kellogg Co. v. National Biscuit Co.* (1938), the Court held that, notwithstanding an expenditure of more than $17,000,000 to make the term "Shredded Wheat" a household word identifying a particular brand of breakfast cereal, the National Biscuit Company had no exclusive rights to the term inasmuch as it had become the generic term for the breakfast cereal. In making that decision, the Court was influenced to some extent by the now-discredited *Singer* doctrine. In *Singer Manufacturing Co. v. June Manufacturing Co.* (1896) the Court held that the term "Singer," by which a patented sewing machine became known, passed into the public domain along with the invention upon expiration of the patent. The implication was that where only one brand of a product was on the market, the public would necessarily tend to use the trademark as a generic term for the product. Subsequent decisions viewed the *Singer* case as having created an irrebuttable presumption that a trademark used during the term of the patent becomes a generic term and thus unprotectible when the patent expires. Section 14(3) of the Lanham Act originally provided for cancellation of a registered mark if it became the "common descriptive name of an article or substance on which the patent has expired."

More recent cases and amendments to the Lanham Act recognize that even if a product is patented or otherwise unique, the sole question is how a term used as a trademark for the product is understood by the consuming public. In 1962, Congress endorsed that view by amending section 14(c) of the Lanham Act so as to delete the words "on which the patent has expired." Through assiduous trademark management and policing a number of manufacturers of formerly patented products have been able to retain rights in their trademark after expiration of the patent. Indeed, in a few cases, businesses have been able to "recapture" trademarks which earlier went generic—the most notable example being the very trademark which gave rise to the *Singer* doctrine. In *Singer Manufacturing Co. v. Briley* (1953), the court held that the persistent efforts of the sewing machine manufacturer to re-educate the consuming public had resulted in its recapturing its trademark from the public domain. Still more recently, Congress sought to legislatively overrule the decision in *Anti-Monopoly, Inc. v. General Mills Fun Group, Inc.* (1982), which invalidated the registration of the trademark "Monopoly" for Parker Brothers' unique real estate trading game because, although a majority of consumers linked the game with its single producer, a larger majority said that in purchasing a game they would not care who made it. The Trademark Clarification Act of 1984, added the following language to what is now section 14(3) of the Lanham Act, 15 U.S.C. § 1064:

A registered mark shall not be deemed to be the common descriptive name of goods or services solely because such mark is also used as a name of or to identify a unique product or service. The primary significance of the registered mark to the relevant public rather than purchaser motivation shall be the test for determining whether the registered mark has become the common descriptive name of goods or services in connection with which it has been used.

The definitions of "trade-mark" and "service mark" in section 45 of the Act, 15 U.S.C.A. § 1127, were likewise amended to explicitly include marks used to identify a unique product or service.

(3) Functional Product and Business Features

Functional product and business features, like generic terms, are deemed wholly unsuitable for use as marks or names. Thus such distinctive product features as the familiar sleigh-shaped dispenser for "Scotch Brand Cellophane Tape," while actually denied registration on the questionable ground that it was not a "device" within the meaning of the Lanham Act's definition of a trademark, see *Ex parte Minnesota Mining & Mfg. Co.* (1952), might more appropriately have been denied registration on the ground that the dispenser was a functional product feature. Cf. *U.S. Golf Association v. St. Andrews Systems, Data–Max, Inc.* (1984) (holding that a marketer of a small computer programmed to calculate a golfer's handicap, using a U.S.G.A.-developed formula, did not thereby employ a false designation of origin in violation of § 43(a) of the Lanham Act, even if the public did associate the formula with the U.S.G.A., because the formula was "functional"). *See also, Wallace International Silversmiths, Inc. v. Godinger Silver Art Co.* (1990) (holding that where basic baroque silverware pattern features are claimed as a mark and granting protection to such features would hinder competition by limiting the range of alternate designs, the aesthetic functionality doctrine operates to deny trademark protection).

The line separating functional from nonfunctional features may vary depending on whether a product feature or some type of trade dress is involved. The color of a product, for example, is often said not to qualify at all for protection, because colors alone are too few in number to be reserved for the exclusive use of any one business. On the other hand, colors that are used in combination with other distinctive design elements and constitute an essential element of a trademark or trade name format are readily protectible as a common law trademark or trade name.

Until recently, the principal difficulty posed in product color cases was determining how much or little in the way of nonfunctional design elements must be added to the element of color in order to qualify for protection. One court held, for example, that the manufacturer of unpatented "tipped" matches, the head and tip of which must be of different colors to enable users to distinguish where the match should be struck, was not entitled to protection against another matchmaker's use of the same colors as the plaintiff used on his matches because the primary colors are but few and it would not take long, if two colors could be appropriated for one brand of matches, for a few vigilant companies to appropriate the rest and thus monopolize the manufacture of tipped matches without any patent whatsoever. *Diamond Match Co. v. Saginaw Match Co.* (1906). See also *Radio Corp. of America v. Decca Records, Inc.* (1943) (in which the court refused to protect a round red phonograph record label as a trademark for RCA's "Red Seal" records, noting that the color red constitutes approximately one-third of the visible spectrum of light), and *Application of David Crystal, Inc.* (1961) (in which the CCPA held there to be no registrable trademark in red and blue bands around the top of men's white socks).

More recently, however, there has been held to be no inherent bar to the registration of the color of goods. Specifically, the color pink, as used for insulation, was held to be non-functional, to have acquired a secondary meaning and thus to be registrable. *In re Owens–Corning Fiberglas Corp.* (1985). But see *Nutrasweet Co. v. Stadt Corp.* (1990) in which the court declined to follow the CAFC's decision in *Owens–Corning* and refused to enjoin a company from packaging its sugar substitute in blue packets that were allegedly confusingly similar to plaintiff's own previously distributed blue packets of artificial sweetener). See also *Inwood Laboratories v. Ivers Laboratories, Inc.* (1982) (upholding as not clearly erroneous a trial court finding that the colors of a brand name prescription drug capsule, for which no secondary meaning was established, were functional, in that they helped patients as well as doctors and hospitals identify the type of drug, and that use of the same colors by drug producers of generic equivalents of the brand name drug helped avoid confusion).

Courts have been more liberal in granting protection for the colors or designs of packaging, business vehicles and buildings. In numerous taxicab cases throughout the country, for example, the use of yellow taxicabs has been enjoined as likely to confuse customers. See, e.g., *Yellow Cab Co. v. Creasman* (1923). See also *White Tower System, Inc. v. White Castle System* (1937) (granting defendant common-law protection for its distinctive "White Castle" hamburger stands). But see, *New York Good Humor v. Standard Commercial Body Corp.* (1932) (holding that the plaintiff had no exclusive rights to the color white for its trucks and employee uniforms). For its part, the PTO has allowed federal registration of such marks as a blue band around a chemical drum, *Ex parte Nuodex Products Co.* (1966) and a yellow band around a package of sausages, *Ex parte Oscar Mayer & Co.* (1940). Similar treatment has been accorded distinctive container designs. In *Ex parte Haig & Haig, Limited* (1958), for example, registration on the Principal Register was granted for the well-known "Pinch Bottle" container for whiskey. While in *Application of Mogen David Wine Corp.* (1967), the court upheld the denial of registration for the configuration of a decanter bottle as a trademark for wines, it emphasized that its reason for doing so was the lack of distinctiveness of the decanter and lack of any evidence that the bottle was ever promoted separate and apart from the word mark "Mogen David" as trademark for the wine. The court explicitly rejected the argument that, because the decanter bottle was the subject of a design patent, it was necessarily functional and thus incapable of being protected as a trademark.

In some instances, a non-functional design embodied in the product itself has been held to be registrable. See, e.g., *In re Levi Strauss & Co.* (1970) (holding that small tab, of whatever color, affixed in a particular location on particular kinds of apparel, was registrable as a trademark). But cf. *Levi Strauss & Co. v. Blue Bell, Inc.* (1984) (holding Levi shirt tabs were not infringed by Blue Bell's, due to lack of evidence of customer confusion).

In order to settle the issue of functionality before going to the expense of developing a secondary meaning for a product or business feature, many businesses make a practice of applying to the PTO for registration of the feature on the Supplemental Register. Supplemental registration, it will be recalled, merely requires that a mark or name be *capable* of distinguishing the applicant's goods or services. A PTO finding of capacity to distinguish is the equivalent of a finding of nonfunctionality. Thus, a mark or name which is granted Supplemental Registration may safely be said to be one which, if secondary meaning is established, will be allowed to be entered on the Principal Register.

3. ASSIGNMENT, LICENSING AND TERMINATION OF RIGHTS IN A MARK OR NAME

Once rights in a mark have been obtained, they remain in existence, and may be transferred from one party to another, until such time as the mark or name is abandoned or loses its distinctiveness. The Lanham Act specifies that the registration of a mark may be cancelled in either event.

Abandonment may occur either through non-use of the mark or name or through such misuse as to cause the mark or name to lose its distinctiveness. Abandonment, in other words, amounts to conduct on the part of the user of a mark or name which cancels one of the prerequisites for acquiring rights in the mark or name initially.

Abandonment through non-use will not be lightly found. As one court put it, "We reject the view that the slightest cessation of use causes a trademark to roll free, like a fumbled football, so that it may be pounced upon by any alert opponent." *Continental Distilling Corp. v. Old Charter Distillery* (1950). Thus, a mere suspension in the use of a mark or name, such as would result from a temporary withdrawal from the marketplace due to business delays or difficulties, will not work an abandonment. Rather, non-use must be of the sort which clearly manifests an intent permanently to abandon rights in the mark or name. Intent to abandon might be inferred, for example, from non-use coupled with a failure to enforce rights against infringers or from an extended period of non-use. Section 45 of the Lanham Act defines abandonment as discontinuance of use "with intent not to resume" and specifies that non-use for two consecutive years will be prima facie evidence of abandonment. 15 U.S.C.A. § 1127. The Lanham Act presumption is rebuttable, however, and in one case, at least, was successfully rebutted where the owner of a business which had been closed for nine years showed that the business premises remained intact, pending sale as a going business, and that use of trademark could be resumed on short notice. *Sterling Brewers, Inc. v. Schenley Industries, Inc.* (1971). But see *Exxon Corp. v. Humble Exploration Co., Inc.* (1983) (holding that where Exxon ceased to use its former mark "Humble" for a three-year period except for a limited number of arranged sales of products either bearing both its old and new marks or no mark at all on the products themselves but only on the invoices for them, these did not constitute sufficient use and the presumption of abandonment was therefore not rebutted).

The Lanham Act presumption of abandonment has also been interpreted as requiring *nationwide* non-use for a period of two years. See *Dawn Donut Co. v. Harts Food Stores, Inc.* (1959) (holding that a failure to license a federally registered mark in a given market area for over 30 years did not work an abandonment of the mark). Common-law rights on a trademark or trade name, on the other hand, may be abandoned in a given trade area through non-use in that area.

Abandonment may also occur through misuse of a mark or name. In contrast to abandonment through non-use, misuse need not be shown to have been intentional in order for it to work an abandonment. Misuse may amount to nothing more than culpable neglect.

Misuse of a mark or name sufficient to work an abandonment may be found where substantial changes are made in the underlying product, service or business or in the format of the mark or name itself. Not every minor variation will work an abandonment, of course. The law recognizes the need for periodic modifications in the underlying product, service or business and so long as these changes are not so extreme as to work a fraud on the consuming public, they will not result in an abandonment. Similarly, modernizing a trademark, service mark or trade name format will not result in an abandonment so long as the modernized mark creates the same commercial impression as the old mark or name.

The Lanham Act is particularly stringent in its insistence that certification marks not be misused. Section 14(5) of the Act provides for cancellation of a certification mark if the registrant does not control the use of the mark, engages in the production or marketing of any goods or services on which the mark is used, permits the mark to be used for purposes other than to certify or discriminately refuses to certify goods or services which meet the registrant's standards for certification.

Claims of abandonment through misuse frequently arise in the context of an attempt to assign or license a mark or name. An assignment consists of an outright transfer of rights, whereas licensing consists merely of a limited permit to another to make use of the mark or name, the underlying rights to which are retained.

Because marks and names symbolize the good will of a product, service or business, they cannot be transferred apart from the good will they symbolize. An attempt to transfer a mark or name apart from the good will it symbolizes is termed an "assignment in gross" which will pass no rights to the assignee and may be treated as an abandonment on the part of the assignor if, as usually occurs, the latter ceases to use the trademark after the attempted assignment.

In order for an assignment in gross to be avoided the sale of rights in a mark must amount to a sale of the good will which the mark or name symbolizes. This is not to say that a transfer of tangible assets of a business or such intangible assets as formulas or customer lists is absolutely essential for a valid assignment of rights in a mark to occur. The test of a valid assignment, rather, is whether the assignee succeeds in producing or distributing a product or service or operating a business with substantially the same characteristics as the product, service or business originally designated by the mark or name.

An equally common method for exploiting rights in a mark or name is by way of licensing. A trademark or service mark license, for example, is at the core of most contemporary franchising schemes. The licensing of trademarks was initially inhibited by the view that trademarks functioned as a designation of a particular physical source of goods. Under that early view, rights in a trademark could not be transferred without a transfer of the source—i.e., a sale of the underlying business. Thus, assignment was the only proper method for transferring rights in a trademark. Eventually, however, the law came to recognize that marks and names may also function as a symbol of quality of a product, service or business, irrespective of the particular source of the product or service. As a result, licensing is now permitted so long as the licensor exercises an adequate degree of quality control over the goods or services sold by the licensee under the mark or name. Uncontrolled (or "naked") licensing, however, like assignments in gross, may cause the mark to lose its significance and thus may constitute an abandonment of the mark.

How much quality control is necessary to avoid naked licensing and what methods of quality control are proper remains unclear. Some courts have held that the mere retention of a right to exercise quality control is sufficient even if the licensor exercises no actual control. Others have upheld licenses when the licensor simply relied on the licensee's own voluntary efforts to exercise quality control. A majority of courts appear to have agreed, however, that the validity of a trademark or service mark license depends on actual control by the licensor and not on the mere retention of a right to control or reliance on the licensee. In addition to setting out product specifications, the prudent trademark licensor will provide for and actually conduct periodic inspections or sampling to insure that the quality of the product is being maintained.

There is a fine line, however, between too little and too much quality control. Certain techniques for maintaining the quality of a product or service may run afoul of the antitrust laws. A licensor who designates a specific source of supplies or ingredients as a means of maintaining quality control over the marked product, for example, runs the risk of being charged with illegally tying the purchase of the product to the purchase of rights in the trademark. See, e.g., *Siegel v. Chicken Delight, Inc.* (1971) (finding an illegal tie-in where a fast food franchisor required franchisees to purchase all equipment from the franchisor). Thus, where alternative sources of supply are available, the licensor must take care to specify a certain level of quality without specifying a particular source of supply.

While an abandonment may consist of either an intentional relinquishment of rights or a culpable failure to preserve rights in a mark or name, rights in a mark or name may be lost irrespective of the intent or culpability of the user of the mark or name. This occurs when a mark or name becomes the generic name for a type of product, service or business. Section 15(4) of the Lanham Act, 15 U.S.C.A. § 1065(4), specifies that no incontestable right will be acquired in a mark which is the "generic name" of an article or substance and section 14(3) specifies that the registration of a mark which becomes the "generic name" of an article or substance may be cancelled.

In order to prevent a mark or name from going generic a prudent trademark manager will: (1) select as fanciful or arbitrary a mark or name as possible; (2) register it as a federal trademark at the earliest possible time; (3) so distinguish it in advertising that the public will recognize it as a trademark (i.e., use distinctive type face, quotation marks, etc., use the term in association with some other term which will function as a generic term and, where registered, use the symbol ®); (4) avoid using corruptions of the term; (5) use the mark on several different but related products; (6) engage in continuous advertising; and (7) aggressively police the mark by challenging misuse of the mark, not only by competitors and other commercial parties, but by the public at large.

To police a mark, one may institute a media monitoring program with follow-up letters of varying degrees of forcefulness reminding editors, publishers, broadcasters and other businesses and public figures who have misused a mark or name, that it is a protected trademark, service mark or trade name. One may also police a mark or name, as we have seen, by utilizing administrative opposition or cancellation proceedings to contest the federal registrability of other marks. In the case of arguably infringing foreign marks or names, one may also seek to bar importation of goods which simulate a federally registered mark or copy the trade name of any domestic company or foreign company located in a country having trademark treaties with the U.S. The ultimate weapon for policing a mark or name, however, is through private lawsuits for infringement. It is to that subject that we now turn.

B. INFRINGING AND NON-INFRINGING USES

A prima facie case of infringement requires proof with respect to two elements: (1) plaintiff's priority in the use of the mark or name as a trademark, servicemark or tradename and (2) defendant's infringing use of an identical or similar mark or name.

Priority, as we have seen, has both a temporal and a territorial dimension. Temporal priority in the right to use a mark or name depends on whether the distinctiveness of the mark or name is inherent or acquired. Territorial priority depends on whether common-law or federal rights are being asserted. For inherently distinctive common-law marks and names, the first business to use the mark or name in a given market area has priority of rights in that market area. For common-law marks and names which lack inherent distinctiveness but have acquired a secondary meaning, the business whose mark or name first acquires secondary meaning in a given market area has priority of rights in that market area. Federal registration of a mark of inherent or acquired distinction establishes nationwide rights in the mark. The registrant is the presumptive owner of the mark throughout the country, with the exception of any market areas in which, prior to the registration, others have acquired common-law priority in the same or a similar mark.

Not every use of another's mark or name constitutes an infringement. Certain "collateral" uses are recognized as privileged. For example, where one business rebottles, repackages or reconditions the trademarked products of another business, the trademark of the original product may remain on the product or be used to describe the altered goods, so long as no deception results. See, e.g., *Champion Spark Plug Co. v. Sanders* (1947) (reconditioner of spark plugs not required to block out "Champion" trademark where spark plug is adequately identified as a used spark plug); *Prestonettes, Inc. v. Coty* (1924) (label of repackaged powder and rebottled perfume allowed to describe contents as composed of Coty constituents, so long as the trademark in no way stands out from that statement of fact). Similarly, one may use another's trademark in comparative advertising or advertising of replacement parts for another's product. See *Smith v. Chanel, Inc.* (1968) (one who creates a fragrance that supposedly duplicates that of Chanel No. 5 perfume may use the "Chanel No. 5" trademark to advertise that fact, so long as it does not constitute a misrepresentation or create the likelihood of confusion); *American–Marietta Co. v. Krigsman* (1960) (maker of sponge mops and replacement sponges may advertise that replacement sponges fit "O–Cedar 76" mops).

Infringement is not limited, on the other hand, to the use of an identical mark or name. Nor is it necessarily limited to the use of confusingly similar marks or names or to the use of similar marks or names in association with goods, services or businesses which are in direct competition with each other. The basic test for infringement of common-law or federally registered trade symbols is whether the defendant's use of the same or a similar trade symbol creates a likelihood of confusion. A number of state trademark statutes, however, have provided an alternative test for infringement of certain inherently distinctive marks and names—namely whether, in the absence of any likelihood of confusion, there is nevertheless a likelihood that the distinctive quality of the mark or name will be diluted by defendant's use of the same or a similar mark or name. These two tests for infringement bear separate discussion.

1. USES CREATING A LIKELIHOOD OF CONFUSION

The common-law test for infringement has been stated as requiring the defendant's trade symbol to be "identical with or confusingly similar to" the plaintiff's. See 3 Restatement, Torts § 717. According to Section 32 of the Lanham Act, 15 U.S.C.A. § 1114 a plaintiff claiming infringement of a federally registered mark must show that the defendant's use of a copy or colorable imitation of the plaintiff's registered mark is "likely to cause confusion, mistake or to deceive." Proof of a likelihood of confusion is thus both necessary and sufficient to establish that a second user has infringed a prior user's common-law or federally registered trade symbol. It is not necessary to show that the second user specifically intended to cause consumer confusion as to the source of a product or service or that such confusion has in fact occurred but only that confusion of some sort is likely to occur. Nor is it necessary to establish that the second user actually used the prior user's trade symbol to identify an identical product, service or business but only that trade symbols of the first and second user are sufficiently similar and the product, service or business they identify are sufficiently related as to create a likelihood of confusion.

a. Proof of Likelihood of Confusion

Although fraudulent intent is generally no longer thought to be a necessary element of proof in establishing an infringement, evidence of fraudulent intent is nevertheless relevant and may well be dispositive of the issue of likelihood of confusion. Courts tend to assume that any intentional attempt to create confusion is likely to be successful. Thus, evidence of an intent to confuse will generally be sufficient evidence of a likelihood of confusion.

Proof of intent will also have a bearing on the remedy awarded for infringement. A showing of fraudulent intent will provide a basis for awarding punitive and compensatory damages or an accounting of defendant's profits. In the absence of evidence of a fraudulent intent, relief may well be limited to an injunction prohibiting infringement in the future.

If an appreciable number of actual or prospective purchasers of a product or service are likely to be confused, that is apparently enough to create liability for infringement. An appreciable number does not necessarily mean a majority. One court has even gone so far as to suggest that the law sets no numerical standard for misguided purchasers and that confusing similarity may be established by evidence of even a small number of actual mistakes made by average consumers. See *McCormick & Co. v. Manischewitz Co.* (1953).

Purchaser confusion as to the source of goods or services is not the only type of proof which will result in a finding of confusion. In 1962, for example, Congress struck out language in the Lanham

Act which had limited the likelihood of confusion, mistake or deception to "purchasers as to the source of origin of such goods and services." Since then, federal registration has been denied and infringement of a federally registered mark found both where purchasers are likely to confuse products after their purchase and where sellers are likely to confuse products either before or during their sale. See, e.g., *American Cyanamid Co. v. United States Rubber Co.* (1966) (upholding denial of registration for insecticide "Cygon," which had been found to be confusingly similar to fungicide "Phygon" due to likelihood that an employee might confuse the words when spoken and damage crops by applying the wrong material); *Syntex Laboratories, Inc. v. Norwich Pharmacal Co.* (1971) (confusion among physicians and pharmacists, rather than source confusion among purchasers of prescription drugs, held sufficient to support a finding of infringement).

Relevant evidence in determining the likelihood of confusion includes not only the subjective intent of the defendant and the degree of actual confusion caused but also the degree of similarity between the plaintiff's and defendant's trade symbols and the relation between the products, services or businesses which these trade symbols identify.

The degree of similarity between trade symbols has traditionally been determined by gauging the degree of similarity in the "sound, sight and meaning" of the two trade symbols, under the actual market conditions in which the trade symbols are used. Two marks may be visually distinguishable but sound identical or confusingly similar. See, e.g., *Esso, Inc. v. Standard Oil Co.* (1938) ("Esso" v. "S.O."); *Brown–Forman Distillery Co. v. Arthur M. Bloch Liquor Importers, Inc.* (1938) ("Old Forester" v. "Old Foster"). Likewise, two trade symbols may be distinguishable to both eye and ear but nevertheless have confusingly similar meanings. Cf. *Hancock v. American Steel & Wire Co.* (1953) ("Tornado" as applied to wire fencing denied federal registration due to confusing similarity with "Cyclone" wire fencing).

In the typical infringement case involving a likelihood of consumer confusion as to the source of goods or services, the courts have generally held that the question is whether an ordinary purchaser of a product or service would be likely to be confused under actual market conditions. Courts have differed over whether the ordinary purchaser is "reasonably discerning" or "hasty, heedless and easily deceived." Suffice it to say that the ordinary purchaser is generally expected to exercise that degree of care appropriate to the kind of choice being made. An ordinary purchaser of chewing gum is not expected to use the same degree of care as the ordinary purchaser of a diamond ring. Nor is a child expected to use the same degree of care as an adult. On the other hand, where a product is typically purchased by professional buyers, considerable discrimination on the part of the buyer may be expected. The fact that a discriminating purchaser might discern a notice of differentiation contained on a product label will not negate a claim of infringement if the ordinary purchaser would not be so discriminating. As one English decision succinctly put it in explaining why it would be impossible for a brewer adequately to distinguish his ales from those of another brewer: "Thirsty folk want beer, not explanations." *Montgomery v. Thompson* (1891). See also *University of Georgia Athletic Ass'n v. Laite* (1985) ("Battlin' Bulldog Beer" held to infringe athletic association service marks notwithstanding notice of differentiation and absence of any competition between defendant's product and plaintiff's services).

Also relevant to the question of a likelihood of confusion is the actual market conditions in which a mark or name is used. Marks might be confusingly similar as applied to identical products sold side by side on the same shelf but not confusingly similar as applied to different products which are marketed in entirely different ways. Similar marks or names are more likely to be confusing if the plaintiff has developed a family of marks and names (e.g., "Kodak," "Kodacolor," "Kodachrome") and less likely to be confusing if the plaintiff has incorporated a common generic or descriptive element in the mark or name.

Perhaps the most difficult questions with respect to likelihood of confusion arise where similar symbols are used to identify products, services or businesses which are not actually competing with each other. Such may be the case where different products, services or businesses in the same geographic market area are in some sense "related" but non-competing or where similar products, services or businesses have different geographic markets.

b. Use of Marks and Names on Related But Non-competing Goods, Services or Businesses

The original common-law view was that there could be no infringement except by use of a confusingly similar mark or name on a competing product, service or business. The harm sought to be avoided was diversion of sales and without competition there could be no such harm.

The Trademark Act of 1905, by contrast, stated the test both for denying registration and finding an infringement as being the use of confusingly similar marks on goods having the "same descriptive properties." The Lanham Act, by dropping the "same descriptive properties" language of the 1905 Act, ultimately broadened the scope of protection for federally registered marks still further.

Influenced by the first of these federal legislative developments, the common law itself came to recognize that confusion as to the identity of a particular product, service or business can pose a threat of economic harm to the reputation or good will of the product, service or business with which it is being erroneously associated, even in the absence of competition between the two. In the seminal case of *Aunt Jemima Mills Co. v. Rigney & Co.* (1917), for example, the Second Circuit Court of Appeals held, apparently as a matter of common law, that the defendant's use of the mark "Aunt Jemima" on its pancake syrup infringed the plaintiff's identical mark identifying its pancake batter. The court concluded that the goods, though different, were so related that complainant's reputation was in effect put in the hands of the defendant.

The Second Circuit subsequently proceeded to utilize the *Aunt Jemima* "related goods" rule not only in common-law infringement cases, but in federal trademark cases as well. Although it conceded that its decision did some violence to the "same descriptive properties" language of the 1905 Act, the court upheld denial of registration for the word "Yale" to identify flashlights, given the opposer's prior use of the word on many sorts of hardware, including locks and keys, but not flashlights and batteries. See *Yale Electric Corp. v. Robertson* (1928). See also *L.E. Waterman Co. v. Gordon* (1934) (upholding a grant of preliminary injunctive relief, apparently on a pendent state law claim of unfair competition, prohibiting the use of "Waterman" on razors due to a likelihood of confusion with "Waterman" fountain pens, a federally registered mark).

Most federal courts, on the other hand, continued to construe the 1905 Act as denying federal jurisdiction over infringement actions in which the infringer used the same or a similar mark on goods of a different descriptive class than that for which federal registration had been granted. In the Lanham Act of 1946, Congress eliminated the "same descriptive properties" language of the 1905 Act and thus signaled its approval of the Second Circuit's use of the *Aunt Jemima* "related goods" rule in federal trademark cases.

Meanwhile, back in the Second Circuit, Learned Hand, the author of the *Yale* decision, had experienced a change of heart. He and his protege, Jerome Frank, became troubled over the effect such expansive trademark protection might have on the competitive process. In order to prevent the creation of judicially sanctioned monopolies in trademarks, Hand and Frank thought that injunctive relief altogether prohibiting the use of a mark in non-competing goods cases ought to be limited to instances where it could be shown that the defendant's product was in fact of inferior quality, thereby posing a likely threat to plaintiff's reputation, or that the plaintiff was actively planning to expand into defendant's product market, thereby posing a likely threat of diverted sales. In *S.C. Johnson & Son, Inc. v. Johnson* (1940), for example, Hand conceded that the defendant had infringed plaintiff's registered mark "Johnson's" (which under the 1905 Act was registrable only because it was rendered in a distinctive script), but concluded that, because the defendant used the mark on a cleaner for fabrics and glazed surfaces, whereas the plaintiff had previously used the mark only on floor wax, relief was to be limited to an injunction merely prohibiting the defendant from using the word "Johnson's" except in conjunction with the word "cleaner" and in juxtaposition with the name of the company and its location.

Another faction on the Second Circuit, which included another Judge Hand (namely Augustus N. Hand), continued to follow Learned Hand's *Yale* opinion using the *Aunt Jemima* "related goods" test in federal as well as common-law trademark cases. The clash between these two factions did not subside with the enactment of the Lanham Act in 1946, for Judge Learned Hand proceeded to apply his restrictive test under the new act even though that act expressly ratified his earlier expansive reading of the old act. See, e.g., *S.C. Johnson & Son, Inc. v. Johnson* (1949) (upholding a refusal to reopen the *Johnson* case, supra, which had been decided under the 1905 Act). As a result, for 20 years (from 1940 to 1960) the Second Circuit was afflicted with what has been described as a case of judicial schizophrenia, with non-competing goods cases turning on which panel of the Court of Appeals the litigants happened to draw. See 2 *McCarthy, Trademarks and Unfair Competition* § 24.9 (1984). Thus, while Judge Learned Hand stoutly refused to enjoin the use of the word "Johnson's" on fabric cleaner merely because S.C. Johnson & Son had previously used the word on floor wax and a variety of other products, Judge Augustus N. Hand equally stoutly upheld an injunction against the use of the mark "Miss Seventeen" on girdles as an infringement of the trademark of "Seventeen" magazine. See *Triangle Publications, Inc. v. Rohrlich* (1948). While these two particular cases can perhaps be distinguished as involving trademarks of different strengths ("Johnson" being at best a secondary meaning mark, whereas "Seventeen" is arguably more suggestive than descriptive), not all Second Circuit case law during this period can be thus harmonized.

By 1961, it appeared that the Second Circuit had finally unequivocally adopted the "related goods" test for use in non-competing goods cases. In *Polaroid Corp. v. Polarad Electronics Corp.* (1961), the court elaborated an extensive list of factors to be considered in assessing whether a non-competitor's use of a mark constitutes an infringement. These factors include the strength of the plaintiff's mark, the degree of similarity between the two marks, the proximity of the products, the likelihood that the plaintiff will expand into the defendant's market, evidence of actual confusion, defendant's good faith or lack thereof, the quality of the defendant's product and the sophistication of buyers of the two products. See, e.g., *McGregor–Doniger, Inc. v. Drizzle Inc.* (1979) (applying the *Polaroid* test to uphold a finding that the use of the mark "Drizzle" to identify expensive women's coats did not infringe the mark "Drizzler" as used on inexpensive men's golf jackets because "Drizzler" is only moderately strong, being just barely suggestive, the competitive distance between the two products is significant, the user of "Drizzler" had no plans to enter the women's clothing market, the user of "Drizzle" adopted its mark in good faith, without knowledge of the prior use of "Drizzler," and purchasers of women's coats tended to be sophisticated and knowledgeable).

The *Polaroid* factors parallel those enumerated in § 731 of the Restatement of Torts as the common-law test for determining whether the goods, services or business of one party are likely to be viewed as associated with the goods, services or business of another party. The Court of Customs and Patents Appeals adopted a similar test for use by the Patent and Trademark Office in determining whether the registration of a mark is likely to cause confusion with mark or name previously used on a non-competing product, service or business. See *Application of E.I. DuPont DeNemours & Co.* (1973) (reversing a PTO refusal to register DuPont's mark "Rally" for a combination polishing, glazing and cleaning agent for automobiles where Horizon Company previously registered the mark "Rally" for use on an all-purpose detergent).

The "Rally" case, supra, illustrates how private contractual arrangements can be utilized to resolve non-competing goods cases. In that case, Horizon Company had originally filed the application for registration of "Rally" for use on a wax and cleaning agent for automobiles but sold its mark, the application and the attendant good will of its car wax business to DuPont, while retaining "Rally" for use on its all-purpose detergent. As part of the bargain, the parties entered into an agreement designed to avoid conflict between the two "Rally" marks. While the CCPA affirmed the PTO's authority to make an independent inquiry into the likelihood of confusion, it concluded that the weight to be given detailed agreements such as the one entered into by DuPont and Horizon should be substantial. The court noted that it is in the pecuniary interest of such companies to avoid confusion and that a refusal to federally register a mark cannot itself prevent confusion (since it does not prevent unregistered use of the mark) and in certain circumstances might even encourage confusion. A refusal to federally register a mark, for example, might simply encourage businesses operating in geographic areas where a disappointed applicant does not currently operate to use the mark on their own identical or closely related products. As we shall see, federal registration serves to eliminate that problem.

c. Use of Marks and Names in Different Geographic Markets

The geographic extent of common-law protection, it will be recalled, is the market in which a mark or name is actually used. Federal registration, on the other hand, constitutes nation-wide constructive notice of an exclusive right to use a mark. Thus, once a mark is federally registered, it is within the registrant's power to prevent further use of confusingly similar marks anywhere in the country, except in areas where the mark was in continuous use prior to the registration. In *Burger King of Florida, Inc. v. Hoots* (1968), for example, the defendant's use of the trademark "Burgerking" was restricted to the single market area in Illinois where it had been used by defendant prior to plaintiff's federal registration of the mark, while the plaintiff's right to exclusive use of the mark extended to the remainder of the country, including the remainder of Illinois.

In order to establish that a non-competing use of a similar mark or name constitutes an infringement, however, the owner of a federally registered mark must nevertheless establish a likelihood of confusion. Such a likelihood was found to exist in the *Burger King* case because the plaintiff company, although it originated in Florida, had subsequently expanded throughout the southeast and into Illinois. Where a defendant uses a mark in an area where the federally registered mark is not currently in use, the owner of the federally registered mark may be denied relief, due to the lack of any likelihood of confusion, until such time as the plaintiff expands into the defendant's trading area. See, e.g., *Dawn Donut Co. v. Hart's Food Stores, Inc.* (1959) (holding there to be no likelihood of confusion arising from use of an identical mark for doughnuts and other baked goods sold in separate trading areas, where there is no present likelihood that plaintiff plans to expand into defendant's area). This is not to say, however, that the defendant in such a case has any permanent right to use the mark. The owner of the federally registered mark in effect holds a sword of Damocles over the defendant's head and may put an end to defendant's right to use the mark merely by commencing use of the mark in the defendant's trading area.

Not surprisingly, disputes over uses of a mark in different geographic areas, like disputes over the use of similar marks on dissimilar but related goods, are often resolved by private agreement between the parties. The Lanham Act encourages such agreements by providing for concurrent registration of marks. Where two businesses have begun using similar marks or names in two different areas of the country, either party (or both) may file an application which is limited to territory and product line. The PTO has power under section 2(d) of the Lanham Act to issue registrations providing for concurrent use of the same or similar marks in different geographic areas of the country.

In *Application of Beatrice Foods* (1970), for example, two companies in different parts of the country began using the mark "Homestead" on their food products and agreed to a division of territory. The CCPA reversed the PTO's refusal to recognize the agreement or grant registration for areas other than actual use, and held that the party which first began using the mark in the United States was entitled to registration covering the entire United States, save for areas of actual use or imminent expansion by the second user and that ordinarily it was not proper to leave territory open, since this would tend to frustrate the Lanham Act's policy of giving nation-wide rights to the senior user of the mark. The court also noted that agreements between the parties should ordinarily be respected by the PTO. If two parties agree to leave an area open, for example, nothing requires the PTO to grant registrations contrary to such an agreement. Only if absolutely necessary to prevent a likelihood of confusion, said the court, should an agreement between the parties be disregarded or territory left open.

The court also emphasized that its holding was limited to those instances where senior user was also first to seek registration. In order to reward those who first seek federal registration, the court noted, there may be valid grounds for allowing a junior user who first seeks federal registration to retain nation-wide protection, subject only to the territory of the first user. See also *Weiner King, Inc. v. Wiener King Corp.* (1980) (holding that a business which federally registered the mark "Wiener King" in unopposed proceedings in 1972 was entitled to nationwide rights in the mark, excepting only the market area of a previous user who did not seek federal registration until 1975).

d. Parallel Imports ("Grey Market" Goods)

Parallel imports (also called "grey market" goods) are genuine goods purchased abroad and imported into the United States by someone other than the party having an exclusive right to use the trademark for the goods in the United States. In *A. Bourjois & Co. v. Katzel* (1923) the Supreme Court held that where a company doing business in France and the U.S. sold its U.S. business, including its U.S. trademarks, to an independent American business, but retained the right to use these trademarks in France, a third party's importation of the French company's goods carrying these marks would infringe the trademark of the authorized U.S. user of the marks. At about the same time as the Supreme Court's decision in *Katzel,* Congress enacted § 526 of the Tariff Act, 19 U.S.C.A. § 1526, which makes it unlawful "to import into the United States any merchandise of foreign manufacture if such merchandise ... bears a trademark owned by a citizen of ... the United States." See also the 1946 Lanham Act § 42, 15 U.S.C.A. § 1124, which provides that no article of imported merchandise which copies or simulates a federally registered mark or the name of any domestic company or foreign company located in a country which by treaty, convention or law accords certain rights to U.S. citizens shall be admitted entry into the U.S. To aid customs officials, section 42 goes on to authorize parties to record facsimiles of their name or federally registered mark with the Department of Treasury, which is to distribute them to customs officials.

Although the *Katzel* decision has been questioned on the ground that if the imported goods are in fact genuine "there would appear to be little confusion, if any" created by the importation, *Bell & Howell: Mamiya Co. v. Masel Supply Co., Inc.* (1983), it still appears to be good law, at least where the U.S. and foreign trademark owners are not closely affiliated and the product's good will in the U.S. is separately promoted and developed by the U.S. mark owner. At the same time, however, section 526 of the Tariff Act has been the subject of a longstanding interpretive controversy which began when the U.S. Department of Justice successfully argued in *United States v. Guerlain, Inc.* (1957) that section 526 does not authorize a U.S. company in a close relationship with a foreign trademark owner to bar parallel imports and that any attempt to bar parallel imports in such a case would constitute a restraint of trade in violation of the Sherman Act. Although *Guerlain* was later vacated and dismissed at the request of the government, which then unsuccessfully sought legislative codification of the *Guerlain* ruling, the Bureau of Customs (now the U.S. Customs Service) revised its Customs Service Regulations so as to preclude the exclusion of parallel imports not only where the foreign and U.S. trademarks are owned by the same entity, but also where the foreign and U.S. owners are parent and subsidiary companies or subject to common control or where a recorded mark or name is applied to the goods by authorization of the U.S. owner of the mark (i.e. a licensing arrangement). See 19 C.F.R. § 133.21. The theory behind these regulations is that a trademark holder's own mark cannot be infringing of itself. In *K*

Mart Corp. v. Cartier, Inc. (1988), the Supreme Court held that the Customs Service regulation is consistent with section 526 insofar as it exempts from the importation ban goods that are manufactured abroad by the same person who holds the U.S. trademark or by a person who is subject to common control with the U.S. trademark holder but that the regulation is invalid insofar as it permits importation of goods bearing a recorded trademark or trade name applied to the goods by virtue of a licensing arrangement with a U.S. owner.

See also *Weil Ceramics and Glass, Inc. v. Dash* (1989) (construing sections 32 and 42 of the Lanham Act as not providing a U.S. subsidiary relief against imports of genuine goods not materially different from those of the U.S. subsidiary, produced by a sister corporation of the Spanish parent company). But cf. *Lever Brothers Co. v. U.S.* (1989) (holding, albeit tentatively, that section 42 of the Lanham Act bars third party importation of goods bearing a trademark identical to a valid U.S. trademark where the goods are physically different from the U.S. goods, regardless of the genuineness of the trademark abroad or the affiliation between the producing firms). See also *Lever Brothers v. U.S.* (1992), holding on remand that section 42 bars the unauthorized importation of foreign goods that bear a mark identical to a valid U.S. mark, notwithstanding an affiliation between the foreign manufacturer and the U.S. trademark owner, at least where the imported goods are materially, physically different from the U.S. goods, and that application of the U.S. Customs Service's affiliate exception to section 42's ban on unauthorized imports is to be enjoined in such cases.

See generally *Duracell, Inc. v. U.S. International Trade Commission* (1985), dismissing a case challenging a presidential rejection of an ITC determination in a grey market goods case brought before the ITC under section 337 of the Tariff Act, which gives the ITC authority to prohibit unfair methods of competition in the import trade of the U.S. In this case the reviewing court stated that in exercising statutorily provided authority to reject ITC determinations, the President did not need to articulate in detail the reasons for rejection, and that in the present case it was sufficient that the President disapproved for his own policy reasons, including the desire to avoid creating conflicting administrative interpretations of the law relating to grey goods.

2. USES CREATING A LIKELIHOOD OF DILUTION

A number of states, including New York, Illinois and California, have enacted statutes similar to section 12 of the Model State Trademark Act, which provides that:

Likelihood of injury to business reputation or of dilution of the distinctive quality of a mark registered under this Act, or a mark valid at common law, or a trade name valid at common law, shall be a ground for injunctive relief notwithstanding the absence of competition between the parties or the absence of confusion as to the source of goods or services.

These anti-dilution statutes, which have no counterpart in the Lanham Act, are designed to grant protection to strong, well-recognized marks and names, even in the absence of any confusion, where the defendant's use of an identical or similar symbol is likely to tarnish, degrade or dilute the distinctive quality of the mark or name. The theory behind the anti-dilution statutes is that even nonconfusing uses of identical or similar trade symbols will gradually erode the distinctive value of a strong mark or name.

The anti-dilution statutes were initially construed quite narrowly. In federal diversity cases governed by the law of a state having an anti-dilution statute, for example, the federal courts often continued to insist on a showing of a likelihood of confusion of some sort, on the ground that the statute merely eliminated the requirement of confusion as to the source of goods or services. In recent years, however, the federal courts have taken a broader view of state anti-dilution statutes. Indeed, some federal courts have tended to go to the other extreme, granting protection against the dilution of marks and names even in the absence of an applicable state anti-dilution statute.

In *Polaroid Corp. v. Polaraid, Inc.* (1963), the court quite properly concluded that "Polaroid" was precisely the type of trade symbol that the Illinois anti-dilution statute was designed to protect and accordingly granted injunctive relief against the use of the word "Polaraid" as a trade name for a business specializing in designing and installing refrigeration and heating systems. In *Mead Data Central, Inc. v. Toyota Motor Sales, U.S.A., Inc.* (1989), however, the court refused to enjoin Toyota's use of "Lexus" on automobiles as either confusingly similar to or a dilution of "Lexis," Mead Data Central's mark for its computerized legal research service, concluding that given the recognized sophistication of lawyers, the principal consumers of the legal research service, it was unlikely that Toyota's "Lexus" would either be confused with or blur the distinctiveness of "Lexis."

In *Chemical Corp. of America v. Anheuser–Busch, Inc.* (1952), on the other hand, the court held that a Texas manufacturer of insecticide-floor wax infringed the federally registered Budweiser beer slogan "Where There's Life ... There's Bud," by using the slogan "Where There's Life ... There's Bugs" on its own products. While the court struggled mightily to demonstrate that beer and floor wax were sufficiently related to create a likelihood of confusion, it revealed what was perhaps the real basis for its decision when it spoke of the injury done to plaintiff by reason of the particularly unwholesome association of ideas when the word "bugs" was substituted for the word "Bud."

Dilution by reason of an unwholesome association has figured prominently in a number of recent decisions in which a likelihood of dilution was found. See, e.g., *Dallas Cowboys Cheerleaders, Inc. v. Pussycat Cinema Ltd.* (1979) (actress attired in a Dallas Cowboys cheerleaders uniform in an X-rated film dilutes the reputation of the plaintiff); *Coca–Cola Co. v. Gemini Rising, Inc.* (1972) ("Enjoy Cocaine" posters in a script similar to that of the "Coca–Cola" trademark held to constitute a dilution under New York law). But see *Girl Scouts of the United States of America v. Personality Posters Manufacturing Co.* (1969) (refusing to find, in the absence of any evidence of a likelihood of confusion, that a poster consisting of a pregnant female in a Girl Scout uniform and the motto "Be Prepared" violated New York's anti-dilution statute). See also *L.L. Bean, Inc. v. Drake Publishers, Inc.* (1987) (holding that the First Amendment bans application of a dilution statute to prohibit a magazine featuring adult erotic entertainment from publishing a sexually explicit parody of a well known mail order catalog).

Several courts and commentators have suggested that the terms of anti-dilution statutes are broad enough to prevent rebottlers and repackagers from making "collateral use" of marks and names, and to prohibit virtually anyone from using a mark or name in a generic sense. See, e.g., 2 *McCarthy, Trademarks and Unfair Competition* § 24.13 at 160–61. Application of the dilution doctrine in those contexts, however, might likewise be held to run afoul of the First Amendment's guarantee of freedom of expression. The Supreme Court, as we have seen, has declared that commercial speech no less than political speech is protected under the First Amendment. See *Virginia State Board of Pharmacy v. Virginia Citizens Consumer Council, Inc.* (1976) (holding that a state may not prohibit the truthful advertising of prescription drug prices). So long as a mark or name has in fact come into common usage as a generic term for a type of product, service or business and no deception or damage to business reputation flows from collateral use of a mark or name in advertising, generic or collateral uses of another's mark or name are arguably constitutionally protected forms of speech. See also *Hyatt Corporation v. Hyatt Legal Services* (1985) (holding there to be a conflict between an interpretation of a state anti-dilution law which allows for a nationwide injunction and the Commerce Clause of the U.S. Constitution).

Quite apart from these constitutional constraints, the most significant limitation on dilution protection is implicit in the dilution doctrine itself. A mark or name must be fairly distinctive before it is capable of being diluted. Marks or names which are already diluted when selected for use as a mark or tradename are not entitled to protection under the anti-dilution statute. See *Esquire, Inc. v. Esquire Slipper Manufacturing Co.* (1957) (because "Esquire" is not a coined word but one firmly established in the English language, the protection accorded to such a weak name is not as broad as that accorded to a strong, coined name such as "Kodak"). Arguably only coined marks and names, such as "Polaroid" and "Kodak," or other inherently distinctive (i.e., arbitrary or suggestive) marks and names such as "Tiffanys" or "Rolls–Royce" which have become extremely well-known, are entitled to protection against dilution.

3. CONTRIBUTORY INFRINGEMENT

Contributory infringement consists of supplying the instruments enabling another to infringe a mark or name, knowing that the other will or can reasonably be expected to commit the infringement. Such conduct amounts to knowingly aiding or inducing the infringement of the mark or name. On the other hand, the mere foreseeability that the instruments supplied could be used by another to infringe a mark or name is not enough to constitute contributory infringement. Compare *Inwood Laboratories, Inc. v. Ives Laboratories, Inc.* (1982) (holding that the manufacturer of a generic drug whose capsules were the same color as those of a competitor's brand name drug was not liable for contributory infringement in the absence of evidence that the generic drug manufacturer continued to supply pharmacists whom it knew or had reason to know were mislabelling the generic drug as the brand name drug) with *Ciba–Geigy Corp. v. Bolar Pharmaceutical Co., Inc.* (1984) (holding that *Inwood Labs* permitted liability under § 43(a) of the Lanham Act for contributory infringement where the supplier of capsules had a "reasonable apprehension" that the capsule colors would facilitate infringements by others).

C. AFFIRMATIVE DEFENSES AND REMEDIES

A plaintiff who has established a prima facie case of infringement may nevertheless be denied all or certain types of relief. To obtain some remedies, the plaintiff must show that the defendant's infringement was willful. Likewise, the defendant may assert certain affirmative defenses, based primarily on various types of plaintiff misconduct, which will serve to bar or limit plaintiff's relief. Finally, there may be policy reasons, having nothing to do with the conduct of the parties, for limiting or denying relief for an infringement.

1. AFFIRMATIVE DEFENSES

Ordinarily, the first line of defense for a defendant in an infringement proceeding is to attack the sufficiency of the plaintiff's prima facie case of infringement. The plaintiff, as we have seen, has the burden of proof on the matter of priority and likelihood of confusion or dilution.

An affirmative defense, on the other hand, raises certain additional grounds for denying or limiting the grant of relief. For these defenses the defendant has the burden of proof. A defense which completely extinguishes plaintiff's rights in a mark or name is generally referred to as a complete or absolute defense. A defense which merely establishes grounds for the exercise of judicial discretion in deciding what relief, if any, is to be granted, is generally referred to as an equitable defense.

The principal affirmative defenses which may be raised to a prima facie case of trademark, service mark or trade name infringement include the three absolute defenses of abandonment, loss of distinctiveness (i.e., genericide), and collateral or fair use which have already been discussed (see pp. 143, 151–7, 159–60 supra), and three equitable defenses: laches, acquiescence and unclean hands.

The Lanham Act purports to limit the defenses that can be raised where a federally registered mark has become "incontestable." Section 15 of the Act, 15 U.S.C.A. § 1065, specifies that a federally registered mark becomes incontestable if (1) the mark has been in continuous use for five consecutive years after registration, (2) there have been no final decisions adverse to the registrant's claim of ownership or right to register, (3) there are no pending PTO or court proceedings, (4) the registrant files a "five year affidavit" with the PTO and (5) the mark is not the generic name of an article or substance.

Section 14 of the Lanham Act, 15 U.S.C.A. § 1064, however, specifies that abandonment and loss of distinctiveness may both be raised "at any time" as a ground for cancelling the registration of a federally registered mark. While section 33(b), 15 U.S.C.A. § 1115(b) states that a registration which has become incontestable is conclusive evidence of the registrant's exclusive right to use the registered mark, it goes on to list seven enumerated defenses, including abandonment and collateral (i.e. fair) use, which can be raised to a claimed infringement of an incontestable mark. The practical effect of these two sections is that abandonment, genericide and collateral use may be raised even though a federally registered mark has become incontestable. The mere descriptiveness of the mark, on the other hand, cannot be contested. *Park 'N Fly, Inc. v. Dollar Park and Fly, Inc.* (1985). How incontestability affects the equitable defenses depends on which defense is being asserted.

Sections 34 and 35 of the Lanham Act, 15 U.S.C.A. §§ 1115–1116, state that the courts are to grant relief for infringement of federally registered marks according to "principles of equity"—which arguably includes the traditional equitable defenses of laches, acquiescence and unclean hands. Each of these defenses, if successful, will function as an estoppel—i.e., they will simply preclude the plaintiff from asserting an otherwise valid claim or obtaining otherwise available relief. They are to be distinguished from absolute defenses, which if successfully asserted, will deprive the plaintiff of all rights in a mark or name.

The defense of laches seeks to prevent unreasonable (i.e., inexcusable and prejudicial) delay in the assertion of rights. The defense of acquiescence, on the other hand, seeks to prevent the assertion of rights after there have been express or implied assurances that they will not be asserted. When acquiescence is implied from a plaintiff's long delay in asserting rights, the defenses of acquiescence and laches in effect merge. Where the defense of acquiescence is not based on plaintiff's delay, it generally amounts to an assertion that in some prior commercial relation the plaintiff expressly or impliedly acquiesced to the defendant's use of the mark or name.

In no case is delay alone enough to establish the defense of laches. That is, it must have been *unexcusable* delay on the part of the plaintiff and *prejudicial* delay as it affects the defendant. What constitutes unreasonable delay cannot be reduced to a precise rule but must be determined by carefully examining the facts of a particular case and balancing not only the competing interests and equities of the parties but also the interest of the consuming public in being protected against deception, confusion and mistake.

Section 19 of the Lanham Act, 15 U.S.C.A. § 1609, expressly provides that in all *inter partes* proceedings before the Patent and Trademark Office the equitable principles of laches, estoppel and acquiescence, where applicable, may be considered and applied. Thus, just as laches and acquiescence may be raised in judicial proceedings as a defense to a federal registrant's claim of infringement, so laches and acquiescence may be raised by a federal applicant or registrant as a defense in an opposition or cancellation proceeding.

Presently unsettled is whether the defense of laches may be raised to a claim of infringement of a federally registered mark which has become "incontestable." Section 33(b) of the Act, 15 U.S.C.A. § 1115(b), specifies that an incontestable registration is conclusive evidence of an exclusive right to use the mark except where one of seven enumerated defenses, laches not among them, is established. As we have seen, however, immediately following section 33 are two sections which empower the courts to grant relief for infringement of federally registered marks and they each specify that relief is to be granted subject to "principles of equity"— including, presumably, the equitable principle of laches. Not surprisingly, some courts have held that laches is no defense where a federally registered mark has become incontestable, while other courts have allowed the defense, notwithstanding the "incontestability" of the mark.

Under the defense of unclean hands, which stems from the maxim that "He who comes into equity must come with clean hands," the plaintiff's own misconduct relative to the matter for which relief is sought operates to defeat the plaintiff's claim for relief. Unclean hands may consist of virtually any sort of immoral or illegal conduct, so long as it relates to the subject matter in litigation. For example, unclean hands may be found and protection denied where a mark misrepresents the ingredients of a product. See, e.g., *Clinton E. Worden & Co. v. California Fig Syrup Co.* (1903) (protection denied mark "Syrup of Figs" which was used on a syrup containing no figs). Courts have also refused to protect the trademark of an illegal lottery, see *Werts Novelty Co. v. Chandler* (1939), or the corporate name of an organization which was found to be the source of bloodshed and despotic rule. See *Knights of Ku Klux Klan v. Strayer* (1929).

Courts are becoming increasingly reluctant, however, to allow the plaintiff's misconduct to defeat the grant of injunctive relief against defendant's infringement, where the effect is to leave the public unprotected from two wrongs rather than one. A court may thus deny monetary relief to a plaintiff with unclean hands but issue injunctive relief against both parties or condition the grant of injunctive relief on the plaintiff's discontinuance of his or her own misconduct.

Section 33(b) of the Lanham Act, 15 U.S.C.A. § 1115(b), enumerates three specific acts of misconduct which may be raised as defenses to an "uncontestable" federal registration. These are: (1) fraud in obtaining the registration or incontestable rights, (2) misrepresentation as to the source of goods identified by the incontestable mark, and (3) use of the mark to violate the antitrust laws. Thus, whether or not laches, acquiescence or other forms of unclean hands are good defenses to an infringement of an incontestable mark, these three types of unclean hands clearly can be raised in such a case.

2. CRIMINAL SANCTIONS AND CIVIL AND ADMINISTRATIVE REMEDIES

a. Criminal Sanctions

The Trademark Counterfeiting Act of 1984 created the first federal criminal penalties of fines up to $250,000 for an individual ($1,000,000 for repeat offenders and non-individuals and $5,000,000 for non-individual repeat offenders) and imprisonment up to five years (15 years for repeat offenders) for intentionally trafficking in goods or services known to bear a counterfeit mark. 18 U.S.C.A. § 2320. A counterfeit mark is defined as one "identical with or substantially indistinguishable from" a federally registered mark, and "the use of which is likely to cause confusion, to cause mistake or to deceive." The Act explicitly excludes parallel imports (or grey goods) as violative of this prohibition. On the other hand, the goods on which or services in connection with which the counterfeit mark appears need not be identical to, or even in competition with, the goods or services of the owner of the registered mark.

b. Civil and Administrative Remedies

The judicial remedies available to the victim of trademark or trade name infringement include injunctive relief, damages and an accounting of the defendant's profits. Also available are such administrative remedies as cancellation of a federal trademark registration and barring importation of goods bearing an infringing mark or name. In addition to section 42 of the Lanham Act, 15 U.S.C.A. § 1124, which enables the owner of a federally registered mark and any domestic and qualifying foreign users of a business name to register with the Customs Service to have infringing imports barred, a party may petition the International Trade Commission, which has authority under section 337 of Tariff Act of 1930, 19 U.S.C.A. § 1337, as subsequently amended in 1974, 1979, 1984 and 1988, to issue (subject to Presidential review) exclusion orders or cease and desist orders, to prevent an unfair method of competition, including trademark or tradename infringement, in the importation of articles into the U.S. or their subsequent sale. See, e.g., *Bally/Midway Mfg. Co. v. United States International Trade Commission* (1983) (upholding an ITC order excluding certain video games and components found to infringe the common-law trademark "PAC MAN" and holding that exclusion was also proper where certain games infringed the trademarked games "Rally–X," which had already lost its popularity).

A party may also petition the U.S. Trade Representative to impose sanctions on foreign countries which give inadequate or ineffective protection to the intellectual property of U.S. nationals. See Chapter 1, supra.

In recognition of the difficulty of proving money damages and the inherent inadequacy of damages to remedy continuing acts of infringement, the courts routinely make the equitable remedy of injunction available in trademark and trade name infringement cases. The scope of injunctive relief, however, may vary, depending on the type of trade symbol involved. An injunction may prohibit the use of an inherently distinctive mark or name, while merely attaching conditions to the use of a geographically descriptive term, personal name or distinctive product feature. See, e.g., *Taylor Wine Company v. Bully Hill Vineyards, Inc.* (1978) (modifying an order broadly prohibiting Walter S. Taylor from using the word "Taylor" in connection with his wine business). Similarly, as a result of the *Sears–Compco* decisions, the grant of injunctive relief in common-law product imitation cases will be limited to requiring distinguishing labels and trade dress. But cf. *Truck Equipment Service Co. v. Fruehauf Corp.* (1976) (upholding an injunction in a case brought under section 43(a) of the Lanham Act to prevent the copying of a side configuration of a grain semi-trailer, where the designer and defendant's engineers testified that the configuration was "useless" and its only function would be to gather road dirt and mud). See also *Boston*

Professional Hockey Association, Inc. v. Dallas Cap & Emblem Manufacturing, Inc. (1975) (holding that the unauthorized, intentional duplication of a professional hockey team's symbol on an embroidered emblem, to be sold to the public as a patch for attachment on clothing, constituted an infringement under the Lanham Act and at common law, and that the district court erred in limiting relief in the case to a requirement that the defendant place a notice on the emblems or their packages that the emblems are not authorized by and have not emanated from the plaintiffs). The *Boston Hockey* case has been criticized. See *International Order of Job's Daughters v. Lindeburg & Co.* (1980) (noting that *Boston Hockey* in effect gives the owner of a trademark a complete monopoly over the trademark's commercial use, including its functional use).

In addition to injunctive relief, the victim of infringement may be entitled to damages for any provable losses resulting from past infringement. In appropriate cases, the plaintiff may also recover defendant's profits. See, e.g., Lanham Act § 35, 15 U.S.C.A. § 1117 (subject to the principles of equity, a plaintiff may recover defendant's profits and any damages sustained). Defendant's profits may be used as evidence of plaintiff's losses where the defendant uses an infringing mark on goods that compete with plaintiff's. Even where plaintiff and defendant do not compete and plaintiff has thus suffered no diversion of sales, however, defendant's profits may be recoverable on a purely restitutionary theory of unjust enrichment. See, e.g., *Maier Brewing Co. v. Fleischmann Distilling Corp.* (1968) (accounting of defendant's profits upheld where defendant infringed plaintiff's federally registered mark for Scotch whiskey by using the mark on defendant's beer). Because an accounting is equitable remedy, however, it is not available as a matter of right but only as the equities of the case demand. Most courts insist that defendant's infringement be shown to have been deliberate and wilful before they will order an accounting.

A lack of deliberate and wilful conduct may also be grounds for denying punitive damages. Most courts also refuse to award punitive damages unless some compensatory damages are awarded. While the Lanham Act does not specifically provide for the award of punitive damages, it does permit courts to award a plaintiff up to treble a plaintiff's actual damages. In fact, section 1117 has two trebling provisions, the first being a kind of statutory liquidated damages provision, while the second is punitive in nature. See section 35, 15 U.S.C.A. § 1117. In 1975 section 35 of the Act was amended to allow the award of attorney's fees to the prevailing party in exceptional cases. The Trademark Counterfeiting Act of 1984 authorizes virtually mandatory awards of treble damages and attorney's fees in civil counterfeiting cases and also authorizes courts to enter as interim relief *ex parte* orders for seizure of goods and counterfeit marks, the means of making such marks, and records concerning any of the above, where the person being proceeded against is likely to destroy, conceal or render inaccessible any of the above.

In awarding compensatory damages, the courts have generally employed liberal damage measures and have not required the extent of damage to be proved with the same degree of certainty as the fact of damage. In *Big O Tire Dealers, Inc. v. Goodyear Tire & Rubber Co.* (1977), for example, the court held that the plaintiffs could recover damages for corrective advertising that would be necessary to dispel the confusion which had been shown to have been created by the defendant's advertising. The court went on to hold that the amount to be awarded could be calculated by taking the amount the defendant spent on the offending nationwide advertising, reducing it by a percentage to reflect the number of states in which the plaintiffs did business and allowing plaintiffs to recover up to 25% of that amount. The 25% limitation was based on the Federal Trade Commission's practice of requiring businesses which engage in misleading advertising to spend 25% of their advertising budget on corrective advertising, and was said to reflect the fact that a dollar-for-dollar expenditure is probably not required to dispel confusion in the consuming public's mind.

CHAPTER FIVE
PRODUCT SUBSTITUTION OR ALTERATION

Although the earliest form of palming off consisted of the deceptive use of another's trademark, that is by no means the only way one merchant might attempt to palm off inferior or less well-known goods as those of another more reputable or better known merchant. As we have seen, any distinctive product or business feature, whether adopted for the purpose of identifying a product or business or not, can be imitated and thus used to deceive the consuming public as to the identity of goods, services or a business. Hence the common law's prohibition against deceptive imitation of such distinctive product and business features as product and packaging designs, advertising slogans and literary or artistic titles and characters.

One form of palming off—namely, deceptive product substitution or alteration—involves neither the deceptive use of another's trade symbol nor the deceptive imitation of a distinctive product or business feature. This particular form of palming off might be accomplished by deceptively substituting less well-known goods for better known goods or inferior quality goods for better quality goods. It might also be accomplished by selling used goods as new or adulterated goods as the original. In each case palming off takes place without deceptive imitation of a distinctive trade symbol or a distinctive product or business feature. Whereas deceptive substitution of services generally requires an infringement of the service mark, trade name or trade dress of another business, deceptive product substitution and alteration is possible precisely because of the absence of any accompanying trade symbols or trade dress and the superficial lack of distinction between the goods requested and those provided.

Here as in previous chapters, it is useful first to identify the type of trade relations which are being protected and then to distinguish actionable from privileged interference with those trade relations.

A. TRADE RELATIONS PROTECTED

The common law governing product substitution and alteration seeks to protect essentially the same trade relations as are protected by the common law of trademarks and trade names—namely, the existing public relations or good will of a business. Whereas the common law of trademarks and trade names specifically seeks to protect any good will generated by the use of distinctive trade symbols, the law governing product substitution and alteration specifically seeks to protect *product* good will, whether generated by a distinctive trade symbol or not.

The reputation of a product, whether spread by word of mouth or advertising, is often enough to stimulate retail customers to request the product by name (e.g., "I'd like a Coke"). A retailer who deceptively substitutes or alters the goods requested not only deceives the customer but also interferes with the good will of the product and the public relations of the manufacturer or distributor of the product (depending on which one created and thus "owns" the good will).

B. ACTIONABLE AND PRIVILEGED SUBSTITUTION OR ALTERATION OF GOODS

Not every substitution or alteration of goods is actionable. Nothing precludes the seller who wishes to substitute or alter goods from attempting to persuade the customer to accept the goods proffered—at least so long as no false representations are made. The only prohibition is against making *unannounced* substitutions or alterations. Unannounced substitution or alteration of goods has long been condemned as a form of unfair competition, even though no deceptive mark or trade dress is used and the goods are in fact clearly marked so as to indicate their actual origin. In practice, however, product substitution or alteration most frequently occurs where goods are unmarked or sold outside their original containers.

1. PRODUCT SUBSTITUTION

Product substitution cases may be divided into those involving the substitution of less well-known goods for better known goods, those involving the substitution of inferior quality goods for better quality goods, and those involving the substitution of another's product as one's own (reverse palming off). The goods most commonly involved in substitution cases of the first type are drugs, food, and beverages. Indeed, much of the case law governing unannounced substitution of less well-known goods for better known goods is the handiwork of the Coca–Cola Company, whose efforts to ensure that the consuming public gets "The Real Thing" when it asks for it are truly prodigious. In the typical case, the Coca–Cola Company brings an action against a retail establishment of some sort, citing instances in which the establishment or its agents have made unannounced substitutions of another carbonated beverage when a customer ordered a "Coke."

So long as the designation by which goods are ordered functions unambiguously as a trademark, the owner of the trademark has little difficulty in obtaining relief, not only against a retailer who substitutes less well-known goods for better known goods, but also against a manufacturer or distributor who can be shown either to have induced, explicitly or by suggestion or insinuation, the substitution of products or to have provided the substitute product knowing that the retailer would or could be expected to engage in unannounced substitutions. Difficulties arise, however, where a trademark has more than one meaning. Such ambiguity can occur in two distinct types of cases. In the first, normally involving a rather unique new product, the plaintiff coins a word to serve as a trademark for its product and the word over time comes to be used as the generic name for the product type. As we saw in Chapter 4, for example, such terms as "aspirin," "cellophane" and "thermos," were all originally used to designate a particular company's product but over time took on a broader meaning and came to be understood as designating an entire class of goods without limitation as to the producer.

Ambiguity may also result from the conscious selection of a mark, such as "Raisin-bran," which is simply descriptive of the product. The nearly descriptive trademark may be thought of as a "weak" trademark because it is chosen as much for its descriptive qualities as for its use as a designation of origin. Trademarks which tend to take on a generic meaning, by contrast, are generally trademarks which were initially "strong" marks, coined to function solely as a designation of origin, which only fortuitously came to have any other meaning.

Because the nearly descriptive and nearly generic trademark have more than one meaning, it is not clear, when a customer asks for a "thermos bottle" or "raisin-bran cereal," whether a particular brand or a particular type of product is being ordered. For that reason it is debatable whether a retailer who is aware of the possibility of confusion should be held liable for palming off where the customer is provided a product which has the same descriptive qualities or falls within the same generic classification as that requested. Such cases in the end must necessarily turn on their particular facts. Where two different brands of hat, for example, are sold under the surname "Stetson" but only one hat maker is responsible for developing the reputation of the "Stetson hat," the ambiguity is more apparent than real and, where a second hat maker named Stetson fails to distinguish his goods from the first, palming off will readily be found. See *John B. Stetson Co. v. Stephen L. Stetson Co., Ltd.* (1936). In such cases, the courts take the view that when in doubt the junior user of the surname must assume that the ambiguous term is being used in its trademark sense and, where necessary, seek to clarify any confusion about what brand is meant. Where the ambiguity is real, however, and the owner of the trademark either created the ambiguity or failed to keep it from developing, the courts have allowed retailers greater latitude. In *DuPont Cellophane Co. v. Waxed Products Co.* (1936), for example, the court found that the trademark "Cellophane" had to a large extent gone generic and held that in filling orders for cellophane it was only necessary for the retailer to state that the product sold is the cellophane of whomsoever is the maker and nothing more. In such cases, the court held, the retailer need not provide free advertising for the originator of cellophane by asking if the originator's product is what is being requested.

Thus far we have been considering substitution cases in which one person's less well-known product is substituted for another person's better known but otherwise similar product. The substituted product need not be of inferior quality because the principal harm sought to be avoided is the direct diversion of sales. In practice, however, the less known product is often of inferior quality as well. One type of product substitution necessarily involves but one product brand and the substitution of inferior quality goods. This type of case arises where "seconds" (i.e., flawed goods of a particular brand) are palmed off as top quality goods of that same brand. Not surprisingly, the courts have held that misrepresenting the quality of one brand of goods, no less than deceptively substituting one brand of goods for another, constitutes palming off. There is no prohibition against dealing in seconds, of course. One is merely required to notify the purchaser of that fact.

The only particular difficulty arising in cases involving palming off "seconds" as top quality goods is the problem of establishing that two such classes of a given brand of goods in fact exist. In *Harris v. Warren & Phillips* (1918), for example, a publisher sought to enjoin the proposed republication of a song written by a popular songwriter long before she had become famous. The plaintiff argued that although the defendant publisher had purchased the rights to the older composition, the song was so lacking in merit that it should not be published in a manner which could lead to a belief that it was one of the songwriter's recent works. The court refused to pass on the relative merit of the songwriter's earlier and later compositions, however, and denied the plaintiff relief.

Just as it is actionable to pass off one's own product as that of another, so it may be actionable to pass off another's product as one's own. See, e.g., *International News Service v. Associated Press* (1918) (dissenting opinion of Mr. Justice Holmes) ("The ordinary case, I say, is palming off the defendant's product as the plaintiff's, but the same evil may follow from the opposite falsehood—from saying, whether in words or by implication, that the plaintiff's product is the defendant's, and that, it seems to me, is what happened here [where one news service copied or paraphrased another news service's stories as they were published on the east coast and then used those stories to compete with the other news service on the west coast]"). Such cases most frequently involve plagiarism of another's literary work. The passing off claim is often accompanied by or subsumed in claims of copyright infringement, misappropriation or invasion of the right of publicity. See, e.g., *Bajpayee v. Rothermich* (1977) (holding that where a president of a research laboratory, without authorization, used an unpublished article, written by a biochemist during the course of his employment with the laboratory, at a professional meeting in such a way as to indicate that it was the work of the president, the biochemist had a cause of action—be it classified as a claim for relief for plagiarism, invasion of a right of publicity or prima facie tort—for violation of his right to be recognized for his work product, even though he claimed no common-law copyright interest in the article and the discovery revealed in the article was the property of the employer).

2. PRODUCT ALTERATION

Under the general heading of unannounced alteration of goods may be grouped two further variations on the unannounced substitution theme— namely selling reconditioned goods as new and adulterated goods as the original. Both forms of unannounced alteration of goods bear a particularly strong resemblance to the substitution of "seconds" for first run goods.

Just as one may legitimately attempt to convince a customer to accept substitute goods and may legitimately deal in seconds, so one may legitimately recondition and resell used goods. One may even resell used goods with the original trademark still affixed, at least so long as the public is aware that the goods are in fact reconditioned. But the danger inherent in the reconditioning of used goods which are to all outward appearances indistinguishable from new goods is that the reconditioned goods are easily palmed off on an unsuspecting public as new. Thus, just as manufacturers and distributors are obligated to anticipate instances in which those they supply are likely to deceptively substitute the supplied brand of goods for another better known or higher quality brand, so those who recondition and resell used goods are obligated to take steps to avoid the danger of customer confusion over whether the goods are new or used.

If the common law of unannounced product substitution owes much to the Coca–Cola Company, so the law governing reconditioned goods owes a similar debt to the Champion Spark Plug Company. In *Champion Spark Plug Co. v. Sanders* (1947), for example, the Supreme Court upheld a claim of trademark infringement and unfair competition against a defendant who reconditioned used spark plugs and sold them under their original "Champion" mark with inadequate notice that they were reconditioned. The case was only a partial victory for Champion, however, because the Court affirmed a modified decree which merely required the defendant to stamp "Repaired" or "Used" on the plugs in such a way as to be clearly and distinctly visible but did not require removal of the word "Champion" from the plug. The Court concluded that, although used, the plugs were nevertheless Champion plugs and not those of some other make and that the defendant was therefore entitled to identify them as such.

At some point, of course, the alteration of the original product may be so substantial that it would be deceptive to continue identifying it by its original trademark. Similarly, product size or configuration may be such that adequate notice of the alteration of the original product will be impossible. In such cases the courts may well order the original mark to be obliterated prior to resale.

A second form of unannounced alteration of goods is the selling of an adulterated form of the original product. This form of palming off, like the unannounced substitution of goods, is most likely to occur when goods are sold outside their containers, but may also involve repackaged goods. The product, of course, must be capable of adulteration. Most frequently involved are drugs, cosmetics, foods and beverages. Just as the Coca-Cola Company has gone to great lengths to prevent unannounced substitutions by those who do not sell Coca-Cola, for example, so it has gone to great lengths to prevent the authorized retailers of its product from secretly diluting the syrup prior to mixing it with carbonated water in the presence of the soda fountain customer.

Somewhat analogous to the right to prevent product adulteration is the right to prevent unannounced alteration of a literary and artistic product. In *Gilliam v. American Broadcasting Companies, Inc.* (1976), for example, the court held that a group of British writers and performers known as "Monty Python" were entitled to a preliminary injunction to restrain ABC from broadcasting edited versions of programs originally written and performed by Monty Python for the British Broadcasting Company (BBC). Although ABC was licensed by BBC to distribute the Monty Python series, the writers and performers complained that ABC's omission of twenty-four of the original 90 minutes constituted an actionable mutilation (or "deformation") of their work.

In addition to holding that there was a substantial likelihood that ABC's editing of the TV recording constituted an infringement of Monty Python's copyright in the underlying script, the court concluded that Monty Python had also stated a cause of action under section 43(a) of the Lanham Act, 15 U.S.C.A. § 1125(a), which creates a federal cause of action against anyone who uses a false designation of origin or a false description or representation in connection with any goods or services put into commerce. (See Chapter 8 infra). The court noted that while American copyright law had not as yet recognized any equivalent of the European civil law concept of *droit moral* (i.e., the right of an artist to have his work attributed to him in the form in which he created it), courts had long granted common-law relief based either on a theory of breach of implied contractual obligation or unfair competition, for misrepresentation of an artist's work. The court expressed doubt that a legend disclaiming Monty Python's approval of the edited version would provide adequate relief for the plaintiffs, since viewers would have no means of comparing the truncated version with the original to make their own determination as to the talents of the plaintiffs and might, in any event, tune in after the disclaimer had been displayed.

C. AFFIRMATIVE DEFENSES AND REMEDIES

The affirmative defenses and remedies for product substitution and alteration are essentially the same as those available in trademark or trade name infringement cases. As there, a defendant in a product substitution or alteration case may establish that the plaintiff's mark or name has been abandoned or lost its distinctiveness or that the plaintiff is guilty of laches, acquiescence or unclean hands. Where a party is held to have made an unannounced product substitution or alteration, the commercial victim may recover provable compensatory damages and obtain an injunction from a court or a cease and desist order from the Federal Trade Commission or an exclusion or cease and desist order from the International Trade Commission, against further substitutions or alterations. In appropriate cases, the plaintiff may also recover punitive damages or restitution of defendant's profits. Because plaintiff's damages and defendant's profits may be particularly difficult to prove in product substitution and alteration cases, the availability of injunctive relief and punitive damages is all the more important.

*

PART III

APPROPRIATION OF INTANGIBLE TRADE VALUES

CHAPTER SIX

APPROPRIATION OF PUBLICLY DISCLOSED TRADE VALUES

The intangible assets of a business may include not only its trademarks, trade names and business good will but also any inventions, literary or artistic works or other commercially valuable ideas or information. Unlike trademarks, trade names and good will, these intangible trade values may be developed by non-commercial as well as commercial parties. What all of these intangible trade values have in common is that they are the product of intellectual effort—and often entail a substantial investment of time and money as well.

Several bodies of federal and state law provide varying degrees of protection for such products of intellectual effort. Article I, Section 8 of the Constitution of the United States, for example, specifically empowers Congress to "promote the progress of science and useful arts, by securing for limited times to authors and inventors the exclusive rights to their respective writings and discoveries." Pursuant to that authority Congress has long provided and periodically expanded patent and copyright protection. Like other federal law enacted pursuant to constitutional authority, U.S. patent and copyright law are declared by the supremacy clause of the Constitution to be the supreme law of the land and may not be undermined by inconsistent state law.

The purpose of federal patent and copyright law is not merely to reward inventors and authors but to secure for the public the benefit of their labors. A patent may be thought of as a contract between an inventor and the public (represented by the federal government), whereby in return for full public disclosure of an invention the public grants the inventor the right to exclude others for a limited time from making, using or selling the invention in the United States. A federal copyright, in turn, may be defined as an intangible right, vesting in the author or originator of certain literary or artistic works, to control for a limited time the multiplication of copies of the work and the publication, adaption, distribution, performance, or display of same in the United States.

Patent and copyright law like the law of trademarks and trade names is strictly territorial. United States patents and copyrights confer no rights outside the United States, nor does a foreign patent or copyright confer rights within the United States. An inventor or author must file separate applications in each country in which patent or copyright protection is desired. The Patent Cooperation Treaty is designed to facilitate parallel patent filings (see pp. 28–29 supra).

Although federal patent protection is the exclusive method for retaining rights in publicly disclosed inventions in the United States, federal patent law has long co-existed not only with state contract law governing the assignment and licensing of patents but also with an amorphous body of state law, generally known as the law of trade secrets and the law of ideas, which protects non-publicly disclosed inventions, ideas or information from unauthorized use or disclosure. (See Chapter 7 infra.) Until 1976, copyright protection of literary and artistic works in the United States was likewise provided through a dual system whereby state common law protected literary and artistic works prior to their general publication and federal statutory law protected specified classes of literary and artistic works after general publication. That approach to copyright protection was modified by the Copyright Act of 1976, 17 U.S.C.A. § 101 et seq., so that today federal copyright protection extends to specified classes of works which have been reduced to tangible form, whether they have been publicly disclosed or not, while common-law copyright protection extends only to ephemeral works or tangible works which are not entitled to federal protection.

Federal patent and copyright law has also had an impact on a body of common law known as the law of misappropriation. Originating in the Supreme Court's decision in *International News Service v. Associated Press,* the famous news piracy case (see Chapter 1, supra), the law of misappropriation purported to supplement both federal and state law by protecting publicly disclosed products of intellectual effort from misappropriation by others. In a closely related development, the common law of privacy emerged at about the same time to protect the exclusive right of individuals to prohibit or authorize the commercial exploitation of their own name or likeness. Although federal patent and copyright law narrow the permissible scope of both of these bodies of law, the common law nevertheless continues to provide protection against the misappropriation of certain publicly disclosed trade values which are not protected by federal law. Likewise, federal law supplements but does not supplant state contract law, which governs the assignment and licensing of patents and copyrights.

An important development in intellectual property protection was the enactment of the Semiconductor Chip Protection Act of 1984, 17 U.S.C.A. § 901 et seq., (hereinafter "the Chip Act"), which represents not simply a new development in patent and copyright law, but, rather, the emergence of an entirely new *sui generis* form of intellectual property protection for semiconductor chip designs, which the Chip Act refers to as "mask works." The Chip Act signals what may be the beginning of a trend toward creating *sui generis* forms of protection for new technologies (in preference to expanding existing patent or copyright protection) and contains provisions specifically designed to encourage other countries to create equivalent forms of legal protection for semiconductor chip design.

The subject matter and owners eligible for protection under the Chip Act are defined in much the same way as they are in U.S. copyright law. Registration, notice, and the duration and nature of the exclusive rights created by the Chip Act, on the other hand, are defined in such a way as to bear a closer resemblance, in a number of important respects, to U.S. patent law than to U.S. copyright law. Finally, the principal limitation placed on these exclusive rights—namely, the reverse engineering limitation—resembles neither U.S. patent nor copyright law but rather the common law of trade secrets. From this summary alone, it is easy to see why the Chip Act is described as having created a hybrid or *sui generis* form of intellectual property.

As in previous chapters, it is useful first to identify what trade relations and trade values are protected by the foregoing bodies of law and then to consider what constitutes actionable and privileged appropriation of those trade relations and values.

A. TRADE RELATIONS AND TRADE VALUES PROTECTED

The trade relations whose protection is the subject of this chapter and the next are the existing or prospective trade relations of a party who has made an investment of intellectual effort and wishes to exploit that investment. The specific concern in this chapter is with those bodies of law which protect the purely prospective commercial relations of a party who wishes to exploit a product of intellectual effort publicly.

Those products of intellectual effort protected by federal patent and copyright law include certain inventions (including designs and certain plants) and literary or artistic works, respectively. A publicly disclosed product of intellectual effort may alternatively be entitled to common-law protection against misappropriation.

1. PATENTABLE INVENTIONS

Federal patent law defines the requirements an inventor must meet in order to be able to take advantage of the public's standing contractual offer to grant exclusive rights in an invention for a limited time in return for its full public disclosure. These requirements may be divided into those which are substantive and those which are procedural. The substantive requirements specify what subject matter constitutes a patentable invention while the procedural requirements specify how patent rights are obtained, transferred and terminated.

a. Subject Matter Protected

Federal patent protection is restricted as a constitutional matter to "inventors" and their "discoveries." The subject matter protected by the federal patent statute is limited still more narrowly to "inventions"—which, notwithstanding the statement in 35 U.S.C.A. § 100 that the term "invention" means invention or discovery, has been construed as being limited to that class of discoveries which produces something that did not previously exist, as opposed to the mere bringing to light of that which previously existed but was unknown. The constitutional requirement of a "discovery," however, does place one important limitation on federal patent protection. Inventions must as a constitutional matter contain an element of novelty. Beyond this all-important constitutional requirement, limitations on the subject matter of federal patent protection are essentially statutory.

The federal patent statute defines a patentable invention in two ways. In order to be patentable, an invention must (1) fall within one of the specified classes of subject matter for which the patent statute provides protection and (2) meet a general standard of newness and non-obviousness. An invention meeting these prerequisites may qualify for one of three types of patent: a utility patent, a design patent or a plant patent. By far the most frequently sought type of patent is the utility patent, which, as the name suggests, requires a showing that the invention is useful, as well as new and non-obvious.

The various classes of subject matter for which a utility patent may be sought include (1) *a process,* (2) *a machine,* (3) *an article of manufacture,* (4) *a composition of matter,* or (5) *an improvement* of any of the foregoing classifications. Courts have construed each of the foregoing classes so as to exclude certain types of subject matter which might otherwise appear to be included. The "process" classification, for example, has been construed as excluding methods of doing business, abstract ideas, scientific principles, mental processes, printing systems, and at least some computer inventions involving programs. See, e.g., *Gottschalk v. Benson* (1972); *Parker v. Flook* (1978) (holding that a mathematical formula used in a computer program is not patentable). *Gottschalk* and *Parker* have subsequently been interpreted, not as having barred patent protection for computer programs per se, but merely for mathematical algorithms (i.e., processes for solving a given type of mathematical problem). Patentability will turn on whether (1) a patent claim directly or indirectly recites an algorithm, and (2) whether the algorithm is applied or implemented in a particular way or simply stated and solved. *Application of Freeman* (1978); *Application of Walter* (1980). A claim containing otherwise statutory subject matter does not become non-statutory merely because it uses a mathematical formula, computer program or digital computer. *Diamond v. Diehr* (1981) (holding that a process for curing synthetic rubber, which in several of its steps uses a mathematical formula, is patentable). The test is to be construed broadly and in favor of patentability. *In re Abele* (1982). For example, a patent issued for a computer program dealing with cash management has been upheld because it claimed a methodology to effectuate a highly efficient business system rather than a mathematical formula. *Paine, Webber v. Merrill Lynch* (1983). The Patent Office is currently issuing "pure" software patents in significant numbers.

An "article of manufacture" has likewise been held to exclude a mere arrangement of printed matter or an article found in nature, while a "composition of matter" has been held to exclude a material found in nature. On the other hand, a live, human-made micro-organism has been held to constitute a "manufacture" or "composition of matter" within the meaning of the statute. *Diamond v. Chakrabarty* (1980).

Inventions falling within (and not judicially excluded from) one or more of the five statutory classes of protectible subject matter must meet the general standard of *novelty, utility,* and *non-obviousness* in order for a utility patent to issue. Novelty is present when an invention is different from the prior art (i.e., information previously available to the public) and is negated if the invention is anticipated in the prior art (i.e., is known or used by others in the United States, patented or published anywhere in the world, or previously abandoned by the inventor). Utility is present when an invention has an obvious and direct benefit to mankind and is negated if the invention is frivolous or injurious to morals, health or good order. An invention is non-obvious if the differences between the subject matter sought to be patented and the prior art are such that the subject matter as a whole would not have been obvious at the time the invention was made to a person having ordinary skill in the art to which the subject matter pertains.

For the two other statutory classes of patentable subject matter—ornamental designs and plants— slightly different standards obtain. Because a design patent is based solely on the appearance of an article of manufacture and not on its utility, the design must be shown to be *novel, original* and *ornamental.* Similarly, in order for a plant patent to issue, the plant must be shown to be a *distinct* and *new* asexually-reproduced variety not found in nature. In addition, however, both designs and plants must be non-obvious as well as new.

The Plant Variety Protection Act of 1970, as amended in 1980, 7 U.S.C.A. § 2401 et seq. provides protection for new plant varieties reproduced sexually, through seeds. For a certificate of plant variety protection to issue, the variety claimed must meet the statutory requirements of *distinctiveness, uniformity* and *stability,* as well novelty. The term of protection is 18 years. The Act is administered by the U.S. Department of Agriculture.

b. Obtaining a Patent

Patent applications are filed with the Patent and Trademark Office (PTO) of the U.S. Department of Commerce. Prior to filing an application for a patent, the inventor will normally retain a patent attorney in order to search PTO records, much as one might search the title of real property. From this search an initial determination of probable patentability is made.

Patent applications must be filed in the name of the actual inventor or inventors. Thus, only natural persons and not corporations may be named as the inventor. This is not to say that a corporation may not apply for the patent, but only that the corporation must file in the name of the inventor. An applicant who is not the named inventor must be shown to be the inventor's legal representative or an entity having a proprietary interest in the patent.

An inventor forfeits the right to obtain a patent if it is not applied for within a year after the invention is "in public use or on sale." 35 U.S.C.A. § 102(b). "Public use" has been construed as use by any member of the public, including the inventor, so long as the use is not purely experimental. Where an invention is made in the U.S., a patent must first be filed in the U.S. and a patent application or registration of a utility model or industrial design or model (two forms of intellectual property protected elsewhere in the world but having no exact equivalent in the U.S.) may not be filed elsewhere until six months has elapsed unless permission is obtained from the PTO.

The application for a patent must be accompanied by a specification, which in full, clear, concise and exact terms describes the invention and states the inventor's specific claims to that invention. In contrast to the practice in other countries, applications are normally kept confidential until such time as the PTO actually issues a patent. Because rejected applications are not made public, the applicant loses nothing by applying for a patent. If any or all of an applicant's claims are rejected by the PTO, the applicant may seek judicial review in the Court of Appeals for the Federal Circuit.

Where two parties, unknown to each other, make the same invention in this country and subsequently file patent applications, the first inventor, not the first applicant, has priority so long as the invention was not thereafter abandoned, suppressed or concealed. In this respect, too, U.S. patent law differs from that of most other countries, which generally grant priority to the first inventor to file a patent application. Harmonization legislation, that would convert U.S. patent law to a first-to-file system, has been proposed.

For patent applications having a right of foreign priority under the Paris Convention, the earliest filing date abroad will be used, upon timely motion, to determine priority if an application for a utility or plant patent is filed in the U.S. within 12 months of the foreign filing, 35 U.S.C.A. § 119, or within 6 months in the case of a design patent, 35 U.S.C. § 172, unless the disclosure in such a filing does not meet the requirements of U.S. patent law. In the absence of a foreign filing, however, evidence of activities abroad is not available to establish a date of invention.

In determining priority of invention, the PTO is to consider not only the respective dates of conception and reduction to practice, but also the reasonable diligence of an inventor who was first to conceive but last to reduce the invention to practice. If due diligence is used to reduce the invention to practice, the first to conceive the invention has priority. Inventions made abroad are treated as having been conceived and reduced to practice simultaneously as of the foreign filing date. In practice, many domestic inventions are treated as having been constructively invented as of the patent application filing date.

c. Transfer and Termination of Patents

Once the PTO issues a patent, the patentee obtains the exclusive right to exclude others from making, using or selling the patented invention in the U.S.—a right which exists for a period of seventeen years in the case of utility and plant patents and fourteen years in the case of design patents, unless prior to its expiration the patent is judicially invalidated. As with other forms of intellectual property, patent rights may be assigned or licensed. An assignment transfers ownership of all or some of the patentee's rights in the invention, while a license merely grants the licensee permission to make, use or sell the invention. Although the patent rights themselves are federally created rights, infringement of which must be litigated in federal courts, the assignment or licensing of patents is largely governed by state contract and property law. Thus, where no diversity of citizenship or federal question exists, patent assignments and licensing agreements will be enforced in state courts.

The common law which regulates patent transfers creates important rights independent of federal patent law. Under the common-law "shop right" doctrine, for example, an employer who can show that an employee developed a patentable invention on company time with company facilities and materials, will be treated as having an implied, irrevocable, non-assignable, non-exclusive, royalty-free license to use the employee's invention. If an employee is hired specifically to engage in research and development, courts will imply an agreement that any discoveries will belong to the employer.

State law governing patent assignments and licenses must, of course, be consistent with federal patent law. Thus, states may not enforce an assignment or license of a patent which has been judicially declared invalid. Nor may states enforce a license provision which attempts to extend the license period beyond the term of the patent. *Brulotte v. Thys Co.* (1964). In a similar vein, the Supreme Court held in *Lear, Inc. v. Adkins* (1969), that states could no longer apply the common law "licensee estoppel" doctrine, which previously prevented licensees from challenging the validity of the patent they had obtained permission to use, nor could states require licensees to pay royalties during the time they litigated patent validity in court. The Court concluded that the licensee estoppel doctrine discouraged legitimate attacks on patent validity by the only parties with sufficient economic incentive to mount the attack. But cf. *Roberts v. Sears, Roebuck & Co.* (1978) (holding *Lear* to be inapplicable and a district court not to have erred in declining to decide the validity of a patent in a suit for fraud, breach of a confidential relationship and negligent misrepresentation in a company's procurement of an assignment of the patent rights of an employee who during his off-duty hours invented a new type of socket wrench).

The transfer of patent rights must also comport with federal antitrust law. Although the patent itself is a legal monopoly, which its owner is free to exploit, it may not be used to create other monopolies or restraints on trade. A recurring controversy in patent licensing is whether license restrictions are reasonably necessary to afford the patent owner the rewards of the patented invention or unreasonably restrain trade.

Federal patent law itself superimposes certain procedural formalities on patent transfers. According to 35 U.S.C.A. § 261, patents and patent applications, or fractional interests therein, may be assigned, but the assignment must be by a written instrument recorded in the Patent Office in order to have full legal effect against subsequent bona fide purchasers. No recording requirement exists for licenses. Oral assignments and unrecorded written assignments function much like a license— they create rights between the parties to the agreement but not rights which are enforceable against third parties.

Classification of an agreement as an assignment or a license is no mere formality. The courts are not bound by how an agreement is labelled but will classify the agreement according to its actual legal effect. The courts have held, for example, that the grant of an exclusive license to make, use or sell the patented invention within and throughout all or a specified part of the United States amounts to an assignment, even if the agreement is labeled a license.

Whether an agreement is an assignment or a license has a number of important practical ramifications, not the least of which is determining who has the right to sue for infringement in federal court. Because the right to sue for infringement is an incident of ownership, it will pass under an assignment but not under a license. In a licensing arrangement the licensor is, in effect, merely agreeing not to sue a licensee for making specified uses of the patented invention. The licensee has no right to sue others for infringement but must depend on the licensor to protect the patent against infringement.

Patent rights terminate upon (1) expiration of the term of the patent or (2) judicial invalidation. A utility or plant patent expires seventeen years after issuance, while a design patent expires in fourteen years. Judicial invalidation of patents prior to their expiration is a frequent and to a certain extent unavoidable feature of federal patent law. Given the confidential and largely non-adversarial nature of the patent application process, the PTO simply cannot discern with any accuracy whether a patent application in fact discloses a novel and non-obvious invention. The problem is exacerbated, however, by the fact that the courts tend to use a more stringent standard of non-obviousness than is used by the PTO. Consequently while the PTO grants about 60% of all patent applications filed, the courts invalidate about 60% of all patents granted. Thus, a PTO rejection of a patent application is likely to be upheld on appeal, but its grant of a patent will more likely than not be invalidated in the course of subsequent infringement proceedings. One reason for creating the Court of Appeals for the Federal

Circuit, which has exclusive jurisdiction to hear appeals of patent application denials and patent infringement proceedings, was to bring about greater uniformity in the test for non-obviousness.

2. COPYRIGHTABLE LITERARY AND ARTISTIC WORKS

Federal copyright law, like federal patent law, spells out both substantive and procedural requirements that must be met in order to obtain protection for literary and artistic works. The substantive requirements specify what constitutes a protectible "writing" of an "author," while the procedural requirements specify how a copyright is acquired, transferred and terminated.

a. Subject Matter Protected

In order to obtain federal copyright protection, a literary or artistic work must come within the constitutional definition of a "writing" and its creator within the constitutional definition of an "author." The constitutional scope of these terms is determined not by reference to their dictionary meaning but by reference to the constitutional policy, embodied in the copyright and patent clause itself, of promoting "Science" and the "Useful Arts" (terms which should be read in their 18th Century sense, as meaning knowledge worthy to be known for its own sake and knowledge useful in achieving some other end, respectively). In keeping with that policy, the Supreme Court has defined a "writing" as any physical rendering of fruits of creative intellectual or aesthetic labor. *Goldstein v. California* (1973). Thus defined, a constitutional "writing" includes virtually any literary or artistic work, including visual works and those created for a purely commercial purpose. Implicit in the court's broad definition of the constitutional term is a judicial policy of deferring to Congress on the question of what works should be copyrighted.

If the constitutional definition of a writing is broad, it nevertheless has its limits, beyond which Congress cannot go in granting copyright protection. The Court has held as a constitutional matter that a "writing" is (1) the fruit of intellectual labor which is (2) reduced to tangible form. The requirement of intellectual labor, it will be recalled, has been held to exclude trademarks (or at least those which are not inherently distinctive) from copyright protection. In the *Trademark Cases* (1872) the Court held that the expenditure of intellectual labor in the creation of a trademark was too trivial to merit copyright protection. While one may criticize the Court's conclusion to the extent that it applies to fanciful and arbitrary as well as secondary meaning marks and names, the requirement of some minimal degree of intellectual labor is itself sound enough, for it serves to exclude common words and phrases from copyright protection. Even if there is no constitutional bar to providing copyright protection for fanciful marks or names, there is a strong policy argument for such a bar—namely to prevent the law of copyrights from rendering superfluous the likelihood of confusion requirement for infringement of a federally registered mark.

The requirement that the product of intellectual labor be reduced to tangible form serves to exclude ephemeral works (i.e., those not fixed in any tangible form) from federal copyright protection. The requirement that writings be the works of an "author" not only limits federal copyright protection to those who expend the intellectual labor to create the writing, but imports a requirement that the fruits of that labor be original with the author and not mere slavish copies of some earlier work.

Pursuant to its constitutional power, Congress has long provided copyright protection and has steadily expanded its scope. The most comprehensive recent expansion came in the Copyright Act of 1976, 17 U.S.C.A. § 101 et seq., as subsequently amended by P.L. 96–517 (Dec. 12, 1980) (specifically providing for and delineating the scope of copyright protection for computer programs) and four 1990 amendments, the Architectural Works Copyright Protection Act, the Visual Artists Rights Act, the Computer Software Rental Amendments Act, and the Copyright Remedy Clarification Act.

The 1976 Act operates prospectively from its effective date of January 1, 1978. Certain provisions of its predecessor, the Copyright Act of 1909, have been allowed to remain in force for works created prior to that effective date. The 1909 and 1976 Acts differ both as to their definition of what constitutes a copyrightable work and as to the procedure whereby copyright is obtained, transferred and terminated.

As we have seen, prior to the 1976 Act, copyright protection was provided through a dual system of state common-law protection prior to general publication and federal statutory protection after general publication. In contrast to the dual system of trademark law, which provides *concurrent* federal and state protection of trade symbols, common-law and statutory copyright provided *alternative* forms of protection, with general publication serving as the all important dividing line between the two. Common-law copyright was based on the right of the author or originator of a literary or artistic work to keep the work secret or place conditions on its limited publication to others, whereas federal copyright law provided the exclusive protection for a work after its unlimited or general publication. Under the 1976 Act, federal copyright protection extends to all otherwise copyrightable literary or artistic works fixed in tangible form, whether generally published or not and to that extent preempts much of what was formerly known as the common law of copyright.

Section 102(a) of the 1976 Act states that copyright protection subsists in original works of authorship fixed in any tangible medium of expression and, as amended by the Architectural Works

Copyright Protection Act of 1990, goes on to enumerate eight specific classes of protectible works of authorship. The legislative history of the 1976 Act reveals that Congress did not intend these classes to be exhaustive but merely to illustrate those works that it clearly intended to protect. On the other hand, Congress disclaimed any intent to create an open-ended class of protectible works. Thus, for a work to be copyrighted under the 1976 Act it must either fall clearly within or be reasonably analogous to one of the following categories of works: (1) *Literary works,* including books, periodicals, pamphlets, lectures, sermons, addresses, scripts, catalogues, directories, product labels, computer programs and data bases; (2) *Musical works,* including any accompanying words; (3) *Dramatic works,* including any accompanying music; (4) *Pantomimes and choreographic works* (reduced, of course, to tangible form); (5) *Pictorial, graphic and sculptural works,* including cartoons, photographs, prints and art reproductions, maps, globes, charts, diagrams, models, architect's drawings, fabric designs and prints for merchandise and non-functional monumental structures; (6) *Motion pictures and other audiovisual works;* (7) *Sound Recordings;* and (as a result of the Architectural Works Copyright Protection Act of 1990) (8) *Architectural Works,* as embodied in any medium of expression, including buildings, architectural plans or drawings.

Several of these classes have no counterpart under the 1909 Act. For example, neither pantomimes, choreographic works, sound recordings nor architectural works (as opposed to architectural plans) were copyrightable under the old Act. Both the old and the new Acts, on the other hand, protect compilations and derivative works. Under the 1976 Act, a compilation is a work formed by the collection and assembling of pre-existing materials or data. A derivative work is any work based on a pre-existing work, and may consist of a translation, fictionalization, motion picture version, sound recording, art reproduction, abridgement, condensation or any other form in which the pre-existing work may be recast, transformed or adapted. Any work based on pre-existing material or data or on a pre-existing work can thus be separately copyrighted so long as the compilation or derivative work has enough originality to constitute an original work of authorship and does not infringe any copyright others may have in the pre-existing work. But see *Feist Publications, Inc. v. Rural Telephone Service Co.* (1991) (holding the white pages of a telephone directory to lack the requisite originality for a copyrightable work).

Certain classes of subject matter are expressly or impliedly excluded from federal copyright protection. In the 1976 Act, for example, Congress expressly incorporated a prior judicial exclusion from the 1909 Act when it provided in section 101 that the design of a useful article shall be considered a "pictorial, graphic or sculptural work" only to the extent that the design incorporates pictorial, graphic or sculptural features that can be identified separately from the utilitarian features of the work. The legislative history, though nothing in the language of the 1976 Act itself, indicates that distinctive type faces are excluded from protection. Likewise, section 102(b) expressly excludes from copyright protection any idea, procedure, process, system, method of operation, concept, or discovery. But see *Apple Computer, Inc. v. Franklin Computer Corp.* (1983) (holding that a computer program, whether in object code or source code, is a literary work capable of copyright protection, even when embedded in an internal permanent memory device, called "Read Only Memory" or ROM, consisting of a semi-conductor chip which is incorporated into the circuitry of a computer). See also P.L. No. 96–517, Dec. 12, 1980 (amending the Copyright Act of 1976 by adding a definition of a computer program and a new § 117 which provides that it is not an infringement for the owner of a computer program to make a copy of it as an essential step in using the program with a machine or for archival purposes). Finally, by not expressly including literary titles as a class of protectible subject matter, Congress has presumably ratified prior case law which excluded literary titles from copyright protection under the 1909 Act.

Works analogous to (and not expressly or impliedly excluded from) one or more of the foregoing statutory classes of protectible subject matter must also constitute (1) an original work of authorship (2) reduced to tangible form. 17 U.S.C.A. § 102. Congress purposely left the phrase "original works of authorship" undefined in the 1976 Act, stating its intention to incorporate without change the standard of originality established by the courts under the 1909 Act. H.Rep. No. 94–1476. Under the 1909 Act originality was held to mean that the particular work owes its origin to the author and is not a mere copy of some earlier work. As did the 1909 Act, however, section 103 of the 1976 Act specifically extends protection to compilations (i.e., collections of preexisting materials or data) and derivative works (i.e., works based upon one or more preexisting works). A work, including a compilation or derivative work, is more than a mere copy of some earlier work if the author contributes something more than a trivial variation, something recognizably the author's own. But see *Feist Publications,* supra.

This minimal requirement of originality stands in marked contrast to the patent law's non-obviousness requirement for obtaining a utility, design, or plant patent. The difference stems from the difference in the constitutional use of the words "authors" and "writings" on the one hand and "inventors" and "discoveries" on the other. The latter implies an element of inventiveness as a prerequisite for protection while the former demands only that the work be original to the author.

The lower standard for copyright protection is said to be necessary to avoid administrative and judicial judgments as to the literary or artistic merit of a particular work. Such judgments are arguably inconsistent with the First Amendment policy—not in issue in granting patent protection—of prohibiting government censorship of speech. Selective protection of expression according to its perceived merit is arguably only marginally less offensive to the First Amendment than direct censorship.

Offsetting the lower standard for copyright protection is the fact that copyright protection extends only to original expression and not to the facts or ideas expressed. This judicially developed doctrine has been codified in section 102(b) of the 1976 Act, which states that in no case does copyright protection for an original work of authorship extend to any idea, procedure, process, system, method of operation, concept, principle, or discovery, regardless of the form in which it is described, explained, illustrated, or embodied in such work.

As a practical matter, drawing the line between unprotected facts and ideas, on the one hand, and protected expression, on the other, is not always an easy task. What the courts treat as protected expression tends to vary with the originality and creativity of the work. The author of a fictional literary work, for example, may obtain protection not only of the literal words in the work but also any reasonably detailed original structural patterns appearing in the work. Similarly, the courts have held that the author of a factual or utilitarian work has a protectible interest not only in any original expression used to convey facts or ideas, but also in any originality in the selection or arrangement of facts. See, e.g., *Whelan Associates, Inc. v. Jaslow Dental Laboratory, Inc.* (1986) (copyright protection of computer programs may extend beyond the programs' literal code to their structure, sequence and organization). But cf. *Hoehling v. Universal City Studios, Inc.* (1980) (historical interpretation of Hindenburg disaster, even if original, is not protected by copyright). As the originality of the author's expression, selection or arrangement of facts or ideas diminishes, copyright protection itself reduces to a mere prohibition against outright copying. Thus, where two authors draw identical maps of the same territory or compile identical directories of information, both can obtain copyright protection for their work and neither has a claim of infringement against the other so long as their works were the product of independent effort. Indeed, a mere alphabetized directory of names, addresses and telephone numbers has been held to lack the requisite originality to constitute a protectible work of authorship, notwithstanding the "sweat of the brow" that went into compiling the directory. See *Feist Publications, Inc. v. Rural Telephone Service Co.* (1991). See also *Financial Information, Inc. v. Moody's Investors Service* (1986) (upholding a finding of insufficient evidence of independent creation to render a daily report containing information on municipal bonds a work of authorship). But cf. *West Publishing Co. v. Mead Data Central, Inc.* (1986) (holding pagination of unofficial law reports copyrightable and sufficiently likely to be infringed by a computerized legal research system keyed to the law reports as to merit the grant of temporary injunctive relief).

The courts and Congress have similarly limited the scope of copyright protection for objects having a utilitarian function. Although any discrete literary or artistic features of a useful object are copyrightable, purely utilitarian features and aesthetic features not capable of existing independently as a work of art are not copyrightable. See, e.g., *Carol Barnhart, Inc. v. Economy Cover Corp.* (1985) (holding that human torso forms used for the display of wearing apparel are works whose aesthetic and artistic features are inseparable from their utilitarian function and are thus uncopyrightable). For such features, only utility or design patent protection is available. Thus, while a statuette which happens to serve as a lamp base is copyrightable, *Mazer v. Stein* (1954), a lamp itself is not, no matter how aesthetic its design. See, e.g., *Esquire, Inc. v. Ringer* (1978). Similarly, while a distinct *fabric* design may be copyrightable, a *dress* design is not. In the Architectural Work Copyright Protection Act of 1990, however, Congress explicitly extended protection to "architectural works," which was defined as the design of a building as embodied in any tangible medium of expression, including a building, as well as architectural plans or drawings.

Also excluded from copyright protection are those tangible forms of expression which function as identifying trade symbols. While one may question whether all such symbols should properly be excluded as a constitutional matter, see p. 22 supra, there are persuasive reasons for excluding trademarks from copyright protection as a policy matter. As the *Sears–Compco* decisions emphasize, the right to be free of confusion in the identification of one's product or service is not necessarily synonymous with the right to the exclusive use of a symbol. In order to highlight that distinction, both the PTO and the courts have concluded that trademark and copyright protection should be alternative and not concurrent. Thus, if a word, symbol or slogan functions as a trademark, it does not constitute a work of authorship. Commercial prints and labels which do not function as a trademark, on the other hand, are copyrightable subject matter. See, e.g., *Drop Dead Co. v. S.C. Johnson & Son, Inc.* (1963) (upholding a finding of copyright as well as trademark infringement where the defendant copied the laudatory and instructional words as well as the design of the label on plaintiff's aerosol furniture wax).

b. Obtaining a Copyright

In order to obtain federal copyright protection under the 1909 Act, it was necessary for an author to publish the work with the required copyright notice. General publication without the required notice constituted an abandonment of rights to the work. That Draconian rule led courts to distinguish between limited and general publication. The performance or broadcast of a play, dance, or musical work, the display of a graphic work of art and the delivery or broadcast of a lecture or speech were all classified as limited rather than general publications, for which copyright notice was not required. See e.g., *King v. Mister Maestro Inc.* (1963) (holding that Dr. Martin Luther King's famous "I Have a Dream" speech, delivered to 200,000 people gathered in front of the Lincoln Memorial in Washington, D.C., did not constitute a general publication).

Common-law copyright protection carried certain distinct advantages. Unlike federal statutory copyright, common-law protection was of unlimited duration, arose automatically upon the creation of a work, extended to all foreign or domestic authors and excluded any use of the protected work by others, whether for profit or not. A perceived need for a more balanced method of protecting unpublished works, including performances and displays, led Congress in the 1976 Act to preempt common-law copyright protection for any works of authorship that are fixed in a tangible medium of expression.

Under the new Act, an "author" obtains federal copyright protection (and loses any common-law protection) automatically upon fixing a work in a tangible medium of expression. Until 1989, it was still necessary to observe certain formalities in order to maintain and enforce one's copyright.

Works published without notice, for example, could lose their copyright protection unless only a relatively small number of copies were involved or certain remedial steps were taken. On March 1, 1989, however, the United States joined the Berne Convention for the Protection of Literary and Artistic Works, which required the United States to provide copyright protection without imposing any formalities. In implementing the Berne Convention, Congress made the use of copyright notice optional, though use of notice will continue to eliminate an innocent infringement defense. 17 U.S.C.A. § 401. Registration and deposit were also made optional for foreign works claiming protection under the Berne Convention, but continue to be required for U.S. or other foreign works as a precondition for bringing an infringement action. The rationale for continuing to require deposit and registration for such works is that it aids in specifying the work for which protection is claimed and in the development of the collection of the Library of Congress.

Under the 1909 Act the copyright term was 28 years, with a right, vesting exclusively in the author or certain of the author's heirs, to renew for an additional 28 years. The new Act provides for a longer single term. For most works under the new Act, the copyright term is the life of the author plus 50 years. For anonymous or pseudonymous works or works made for hire the term is 75 years from the date of publication or 100 years from creation, whichever expires first.

For existing works already under federal copyright protection when the new Act went into effect, the term has been extended to the remainder of the initial term plus 47 years or, if the work is in its renewal term, a total of 75 years from the date of first publication. For existing works subject to common law copyright protection when the new Act went into effect, the term is the same as if the work had been created after the effective date of the new Act or until specified dates in the 21st century, whichever is longer.

Under § 104 of the 1976 Act unpublished works are subject to protection without regard to the nationality or domicile of the author. Published works, on the other hand, are protected only if when first published (1) one or more of the authors was a national or domiciliary of the U.S. or of a foreign national that is a party to a copyright treaty to which the U.S. is also a party; (2) the work was first published in the U.S. or a foreign nation that on the date of first publication was a party to the Universal Copyright Convention (U.C.C.); (3) the work was first published by the U.N., any of its agencies or the Organization of American States; (4) the work is a Berne Convention Work; or (5) the work comes within the scope of a Presidential proclamation based on a finding that a foreign nation extends non-discriminatory copyright protection to U.S. nationals.

Although according to section 201(a) of the 1976 Act, copyright vests initially in the author or authors of a work, section 201(b) specifies that in the case of a work made for hire, the employer or other person for whom the work is prepared is considered the author and, unless the parties have expressly agreed otherwise in a written and signed instrument, owns all of the rights comprised in the copyright. A "work made for hire" is defined in section 101 as a work prepared by an employee within the scope of employment or a work specially ordered or commissioned for any one of nine enumerated uses if the parties expressly agreed in a written and signed instrument that the work is a work made for hire. In deciding whether a person is an employee or independent contractor, general principles of the common law of agency are to be used. *Community for Creative Non-Violence v. Reid* (1989) (holding a sculptor to be an independent contractor and the sculpture not to be a work made for hire since it did not fall within one of the nine enumerated classes, but stating in dictum that the sculpture may be a joint work, since CCNV contributed the base of the sculpture).

c. Transfer and Termination of Copyright

So long as certain formalities are observed, the copyright in a work may be transferred in whole or in part from one party to another throughout the term of the copyright. The owner of a copyright may license others to multiply copies of or distribute, perform or display the copyrighted work. As with trademarks and patents, the validity of copyright assignments and licenses is largely governed by common-law property and contract principles, including the common-law "shop-right" doctrine. See p. 224, supra. See also *Morseburg v. Balyon* (1980) (holding that the California Resale Royalties Act, which requires the payment of a royalty upon the sale of a work of fine art whenever the seller resides in California or the sale takes place in California, was not preempted by the 1909 Copyright Act). As a matter of federal law, however, neither an assignment nor an exclusive license will be valid unless conveyed by written instrument signed by the owner of the rights conveyed or by the duly authorized agent of the owner. 17 U.S.C.A. § 204(a). A non-exclusive license, by contrast, may be conveyed orally or by mere conduct. An assignment or exclusive license must be recorded in the Copyright Office in order to be enforceable against anyone other than the parties to the transfer. 17 U.S.C. § 205.

Rapid technological advances in communications media have complicated the interpretation of assignments or licenses which by their terms are limited to a particular medium. Does the transfer of motion picture rights, for example, include or exclude the right to exhibit motion pictures on television? For that matter does the transfer of television rights include or exclude the right to produce videotapes or video discs? As a practical matter, these issues are largely resolved by negotiation and the inclusion of explicit provisions in the assignment or license.

In addition to allowing for voluntary copyright licensing, the new Act contains five separate compulsory licensing provisions. The first two of these provisions are limited to the compulsory licensing of non-dramatic musical works for the purpose of (1) making and distributing phonorecords after a phonorecord of the work has been distributed under the authority of the copyright owner and (2) publicly performing the work on juke boxes. The other three compulsory licensing provisions are concerned, respectively, with the licensing of published pictorial, graphic, sculptural and non-dramatic musical works for non-commercial broadcasts, the licensing of works for cable television transmission, and, as a result of a 1988 amendment, the temporary licensing of TV signals for retransmission by satellite carriers.

To obtain a compulsory license, the prospective licensee of a non-dramatic musical work serves notice on the copyright owner of the work. If the prospective licensee wishes to perform the work on a juke box, he also files an application with the Copyright Office. Monthly royalties on sales of phonorecordings, calculated at a rate of 2¾ per recording or ½ per minute of playing time (whichever is larger) are paid directly to the copyright owner, while royalties for juke box performances, calculated at a yearly rate of $8 per juke box, are deposited with the Copyright Office for later distribution by the Copyright Royalty Tribunal.

Recognizing that the Berne Convention "apparently does not permit compulsory licensing of non-broadcast performances," H.R.Rep. No. 609, 100th Cong., 2d Sess. 47 (1988), Congress in the Berne Implementation Act of 1988, enacted a new section 116A to encourage representatives of companies and jukebox operators to negotiate licenses or submit to arbitration. If such negotiations fail, the compulsory licensing provisions in section 116 would remain in effect. The Chairman of the Copyright Royalty Tribunal is empowered to schedule negotiations between copyright owners and jukebox operators.

Subject to the terms of any voluntary license agreements that have been reached, compulsory royalty rates for non-commercial broadcasts and methods of paying same are set by the Copyright Royalty Tribunal. A compulsory license for the cable television transmission of copyrighted works may be obtained by filing with and periodically reporting to the Copyright Office. The royalty fee is generally a specified percentage of the cable system's gross receipts, and is deposited with the Copyright Office for later distribution by the Copyright Royalty Tribunal to qualifying copyright owners. Royalty fees for satellite retransmissions are based the numbers of subscribers receiving each transmission. After December 31, 1992, royalty fees for satellite retransmissions will be established through voluntary negotiations.

Under both the old and the new Act, authors (or their heirs) are granted an opportunity to regain their original rights after an initial transfer of ownership or license of rights. Under the old Act, it will be recalled, the renewal right vested exclusively in the author or certain of the author's heirs. Under the new Act, with its single term, the author or certain of the author's heirs (spouse, children and grandchildren) may terminate, at a certain point prior to the end of the copyright term, any initial copyright transfer or license, whether or not a right to terminate was contractually reserved or contractually relinquished in the original agreement. (Under the old Act, the courts had held that the renewal right, like the copyright itself, could be assigned). The object behind the renewal/termination right is to safeguard authors against unremunerative transfers resulting from either the weak bargaining position of the author or the impossibility of accurately valuing a literary or artistic work prior to its exploitation. Rights in a work made for hire are not subject to termination by the hired author. However, parties may not stipulate in a contract that a work is made for hire simply as a means of extinguishing the termination right.

A notice of termination must be served on the grantee or the grantee's successor in title and, as with the transfer itself, must be recorded in the Copyright Office. If the parties entitled to terminate a transfer of ownership or license fail to serve notice of termination within the specified time period or fail to observe the requisite formalities, no termination will occur and the initial grant will continue in force.

3. MASK WORKS

In order for subject matter to be eligible for protection under the Semiconductor Chip Act of 1984, both the subject matter itself and the owner seeking to obtain protection must fall within the terms of section 902. These two requirements will be dealt with separately.

a. Subject Matter Protected

Section 902(a) of the Chip Act, 17 U.S.C.A. § 902(a) identifies the subject matter of protection as a "mask work fixed in a semiconductor chip product." In other words, a "mask work" is the protected subject matter and the material object in which it must be embodied in order to be protected is a "semiconductor chip product." Both of these terms, which are defined in some detail in section 901 of the Act, are drawn from the technical terminology of the electronics industry. Masks are stencils or templates used in the manufacture of semiconductor chips. A set of masks contains all the patterns of a chip layout. Each mask represents the topography of the chip product at a given stage in the manufacturing process. Masks can be translated into digital form by storing the relevant coordinates on a computer tape, which can then be used to control a light or electron beam used in the etching process. Because coordinates on a computer tape are not fixed in a chip product, however, the tape itself is not protectible subject matter under the Chip Act, though it would constitute a protectible work of authorship under the 1976 Copyright Act.

The manufacturing process can be compared to converting a topographical map into a three dimensional model by tracing a set of stencils of the various elevations on the map and then using the stencils to cut out pieces of wood to represent these elevations. The topography of a semiconductor chip, however, is considerably more complex than that of natural terrain—more like the topography of, say, an entire city, including all of the interior and subterranean electrical, plumbing and ventilation systems in and between every building. Imagining a set of stencils of such complexity reduced to the size of a finger nail gives a rough idea of what is meant by a mask work.

Although a great deal of effort and expense goes into the design of a semiconductor chip, it is a relatively simple matter for competitors to purchase a semiconductor chip product and disassemble it by removing the plastic or ceramic casing, photographing the top metal connection layer, dissolving the metal away with acid and photographing the various translucent layers of semiconductor material by varying the depth of focus of the camera, thus ascertaining how to manufacture a compatible chip.

Until enactment of the Chip Act, there was no legal basis for prohibiting competitive copying of a chip, except where the chip product stored a computer program essential to its functioning and was thus protected under the 1976 Copyright Act, as amended in 1980 to provide explicit protection for computer programs. Any other aspect of a chip would constitute a useful article whose design is protectible only to the extent that it can be identified separately from, and is capable of existing independently of, the utilitarian aspects of the article.

Section 902(b) of the Chip Act excludes from protection any mask work that is not original or consists of staple, commonplace or familiar designs or variations of such designs combined in such a way that, taken as a whole, is not original. While the originality requirement is likely to be read *in pari materia* with section 102 of the 1976 Copyright Act as meaning only that the mask work design owes its origin to the designer and is not a copy, the exclusion of staple, commonplace or familiar designs is more reminiscent of the statutory language limiting the scope of contributory patent infringement. See p. 269 infra.

Section 902(c), in turn, specifies that in no case does protection extend to any idea, procedure, process, system, method of operation, concept, principle, or discovery embodied in a mask work. Because the language of section 902(c) is identical to that contained in section 102(b) of the 1976 Copyright Act, courts attempting to distinguish unprotectible ideas from protectible expression in chip design are likely to look to case law construing section 102(b) of the 1976 Act, particularly as it applies to computer software, for guidance.

b. Obtaining Protection

The "owner" of a mask work is defined in section 901 as the creator, employer of one who created a mask work within the scope of employment, or a transferee of *all* rights created by the Chip Act. Unlike U.S. copyright law, ownership of less than all of the various exclusive rights in a protected work cannot be held by more than one person. The owner may, of course, license others to exercise one or more but less than all of the exclusive rights, but the licensee will lack standing to sue for infringement of these rights.

According to section 902(a)(1) of the Act, a mask work is protectible (1) regardless of whether or where the work has been commercially exploited, if on the date of registration or first commercial exploitation anywhere in the world, whichever occurs first, the owner is a U.S. national or domiciliary, a stateless person or a national, domiciliary, or sovereign authority of a foreign nation that is a party to a treaty, to which the U.S. is also a party, affording protection to mask works, or is the subject of a Presidential proclamation issued under paragraph (2) of section 902; and (2) regardless of the citizenship or domicile of the owner, if the work is first commercially exploited in the U.S. Up to this point, ownership under section 902 is simply modelled on section 104 of the Copyright Act of 1976. See p. 242 supra.

The scope of Presidential proclamations that may issue under section 902 of the Chip Act, however, is substantially different from section 104 of the Copyright Act—and becomes still more so after one takes into account an apparent ambiguity in section 902(a)(2). This section states that whenever the President finds that a foreign nation extends protection to mask works of U.S. nationals or domiciliaries (A) on substantially the same basis as it extends protection to mask works of its own citizens and domiciliaries and mask works first commercially exploited in that nation, or (B) on substantially the same basis as provided in the Chip Act, the President may by proclamation extend protection under the Chip Act to mask works of owners from that nation or owners who first exploit the mask work in that nation.

Clause (A), like the Universal Copyright Convention and U.S. copyright law, merely specifies that a foreign nation provide "national (i.e., non-discriminatory) treatment" for mask works of U.S. citizens or domiciliaries—which means that, as long as the foreign nation provides no protection for the mask works of its own citizens and domiciliaries, it need not provide any protection for those of U.S. citizens and domiciliaries. Clause (B), on the other hand, comes closer to requiring "reciprocal treatment" as the basis for a Presidential proclamation—that is, the President is to accord protection to mask works of foreign nationals if and only if their countries accord substantially the same protection as the U.S. does to mask works of U.S. nationals. The meaning of the word "or" which connects the two clauses is thus unclear.

To date, no Presidential proclamations have issued under section 902(a)(2). Japan, various members of the European Economic Community, and other European nations have enacted a *sui generis* law substantially similar to the U.S. Chip Act—and in addition the existing copyright laws of the United Kingdom, Australia, and perhaps the Netherlands and Sweden could presently be found to protect mask works on substantially the same basis as the U.S. Chip Act does.

In addition to section 902(a)(2), however, the Chip Act contains a provision which permits the grant of interim protection for foreign mask works where a foreign nation is moving toward reciprocity. Section 914(a) authorizes the Secretary of Commerce (who has delegated his power to the Commissioner of Patents and Trademarks) to issue an order extending interim protection to nationals, domiciliaries, and sovereign authorities of a foreign country if the Secretary finds (1) that the foreign nation is making good faith efforts and reasonable progress toward entering a treaty or enacting legislation of the sort specified in section 902; (2) that the nationals, domiciliaries, and sovereign authorities, and persons controlled by them, are not engaged in the misappropriation, or unauthorized distribution or commercial exploitation of mask works; and (3) that issuing the order would promote the purposes of the Act and international comity with respect to the protection of mask works. At the moment, the mask works of at least eighteen countries, including Japan, Finland, Sweden, Australia, Canada, Switzerland and member countries of the European Economic Community, have been ruled eligible for interim U.S. protection.

Quite apart from these efforts by the United States to promote bilateral arrangements to protect mask works, the World Intellectual Property Organization (WIPO) prepared a draft treaty on the Protection of Intellectual Property in Respect of Integrated Circuits. Adoption of the draft treaty was delayed for several years, however, because developing countries voiced strong objections to it, questioning whether there is a need for such a treaty and whether it adequately takes the need of developing countries into account. Although approximately forty nations at a WIPO sponsored conference in May, 1989, ultimately adopted a modified version of the 1985 draft treaty, the U.S. and Japan—the world's two largest chip producers—voted against the treaty. In the meantime, the European Commission adopted a directive requiring members of the European Economic Community to protect the topographies of semiconductor products. The terms of the directive are generally compatible with those of the U.S. Chip Act.

Pursuant to section 908 of the Chip Act, an eligible owner of a mask work fixed in a semiconductor chip product may apply to the Register of Copyrights for registration of a claim of protection in the mask work. In contrast to U.S. copyright law (though like U.S. patent law), the Chip Act requires prompt registration in order to avoid forfeiture of rights. Section 908(a) of the Chip Act states that protection under the Act shall terminate if application for registration of a claim is not made within two years after the mask work is first commercially exploited anywhere in the world. Section 901(a)(5), in turn, states that to "commercially exploit" a mask work is to distribute a semiconductor chip product embodying the mask work to the public for commercial purposes or making a written offer to sell or transfer a semiconductor chip product after the mask work has been fixed in the product.

Although section 908(e) requires the Copyright Office to examine applications for registration of mask works, the legislative history makes it clear that this provision "does not mandate an examination system for chips like that provided for patent applications." H.R.Rep. No. 98–781, 98th Cong., 2d Sess., at 19 (1984). The Copyright Office need only examine the application for facial validity.

The notice requirements of the Chip Act, contained in section 909, makes the use of the prescribed notice symbol (the words "mask work," the symbol *M*, or the letter M within a circle) optional rather than mandatory. The consequences of failing to provide such notice are not severe, but use of the notice symbol constitutes prima facie evidence of notice of protection.

4. OTHER INVESTMENTS OF INTELLECTUAL EFFORT: NEWS, EPHEMERAL PERFORMANCES, PUBLICITY

The common law protects a variety of publicly disclosed products of intellectual effort which do not qualify for federal patent or copyright protection. In the seminal case of *International News Service v. Associated Press* (1918), for example, the Supreme Court held that a news service had a "quasi-property" interest in the news it had gone to the expense of collecting and could thus prevent a rival news service from appropriating that news for a competitive purpose even after the news had become public. The misappropriation doctrine enunciated *INS v. AP* was subsequently applied to a variety of other products of intellectual effort which at the time did not qualify for federal patent or copyright protection. See, e.g., *Waring v. WDAS Broadcasting Station* (1937) (protecting a musical group against unauthorized broadcast of their phonograph records); *Metropolitan Opera Association v. Wagner–Nichols Recorder Corp.* (1950) (protecting an opera company against unauthorized recording of their radio broadcasts); *Dior v. Milton* (1956) (protecting a dress designer against unauthorized copying of dress designs).

Judicial reaction to the misappropriation doctrine, however, was not entirely positive. In his dissent in *INS,* for example, Mr. Justice Brandeis pointed out that news was not the sort of subject matter which the common law had theretofore treated as property and that appropriation of publicly disclosed information for a competitive purpose had not theretofore been considered wrongful. Copyright law merely protected original expression and not the news itself, while the law of trade secrets merely protected those facts or ideas which had not been publicly disclosed. The longstanding rule, in short, had been that, after unrestricted disclosure, facts and ideas and their unpatented or uncopyrighted expression are "free as the air to common use." Brandeis questioned whether the courts were the appropriate agency of government to change that fundamental legal concept.

The misappropriation doctrine met with an equally hostile reception in some lower federal courts. The Second Circuit in particular consistently refused to apply the *INS* case to facts not substantially similar to those in *INS*. In *Cheney Brothers v. Doris Silk Corp.* (1929), for example, the court refused to apply the *INS* doctrine to the copying of dress designs. The court concluded that to extend *INS* beyond its particular facts would be to create a common-law patent or copyright and would thus usurp the power of Congress to decide what products of intellectual effort are to be protected.

In *Erie Railroad Co. v. Tompkins* (1938), the Supreme Court abandoned the accumulated corpus of federal common law of which *INS* was a part, intimating that its prior practice may have been an unconstitutional usurpation of *state* lawmaking power, and directed the lower federal courts in the future to apply state substantive law in federal diversity cases. While *INS* was no longer authoritative federal common law, however, a number of state courts, both before and after *Erie,* cited *INS* with approval as an accurate expression of their state's common law. See e.g., *Waring v. WDAS Broadcasting Station, Metropolitan Opera Association v. Wagner–Nichols Recorder Corp.,* and *Dior v. Milton,* supra. Thus in federal diversity cases where the substantive law of those states applied, *Erie* commanded the federal courts to follow *INS* as an authoritative expression of state common law even as it forbade them to follow it as an authoritative expression of federal law.

In the view of some lower federal courts, however, the Supreme Court, in its *Sears–Compco* decisions in effect preempted the common law of misappropriation when it stated (albeit by way of dictum insofar as copyright law was concerned) that a state may not prohibit the copying of an article which is unpatented and uncopyrighted. In *Columbia Broadcasting System Inc. v. DeCosta* (1967), for example, the court refused to grant the originator of the character "Paladin" any common-law protection against the appropriation of the character by the makers of the television series

"Have Gun Will Travel". Other federal courts took the position that, notwithstanding *Sears–Compco,* where Congress could grant protection to a work but has not, the courts are free to grant common-law protection. In their view, only where Congress expressly grants protection or expressly or impliedly proclaims certain subject-matter to be unprotectible, does federal law preempt the common law. While federal patent law seemed to indicate both what Congress wished to protect and what it wished to remain free, the same was not thought to be true of federal copyright law, which had simply left many areas unattended.

In *Goldstein v. California* (1973), the Supreme Court opted for the latter view. In that case the Court confirmed that the states retain power to protect literary and artistic works, so long as that protection does not conflict with federal copyright law, and went on to hold that the mere failure of Congress to grant copyright protection to a given class of literary or artistic works did not mean that Congress intended to place such works in the public domain or to prevent the states from protecting them. Thus, state record and tape piracy statutes, which provide criminal penalties for the misappropriation of sound recordings, were held not to conflict with federal copyright law prior to the time it was amended to grant protection to sound recordings. By extension, it appeared that the states were free to protect, either by statute or by common law, any other creative effort falling within the constitutional definition of a writing but left unprotected by Congress.

In section 301(a) of the Copyright Act of 1976, Congress expressly preempted state law to the extent that state law granted rights equivalent to copyright in works falling within the subject matter of federal copyright protection. Section 301(b) expressly permits state regulation with respect to (1) subject matter not covered by the Act or (2) the extension of rights not equivalent to those created by the Act.

By way of illustrating what constitutes nonpreempted subject matter, a House Report on an earlier version of section 301 that contained specific examples of state law doctrines not preempted by the Act noted that states retain the power to protect ephemeral performances and the sort of "hot" news that was involved in the *INS* case. H.Rep. No. 94–1476 (1976). The express language of section 301(b), however, is far broader. It permits states to protect not only any subject matter which is not a constitutional "writing," but also any constitutional writing which is excluded from copyright protection purely as a statutory matter. Section 301(b) even permits states to protect statutorily copyrightable subject matter, so long as the rights extended are not equivalent to those created by the Act.

By way of illustrating what constitutes rights not equivalent to those created by the Act, the above-mentioned House Report noted that the common law tort of misappropriation is not necessarily synonymous with copyright infringement and that the evolving common-law rights of "privacy" and "publicity," as well as the common law of trade secrets, defamation and fraud remain unaffected so long as the causes of action contain elements, such as an invasion of personal rights or a breach of trust or confidentiality, that are different in kind from copyright infringement. While the common law of trade secrets, defamation and fraud clearly contain such elements, the common-law tort of misappropriation and the common-law rights of privacy and publicity are not always easy to distinguish from copyright.

The Justice Department took the position during debates on the 1976 Act, that inclusion of a reference in the Act to misappropriation as exempted from preemption would be a serious mistake and might defeat the purposes of section 301 and encourage states to pass misappropriation laws. See 122 Cong.Rec.H. 10910 (Sept. 22, 1976). As a result of this objection, all of the illustrations of state law not preempted by section 301 were ultimately deleted from section 301(b). It is thus left to the courts to decide what is and is not preempted under section 301. See, e.g. *Financial Information, Inc. v. Moody's Investors Service* (1986), holding that even though information contained in plaintiffs "Daily Bond Cards" were unprotectible facts under federal copyright law, plaintiff's misappropriation claim was nevertheless preempted. The court noted that the plaintiff "proved neither the quantity of copying nor the immediacy of distribution necessary to sustain a 'hot' news claim", and that the House Report states that as long as the work fits within one of the general subject matter categories of sections 102 and 103, the Act prevents states from protecting it even if it fails to achieve federal copyright protection. H.Rep. No. 94–1476 (1976).

The right of privacy, like the misappropriation doctrine, is a creature of the early twentieth century. Unlike the tort of misappropriation, which owed its origin to a federal judicial decision, the right of privacy was stimulated by a law review article—co-authored, ironically, by Louis Brandeis, who would later dissent in the case which originated the misappropriation doctrine. See Warren & Brandeis, The Right to Privacy, 4 Harv.L.Rev. 193 (1890). As a result of that article, the right of privacy soon received widespread judicial and legislative recognition. See, e.g., *Pavesich v. New England Life Insurance Co.* (1905) (holding that an insurance company invaded plaintiff's common-law right of privacy when it used plaintiff's name and picture, as well as a spurious testimonial from him, in its advertising). See also N.Y. Civil Rights Law §§ 50–51 (making it both a misdemeanor and a tort to make use of the name or picture of any person for "advertising purposes or the purposes of trade" without the person's written consent).

Over the years the tort of invasion of privacy has since evolved into a number of distinct legal wrongs. The intrusive invasion upon a person's physical solitude by such means as electronic eavesdropping, for example, is to be distinguished from the public disclosure of highly embarrassing private facts or facts which place a person in a false (albeit nondefamatory) light in the public eye. See W. Prosser, Law of Torts 849–869 (5th ed. 1984). From its inception, however, the right of privacy has prominently included a right to prohibit the unauthorized commercial appropriation of one's own name or likeness. See, e.g., *Pavesich v. New England Life Insurance Co.,* and N.Y. Civil Rights Law §§ 50–51, supra.

Where a person has no interest in exploiting the commercial value of his or her name or likeness, the right to prevent others from doing so amounts to a purely personal right to be free of unwanted publicity. Where a person would like to exploit the commercial value of his or her name, on the other hand, the right to prohibit unauthorized commercial exploitation by others is more appropriately characterized as a right to the publicity value of the name or likeness. This right of publicity is often described as a "property right" and its violation is said to be more akin to the tort of misappropriation than it is to other types of invasion of privacy. See, e.g., *Zacchini v. Scripps–Howard Broadcasting Co.* (1977) (recognizing that the common-law right of publicity is "an entirely different tort" than other forms of invasion of privacy, being analogous to and having the same goals as the federal patent and copyright laws).

The right of publicity remains largely unpreempted by the Copyright Act of 1976. This is so, not because it is not equivalent to rights created by the 1976 Act but because personal names and likenesses (as opposed to particular pictorial renditions of a likeness) are not copyrightable subject matter under the Act. But cf. *Baltimore Orioles, Inc. v. Major League Baseball Players Ass'n* (1986) (holding that telecasts of major league baseball games are copyrighted works made for hire owned by the major league baseball clubs and that the players' right of publicity in their game-time performances was preempted under section 301(a) of the 1976 Act.) State protection of the right of publicity has also been held not to violate the First Amendment. In *Zacchini v. Scripps–Howard Broadcasting Co.*, supra, the Supreme Court held that the First Amendment provided no defense to a claim that a television station, by making an unauthorized broadcast of an entire 15 second "Human Cannonball" act, appropriated the human cannonball's right of publicity.

Even though the common-law right of publicity has largely avoided federal statutory and constitutional preemption, debate nevertheless rages over whether and to what extent, as a matter of sound state policy, a distinct right of publicity should in fact be recognized. Some courts, for example, have extended the right of publicity to prevent the use of a person's nickname, *Hirsch v. S.C. Johnson & Son, Inc.* (1979) (holding that the use of the term "Crazylegs" on a moisturizing shaving gel for women constituted an actionable appropriation of a well-known athlete's nickname); to prevent imitations of a well-known singer's voice in a commercial advertisement, *Midler v. Ford Motor Co.* (1988); and even to prevent the commercial use of a photograph of a well-known racing driver's car as an appropriation of an attribute of the driver's identity. *Motschenbacher v. R.J. Reynolds Tobacco* (1974). A second question as to the extent of protection for one's right of publicity is whether such a right is a descendible property right. The argument in favor of descent is that it will further the social policy underlying the right of publicity itself—namely that of encouraging individual enterprise and creativity. At least one court has recognized the descendibility of the right simply because it could discern no logical reason to terminate the right upon the death of the person protected. *Price v. Hal Roach Studios, Inc.* (1975) (holding that the rights of the widows of Laurel and Hardy were invaded by an attempt by producers of Laurel and Hardy films to assign merchandising rights in the names and likenesses of Laurel and Hardy).

Other courts, viewing the descendibility of the right of publicity as a marginal incentive which poses a threat to the countervailing societal interest in the free dissemination of ideas, have either hedged the descendibility of the right with restrictions or flatly denied its descendibility. A number of courts, for example, have stated that in order for the right of publicity to be descendible, a person must have exploited the right by translating it into a contractual right during his or her own lifetime. See, e.g., *Lugosi v. Universal Pictures* (1979) (holding that because Bella Lugosi, famed for his movie role as Count Dracula, never exercised his right to exploit the commercial value of his likeness as Count Dracula during his life, he had not converted his personal right into a descendible thing of value and the mere unexercised opportunity was not descendible). But see California Civil Code § 990 (1984) (legislatively overruling *Lugosi* and creating a descendible 50 year right of publicity).

Several courts have rejected even that limited form of descendibility, citing, in addition to the potential conflict with the First Amendment, the difficulty of defining the scope and duration of the right. See *Memphis Development Foundation v. Factors Etc., Inc.* (1980) (refusing to recognize a descendible right in Elvis Presley's name and likeness, even though it was exercised during his lifetime). *Factors Etc., Inc. v. Pro Arts, Inc.* (1981) (holding that *Memphis Development Foundation v. Factors Etc., Inc.* stated controlling Tennessee law governing the descendibility of Elvis Presley's right of publicity).

The Supreme Court of Georgia, on the other hand, has held that the right of publicity survives the death of its owner even if the owner has not exploited the right during his lifetime. *Martin Luther King, Jr., Center for Social Changes, Inc. v. American Heritage Products, Inc.* (1982). See also

California Civil Code § 990 (1984) (creating a descendible right of publicity in a deceased personality's name, voice, signature, photograph or likeness, whether or not the deceased personality exploited his or her name during his or her lifetime).

From a policy perspective, it is difficult to imagine that either a poor boy from Tupelo, Mississippi, intent upon becoming the King of Rock 'n Roll, or a young Baptist clergyman in Montgomery, Alabama, intent upon securing equal rights for black people in the South, would be much influenced in their respective career decisions by the knowledge that their common-law right of publicity was or was not descendible. Even those who favor the descendibility of the right of publicity recognize that the right should not be of unlimited duration, but only long enough to provide for heirs living at the time of the public figure's death. It has been suggested, for example, that the courts themselves or state legislatures should limit the duration of the right of publicity to a term equivalent to that specified in the 1976 Copyright Act—namely life of the creator plus fifty years. See California Civil Code § 990 (1984) (50 year right of publicity in a deceased person's name, voice, signature, photograph or likeness).

B. ACTIONABLE AND PRIVILEGED APPROPRIATION

The Constitution provides that authors and inventors are to obtain "exclusive rights" in their respective writings and discoveries. The common law provides analogous rights to products of intellectual effort which do not qualify for federal patent or copyright protection. Not every use of another's federally patented or copyrighted work, however, constitutes an infringing use. Nor does every appropriation of another's unpatented or uncopyrighted investment of intellectual effort constitute a misappropriation. In order to distinguish those uses which are actionable from those uses which are privileged we will first identify the exact extent and limits of the exclusive rights in a given work and then identify what admitted invasions of those rights might nevertheless be privileged and what remedies are available where an infringement or misappropriation is found.

1. PATENT INFRINGEMENT

In patent law, one's exclusive right consists of the right to exclude others from making, using or selling the patented invention or design or, in the case of a plant patent, the exclusive right to asexually reproduce the patented plant. The right to exclude others from making, using or selling an invention is not necessarily the same as an exclusive right on the part of the patent owner to make, use or sell his or her own patented invention. It may well be that the patented invention consists of an improvement on another patented invention. Thus, the inventor's exclusive right in the improvement is limited to preventing others (including the original inventor) from using the improvement without permission. In such cases, cross-licensing agreements between the two patent owners is common.

Infringement, as we have seen, is an act which violates the exclusive intangible intellectual property rights of another. Patent infringement does not depend on proof that the actor knew of the owner's rights. Patent infringement will occur when anyone either (1) makes, uses or sells a patented invention or design within the United States during the term of the patent without authority; (2) actively induces infringement of a patent; or (3) contributes to an infringement by selling a component of a patented machine, manufacture, combination or composition, or material or apparatus for use in practicing a material part of a patented process, knowing it to be specially made or adopted for such use and not a staple article or commodity available for a variety of uses. 35 U.S.C.A. § 271(a)–(c). Plant patent infringement occurs whenever unauthorized asexual reproduction (e.g. a cutting) of the actual patented plant occurs.

As a result of the Patent Law Amendments Act of 1984, it is also an infringement to supply in or from the U.S. all or a substantial portion of the uncombined components of a patented invention in such a manner as to actively induce the combination of such components outside the U.S. in a manner that would infringe the patent if such combination occurred within the U.S. 35 U.S.C.A. § 271(f). As a result of a provision in the Omnibus Trade and Competitiveness Act of 1988, it is an infringement to import into the U.S. or sell or use within the U.S. a product which is made outside the U.S. by a process patented in the U.S. 35 U.S.C.A. § 271(g).

While one does not infringe another's patent by studying the specifications of the patented invention and designing an invention that will accomplish the same result in a different way, an infringement will be found if two inventions accomplish substantially the same result in substantially the same way, even though the inventions differ in some respect and the junior inventor arrived at his invention independently (the "doctrine of equivalents"). Similarly while one does not infringe a patent merely by repairing a patented invention, completely rebuilding the invention does constitute an infringement.

Finally, while a purely experimental use as opposed to a commercial use of the patented invention will not constitute an infringement, an experiment to determine the commercial feasibility or practicability of the patented invention will be regarded as an infringing commercial use. It is not an infringement, however, to make, use or sell a patented invention (other than certain new animal drugs or veterinary biological products) solely for uses reasonably related to the development and submission of information under a federal law which regulates the manufacture, use or sale of drugs or veterinary biological products. 35 U.S.C.A. § 271(e).

As a result of section 156, added in 1984, and amended in 1988, the term for certain human and animal drugs and other federally regulated products can be extended to compensate for the time lost in federal regulatory review of the products.

2. COPYRIGHT INFRINGEMENT AND FAIR USE

The exclusive right protected by federal copyright law consists, as one might expect, of a right to prevent others from copying the protected work. Unlike the exclusive patent rights, copyright does not include a right to exclude others from making, using or selling a substantially similar work which was created without reference to the protected work. As the term "copyright" suggests, infringement generally involves unauthorized copying. Specifically, the owner of a federal copyright is granted the exclusive right to do or authorize any of the following:

With respect to all copyrightable subject matter,

(1) the right to *reproduce* the work (the reproduction right);

(2) the right to *prepare derivative works* in the same or a different medium (the adaptation right); and

(3) the right to *distribute copies* of the work to the public (the distribution right).

With respect to all copyrightable subject matter except pictorial, graphic and sculptural works and sound recordings,

(4) the right to *perform* the work publicly.

With respect to all copyrightable subject matter except motion pictures, audiovisual works and sound recordings,

(5) the right to *display* the work publicly.

17 U.S.C.A. § 106.

As a result of the Visual Artists Rights Act of 1990, the author of a visual work of art has the exclusive right (1) to *claim authorship* (the attribution right) and (2) to *prevent* any intentional *distortion, mutilation* or other *modification* of a qualifying work of visual art or any intentional or grossly negligent *destruction* of a work of recognized stature (the right of integrity). 17 U.S.C.A. § 106A. Section 301 has been amended to preempt any equivalent rights created by state law with respect to workers of visual art.

Each of the foregoing rights exist independently. For example, it is an infringement of the adaptation right, although not of the reproduction right, to cut pictures from a commemorative art book and mount them on ceramic tiles for sale at retail. *Mirage Editions, Inc. v. Albuquerque A.R.T. Co.* (1988). Similarly, a visual artist's attribution right and right of integrity exist independently of the exclusive rights enumerated in section 106.

Each of the foregoing rights is also subject to various exemptions and qualifications which collectively serve as "safe havens," defining what is clearly fair use and not infringement. Both the reproduction and the distribution right, for example, are subject to an exemption enabling libraries and archives with open collections to make or distribute isolated and unrelated single copies of literary, dramatic, choreographic work, pantomimes, and sound recordings, for the noncommercial purpose of preserving an unpublished work, replacing the published work or meeting a user request for a small part of an available work or a copy of an unobtainable work. 17 U.S.C.A. § 108.

The reproduction and distribution rights are also qualified by the provision for compulsory licensing of non-dramatic musical works in the making of phonorecords for distribution to the public for private use. 15 U.S.C.A. § 115. A licensee under this provision may also make a musical arrangement of the licensed work to the extent necessary to conform the work to the style or manner of interpretation of the performance involved. The arrangement cannot, however, change the melody or fundamental character of the work. The reproduction and distribution rights in a work do not otherwise include a right to make adaptations of the work. Thus a copyright owner who has licensed the reproduction or distribution rights in a work may sue the licensee for infringement where unauthorized changes are made in the work. See, e.g., *Gilliam v. American Broadcasting Companies* (1976) (upholding the grant of preliminary injunctive relief in favor of "Monty Python" scriptwriters, who claimed that editing by an American television company licensed by the British Broadcasting Company to distribute certain BBC programs infringed their copyright in the script).

The distribution and display rights are subject to the "first sale" limitation of section 109, which specifies that the owner of a particular copy or phonorecord embodying a copyright work may sell or otherwise dispose of the copy or phonorecord and the owner of a copy of a copyrighted work may publicly display it to viewers present at the place where the copy is located. In section 109(b) the first sale doctrine is expressly limited to bar rentals or leases of phonorecords or computer software, because such rentals or leases are likely to be for the purpose of unauthorized copying. Likewise, the first sale doctrine does not permit the owner of a particular copy of a book to prepare derivative works by mounting pictures on ceramic tiles for sale at retail, because section 109 limits only the distribution and display rights, not the adaptation right. *Mirage Editions, Inc. v. Albuquerque A.R.T. Co.* (1988).

The purpose of the first sale limitation is to prevent a copyright owner from trying to exercise "remote control" over the pricing or other business conduct of purchasers once a copy of the copyrighted work passes into their hands. Thus, the limitation has been applied not only to sales denominated as such but also to non-sale transactions that appear designed to try to avoid the first sale limitation. For example, mass marketers of computer software frequently seek to avoid the strictures of section 109 by purporting not to sell, but only to license or bail software diskettes. At least two states, Illinois and Louisiana, have enacted statutes explicitly upholding the enforceability of these so-called "shrink-wrap licenses" that typically appear on the packages containing software diskettes. A federal court, however, has held the Louisiana statute to have been preempted by section 117 of the Copyright Act which gives the owner of a copy of a computer program the right to make another copy or an adaptation as an essential step in utilizing the program or for archival purposes. *Vault Corporation v. Quaid Software Limited* (1988). The case has been criticized for preempting a state statute dealing with licensing because it interfered with a federal statute conferring certain rights on *owners* of copies of software.

The performance and display rights are limited to *public* performances and displays. For example, it is an infringement of the public performance right to exhibit copyright video cassettes in private booths on commercial premises devoted to that purpose, *Columbia Pictures Industries, Inc. v. Redd Horne, Inc.* (1984), but not for a hotel to rent videodiscs to guests for viewing on videodisc players in individual rooms, *Columbia Pictures Industries, Inc. v. Professional Real Estate Investors, Inc.* (1989).

The performance and display rights are also subject to a number of exceptions for the performance or display of specified works during the course of such activities as classroom instruction, educational broadcasting, religious services, certain non-profit and ancillary commercial activities, and transmissions to blind or deaf audiences. 17 U.S.C.A. § 110. These rights are also qualified by the provisions for compulsory licensing of the public performance of non-dramatic musical works on juke boxes, 17 U.S.C.A. § 116, and the public performance or display on non-exempt cable television transmissions. 17 U.S.C.A. § 111.

The exclusive rights in sound recordings, it will be noted, are limited to reproduction, adaptation and distribution rights and do not include a performance or display right. Thus, one does not infringe the copyright of a sound recording by playing the recording publicly. If a copyright is infringed it will be the copyright of the underlying literary or artistic work. Likewise, the royalties collected under the Act's compulsory licensing system for the public playing of a sound recording on a juke box or as a part of a cable television transmission will go to the owner of the underlying copyrighted work, not to the owner of the copyright in the sound recording.

The exclusive right in an architectural work does not include the right to prevent the making of pictures or photographs of a publicly visible architectural work. Nor does it include the right to prevent the owner of a building embodying the work from altering or destroying the building.

All of the exclusive rights in published pictorial, graphic, sculptural and non-dramatic musical works are subject to compulsory licensing for non-commercial broadcasts. In addition, the exclusive rights in copyrighted works of all types are subject to a broad "fair use" exemption contained in section 107 of the Act. Almost as important a limitation on the reproduction right as the fair use exemption is another that does not appear in the 1976 Copyright Act at all, but in its legislative history. See H.R.Rep. No. 94–1476, 94th Cong., 2d Sess. 68–72 (1976); Conf.Rep. No. 1733, 94th Cong., 2d Sess. 70 reprinted in 1976 U.S.Code Cong. & Ad.News 5810, 5811 (1976), which recognizes a set of guidelines, drafted by an ad hoc committee of educators, authors and publishers, for teacher and classroom copying in not-for-profit educational institutions. Strongly criticized by the American Association of University Professors and the Association of American Law Schools as too restrictive, the guidelines specify the quantity and conditions under which both a single copy of a work may be made for teachers and multiple copies may be made for classroom use. Although these guidelines are described in the legislative history as "minimum standards" and not the outer limits of fair use, courts have nevertheless tended to treat the guidelines as "instructive" on the issue of fair use. See, e.g., *Marcus v. Rowley* (1983) (holding that a foodservice teacher whose copying from another teacher's book on cake decorating greatly exceeded the "brevity" and "spontaneity" guidelines, though not those concerned with "cumulative effect," did not constitute fair use but constituted copyright infringement as a matter of law). Cf. *Encyclopaedia Britannica Educational Corp. v. Crooks* (1978) (rejecting a fair use defense on the ground that, although defendants were involved in noncommercial copying of broadcasts of educational programs for permanent retention for use in area school systems, the copying fell outside the relevant statutory "safe havens" and constituted the copying of entire copyrighted films, which was too extensive for the fair use defense to apply).

In order to understand the privilege of fair use, it is first necessary to consider what constitutes an infringement of any of the foregoing exclusive rights. To establish an infringement, the plaintiff must prove (1) plaintiff's ownership of one or more of the exclusive rights in a work and (2) defendant's "copying" of the copyrighted work in a manner the plaintiff has a right to prevent. Copying may be established by proving defendant's access to the copyrighted work and a substantial similarity between the plaintiff's and defendant's work. Of the two elements of proof, substantial similarity is the more important. Access may simply be inferred where the similarity of the two works is sufficiently striking.

Determining how much similarity is necessary to constitute substantial similarity is one of the most vexing questions in copyright law. Substantial similarity may be found even though something less than literal similarity is shown. Either comprehensive non-literal similarity or fragmentary literal similarity may be enough to constitute an infringement.

Where the similarity is literal but fragmentary, the focus is simply on whether the segments copied constitute a substantial amount or a substantially important portion of plaintiff's work. Where the similarity between two works is comprehensive but non-literal, the task is to determine whether the substantial similarity is between protected expression or unprotected facts and ideas. Compare, *Hoehling v. Universal City Studios* (1980) (holding that interpretations of an historical event are not copyrightable as a matter of law) with *Saul Steinberg v. Columbia Pictures Industries* (1987) (finding striking stylistic similarities between a magazine cover illustration depicting an "egocentrically myopic" bird's eye view of New York City and the rest of the world, facing west, and a movie poster depicting a similar view of New York City and the rest of the world, facing east). Evaluating the propriety of comprehensive non-literal similarity is thus to confront in an adversary context the distinction alluded to earlier (see pp. 236–37 supra) between protected expression and unprotected facts or ideas.

While each case must turn on its own facts, literary and artistic works may be described as embodying a hierarchy of patterns of increasing generality. Those detailed patterns which contain something recognizably the author's own are likely to be regarded as protected expression, the duplication of which constitutes an infringement, while the more abstract patterns which might equally characterize other works are likely to be regarded as unprotectible ideas in the public domain. Likewise, the more factual or utilitarian the work, the narrower the range of non-literal copyrightable expression. (See pp. 236–38 supra).

A corollary of the notion that not every similarity between two works constitutes an infringement of protected expression is the notion that some instances of manifest copying do not constitute an infringement but are rather a fair use of the copyrighted work. Prior to the passage of the 1976 Act, the courts long recognized a privilege of fair use. In section 107 of the 1976 Act, Congress explicitly recognized and essentially restated the judicially developed fair use privilege. While the 1976 Act contains a narrowly drawn provision (section 108) expressly permitting certain reproductions by libraries and archives, neither this nor other specific exemptions in the Act are intended to curtail the fair use privilege. Their purpose is merely to define clearly permissible uses, not to proscribe all other uses as infringing uses.

Section 107 of the 1976 Act states that the use of a copyrighted work for purposes such as criticism, comment, news reporting, teaching (including multiple copies for classroom use), scholarship, or research, is not an infringement of copyright. In determining whether the use made of a work in any particular case is a fair use, a court is to consider

(1) the *purpose* and *character* of the use, including whether the use is of a commercial nature or is for non-profit educational purposes;

(2) the *nature* of the *copyrighted work,* including its intended purpose and availability to the potential user;

(3) the *amount* and *substantiality* of the portion used in relation to the copyrighted work as a whole; and

(4) the *effect* of the use upon the *potential market* for or *value* of the copyrighted work.

While no one of these factors is determinative, the last factor is implicit in the other three. If a particular use of a copyrighted work serves a sufficiently distinguishable function that does not significantly impair the value of the work, then the use of even a substantial portion of the copyrighted work will be deemed a fair use and not an infringement. See, e.g., *Triangle Publications v. Knight–Ridder Newspapers, Inc.* (1980) (holding that the use of a copyrighted cover of "TV Guide" in a comparative advertisement for a competing booklet constituted fair use because defendant's use of the cover did not by itself affect the value of the plaintiff's copyright). Similarly, use of a relatively small portion of a copyrighted work in another work reflecting substantial independent effort on the part of its author is unlikely to undermine the commercial value of the quoted work, even where the two works compete for the same market. Cf. *Rosemont Enterprises, Inc. v. Random House, Inc.* (1966) (holding that an unauthorized Howard Hughes biographer who used a copyrighted magazine article did not infringe the copyright even though the copyright owner was the authorized biographer of Howard Hughes).

On the other hand, unauthorized use of even a small part of an unpublished work may be infringing where an adverse impact on the marketability of the copyrighted work can be shown. *Harper & Row Publishers Inc. v. Nation Enterprises* (1985) (news magazine's unauthorized use of quotations totalling 300–400 words of an unpublished 200,000 word manuscript of autobiography of former President Gerald R. Ford held to constitute infringement where another news magazine cancelled agreement to publish excerpts as a result of the premature disclosure). Cf. *West Publishing Co. v. Mead Data Central, Inc.* (1985) (holding pagination of unofficial law reports copyrightable and sufficiently likely to be infringed by a computerized legal research system keyed to the law reports as to merit the grant of temporary injunctive relief). At the same time, off-the-air copying of an entire work on a home video cassette recorder (VCR) for the non-commercial purpose of delayed viewing is not an infringement but rather a fair use, at least in the absence of some meaningful likelihood of future harm to the copyright owner, and because VCRs are widely used for this legitimate purpose, the sale of VCRs does not constitute contributory infringement even though some VCR owners also accumulate libraries of copyrighted programs. *Sony Corporation of America v. Universal City Studios, Inc.* (1984). But videotaping TV news broadcasts and selling the tapes to the subjects of the news reports does constitute an infringement. *Pacific and Southern Co. Inc. v. Duncan* (1984).

Two areas of controversy reflect the dangers of too narrow or too broad a reading of the fair use privilege: These are burlesque, parody and satire, on the one hand, and library photocopying on the other. Because burlesque, parody and satire all involve varying degrees of mimicry, they necessarily copy substantial portions or indeed the entire outline of a copyrighted work. Nevertheless, they are judicially recognized as deserving of substantial protection, both as a form of social and literary criticism and as a form of entertainment. See, e.g., *Berlin v. E.C. Publications, Inc.* (1964) (holding that "Mad" Magazine's parody of popular songs did not constitute copyright infringement). Arguably, only where the mimicry reveals a surprise ending or is otherwise shown to injure the commercial value of the underlying work should the copying be held to constitute an infringement. Some courts, however, have given the impression that as a form of entertainment, parodies are unprivileged. In *Loew's Inc. v. CBS* (1955), for example, the courts found an infringement where comedian Jack Benny performed a television parody of the movie "Gaslight." The district court distinguished television parody from more scholarly endeavors, emphasizing the commercial nature of the TV parody while the court of appeals focused on the wholesale nature of the appropriation. Neither of these factors, however, should be determinative. Both courts would have been better advised to inquire more extensively into the effect of the parody on the value of the copyrighted work.

The other area of controversy, not wholly resolved by the 1976 Act, is that of library photocopying. In *Williams & Wilkins Co. v. United States* (1973), the Court of Claims held that photocopying, by the National Institute of Health and the National Library of Medicine, of entire articles from medical and scientific journals constituted fair use and not copyright infringement. Described in dissent as "the Dred Scott decision of copyright law," the case appears not to have given serious consideration to the effect of defendants' practices on plaintiff's potential market, but focused exclusively on the role defendants' copying played in the advancement of medical and scientific research. As we saw in the case of television parody, however, the presence or absence of a scholarly purpose should not be determinative of fair use. The question, rather, is the extent to which defendant's copying affects the potential value of plaintiff's work.

On the other hand, the mere absence of measurable pecuniary damage does not require a finding of fair use, and where the copying is substantial and for the same intrinsic purpose, even copying for a non-profit educational use may constitute copyright infringement as a matter of law. See *Marcus v. Rowley* (1983) (holding that verbatim copying of 50% and virtually all of the substance of plaintiff's cake decorating book constituted copyright infringement as a matter of law, notwithstanding the non-profit educational purpose for the copying).

The judicially recognized test for contributory infringement of a copyright is the same as the statutory test for contributory infringement of a patent. See pp. 269, 283 supra and 288–89 infra.

3. MASK WORK INFRINGEMENT AND FAIR USE

Registration of a mask work secures for the owner, for the ten year period specified in 17 U.S.C.A. § 904, all of the exclusive rights enumerated in section 905. The basic exclusive rights are three—namely the right to prohibit others from 1) reproducing the mask work in any form; 2) importing semiconductor chip products embodying the mask work; and 3) distributing semiconductor chip products embodying the mask work. These three basic rights are supplemented by a further pair of rights: the right to prohibit others from inducing or knowingly causing any person to violate any of the owner's exclusive rights. Significantly absent is any mention of an exclusive adaptation right.

The broadest (and potentially most troublesome) of the three basic rights is the reproduction right. Section 905(1) gives the owner of a mask work the exclusive right to "reproduce the mask work by optical, electronic, or any other means." This language differs slightly from section 106 of the 1976 Copyright Act, which gives the owner of a copyrighted work the exclusive right to "reproduce the copyrighted work *in copies.*" The failure of section 905(1) to limit the reproduction right to the reproduction of copies raises the question whether independent creation of an identical or substantially similar mask work would be infringing (as it is for patents) or non-infringing (as it is for copyrights).

As a practical matter, identical or substantially similar layouts of complete chips are virtually certain to be the result of copying. On the other hand, relatively simple cells or other small modules of a chip may well be independently created and yet identical or substantially similar. Here, however, the layout is likely to be unregistrable, either because it consists of a staple, commonplace, or familiar design, or because its form is dictated by function, in which case, as both the legislative history of the Chip Act and a long line of copyright cases make clear, "idea" and "expression" merge and the design is unprotectible. In the relatively rare case of identical or substantially similar cells whose layouts are simple but neither commonplace nor functionally dictated, the question whether the statutory term "reproduce" is limited to copying or extends to independent creation might become relevant.

A related but broader question that will arise in all cases where the reproduction right is in issue is how similar two chip layouts must be in order for there to be an infringement. The legislative history of the Chip Act, recognizing that under U.S. copyright law the degree of similarity necessary to constitute infringement of a copyrighted work varies, depending on whether the copyrighted work is a highly imaginative "non-factual" work in which case protection extends beyond literal expression to any reasonably detailed structural patterns, or is merely a minimally original "factual" work, which will only be protected from almost identical copying, concludes that "[t]he case of semiconductor chips falls between these two extremes." S.Rep. No. 98–425, 98th Cong., 2d Sess. 18 (1984).

A final evidentiary difference between the reproduction rights of the Chip Act and U.S. copyright law is with respect to the role of expert testimony in determining whether two works are substantially similar. In copyright cases, a number of courts have required the use of a subjective, "lay observer" test for determining whether works are substantially similar. The legislative history of the Chip Act, on the other hand, makes it clear that expert testimony on the question of substantial similarity of mask works should ordinarily be admitted.

The exclusive right under section 905(2) to distribute a semiconductor chip product embodying a registered mask work extends not only to sales but also to leases, bailments or other transfers or offers to sell, lease, bail, or otherwise transfer the product. Section 901(b) extends the distribution right, as well as section 905(2)'s accompanying exclusive importation right, to the distribution or importation of a product incorporating a semiconductor chip product. The distribution right itself, however, as opposed to the prohibition against inducing an infringing distribution under section 905(3), can be infringed only by the distributor, not the distributee.

Section 905(3) of the Chip Act makes it a violation of the exclusive rights of the owner of a mask work to "induce" or "knowingly to cause" another person to violate any of the three basic rights enumerated in paragraphs (1) and (2) of section 905. Although paragraph (3) has no analogue in the 1976 Copyright Act, it does have an analogue in section 271 of the Patent Act, which states that whoever "actively induces infringement of a patent shall be liable as an infringer" and that whoever "sells a component of a patented machine ...

knowing the same to be especially made or especially adapted for use in an infringement of such patent, and not a staple article or commodity of commerce suitable for substantial noninfringing use, shall be liable as a contributory infringer." Likewise, in copyright and trademark infringement cases, the courts have judicially recognized similar but not identical doctrines of contributory infringement. Compare pp. 184–85, supra, with p. 283, supra.

The legislative history of the Chip Act makes it clear that the "knowingly to cause" language of section 905(3) is designed to make the doctrine of contributory infringement, as applied in patent and copyright infringement cases, equally applicable in cases of infringement of a mask work. As the language of section 271 of the Patent Act makes clear, contributory infringement of a patent consists of supplying an infringer with a product that is not suitable for a substantial non-infringing use, knowing it to be especially adapted for infringing use. The same test is used for contributory copyright infringement.

Both the distribution and the importation right in the Chip Act are subject to the first sale limitation of section 906(b), which is modelled on section 109(a) of the 1976 Copyright Act. Two additional limitations on the exclusive rights to a mask work are the reverse engineering and innocent infringement limitations. Of the three, only the reverse engineering limitation, which is entirely new and unique to mask work infringement claims, limits all three of the basic exclusive rights. Innocent infringement, like the first sale limitation, merely permits what would otherwise be an infringing distribution or importation.

Section 906(a) of the Chip Act states that it is not an infringement of the exclusive rights of a mask work owner for a person to reproduce the mask work solely for the purpose of teaching, analyzing, or evaluating the concepts or techniques embodied in the mask work or the circuitry, logic flow, or organization of components used in the mask work, or for such a person to incorporate the results of such conduct in an original mask work which is made to be distributed. Unlike the first sale and innocent infringement limitation, which limit only the distribution and importation rights, reverse engineering thus limits the reproduction right as well.

According to the legislative history of the Chip Act, it is an established industry custom to photograph chips of competitors in order to analyze them and design similar, but hopefully improved, and thus not substantially identical, chips. The custom is deemed fair, so long as "substantial analysis and study" and not simply plagiarism occurs, because it produces additional sources for a particular chip and promotes competition in the industry as a whole.

The legislative history makes it clear that to fall within this limitation, the allegedly infringing chip must be shown 1) to be the product of substantial analysis and study—which is to say, the product of a substantial expenditure of time and money; 2) not to be substantially identical to the first chip; and 3) to embody an "original" mask work. Of the three requirements, only the third is expressly stated in section 906(a) itself; but of the three, it poses the biggest problem.

The word "original" is used three times in the Act—namely, in sections 902(b)(1) and (2), and 906(a)(2)—and in each case arguably means something slightly different. A definition of the word "original," contained in earlier versions of the Act, was deleted without explanation from the final bill.

In section 902(b)(1), which bars protection of subject matter that is not original, the term "original" is apparently used, as it had originally been defined in the earlier version of the Act and as it is commonly understood in U.S. copyright law, to mean an independent creation by one who did not copy the work from another person. In section 902(b)(2), which bars protection for chips that are merely variations of staple, commonplace, or familiar designs, "combined in such a way that, taken as a whole, is not original," the term seems to connote an element of inventiveness, over and above independent creation without copying. Finally, in section 906(a)(2), which requires a mask work based on reverse engineering to be "original," the term clearly does not connote independent creation, as the whole purpose of the reverse engineering defense is to permit chip designers to utilize the designs of others and incorporate features of those designs in their own.

The best analogy in the reverse engineering situation is the test used in copyright law for determining whether a derivative work is sufficiently different from the original to support an independent claim of copyright protection. Unlike copyright (or for that matter, patent) law, however, the reverse engineering limitation of the Chip Act permits one person to make a derivative work (or, in the language of patent law, exploit an improvement) without the authorization of, or recompense to, the owner of the original work. Buttressing this conclusion is the absence of an exclusive adaptation right with respect to chip designs.

Under section 907 of the Chip Act, an innocent purchaser of an infringing chip product incurs no liability with respect to the importation or distribution of units of the product that occurs before the innocent purchaser has notice of protection with respect to the mask work embodied in the product, and the innocent purchaser is liable only for a reasonable royalty on each unit of the infringing product that the innocent purchaser purchased prior to notice but imports or distributes after having such notice. Section 907 goes on to state that the limitation extends to any person (whether "innocent" or not) who directly or indirectly purchases an infringing chip product from an innocent purchaser.

Section 901(a)(7), in turn, defines an innocent purchaser as a person who purchases a chip product in good faith and without having notice of protection with respect to the chip product, and section 901(a)(8) defines "notice of protection" as having actual knowledge that, or reasonable grounds to believe that, a mask work is protected under the Act. Although use of the notice specified (though not required) by section 909(a) constitutes prima facie evidence of notice of protection, the definition of "notice of protection" makes it clear that use of such notice does not serve as constructive notice of an owner's claim of protection. Thus, it remains open for the alleged infringer to prove lack of actual notice, notwithstanding the owner's use of the notice symbol.

4. MISAPPROPRIATION

A prima facie case of misappropriation is apparently established at common law merely upon pleading and proving that (1) plaintiff has made a substantial investment of time, money or intellectual effort, (2) defendant has appropriated the product of plaintiff's investment, and (3) defendant's appropriation has injured the plaintiff. These elements, notable chiefly for their vagueness and ambiguity, must be qualified considerably as a result of the preemptive effect of federal patent and copyright law. Where a product of intellectual effort falls within one of the classes of patentable subject matter enumerated in the federal patent statute, for example, states cannot prohibit its appropriation by others once it has been publicly disclosed. See *Sears–Compco* (1964) and *Bonito Boats, Inc. v. Thunder Craft Boats, Inc.* (1989), discussed in Chapter 1 supra. Likewise, where a product of intellectual effort constitutes a federally copyrightable work of authorship, states cannot prohibit its appropriation once it has been reduced to tangible form.

Even for those products of intellectual effort that states clearly can protect, the terms "appropriation" and "misappropriation," have taken on no fixed legal meaning but have been used, rather, as blanket terms denoting a number of distinct types of harm to a number of distinct interests. Some misappropriation cases, for example, simply appear to be palming off cases by another name. The intangible business value being protected is a distinctive product, service or business identifier and the defendant's "misappropriation" consists of making deceptive use of it. In *Chaplin v. Amador* (1928), for example, the court, citing the *INS* case, held that Charlie Chaplin had a right to be protected against defendants' scheme to make motion pictures starring an actor with the stage name of "Charles Aplin," playing a character dressed like the character Chaplin had previously made famous. See also *Metropolitan Opera Association v. Wagner–Nichols Recorder Corp.* (1951), where the court enjoined the unauthorized recording of an opera company's radio broadcasts, noting that even though a failure to allege palming off would not be a fatal defect in the plaintiff's complaint, one of the inferences which could fairly be drawn from the complaint and prayer for relief was that the defendants misled the public into believing that the recordings were made with the cooperation of the opera company and under its supervision.

Other misappropriation cases contain elements of invasion of commercial privacy, appropriation of trade values prior to their unrestricted publication and improper interference with contracts. In the *INS* case itself, for example, the lower court enjoined INS from obtaining the news by bribing employees of AP's members or inducing members themselves to breach the association's by-laws and permit INS to obtain news before its publication. Likewise, in *Pittsburgh Athletic Co. v. KQV Broadcasting Co.* (1938) the court, citing the Supreme Court opinion in the *INS* case, enjoined a radio station from broadcasting the plaintiff's baseball games from a vantage point outside the enclosed ball park. The court noted that the plaintiff had at great expense acquired and maintained the baseball park and paid the players and had entered into a contract granting a third party the exclusive right to broadcast the games. See also *Bajpayee v. Rothermich* (1977), holding that where a president of a research laboratory, without authorization, used an unpublished article, written by a biochemist in the course of his employment with the laboratory, at a professional meeting in such a way as to indicate that it was the work of the president, the biochemist had a cause of action—be it classified as a claim for relief for plagiarism, invasion of a right of publicity or prima facie tort—for violation of his right to be recognized for his work product, even though he claimed no common-law copyright interest in the article and the discovery revealed in the article was the property of the employer.

In contrast to the foregoing cases, the type of misappropriation made actionable by the Supreme Court in the *INS* case amounted to no more than a non-deceptive appropriation of a trade value after its unrestricted publication. The wrong identified in *INS* was simply the diversion of profits from one who had gone to the expense of collecting the news to one who had not.

Even this distinct type of misappropriation is capable of a number of further variations. The Court's rationale for finding an actionable misappropriation in the *INS* case, for example, appears to have been based not merely on the parasitic nature of the defendant's conduct but on its tendency to "kill the goose that lays the golden egg." By using AP's news stories to compete with AP, INS could avoid the cost of gathering the news and could thus charge a lower price for the news it sold. That, in turn, could conceivably render AP's own newsgathering venture unprofitable. If AP were driven out of business, INS would arguably not be able to provide the public with news of the war that was then going on, because INS had been expelled from England for refusing to submit to British censorship (which was apparently the reason INS resorted to pirating AP's news in the first place).

A similar concern over "goose-killing" parasitism underlies the statutory prohibitions against record and tape piracy. In *Goldstein v. California* (1973), for example, the Court noted that the cost of producing a single long playing record of a musical performance may exceed $100,000, while for that same performance the record pirate would pay only the retail cost of a long playing record.

Not all parasitic conduct, however, poses so dire a threat either to the public or to the business whose profits are being diverted. Indeed, where the appropriator does not compete with the business whose intangible assets are being appropriated, there may be no diversion of profits from existing trade relations at all. The only injury to the plaintiff is the diversion of a prospective business opportunity.

Not surprisingly, a number of courts have held that there can be no misappropriation in the absence of competition between plaintiff and defendant. See, e.g., *U.S. Golf Association v. St. Andrews Systems, Data–Max, Inc.* (1984) (holding that a marketer of a small computer programmed to calculate a golfer's handicap, using a U.S.G.A.-developed formula, could not be found to have misappropriated the U.S.G.A. formula inasmuch as the U.S.G.A. is not in the business of selling handicaps to golfers, but is primarily interested in promoting the game of golf and itself as the governing body of amateur golf). But see *Board of Trade of City of Chicago v. Dow Jones & Co.* (1983) holding that offering a commodity futures contract based on the Dow Jones Industrial Average (DJIA) without the consent of Dow Jones & Co. would misappropriate a valuable business asset of Dow Jones & Co., even though the latter did not deal in commodity futures contracts, and that any detriment to the public from not being allowed to use the DJIA is outweighed by the encouragement the court's holding will give to the development of new indexes specifically designed for the purpose of assisting in the marketing of commodity futures contracts.

A competition requirement, however, is arguably still too broad if the courts do not require plaintiffs to show that the defendant's competitive conduct actually threatens the viability of the plaintiff's enterprise. In the *INS* case itself, for example, the Court required no actual proof that the profitability of AP's newsgathering effort was threatened. Without such proof there is a danger that the misappropriation doctrine will itself be used to eliminate competition or preserve a monopoly. As Brandeis pointed out in dissent in the *INS* case, for example, for all that appeared in the record, INS and its subscribers may have previously sought and been denied membership in the Associated Press. Brandeis was apparently adverting to the fact that the AP by-laws at the time gave members veto power over applications by competitors for membership in the association. A number of years later, these same by-laws were held to violate the Sherman Antitrust Act. See *United States v. Associated Press* (1945). See also *FTC v. Sperry & Hutchinson Co.* (1972) (holding that it was within the power of the Federal Trade Commission to find that the largest and oldest trading stamp company in the country engaged in an unfair method of competition when it adopted the practice of bringing lawsuits for misappropriation—which were almost invariably successful—as a means of suppressing the operation of independent trading stamp exchanges). Cf. *Bonito Boats, Inc. v. Thunder Craft Boats, Inc.* (1989), in which the Supreme Court held that a state statute prohibiting the unauthorized use of direct molding to duplicate for the purpose of sale any manufactured boat hull made by another conflicted with, and was thus preempted by, federal patent law.

There is also a danger that the misappropriation doctrine will be employed to curtail the free use of knowledge and ideas. To that extent it may run afoul of federal copyright law or the First Amendment. Merely because section 102(b) of the 1976 Copyright Act expressly excludes facts and ideas as copyrightable subject matter does not necessarily mean that a state law granting exclusive rights in publicly disclosed facts and ideas will never be found to conflict with the federal copyright policy of not protecting ideas or with the First Amendment's prohibition against government abridgements of speech and press. The Supreme Court's decision in *Goldstein v. California,* supra, that a state record and tape piracy statute did not conflict with federal copyright law, for example, emphasized that the state statute did not place any restraint on the use of an idea or concept. Similarly, even though the Court held in *Zacchini v. Scripps–Howard Broadcasting Co.* (1977) that the First Amendment provided no defense to a claim that a television station misappropriated a 15 second "Human Cannonball" act by making an unauthorized newscast of it, the Court noted that entertainment can be important news whose dissemination is protected by the First Amendment and emphasized that the station did not merely make incidental use of plaintiff's name or picture, but appropriated plaintiff's entire act, the effect of which was similar to preventing plaintiff from charging an admission fee. The Court also noted that the plaintiff was not seeking to enjoin dissemination of the newscast but was merely seeking damages for the misappropriation. See also *Hoehling v. Universal City Studios* (1980) (holding that where historical facts, themes, and research which have been deliberately exempted from the scope of copyright protection to vindicate the overriding goal of encouraging contributions to recorded knowledge, the states are pre-empted from removing such material from the public domain).

C. AFFIRMATIVE DEFENSES AND REMEDIES

Affirmative defenses which may be raised to a patent infringement suit include (1) patent invalidity and (2) the equitable defenses of laches, acquiescence and unclean hands. In determining the validity or invalidity of the patent, the courts acknowledge that a presumption of validity technically attaches to a patent once it is issued by the PTO, but they generally proceed to make their own determination as to the utility, novelty and nonobviousness of the invention. As we have seen, a large percentage of patents issued by the PTO are later invalidated by the courts.

The equitable defenses of laches, acquiescence and unclean hands are essentially the same as those which may be raised to a claim of trademark infringement. See Chapter 4 supra. The patent statute, however, does place limits on the defense of unclean hands by spelling out certain types of conduct which do not constitute patent misuse. See 35 U.S.C.A. § 271(d). See also *Dawson Chemical Co. v. Rohm & Haas Co.* (1980) (holding that an owner of a patented process was not guilty of patent misuse in refusing to license those who would not agree to purchase all of their requirements of an unpatented substance needed to carry out the process, where the only known use of the substance is in the patented method).

The judicial remedies available for patent infringement are likewise similar to those available for trademark infringement (including provision for treble damages in appropriate cases), except that the patent statute sets as a minimum damage award a sum no less than a reasonable royalty for the use made of the invention by the infringer, and makes no provision for recovery of defendant's profits. Pursuant to section 337 of the Tariff Act of 1930, 19 U.S.C.A. § 1337, a U.S. patent owner may petition the International Trade Commission (ITC) to order subject to review by the U.S. Trade Representative (USTR) and the President, the exclusion of imports which infringe the patent. A U.S. patent owner may also petition the USTR to impose sanctions on foreign countries providing inadequate or ineffective protection to the intellectual property of U.S. nationals.

The Copyright Remedy Clarification Act of 1990 amended section 501(a) of the 1976 Copyright Act to make it clear that states, state instrumentalities and state officers or employees acting in their official capacities can be held liable for copyright infringement in the same manner as anyone else.

A defendant in a copyright infringement proceeding may raise the same equitable defenses of laches, acquiescence and unclean hands as may be raised in trademark and patent infringement cases. The remedies for copyright infringement are likewise similar to those available for trademark and patent infringement, except that both the 1909 and the 1976 copyright acts specifically provide for a purely discretionary award of attorney's fees, impoundment of allegedly infringing works during the pendency of the infringement proceeding and provide for recovery of statutory damages (in a sum under the 1976 Act of not less than $250 or more than $10,000, as the court considers just), in lieu of actual damages. Like the Lanham Act and unlike the patent statute, both the old and the new copyright acts provide for the recovery of an infringer's profits. Unlike the Lanham Act, however, the copyright acts allow only alternative and not cumulative recovery of damages and profits. As with patents, the holder of a U.S. copyright may petition the ITC, pursuant to section 337 of the Tariff Act of 1930, to order the exclusion of imports which infringe the copyright and may petition the USTR for sanctions where foreign copyright protection for U.S. nationals is inadequate or ineffective.

The principal affirmative defenses that may be raised to the tort of misappropriation are that of federal preemption and First Amendment freedom of commercial speech. Where neither of these defenses applies, the full panoply of legal and equitable remedies is available.

CHAPTER SEVEN

APPROPRIATION OF NON-PUBLICLY DISCLOSED TRADE VALUES

Some intangible products of intellectual effort may be exploited without being publicly disclosed. Whether publicly disclosed or not, they may be entitled to legal protection. An inventor, for example, may have an option between obtaining federal patent protection or common-law trade secret protection for an invention. Whereas a patent protects an invention for a limited time after public disclosure, state trade secret law offers protection for so long as the invention remains a secret.

The American law of trade secrets began, for all practical purposes, with the case of *Peabody v. Norfolk* (1868). In that case, the executors of a manufacturer who had developed a certain manufacturing process obtained an injunction forbidding a former employee, who became "confidentially possessed" of knowledge of the process and later signed a contract with the manufacturer agreeing not to divulge information about it, from disclosing the process to others. In a supplemental bill of complaint, the executors also sought to enjoin a would-be competitor who was allegedly proceeding, with full knowledge of the former employee's relation with the manufacturer and the injunction forbidding disclosure, to replicate the secret manufacturing process, using information provided by the former employee.

In demurring to the executors' supplemental bill of complaint, the prospective competitor in *Peabody* raised virtually all of the defenses that have subsequently been proffered in trade secret litigation. Counsel for the prospective competitor contended that the manufacturer's contract with the former employee was void for lack of consideration, for lack of certainty (due to the indefinite length of the former employee's obligation), and as an unlawful restraint on trade. Counsel also contended that the manufacturing process was not a secret, given the number of operatives and public inspectors who might be familiar with the process, and was not property which could pass by will or inheritance. Finally, counsel contended that because the secret was not acquired surreptitiously, its disclosure was at most a breach of contract giving rise to an action for damages against the disclosing party; but that a grant of injunctive relief would be against the policy of the patent laws (given evidence that the process was patentable but not in fact patented) and in any event should not extend to a stranger to the employment contract.

The court in *Peabody* rejected all of these arguments, holding (1) that a person who invents or discovers and keeps secret a process of manufacture, whether a proper subject for a patent or not, has an assignable property interest in it, which a court of equity will protect against one who in violation of contract and breach of confidence undertakes to apply it to his own use or to disclose it to third persons; (2) that an employee may be bound even beyond the term of employment by a promise not to disclose a secret imparted to him during the course of his employment; (3) that a trade secret does not lose its character by being confidentially disclosed to agents or servants without whose assistance it could not be made of any value; and (4) that a third party who has notice of the confidential relation but nevertheless makes arrangements to have the secret communicated to him may be enjoined from carrying out the arrangement.

A number of theories for granting legal protection to trade secrets have subsequently been advanced. Some courts, influenced no doubt by the law of patents, copyrights and trademarks, emphasize that trade secrets are a protectible form of intellectual property. See, e.g., *Cincinnati Bell Foundry Co. v. Dodds* (1887). Cf. *Ruckelshaus v. Monsanto Co.* (1984) (holding that disclosure or use by a government agency of trade secret information submitted by a private company could constitute a taking of property requiring compensation under the Fifth Amendment of the U.S. Constitution). For most courts, however, the starting point for the law of trade secrets has been the breach of a confidential relation. As Mr. Justice Holmes noted in *E.I. Du Pont De Nemours Powder Co. v. Masland* (1917):

> The word property as applied to trademarks and trade secrets is an unanalyzed expression of certain secondary consequences of the primary fact that the law makes some rudimentary requirements of good faith. Whether the plaintiffs have any valuable secret or not the defendant knows the facts, whatever they are, through a special confidence he accepted. The property may be denied but the confidence cannot be.

See also *Ruckelshaus v. Monsanto Co.* (1984) (where trade secret information was submitted to a government agency and used or disclosed by it, a taking of property requiring compensation under the Fifth Amendment of the U.S. Constitution could only be found where information was submitted under a guarantee of confidentiality and not where the information was voluntarily disclosed to the agency).

Still other courts have emphasized the impropriety in the method of ascertaining the secret. In *Tabor v. Hoffman* (1889), for example, the inventor and manufacturer of a rotary pump whose patent had expired, obtained an injunction restraining defendant from manufacturing the pumps using certain patterns which had remained secret and had been surreptitiously copied by an agent of the defendant while the patterns were in his custody for repairs. The trial court found that although a competent pattern maker could make patterns from the pump itself, the process would be time-consuming and expensive, since the pumps expanded unevenly in casting and thus did not have the same measurements as the patterns. The appellate court upheld the grant of injunctive relief in *Tabor,* noting that even if resort to the patterns was more of a convenience than a necessity, the patterns were nevertheless a secret which had not been disclosed by "publication" of the pump, and that the defendant had no right to obtain the patterns by unfair means (i.e., surreptitious copying) or to use them after they were thus obtained. See also *E.I. duPont deNemours & Co. v. Christopher* (1971) (holding that aerial photography of plant construction was an improper means of obtaining another's trade secret). Inducing another to breach a contract of confidentiality would also constitute an improper means of obtaining a trade secret. As the court's disposition of the supplemental bill of complaint in *Peabody v. Norfolk* illustrates, however, liability for trade secret misappropriation is not limited to those who breach confidential relations or improperly obtain another's trade secret but extends as well to those who make use of a trade secret knowing it to have been improperly disclosed by another.

For a time after the Supreme Court's decision in the *Sears–Compco* cases, there was considerable debate over whether and to what extent the common law of trade secrets had been pre-empted by federal patent law. In *Kewanee Oil Co. v. Bicron Corp.* (1973), however, the Supreme Court purported to resolve the controversy over federal preemption of state trade secret law. The Court held that, because an inventor of a clearly patentable invention is unlikely to rely on trade secret law and after one year forfeit any right or patent protection, state trade secret law does not undermine federal patent law and is thus not preempted by it even where trade secret protection is granted a patentable but unpatented invention. See also *Roberts v. Sears, Roebuck & Co.* (1978) (holding *Lear* to be inapplicable and a district court not to have erred in declining to decide the validity of a patent in a suit for fraud, breach of a confidential relationship and negligent misrepresentation in a company's procurement of an assignment of the patent rights of an employee who during his off-duty hours invented a new type of socket wrench). The Court's opinion in *Kewanee Oil* has been criticized because in that case the creator of a synthetic crystal and a number of associated processes did exactly what the Court said an inventor was unlikely to do—namely opt for trade secret protection rather than obtaining a patent. In *Aronson v. Quick Point Pencil Co.* (1979), the Court went on to hold that federal patent law did not preempt state contract law so as to preclude enforcement of an agreement to pay royalties to a patent applicant for as long as the contracting party sells articles embodying the putative invention, with a reduced royalty if the patent is not granted. As a result of the *Kewanee* and *Aronson* decisions, it now appears clear that state trade secret law may continue to provide an alternative to patent law as a source of legal protection for inventions.

The subject matter of state trade secret protection, however, is not limited to inventions. Nor is state trade secret law the only body of law protecting trade values which have not been publicly disclosed. At the same time the law of trade secrets was developing, there emerged a parallel body of law known as the law of ideas, which provided a degree of protection to those who, whether in business themselves or not, submitted ideas to a business for its consideration. As with trade secrets, courts have on occasion characterized such ideas as a protectible form of intellectual property. See, e.g., *Hamilton National Bank v. Belt* (1953) (holding that a person has such a property right in his own idea as enables him to recover damages for its appropriation or use when the idea is original, concrete, useful and is disclosed in circumstances which, reasonably construed, clearly indicate compensation is contemplated if it is accepted and used). Most courts, however, have tended to echo the view expressed in *Bristol v. Equitable Life Assurance Society of the United States* (1892), where the court, while not denying that there may be property in an idea or trade secret, concluded that the originator or proprietor must himself protect it from disclosure and if it cannot be sold or negotiated or used without disclosure, a contract should guard or regulate the disclosure; otherwise the idea or secret becomes the acquisition of whoever receives it.

Even before the development of the law of trade secrets and ideas, the common-law courts had begun protecting unpublished writings, including those containing trade secrets and ideas. Thus, in *Yovatt v. Winyard* (1820), the court enjoined the use or disclosure of certain recipes for veterinary medicine which the defendant, while in the plaintiff's employ, had surreptitiously copied. Similarly, in *Abernathy v. Hutchinson* (1825) the court enjoined as a breach of confidence the publication of unpublished lectures of a distinguished surgeon, holding that persons attending the lecture, although privileged to take notes for their own use could not publish the lectures for a profit. This form of protection came to be known as common-law copyright.

Under the Copyright Act of 1976, 17 U.S.C.A. § 203(a), federal copyright protection now attaches to any original literary or artistic work created on or after January 1, 1978, from the moment it is fixed in some tangible form, whether or not it is actually published. To that extent common-law copyright has been preempted. For unpublished works created prior to January 1, 1978 or unpublished works not fixed in tangible form, however, common-law copyright protection remains available.

The classes of subject matter protected under the 1976 Copyright Act and the exclusive rights it confers on a copyright holder are discussed in Chapter 6, supra. All that need be added here is that the owner of an unpublished copyrightable work embodying a trade secret may avail himself of all the rights and remedies of the federal copyright law in seeking to prevent unauthorized copying of the work embodying the trade secret. Although registration and deposit with the Library of Congress is required of a U.S. created or non-Berne Convention work before an action for infringement may be brought, and the Library's records are open to the public, the Register of Copyrights may exempt certain works from the deposit requirements and the Copyright Office has promulgated regulations which protect trade secrets in certain cases. See 37 C.F.R. §§ 202.19(e) and 202.20(c)(2)(vi) and (vii) (1991) (enabling copyright holders to seek special relief in the form of an exemption from the required deposit with the Library of Congress; to obtain prompt return by the Copyright Office after examination of any "secure test," such as the LSAT, deposited as a part of registration; and to deposit identifying portions, rather than an entire copy, of any computer program sought to be registered, with any trade secret material contained in the program blocked out).

The primary focus of this chapter will be on the protection which the common law of trade secrets and ideas gives to the secret or idea itself. The theory that has prevailed, as we have seen, is that liability for misappropriation of trade secrets and ideas rests essentially on three bases: (1) breach of contract or confidence; (2) impropriety in the method of ascertaining a secret or idea; and (3) use of a trade secret or idea known to have been improperly disclosed by another. Accordingly, it will be useful, first, to identify the types of contractual and confidential trade relations and the types of trade secrets and ideas that the law will protect and then to identify the types of unauthorized acquisition, disclosure or use that will give rise to a claim for relief.

A. TRADE RELATIONS AND TRADE VALUES PROTECTED

1. CONTRACTUAL AND CONFIDENTIAL RELATIONS

As the *Peabody* and *Bristol* cases illustrate, the law of trade secrets and ideas seek among other things to protect contractual and confidential trade relations. As with contractual relations generally, confidential relations may exist between a business and its employees, between partners in a business, between a corporation and its officers and directors, or between a business and some other commercial or non-commercial party.

Confidential relations may be created by express contract or they may be implied from the particular trade relations existing between the parties. Express contractual provisions for the protection of trade secrets or ideas may consist of a mere promise not to use or disclose a trade secret or idea or may include a covenant not to compete as well. As noted in Chapter 3, supra, courts recognize that often the only practical method for a business to prevent unauthorized use or disclosure of such trade secrets as a secret manufacturing process or a confidential customer list is to have the party to whom it is disclosed agree not to compete with the business for a period of time after the trade relation terminates. Courts will enforce an express covenant not to compete as a permissible means of protecting trade secrets, so long as the covenant is no broader than is required for the protection of the trade secret and does not impose undue hardship on the party restricted. Where no express covenant not to compete exists, however, courts will not imply one. The only implied obligation with respect to the protection of trade secrets is not to make unauthorized use or disclosure of trade secrets or ideas which were learned in the course of a confidential relation.

Not every trade relation is necessarily a confidential one. Courts have been willing enough to imply a covenant on the part of a prospective purchaser of a business not to disclose or exploit information disclosed in the course of negotiations should the sale not go through. See e.g., *Smith v. Dravo Corp.* (1953). See also *Hamilton National Bank v. Belt* (1953) (implying a contract on the part of a sponsor of a radio program to compensate the originator of the idea for the program even though an express contract to purchase the idea and hire its originator had been terminated when it appeared for a time that the idea could not be implemented) and *Landsberg v. Scrabble Crossword*

Game Players, Inc. (1986) (upholding a finding that the initial disclosure of a manuscript on strategy for winning at the Scrabble boardgame for the limited purpose of requesting permission to use the Scrabble trademark, was confidential and that, given the author's expressed intent to exploit the manuscript commercially, defendants' use of any portion of it was conditioned on payment). Merely entering into another's employment, on the other hand, does not by itself give rise to a confidential relation. Nor does the unsolicited submission of an idea. Cf. *Hisel v. Chrysler Corp.* (1951) (refusing to imply a relationship of trust and confidence where an idea was submitted to a corporation after the originator of the idea was informed that the corporation's policy with regard to the submission of ideas was to assume no obligation). See also *Smith v. Snap–On Tools Corporation* (1987) (holding that the proprietor of a trade secret may not unilaterally create a confidential relationship without the knowledge or consent of the party to whom the secret is disclosed and that reliance on confidentiality must exist at the time the disclosure is made and may not be established after an initial disclosure). In both employment relations and idea submissions there must be additional circumstances from which a confidential relation may be implied. While courts are generally willing to imply an employee pledge of secrecy when an employer turns over a trade secret to the employee, they are less willing to imply such a pledge when an employee turns over to an employer a trade secret which he, the employee, has developed in the course of his employment. See, e.g., *Wexler v. Greenberg* (1960) (holding that an employee violated no trust or confidential relationship in disclosing or using formulas which the employee himself had developed). In such cases, there must be some further evidence, such as the fact that the employee was hired specifically to develop such information as a trade secret, before the court will imply an obligation of confidence.

2. TRADE SECRETS AND IDEAS

Not all information disclosed in the course of a confidential relation necessarily constitutes a trade secret or a protectible idea. See, e.g., *Religious Technology Center v. Wollersheim* (1986) (holding that confidential religious materials do not constitute a trade secret). A trade secret may be thought of as any commercially valuable information, whether in the form of an *invention* (such as a machine or process) an abstract *industrial or commercial idea* (such as a new product concept or advertising scheme), or a *compilation of data* (such as a list of customers or sources of supply). The Uniform Trade Secrets Act, which has been adopted in at least 35 states, defines a trade secret as information, including a formula, pattern, compilation, program, device, method, technique or process that 1) derives independent actual or potential economic value from not being generally known or readily ascertainable by proper means and 2) is the subject of reasonable efforts to maintain its secrecy. A number of courts have limited the use of the term "trade secret" to information which is used in one's business and gives one an opportunity to obtain an advantage over competitors who do not know or use it. The law protecting other ideas and information, such as ideas submitted to a business by another party, is often treated as a separate body of law. See, e.g., *Hamilton National Bank v. Belt,* supra (treating the protection of ideas as distinct from the protection of inventions, literary productions and trade secrets).

Whatever the type of information, it must have been guarded from disclosure. This means both that adequate physical security and adequate notice of the confidentiality of information must be provided. The information protected, moreover, must not be common knowledge. Matters of public knowledge or general knowledge in an industry or trade cannot be protected, regardless of the precautions taken. Likewise, matters which are completely revealed in a patent or a product design are not secret once the patent has been issued or the product has been publicly distributed.

Absolute secrecy on the other hand, is not required. Commercial privacy need only be protected from espionage that can reasonably be anticipated and prevented. A trade secret or idea may be disclosed to employees and others, so long as it is understood that the disclosure is a confidential one. Where a patent or public distribution of a product does not completely reveal all there is to know about a secret or idea, it remains to that extent protectible. See *Tabor v. Hoffman,* supra. See also *Smith v. Dravo Corp.* (1953) (holding there to be a protectible trade secret in certain blueprints and models of cargo containers, even though 100 of the containers were in public use at the time the blueprints and models were disclosed, where the defendant failed to show that it actually inspected any of the containers before commencing manufacture of similar containers). But see *Van Products Co. v. General Welding & Fabricating Co.* (1965) (holding that no trade secret exists where information could have been ascertained by permissible means). Further, a patent application (as opposed to the patent itself) does not constitute a general disclosure, since Patent and Trademark Office regulations provide that applications are to be kept confidential. See 37 C.F.R. § 1.14 (1991). Finally, the fact that others may have independently discovered the trade secret or had the idea will not deprive the secret or idea of protection so long as the other parties are not too numerous and also keep the matter secret.

A number of courts have indicated that while a trade secret need not amount to an invention in a patent law sense, it must at least possess an element of novelty. Similar statements have been made with respect to business ideas. See, e.g., *Hamilton National Bank v. Belt,* supra (stating that in order to be protectible, a business idea must be new, novel or original, and concrete). As a practical matter, however, such a requirement seems only to be another way of saying that the information or idea must not be common knowledge. The novelty, usefulness and concreteness of an idea are also relevant circumstances in determining the existence of an implied understanding that compensation is contemplated if the idea is accepted and used. Compare *Murray v. National Broadcasting Co.* (1988) (holding that an idea must be original or novel in order to be protected as property and that no promise to pay for an idea may be implied if the elements of novelty and originality are absent) with *Landsberg v. Scrabble Crossword Game Players, Inc.* (1986) (holding that a breach of contract claim rests not upon the existence of a protectible property interest but upon the implied promise to pay the reasonable value of the material disclosed and that if disclosure occurs before it is known that compensation is a condition of its use, no contract will be implied). Comment (b) to 4 Restatement of Torts, § 757 (1939) indicates that regular use is a prerequisite for finding that a protectible trade secret exists. Because regular use is not required either by the federal law of patents or the common law of ideas, however, many courts have not demanded regular use as a condition of granting relief in trade secret cases.

Trade secrets and ideas, like distinctive trade symbols, patents, copyrights and other investments of intellectual effort, may be assigned or licensed. Unlike other forms of intellectual property, however, it is essential that the confidentiality of the secret or idea be maintained. Loss of secrecy, whether due to the neglect of the owner of the secret or idea or to independent discovery and publication by another business, will result in a loss of rights, except as against those who have expressly agreed to pay royalties for so long as an invention, idea or information is used. See *Aronson v. Quick Point Pencil Co.,* supra.

B. ACTIONABLE AND PRIVILEGED APPROPRIATION

Not every appropriation of another's trade secret or commercially valuable idea is actionable. As we have seen, liability rests on breach of contract or confidence in the use or disclosure of a secret or idea or impropriety in the method of acquiring the secret or idea. Liability is not limited, however, to those who breach a contract or confidence or acquire a trade secret or idea by improper means, but extends as well to those who knowingly use a trade secret improperly acquired or disclosed by a third party.

We have already discussed the circumstances in which a court will enforce an express or implied obligation not to use or disclose information or ideas obtained in confidence. Remaining to be considered are: (1) What constitutes impropriety in the method of acquiring a trade secret or idea; (2) What constitutes an unauthorized use or disclosure of a trade secret or idea; and (3) What constitutes a knowing use of a trade secret or idea improperly disclosed by a third party.

1. IMPROPRIETY IN THE METHOD OF ACQUIRING A TRADE SECRET OR IDEA

Certain methods of acquiring another's trade secret or idea are clearly improper. Surreptitious copying, as in *Tabor v. Hoffman, supra,* or industrial espionage carried out by means of electronic surveillance, planting industrial spies or bribing another's employees, for example, will subject one to civil liability and may result in criminal liability as well. Likewise, inducing former employees to breach an express or implied contract not to disclose their former employer's trade secrets after termination of employment will be actionable under the same circumstances that interference with any other type of express or implied contract is actionable. (See Chapter 3, supra.) The Uniform Trade Secrets Act states that "improper means" includes theft, bribery, misrepresentation, breach or inducement of a breach of a duty to maintain secrecy, or espionage through electronic or other means.

Impropriety in the method of acquiring a trade secret may be found even in the absence of evidence of trespass, illegal conduct or interference with the contractual relations of another. In a case characterized as one in which "an airplane is the cloak and a camera the dagger," for example, the court found there to be sufficient impropriety to warrant an injunction compelling disclosure of an aerial photographer's client, even though the plane used to take pictures of plaintiff's plant construction site was at all times located in public airspace. See *E.I. duPont deNemours & Co. v. Christopher* (1970). The court concluded that discovery of another's trade secret by any means other than one's own independent research efforts or inspection and analysis of a publicly distributed product (i.e., reverse engineering) is improper unless the other party voluntarily discloses the secret or fails to take reasonable precautions to ensure its secrecy. The court emphasized that judicial tolerance of espionage must cease when the protection required to prevent another's spying costs so much that the spirit of inventiveness is dampened. To require the plaintiff to put a roof over the unfinished plant to guard its secret, said the court, "would impose enormous expense to prevent nothing more than a school boy's trick." The court thus appeared to be doing a cost-benefit analysis to determine the propriety of the means employed.

If the *Christopher* case defines what constitutes improper means of acquiring another's trade secret, it also suggests by way of dictum what would constitute privileged appropriation of another's trade secret. Reverse engineering, independent discovery and surveillance of operations which have not been reasonably shielded from public view are all characterized as permissible. See also *Chicago Lock Co. v. Fanberg* (1982) (holding there to be no impropriety in procuring tubular lock serial number-key code correlations from various locksmiths who had reverse engineered the locks, and publishing a compilation of same).

2. UNAUTHORIZED USE OR DISCLOSURE OF A TRADE SECRET OR IDEA

Perhaps the most difficult question plaguing the law of trade secrets is whether a former employee's use of knowledge or skill gained in the course of his or her former employment constitutes an actionable appropriation of a trade secret. Courts have held that employees may carry away their own faculties, skill and experience but may not reveal information gained solely through their employment. Often, however, the two are intertwined. In deciding such cases courts are influenced by the extent to which the former employee will be handicapped in seeking new employment if not permitted to utilize certain knowledge. They are also influenced by the extent to which the information the former employer is seeking to protect was developed as a result of the employee's own initiative. As with patents and copyrights, if the employee was hired specifically to develop the information, it will generally be held to belong to the employer. Otherwise, the employee may be able to claim it as a product of his own knowledge and skill, subject only to a common-law "shop-right" (i.e. an implied, irrevocable, non-exclusive, non-assignable, royalty-free license) in favor of the employer, where company time or materials were used in developing the secret or idea.

Also relevant is the extent to which the employer gave the employee notice of restrictions on disclosure of information. The courts generally hold that the employer bears the burden of making such restrictions explicit. These restrictions, in turn, must be reasonable both as to their geographic scope and their temporal duration. Finally, the courts may also be influenced by the extent of the employer's investment in the information for which protection is sought. The greater the investment, the more likely the court is to find an actionable appropriation.

All of these factors were considered in the case of *Wexler v. Greenberg* (1960), where the court permitted a former employee who had been hired to analyze and duplicate a competitor's products but was under no express contractual duty not to use that information after termination of employment, to use the information in the employ of a competing firm of which he was part owner. The court held that the former employee had violated no confidential relationship in disclosing or using the formulas which he himself had developed as a routine part of his work.

Similarly, where former employees who have had access to confidential customer lists solicit former customers, most courts hold that an employee may use any part of a list he can remember, so long as he has not made a deliberate effort to memorize it, but that he may not copy the list. See, e.g., *Leo Silfen, Inc. v. Cream* (1972) (dismissing a claim against a former employee, where the employer failed to sustain its allegation that the employee had copied the employer's confidential files, having shown only that the former employee's solicitation of plaintiff's customers was at most a product of casual memory).

The casual memory rule is of little value to an employer where a former employee made deliveries over an established route and is now soliciting customers on that route. In such cases the employer's best protection is to have employees enter into an express covenant not to compete. Such covenants are deemed an appropriate method of protecting the employer's good will, but will be voided as an unreasonable restraint on trade where their scope is greater than necessary to protect the employer's good will in the route or imposes undue hardship on the employee. See Chapter 3, supra.

3. KNOWING USE OF AN IMPROPERLY DISCLOSED TRADE SECRET OR IDEA

The *Christopher* court's dictum that the only proper method of obtaining another's trade secret is through reverse engineering, independent discovery or surveillance of activities not reasonably shielded from public view, raises the question whether the knowing receipt and subsequent use of another's trade secret, even by a business which did not engage in espionage or induce a breach of contract to obtain the secret, is improper. This question commonly arises when an employee voluntarily discloses information which was acquired during previous employment.

Where a former employee's use of confidential information is not privileged, a subsequent employer who has not changed his or her position in ignorance of the confidential nature of the material will be held liable for knowingly receiving the trade secret or continuing to use it after its trade secret status becomes known. Courts will generally impute knowledge where the second user is a corporation organized by a person owing a duty not to disclose the secret, and under some circumstances will impute knowledge to a second user merely because it should have known that the first user's former employee or some other party owing the first user a duty of non-disclosure was breaching that duty.

In *Carter Products, Inc. v. Colgate–Palmolive Co.* (1955), for example, the court imposed liability despite the absence of any direct evidence that a business, which had been seeking to reverse engineer plaintiff's successful "Rise" shave bomb and had hired a former employee of the independent research chemists who had developed the plaintiff's shave bomb, induced the employee to disclose plaintiff's trade secrets after the defendant business employed him. The court concluded that because the defendant must have known that the employee was bound by a non-disclosure agreement between his former employer and the plaintiff, it was obligated to do more than it did to ascertain what the employee could or could not disclose to the defendant before assigning him to do work which was known to be in direct competition with the work he had done for his former employer. The court's decision in *Carter Products* appears to have amounted to finding that the defendant either negligently or recklessly interfered with the contractual relations of the plaintiff. The Uniform Trade Secrets Act, by stating that a party must have "had reason to know" that information provided it was the trade secret of another, seems to require proof of a reckless disregard of the trade secrets of another.

C. AFFIRMATIVE DEFENSES AND REMEDIES

The Supreme Court eliminated the principle affirmative defense to a claim of trade secret misappropriation when it held in *Kewanee Oil Co. v. Bicron Corp.*, supra, that state trade secret law does not undermine federal patent law and is thus not preempted by it, even where the trade secret may be patentable. While federal patent law does not preempt any of the substance of state trade secret law, however, it arguably limits the scope of remedies that may be provided for trade secret misappropriation.

Prior to the *Sears–Compco* decisions, courts tended to grant permanent injunctive relief in trade secret cases as a matter of course, without placing any limits on the prohibition against further use of the trade secret. See, e.g., *Shellmar Products Co. v. Allen–Qualley Co.* (1936) (refusing to modify an injunction against further use of a trade secret, even though the secret had become public). Even before *Sears–Compco*, however, at least one lower court concluded that injunctive relief is precluded once a trade secret has become public and that thereafter only monetary relief (i.e., damages or an accounting) is appropriate. See *Conmar Products Corp. v. Universal Slide Fastener Co.* (1949), holding that issuance of a patent, which was subsequently declared invalid, precluded the grant of injunctive relief against a defendant who had come into possession of the invention prior to its public disclosure. The *Conmar* court went on to hold that a defendant who makes innocent use of a machine before learning that it is protected by a trade secrecy agreement between the employee who developed it and a former employer, is excused from liability for the period of innocent use. Because in *Conmar* the defendant's use was innocent until the moment the invention became public, the defendant escaped liability altogether.

After the *Sears–Compco* decisions, some lower courts concluded that in order to avoid undermining federal patent law, injunctive relief in trade secret cases must be limited even more narrowly than it was in *Conmar* to that period of time which would be required to discover the trade secret by proper means, such as reverse engineering or independent discovery. See, e.g., *Hampton v. Blair Manufacturing Co.,* supra, where the court concluded that as a result of *Sears–Compco* even a former employee who surreptitiously obtained blue prints and disobeyed a court order to turn them over to the court could not be permanently enjoined from copying unpatented farm implements but could only be enjoined for such time as would be required to reproduce the implements without the wrongful use of the blueprints.

While the Supreme Court did not discuss the question of relief in *Kewanee Oil,* it did order the appellate court to reinstate the trial court's injunction prohibiting disclosure or use of a trade secret until such time as the trade secret had been released to the public or had otherwise become available to the public or had been obtained by the defendant from sources having a legal right to convey the information. That grant of injunctive relief clearly permits the defendant to use the secret once it becomes public or has been independently discovered by a third party but does not explicitly limit the period of the injunction to the time it would have taken the *defendant* to independently discover the secret. The appropriate scope of injunctive relief in trade secret cases thus remains unclear.

In *Aronson v. Quick Point Pencil Co.* (1979), the Court went on to hold that federal patent law did not preclude state enforcement of a contract to pay royalties to a patent applicant for so long as the contracting party sells articles embodying the putative invention, if the patent is not granted. Implicit in that holding is that contract liability for royalties may continue even after the unpatented invention is publicly disclosed. In the absence of a contractual obligation to pay royalties, however, money liability should arguably be limited to the plaintiff's losses or the defendant's profits during the period of wrongful use. Such a rule excludes damages for innocent use or for use after the secret has become public.

In addition to the foregoing judicial remedies, a trade secret holder may petition the International Trade Commission, which has authority, subject to Presidential review, to issue cease and desist or exclusion orders to bar unfair methods of competition in the import trade, to prevent the importation of goods which misappropriate the trade secret. The Omnibus Trade and Competitiveness Act of 1988 declared one of the primary objectives of U.S. international trade negotiations to be ensuring adequate protection of trade secrets in foreign countries.

PART IV
INJURIOUS PROMOTIONAL AND PRICING PRACTICES

CHAPTER EIGHT
INJURIOUS PROMOTIONAL PRACTICES

The efforts of a business to market its product or service may be hampered if other businesses are not precluded from falsely advertising or otherwise unfairly promoting their products or services. Obtaining legal redress for such practices, however, has not always been easy. At common law, a business which is unable to establish that it has or is likely to suffer specific injury as a result of the deceptive or unfair promotional practices of another business will likely be denied relief, even though the practice complained of manifestly undermines the bargaining or competitive processes as a whole. Thus, the principal legal redress for many deceptive or unfair promotional practices has been provided by state or federal statutes. These statutes either relax the common-law requirements for obtaining private relief or provide for public regulation of injurious promotional practices.

The pricing practices of businesses have also been the subject of state and federal legislation. Regulation of pricing practices is to be distinguished from regulation of promotional practices. Although pricing may be used as a means of promoting a product or service, some pricing practices are unfair precisely because they are *not* designed to promote a product or service but rather to achieve some illicit objective. For that reason, injurious pricing practices will be considered separately in Chapter 9. The present chapter will focus on those business practices which are undertaken for the legitimate purpose of promoting a product or service but are nevertheless deemed deceptive or otherwise unfair.

It should be noted that a substantial body of law governing deceptive promotional practices—namely the law of trademarks and trade names and the law governing product substitution and alteration—has already been introduced in Part I. Those bodies of law are primarily concerned with providing private remedies to protect the existing good will of businesses against deceptive diversion or reputational injury. The body of law which is the subject of this chapter protects prospective as well as existing trade relations against unfair as well as deceptive promotional practices and provides for public as well as private remedies.

A. TRADE RELATIONS PROTECTED

Much of the law considered in this chapter protects prospective as well as existing trade relations of a business. These trade relations may include the employment and commercial customer relations of a business as well as its public relations. The common law of defamation and trade disparagement, for example, protect businesses against injurious falsehood, regardless of whether the falsehood interferes with an existing or purely prospective employment, commercial or consumer relation. Likewise, the largely statutory body of law prohibiting other types of deceptive or unfair advertising and promotional practices serves to protect various types of trade relations, prospective as well as existing. State statutes modeled on the Uniform Deceptive Trade Practices Act and the Unfair Trade Practices and Consumer Protection Law, for example, not only codify the common law's prohibitions against trademark and trade name infringement, palming off and trade disparagement but also prohibit other types of false advertising practices, such as bait-and-switch tactics, which are generally not actionable at common law. Similarly, section 43(a) of the Lanham Act provides a private remedy for any person likely to be damaged by the use of false designations of origin or by the use of false or misleading descriptions or representations of fact with any goods or services put into commerce. The Federal Trade Commission

Act and various other state and federal statutes provide public remedies for virtually all forms of false or misleading advertising and product labelling. Federal and state laws also provide various public and private remedies for such unfair practices as the bribery of an employee of another business in the course of bargaining relations with that business and the use of lotteries and certain types of games, contests, giveaways, premiums and trading stamp schemes in the course of one's consumer relations.

B. ACTIONABLE AND PRIVILEGED PROMOTIONAL PRACTICES

A promotional practice causing only economic injury is actionable if, but only if, in addition to doing private injury, it undermines bargaining or competition on the merits. Actionable promotional practices may be divided into those which are deceptive and those which, although not deceptive, have nevertheless been found to be unfair because of their tendency to undermine the bargaining or competitive processes.

1. DECEPTIVE PROMOTIONAL PRACTICES

Deceptive promotional practices threaten harm not only to those businesses or consumers being deceived but also those businesses which are denied an opportunity to bargain or compete as a result of the deception. Private legal redress for the latter type of harm, however, has not always been available. The common-law remedies for commercial victims of consumer-aimed false advertising, for example, are basically limited to those forms of false advertising, such as palming off, defamation and trade disparagement, which specifically identify the commercial victim of the third party deception. Other types of false advertising are actionable at common law only in the unusual case when one business can show that its customers have been or will be diverted by the false claims that another business is making about its own product, service or business. While state and federal statutes have broadened the private relief available for other types of deceptive advertising and promotional practices, often the only effective remedy is public regulation. Accordingly, the discussion which follows will first describe those deceptive promotional practices (other than trademark infringement and palming off) which are privately actionable at common law or by statute, and then describe the public regulation of potentially deceptive promotional practices.

a. Privately Actionable Deceptive Practices

(1) Defamation

The law of defamation protects the reputation of a person or business from communications which tend to lower the person or business in the eyes of the community or deter third parties from associating or dealing with them. Actually, the term "defamation" is simply a generic term which refers to the common-law torts of libel and slander.

Generally speaking, a slander is an ephemeral (usually oral) defamation, while libel is a written or otherwise tangibly transcribed defamation. Due to a presumably greater capacity to do harm, libels—or at least those whose defamatory meaning is apparent on the face of the statement—were traditionally actionable even in the absence of proof of special (i.e., actual pecuniary) damages, whereas an action for slander generally required proof of special damages. One exception to the requirement of special damages in actions for slander, however, was with regard to oral statements about another's trade or business. Where such slanders were defamatory on their face, they like libels were presumed to cause harm.

The victim of a defamation of either sort was not traditionally required to prove the falsity of the defamatory statement. Rather, the burden was on the maker of the statement to prove that the statement was true or that the maker had a good faith belief in its truth and some justification, such as self defense, defense of another or defense of the public interest, for having made the statement.

The practical effect of the foregoing rules was that the maker of a facially defamatory statement about another's business who could not prove it to be true or otherwise justified, would be held liable without regard to the maker's actual fault or the victim's actual injury. Even where a statement could be shown to have been made in defense of some legitimate private or public interest, victims of defamation were allowed to recover damages where the defendant published the statement more widely than was necessary or acted out of "actual malice." At common law, "actual malice" was defined as a desire to cause injury or a knowing or reckless disregard of the falsity of the statement. Proof of actual malice not only defeated an attempted justification for a defamatory statement but also permitted the recovery of punitive damages.

In *New York Times v. Sullivan* (1964) and *Gertz v. Robert Welch, Inc.* (1974), the U.S. Supreme Court in effect rewrote the law of defamation. In *New York Times v. Sullivan,* the Court held that the First Amendment prohibits a public official from recovering damages for a defamatory statement relating to his or her official conduct unless the official can prove that the statement was made with "actual malice"—which the Court defined as knowledge or reckless disregard of the statement's falsity. Constitutional "actual malice" is thus narrower than common law "actual malice" which, as we have seen, is defined as either a desire to injure or knowledge or reckless disregard of the falsity of the defamatory statement. The Court in *New York Times* expressly held that its rule applied to defamation actions brought against non-media as well as media defendants. In subsequent cases, the Court held that the *New York Times* rule applied in suits brought by public figures as well as in suits brought by public officials.

In *Gertz v. Welch,* the Court confirmed that the *New York Times* standard applied to actions brought by "public figures" but proceeded to limit its definition of "public figures" to those who have thrust themselves to the forefront of particular public controversies in order to influence the resolution of the issues involved. Intervening cases had indicated that anyone who found himself involved in a matter of public interest was a public figure. In *Gertz,* the plaintiff, a lawyer who represented the family of a shooting victim in a wrongful death action against a policeman who in unrelated criminal proceedings was convicted of the victim's murder, was held not to be a public figure merely because his representation of a client involved him in a matter of public interest. The Court in *Gertz* went on to hold that for defamation actions brought by persons who were not public figures the states were free to define for themselves, either by statute or judicial decision, the appropriate standard of liability so long as they (1) did not impose liability without fault, but required at least a showing of negligence on the defendant's part and (2) limited damages to the actual injury sustained in any case in which liability was based on a standard less exacting than the "actual malice" standard of *New York Times v. Sullivan.*

Unlike the *New York Times* decision, *Gertz* did not indicate whether the strictures it placed on defamation actions brought by private individuals applied only to cases brought against media defendants or to all cases of defamation. A number of state supreme courts, and now, the U.S. Supreme Court as well, have held that the *Gertz* strictures do not apply to defamation cases brought by private individuals against non-media defendants, at least where the defamation did not involve a matter of public concern, see *Dun & Bradstreet, Inc. v. Greenmoss Builders, Inc.* (1985) (holding that permitting recovery of presumed and punitive damages does not violate the First Amendment when the defamatory statements by a credit reporting agency falsely reporting that a construction company had filed a voluntary petition for bankruptcy was a purely private matter that did not raise matters of public concern). However, at least one state supreme court (albeit believing that the first part of its decision was required by *Gertz*) has opted to abolish the common-law rule allowing liability without regard to fault or injury, and has required instead a showing of negligence and, where the speaker enjoyed a conditional privilege as a former employer of the defamed person, a reckless disregard of the truth. See *Jacron Sales Co., Inc. v. Sindorf* (1976). Thus, the basis for imposing liability on a private non-media defendant for defamatory remarks about another's trade or business will vary from state to state and may or may not require a showing of the defendant's fault or the plaintiff's actual damage.

Although the Supreme Court in *Virginia State Board of Pharmacy v. Virginia Citizens Consumer Council, Inc.* reversed a long line of precedents holding that "commercial speech" (i.e. advertising) was not protected under the First Amendment, a footnote in the opinion and subsequent cases have made clear that the constitutional protection provided commercial speech is much more limited than that provided other forms of speech. In *U.S. Healthcare, Inc. v. Blue Cross of Greater Philadelphia* (1990), for example, a lower court held that comparative advertising raising community health issues of public concern was nevertheless commercial speech which, because it was less likely than other forms of speech to be chilled by the threat of legal liability, did not require the protection of the *New York Times* "actual malice" standard. The court went on to hold that, notwithstanding *Gertz,* companies engaged in such advertising were not public figures and that the *Gertz* test is simply "not helpful in the context of a comparative advertising war." Rather, the First Amendment requires no higher standard of liability for comparative advertising than is mandated by the substantive law of defamation, commercial disparagement, or unfair competition.

Whatever the requirements with regard to fault and damages, a defamatory statement must at least be shown to refer to a particular plaintiff. In *Fowler v. Curtis Publishing Co.* (1950), for example, an article which characterized Washington cab drivers as ill-mannered and dishonest and included a picture of one of plaintiff's fleet of cabs was held not to defame the owners of taxi cab companies (since it did not imply they were dishonest) nor any particular taxi cab driver (since it referred to them as a group).

Quite apart from any First Amendment protection, a defamation defendant may be privileged, purely as a matter of common law, to make what would otherwise be actionable defamatory statements. For example, a patent holder is privileged to publish its reasonable belief that another has infringed its patent, even if the other party is later found not to have infringed, so long as the patent holder acted without common-law actual malice. *Kemart Corporation v. Printing Arts Research Labs., Inc.* (1959).

Not every derogatory statement about a particular business is defamatory. A statement disparaging the quality of a product or service may be found to defame its producer but that is not always the case. In recognition of the difference between the basically personal interest in the integrity of one's reputation and the basically pecuniary interest in the reputation of a product or service, the courts have held that a disparaging statement about a product or service will not be considered defamatory per se of its producer unless by fair construction and without the aid of extrinsic evidence it imputes fraud, deceit, dishonesty or morally reprehensible conduct on the part of the producer in relation to the product or service. The mere denigration of the quality or value of a product or service has been held as a matter of law not to amount to a defamation. See *National Refinery Co. v. Benzo Gas Motor Fuel Co.* (1927) (holding a statement that benzol/gasoline mixture would corrode automobile engines did not amount to a charge that a producer of the mixture knowingly manufactured an unfit product and was thus not libelous). If one has a cause of action at all for such derogatory statements, it is for trade disparagement.

(2) Trade Disparagement

In order to make out a case of trade disparagement, plaintiffs have traditionally been required to plead and prove (1) the falsity of the disparaging statement, (2) common-law "actual malice" on the part of the defendant (i.e. desire to cause injury or knowing or reckless disregard of falsity of a statement), and (3) special damages resulting from the disparagement. These burdensome pleading and proof requirements have severely limited the action for trade disparagement and have led the victims of trade disparagement to attempt to characterize disparaging statements as defamatory wherever possible.

It is not always easy to distinguish statements which may be said to impute fraud, deceit, dishonesty or morally reprehensible conduct, from those which merely disparage the quality of a product or service. In the venerable case of *Dickes v. Fenne*

(1639), for example, it was held not to be actionable in the absence of proof of special damage, for one brewer to say, in reference to another brewer's product, that "he would give a peck of malt to his mare, and she should pisse as good beare as Dickes doth Brew." See also *National Refinery Co. v. Benzo Motor Fuel Co.*, supra (statement that benzol/gasoline mixture would corrode automobile engines held not libelous).

In *Harwood Pharmacal Co. v. National Broadcasting Co.* (1961), on the other hand, the court held it to be defamatory per se to say of plaintiff's product: "SNOOZ, the new aid for sleep. SNOOZ is full of all kinds of habit-forming drugs. Nothing short of a hospital stay will make you stop taking SNOOZ. You'll feel like a run-down hound dog and lose weight." Likewise in *Meyerson v. Hurlbut* (1938) an oral statement that plaintiff was cutting prices and selling below cost was held to be slanderous per se because it implied that plaintiff was violating statutes prohibiting such conduct and engaging in conduct widely disapproved of in the trade.

Some disparaging statements, however, are clearly not defamatory. For example, it is disparaging but not defamatory per se to falsely state that a person has gone out of business or to falsely imply that a music publisher's songs are not hits. Cf. *Advance Music Corp. v. American Tobacco Co.*, Chapter 1 supra. For statements of this sort, there can be no money recovery except upon proof of special damages. While some courts have insisted that a plaintiff be able to show the loss of particular customers by name, most courts today will also allow evidence of a general diminution in business and extrinsic facts showing that the business losses were a result of the false statement. Where there is more than one explanation for a diminution in business, however, the plaintiff bears the burden of proving what injuries were caused by the disparagement. In *Houston Chronicle Publishing Co. v. Martin* (1933), for example a jury verdict against a newspaper which had disparaged the quality of certain Brahma bulls imported by the plaintiff was reversed where it appeared that news of an outbreak of hoof and mouth disease among bulls purchased from plaintiff and a high mortality rate among Brahmas during freezing weather might have accounted for some or all of plaintiff's business losses.

For a time, virtually any person who was "newsworthy" would be a "public figure" subject to the stringent proof requirements imposed by the *New York Times* case. In *Gertz v. Welch,* however the Court narrowed the definition of a "public figure" to those who brought themselves to the forefront of public controversies. It would thus appear that businesses which do not come within that definition are not obliged as a constitutional matter to prove a knowing or reckless disregard of the falsity of a disparaging statement in order to make out a claim of disparagement against a media defendant. On the other hand, the *Gertz* prohibition against imposing liability without fault and its limitation of damages to the actual injury sustained in any case in which liability is based on a standard less exacting than that of *New York Times* would apparently apply to disparagement as well as defamation actions—at least where the claim is brought against a media defendant. As we have seen, however, the common law itself limits the action of disparagement still more narrowly, by requiring proof of both common-law actual malice and actual pecuniary injury. Where a disparaged business does come within the *Gertz* definition of a public figure, of course, the business will have to prove by clear and convincing evidence that the disparager acted with constitutional actual malice—i.e., a knowing or reckless disregard of the disparaging statement's falsity. *Bose Corporation v. Consumer's Union of the United States, Inc.* (1984) (holding that, particularly where a statement that certain stereo speaker sounds "tended to wander about the room" tread the line between fact and opinion, review of a trial court's actual malice determination is not limited to the clearly erroneous standard of Federal Rule of Civil Procedure 52(a) but must amount to de novo review, independently examining the record to ensure that the district court has applied properly the governing constitutional law and that the plaintiff has indeed satisfied its burden of proof). See also *U.S. Healthcare, Inc. v. Blue Cross of Greater Philadelphia* (1990) (holding that the *Gertz* public figure test is not applicable in the context of a comparative advertising war and that such speech is not in need of a higher standard of liability than is imposed by the substantive law of defamation, disparagement or unfair competition).

Although defamation has been the preferred legal theory for plaintiffs seeking to recover damages for derogatory statements about their product, service or business, disparagement has been the preferred theory where injunctive relief is being sought. Equity courts have historically been extremely reluctant to enjoin libels, basing their refusal to grant such relief on a variety of equitable maxims, such as equity's refusal to protect purely personal rights or to grant equitable relief where legal remedies (i.e., damages) are adequate. The judicial unwillingness to enjoin libels took on constitutional significance with the Supreme Court's decision in *Near v. Minnesota* (1931), where the Supreme Court struck down as unconstitutional a statute authorizing injunctions against defamatory publications. *Near* established as a broad First Amendment principle that, even though damages may be awarded for defamatory speech, the constitutionally protected interest in free dissemination of ideas forbids state imposed prior restraints on speech.

For a time, equity courts also declined to enjoin commercial disparagement. See, e.g., *Kidd v. Horry* (1886); *Marlin Firearms Co. v. Shields* (1902). Some courts, however, were willing to grant injunctive relief where a disparagement could be characterized as but a part of a broader course of tortious misconduct. See, e.g., *Emack v. Kane* (1888) (injunction issued against a patent owner for maliciously and in bad faith publishing a circular charging complainant with patent infringement and attempting to intimidate complainant's customers with threats of patent infringement if they used complainant's product). Eventually, even in cases where nothing more than a simple disparagement of goods was involved, some courts took the position that disparagement stood on a different footing than defamation and that injunctive relief should be made available for the protection of product, service or business good will in disparagement cases, just as it was available in cases of trademark infringement. See, e.g., *Black & Yates v. Mahogany Association* (1942) (stating that the action of disparagement of property has a place of its own in the law and is not a mere branch or special variety of the action for defamation of personal reputation or of the action for deceit). See also *Perma–Maid v. FTC* (1941), where the court upheld an FTC order forbidding a distributor of stainless steel cooking utensils from disparaging aluminum cooking utensils. But see *Scientific Manufacturing Co. v. FTC* (1941) (holding that the FTC was without power under the FTC Act to forbid a business having no connection with the manufacture or distribution of cooking utensils of any kind from publishing or distributing certain pamphlets disparaging aluminum cooking utensils).

The foregoing cases were decided before the Supreme Court held in *Virginia State Board of Pharmacy v. Virginia Citizens Consumer Council, Inc.* (1976) that commercial speech is protected under the First Amendment. That decision, however, apparently did little to alter the availability of injunctive relief in disparagement cases. The Court noted in its opinion that the prohibition against prior restraints on speech may well be inapplicable to commercial speech and that it foresaw no obstacle to a state's dealing effectively with the problem of deceptive or misleading commercial speech. The Court held only that a state may not forbid *truthful* price information.

Commercial speech, however, may need a certain amount of "breathing room," even though less than other forms of speech. At common law, for example, some derogatory statements about another's trade or business are held to be neither defamatory nor disparaging. General statements which take the form of an unfavorable comparison of products or services or which "puff" or exaggerate the quality of one's own product or service, for example, are not ordinarily actionable. The reason typically given is that such statements are mere expressions of opinion, the truth or falsity of which are impossible to ascertain. See, e.g., *White v. Mellin* (1895) (holding it not to be actionable to advertise "Dr. Vance's prepared food for infants and invalids," as being "far more nutritious and healthful than any other preparation yet offered.") Only where an unfavorable comparison makes assertions of specific facts will a disparagement be found. See, e.g., *Testing Systems, Inc. v. Magnaflux Corp.* (1966) (statement that plaintiff's product "is no good" and that "the government is throwing them out" held actionable). Likewise, one may be privileged, purely as a matter of common law, to make what would otherwise be disparaging statements. Cf. *Kemart Corporation v. Printing Arts Research Lab., Inc.* (1959) (holding a patent holder charged with "trade libel" to be privileged to publish its reasonable belief that another has infringed its patent, even if the other party is later found not to have infringed, so long as the patent holder acts without common-law actual malice).

The courts have been particularly solicitous of opinions expressed by consumer testing and rating organizations. Courts have not only refused to enjoin publication of unfavorable ratings, but have granted rating organizations injunctive relief to prevent businesses from publishing misleading or exaggerated reports of favorable ratings. See, e.g., *Consumers Union of the United States, Inc. v. Theodore Hamm Brewing Co.* (1970) (brewer temporarily enjoined from advertising that its beer had been rated "top beer in the country" by "Consumer Reports," when the beer was merely given a first class rating along with other brands of beer). Even here, however, it has been recognized that some puffing of a favorable rating may be permissible in advertising, and that rating organizations, no less than businesses puffing their own product, may be liable for recklessly disregarding facts.

See, e.g., *Advance Music Corp. v. American Tobacco Co.,* Chapter 1 supra (upholding a complaint alleging that ratings for songs used on the radio program "Hit Parade" were based on "caprice.").

(3) Other Deceptive Advertising and Promotional Practices

(a) Common Law Remedies for False Advertising. At one time, the common-law courts took the position that in the absence of evidence of palming off, defamation or disparagement, businesses simply had no cause of action for the consumer-aimed false advertising of rival businesses. See, e.g., *American Washboard Co. v. Saginaw Manufacturing Co.* (1900) ("It is doubtlessly morally wrong and improper to impose upon the public by the sale of spurious goods, but this does not give rise to a private right of action unless the property rights of the plaintiff are involved. There are many wrongs which can only be righted through public prosecution, and for which the legislature, and not the courts, must provide a remedy.")

In *Ely–Norris Safe Co. v. Mosler Safe Co.* (1925) the court created a narrow exception to the common-law rule, holding that if a tradesman falsely foists on a customer a substitute for what the plaintiff alone can supply, the plaintiff is not without remedy, if he can show that the customer would certainly have come to him, had the truth been told. While the *Ely–Norris* "single source" requirement was apparently met in the earlier *American Washboard* case, where the sole manufacturer of aluminum washboards had sought to enjoin a manufacturer of zinc washboards from falsely representing them as being made of aluminum, it was not met in the *Ely–Norris* case itself. In *Mosler Safe Co. v. Ely–Norris Safe Co.* (1927), the Supreme Court reversed the lower court decision, noting that although the plaintiff manufactured certain patented safes which had as their distinctive feature an explosion chamber designed for protection against burglars, there were apparently other safes with explosion chambers besides the plaintiff's. For that reason, the plaintiff failed to state cause of action.

Seldom have plaintiffs in common-law false advertising cases been any more successful. In one of the few cases where the plaintiff did succeed in stating a cause of action, *Electronics Corp. of America v. Honeywell, Inc.* (1970), the plaintiff alleged that the defendant, who manufactured a "programmer" designed to work in plaintiff's safety control system and compete with plaintiff's own programmers, utilized a brochure which misrepresented the ease with which defendant's programmer could be installed in plaintiff's system. The court noted that while there were other control system manufacturers besides the plaintiff, defendant's brochure and promotional activity was aimed at plaintiff's control system and that, as far as owners of plaintiff's system were concerned, the "programmer" market was effectively a two-firm market shared by plaintiff and defendant.

One limited exception to the *Ely–Norris* "single-source" requirement arises where a seller falsely advertises his goods as coming from a locality generally known for superior quality goods. In *Pillsbury–Washburn Flour–Mills Co. v. Eagle* (1898), for example, various flour manufacturers from Minneapolis, Minnesota, whose flour had built up a reputation for quality, succeeded in enjoining the defendant from falsely advertising his flour as coming from that city. See also *Grand Rapids Furniture Co. v. Grand Rapids Furniture Co.* (1942) (furniture manufacturers from Grand Rapids, Michigan allowed to bring a class action and held to have stated a cause of action entitling them to preliminary injunctive relief against a Chicago furniture store which falsely advertised its furniture as having come from Grand Rapids).

Beyond narrowly defined geographic limits, however, the courts have not been willing to go. In *California Apparel Creators v. Wieder of California, Inc.* (1947), for example, the court refused to allow a trade association and some seventy-five California wearing apparel manufacturers to bring a class action against three New York wearing apparel businesses who used the term "California" in connection with their business. The court distinguished *Grand Rapids,* supra, noting that the number of potential California plaintiffs was greater, their products had no obvious connection with the locality and there were no definite standards of quality or grading for California wearing apparel. The court also noted that the fact of injury had not and could not be shown, given the thousands of other California manufacturers and the unlikelihood of proof that specific customers had been diverted from specific plaintiffs through the actions of the defendants.

(b) State Deceptive Trade Practices Statutes. Dissatisfaction with the common-law remedies for false advertising led to the widespread enactment of state statutes providing businesses with a private right of action for the consumer-aimed deceptive practices of other businesses. Many states, for example, have enacted one version or another of the Uniform Deceptive Trade Practices Act (UDTPA). The UDTPA is comprehensive in its substantive coverage but limited in the type of relief it provides. As we noted earlier, the UDTPA not only codifies the common law's prohibitions against trademark and trade name infringement, palming off and trade disparagement, but also prohibits false advertising and a variety of other deceptive trade practices, such as bait and switch tactics, which are generally not actionable at common law. Any person who is likely to be damaged by the deceptive trade practices of another may obtain relief under the Act. The UDTPA specifies that neither monetary damage, loss of profits nor the defendant's intent to deceive need be proved. The only remedy available under the UDTPA, however, is injunctive relief—though the courts may be authorized to award attorney's fees to the prevailing party if the party bringing the claim knew it to be groundless or the party charged has been shown to have willfully engaged in an unfair trade practice knowing it to be deceptive. Some

states adopting the UDTPA have authorized damages for violation of the Act.

The Unfair Trade Practices and Consumer Protection Law (UTPCPL), by contrast, provides a much broader array of public and private remedies for consumers, and often for commercial parties as well, against deceptive and other unfair practices. State statutes modelled on the UTPCPL are often called "Little FTC Acts," both because the UTPCPL was proposed by the FTC for adoption by the states and because its provisions generally parallel the Federal Trade Commission Act and frequently provide that state courts are to give great weight to opinions of the federal courts and the FTC defining unfair and deceptive acts under the FTC Act. The latter provision has the effect of incorporating FTC law into the substantive law of each state.

(c) Federal Statutory Remedies: Section 43(a) of the Lanham Act and RICO. To recover damages as well as injunctive relief for consumer-aimed deceptive practices, businesses have increasingly relied on a once obscure provision of the Lanham Act. Section 43(a) of the Lanham Act, 15 U.S.C.A. § 1125(a), as amended by the Trademark Revision Act of 1988, applies to four types of statements— namely 1) any word, term, name, symbol, or device, or any combination thereof; 2) any false designation of origin; 3) any false or misleading description of fact; or 4) any false or misleading representation of fact. The amended section 43(a) goes on to prohibit two sorts of misconduct. To be action-

able the statement must either 1) be likely to cause confusion or mistake or to deceive as to the relationship between the person making the statement and another person or their goods, services or commercial activities, or 2) misrepresent in commercial advertising or promotion the nature, characteristics, qualities or geographic origin of the goods, services or commercial activities of either the person making the statement or of another person. Statements of the first two types seem to relate to misconduct of the first sort, while statements of the second two types seem to relate to misconduct of the second sort. The two sorts of misconduct defined by amended section 43(a) may be thought of as 1) any form of product, service or business misidentification of the palming off variety, and 2) any other form of false or misleading advertising, whether disparaging of another's product, service or business or falsely describing or representing one's own.

These two substantive prohibitions differ in significant respects from the original section 43(a). To understand the changes brought about by the 1988 amendment to section 43(a) some reference to interpretive problems that arose under the original version of the statute is required.

At first, courts viewed section 43(a) merely as a codification of the common-law rule that a commercial plaintiff complaining of false advertising must be either the victim of palming off, the "single source" of the goods falsely advertised, or the producer of goods in a limited geographic area whose designation was being misused. See, e.g., *Chamberlain v. Columbia Pictures Corp.* (1951). The prevailing view however, was that section 43(a) created a sui generis federal statutory tort which is not limited by the common law. See, e.g., *L'Aiglon Apparel v. Lana Lobell, Inc.* (1954) ("Congress has defined a statutory civil wrong of false representation of goods in commerce and has given a broad class of suitors injured or likely to be injured by such wrong the right to relief in the federal courts").

The principal interpretive problems with respect to section 43(a) were over who had standing to sue, what sorts of misconduct were actionable, and under what circumstances monetary as well as injunctive relief could be obtained. By its terms, the original section 43(a) protected two classes of plaintiffs against two types of misconduct. The section prohibited (1) false designations of origin of goods or services and (2) false descriptions or representations of the same and provided a civil action for (1) any person doing business in the locality falsely indicated and (2) any person who believes that he is or is likely to be damaged by the use of any such false description or representation.

In determining who had standing to sue, the courts concluded that "any person" included not only direct competitors but trade associations. In *Mutation Mink Breeders Association v. Lou Nierenberg Corp.* (1959), for example, an association of over 5,000 mink breeders was allowed to bring an action for damages, injunctive relief and an accounting for profits against certain defendants who allegedly manufactured garments designed to simulate mink and falsely represented that the garments were made of mink or had the characteristics of mink. Another court held that "any person" included the state of Florida in its capacity as the owner of "Sunshine Tree," a common-law certification mark for citrus-fruits, even though the state was not a competitor of the defendant. *Florida v. Real Juices, Inc.* (1971).

On the other hand, a majority of the courts concluded that "any person" did not include consumers, even though they too are "likely to be damaged" by false representations. See, e.g., *Colligan v. Activities Club of New York, Ltd.* (1971) (relying heavily on section 45 of the Lanham Act, 15 U.S.C.A. § 1127, which states in pertinent part that "The intent of this Act is ... to protect persons engaged in commerce against unfair competition"). See also *Florida ex rel. Broward County v. Eli Lilly & Co.* (1971) (State of Florida does not have standing to sue on behalf of a class of consumers for certain false representations allegedly made by the defendant pharmaceutical firm). But see *Arnesen v. Raymond Lee Organization, Inc.* (1971) (Inventor allowed to bring a class action against a "patent service" for alleged false representations about the nature of its business); *Thorn v. Reliance Van Co., Inc.* (1984) (rejecting *Colligan* as contrary to the plain meaning of the statute and holding that an individual investor had standing to maintain an action under § 43(a)). See also section 45 of the Lanham Act, 15 U.S.C.A. § 1127, which states that another purpose of the Act is to "prevent fraud and deception in ... commerce." The proposed amended version of section 43(a) contained in the bill that was to become the Trademark Revision Act of 1988 originally included a provision making it clear that consumers had standing to sue under section 43(a). As a result of a political compromise, however, this provision was deleted, thus leaving the matter of consumer standing unsettled. See Cong.Rec. H1207–02 (April 13, 1989).

As we have seen, the types of misconduct actionable under the original section 43(a) fell into two broad groups: False designations of origin and false descriptions or representations. The principal interpretive question with respect to false designations of origin was whether section 43(a) extended merely to false designations of *geographic* origin or to false designations of origin generally. In *Federal–Mogul–Bower Bearings, Inc. v. Azoff* (1963) the court held that the language of section 43(a) was not limited to false designations of geographic origin and that plaintiff could bring an action for deceptive imitation of his product and packaging. That case was criticized for having ignored the fact that section 43(a) defined the class of plaintiffs who may sue for false designations of origin as those doing business in the locality falsely indicated. This limiting language suggested that the original section 43(a) was merely codifying a specific line of common-law cases (namely the geographic origin cases discussed on p. 352 supra) and not engulfing the entire field of unfair competition.

On the other hand, the language of section 43(a) itself went on to specify that its prohibition of false descriptions or representations included "words or other symbols tending falsely to describe or represent" goods or services and that an action for such false descriptions or representations could be maintained by any person who believes he is or is likely to be damaged by the false description or representation. This language, together with section 45's statement that the intent of the Lanham Act is to protect persons engaged in commerce against unfair competition indicated that the purpose of section 43(a) was not as narrow as the critics of the *Federal–Mogul–Bower Bearings* case suggest.

In any event, the original section 43(a) was subsequently broadly construed as a vehicle for obtaining relief for a wide variety of common-law palming off claims, including deceptive product imitation, deceptive packaging and trade dress, deceptive imitation of unregistered marks and names, deceptive association of non-competing products, deceptive literary and artistic titles. Section 43(c) was also used as the basis for asserting more novel claims, such as the claim by one who has abandoned a mark that another is nevertheless using it as a "false designation of origin," see *Exxon Corp. v. Humble Exploration Co., Inc.* (1983) (dictum); *Manhattan Industries, Inc. v. Sweater Bee by*

Banff, Ltd. (1980) (dictum), and a claim by a creative group that a TV network engaged in deceptive mutilation of an artistic work. *Gilliam v. American Broadcasting Companies, Inc.* (1976) (holding that writers and performers of TV Show "Monty Python" were entitled to preliminary relief under section 43(a) to prevent a broadcasting company licensed to distribute the series from broadcasting edited versions of the show). But cf. *Girl Scouts of the United States of America v. Personality Posters Manufacturing Co.* (1969) (no cause of action under section 43(a) for a poster composed of a pregnant girl in a Girl Scout uniform and the Girl Scout motto "Be Prepared," in the absence of evidence of customer confusion over the origin of the goods). See also *U.S. Golf Association v. St. Andrews Systems, Data–Max, Inc.* (1984) (holding that a marketer of a small computer programmed to calculate a golfer's handicap, using a U.S.G.A.-developed formula, did not employ a false designation of origin by marketing the computer, even if the public did associate the formula with the U.S.G.A., because the formula was "functional"). By retaining the "false designation of origin" language of the original section 43(a) but omitting "any person doing business in the locality falsely indicated" as a specific class of persons entitled to sue, the amended section 43(a) in effect codifies the earlier cases construing the original section 43(a) broadly to reach all forms of palming off. In addition, by extending the scope of the prohibition to reach misleading statements about one's own or another's "goods, services or *commercial activities*," the amended section 43(a) appears to provide a federal remedy for trade name infringement.

Section 43(a)'s original prohibition against "any false description or representation" of goods or services was also used as the basis for bringing a wide variety of false advertising claims for which there may have been no common-law remedy. In some of these cases the defendant's false description or representation also constituted an appropriation of the results of plaintiff's investment of money and labor, while in others, the defendant simply claimed attributes for its own product which the product did not possess.

Included in the first type of false description or representation were cases such as *L'Aiglon Apparel, Inc. v. Lana Lobell, Inc.,* supra, in which the plaintiff was held to have a cause of action against a defendant who allegedly used a photograph of plaintiff's more expensive dress to advertise defendant's inferior and less expensive dress. See also *Boston Professional Hockey Association, Inc. v. Dallas Cap and Emblem Manufacturing, Inc.* (1975) (holding that defendant's reproduction of a professional hockey team's symbol on an embroidered emblem to be sold to the public as a patch for attachment on clothing, amounted to a false representation under section 43(a)).

In a number of cases, such as *Mutation Mink Breeders Association v. Lou Nierenberg Corp.,* supra, plaintiffs were held to have stated a claim under section 43(a) against defendants charged merely with claiming attributes for their own product which it did not in fact possess. Section 43(a)'s prohibition against false descriptions or representations of that sort was construed to extend to misleading as well as demonstrably false statements. In *Yameta Co. v. Capitol Records, Inc.,* for example, the singer Jimi Hendrix and the record company with which he was then associated were held to have stated a section 43(a) claim against another record producer who displayed the name and picture of Hendrix on a record album cover, thereby allegedly creating the impression that Hendrix was the featured performer, when he was merely the accompanist. See also *Follett v. Arbor House Publishing Co.* (1980) (holding that section 43(a) was designed not only to prevent distortion of an author's work but to prevent attributing principal authorship to a writer who merely rewrote, edited and added to a preexisting manuscript).

The amended section 43(a) codifies the foregoing cases by extending the scope of section 43(a)'s prohibition to reach "false or *misleading*" descriptions or representations.

Often, a defendant will be found to have made false or misleading representations in the course of comparing its product with others. In *Bernard Food Industries, Inc. v. Dietene Co.* (1969), the court held that it was not sufficient for a section 43(a) claim that the defendant disparaged (i.e., made false or misleading representations about) plaintiff's product. Defendant must have made false representations about its own product as well. This conclusion was thought to be mandated by the language of section 43(a) itself, which required that the false description or representation be in connection with goods or services which the person making the false description or representation caused to enter into commerce. But cf. *Skil Corp. v. Rockwell International Corp.* (1974) (holding that the plaintiff stated a cause of action under section 43(a) against a defendant for statements made in advertisements comparing portable electric tools since the defendant allegedly misrepresented its own product as well as disparaging plaintiff's). See also *American Home Products Corp. v. Johnson & Johnson* (1977) (comparative advertisement claiming that Anacin worked faster and relieved inflammation better than Tylenol held to be actionable under section 43(a)).

The amended section 43(a) explicitly prohibits misrepresentations concerning "the nature, characteristics, qualities or geographic origin of his or her or *another person's* goods, services, or commercial activities." Thus, a cause of action for disparagement, presumably shorn of the common-law requirements of malice and special damages, is now available as a matter of federal law.

Just as the original section 43(a) did not extend to disparaging statements, so it was held not to prohibit truthful comparative claims. See, e.g., *Societe Comptoir De L'Industrie Cotonniere Estab-*

lissements Boussac v. Alexander's Department Stores, Inc. (1962) (truthful assertion that one's dresses are copies of original "Dior" dresses not actionable under section 43(a)). A more debatable issue was whether a defendant who made no affirmative representations at all but merely failed to disclose an arguably material fact could be held liable under section 43(a). In *Alfred Dunhill Ltd. v. Interstate Cigar Co., Inc.* (1974) the court, holding that section 43(a) applied only to actual representations made, reversed a lower court's conclusion that sales of damaged tobacco in original tins bearing trademarks associated with high quality tobacco goods, without adequate warnings to customers that the goods are damaged, constituted false representations of their quality. Similarly, in *Universal City Studios, Inc. v. Sony Corp. of America* (1977) the court held that defendant's failure to warn purchasers of the Betamax recorder that use of the recorder to copy TV programs could violate copyright laws, failed to state a claim under section 43(a). In *Bohsei Enterprises Co. v. Porteous Fastener Co.* (1977), on the other hand, the court held that failure to name the country from which an imported product originated could constitute a violation under section 43(a). See also *Boston Professional Hockey Association v. Dallas Cap & Emblem Manufacturing, Inc.,* supra (holding that the mere duplication of a professional hockey team's symbol on an embroidered emblem to be sold to the public as a patch for attachment on clothing constituted a false representation within the meaning of section 43(a)). Even after the 1988 amendment, the issue of liability under section 43(a) for deceptive nondisclosures remains unsettled.

A final interpretive problem arising under the original section 43(a) was with respect to the remedies which were available for its violation. Section 43(a) says nothing about what relief may be awarded, and the other remedies provisions of the Lanham Act were originally concerned exclusively with providing remedies for infringement of federally registered marks. The courts were thus left to formulate their own remedial guidelines. To obtain injunctive relief a plaintiff needed only to show a likelihood of damage as a result of a material false representation (i.e., a false representation that was likely to deceive consumers). This test was similar to that governing the availability of injunctive relief for trademark infringement. The recovery of damages, on the other hand, was held to depend on proof that the public has in fact been deceived and that the plaintiff has in fact suffered a loss. Proof of loss, however, was not limited to proof of specific lost sales, as it would be in common law false advertising cases. In *L'Aiglon Apparel, Inc. v. Lana Lobell* (1954), for example, the plaintiff was awarded $17,500 in compensatory damages for the forced sale of its dresses and piece goods after it abandoned the particular dress style and for loss of good will resulting from defendant's acts. At least one court, moreover, drew an analogy to antitrust cases, where the courts do not require as high a degree of proof of the extent of damages as they do of the existence of damage. See *Bangor Punta Operations, Inc. v. Universal Marine Co., Ltd.* (1976) (upholding a $200,000 jury verdict for common law copyright infringement and a section 43(a) violation). In *Rickard v. Auto Publisher, Inc.* (1984) the court held that the express purpose and intent of the Lanham Act was best served by permitting all of the § 35 remedies, including attorney's fees, in § 43(a) cases. The 1988 amendment codified the foregoing view by amending sections 34(a), 35(a) and 36 of the Lanham Act to make it clear that the remedies provided in these sections (namely injunctions, profits, damages, including possible treble damages as a form of liquidated damages, costs, attorney fees in exceptional cases, and destruction of infringing articles) apply to cases brought under section 43(a). See, e.g., *Alpo Petfoods, Inc. v. Ralston Purina Co.* (1990) (holding that an award of profits in a section 43(a) case, as in cases involving infringement of registered marks, requires proof of bad faith or willful misconduct, and that damages can include profits lost by the plaintiff on sales actually diverted or sales at reduced prices resulting from the false ads, cost of counter ads, and quantifiable harm to good will).

A second federal statute to which increasing numbers of victims of deceptive promotional practices are turning is the Racketeer Influenced and Corrupt Organizations Act (RICO), 18 U.S.C. §§ 1961–1968, which allows the recovery of treble damages by any person injured in his business or property as a result of certain activities constituting "*a pattern of racketeering activity*," which is defined to include (among other things) two or more acts violating federal mail fraud and wire fraud statutes, 18 U.S.C.A. §§ 1341, 1343. Virtually any false communication, including false advertising and deceptive promotional practices, would violate the language of the federal mail and wire fraud statutes. See, e.g., *Sutliff v. Donovan Companies, Inc.* (1984) (holding that two oil wholesalers who created a false impression of a supplier's solvency in order to induce the extension of credit to the financially troubled firm, which the wholesalers controlled, constituted fraud in its commonest form and was thus actionable under RICO).

b. Public Regulation of Promotional Practices

Public regulation of promotional practices may take the form of criminal legislation or legislation creating a special government regulatory agency. Although criminal statutes modelled on the Printers Ink Model Statute (so named because it was drafted for an advertising industry trade journal named "Printers Ink") have been widely adopted, they have generally been ineffective—due partly to the strict construction given them by the courts on account of their penal nature and partly to the failure of public prosecutors to enforce them. The enforcement efforts of state and federal regulatory agencies, by contrast, have been more extensive and wide-ranging. The most prominent of these government agencies is the Federal Trade Commission. The International Trade Commission has been given somewhat narrower authority to regulate trade practices in the import trade of the U.S.

The Federal Trade Commission (FTC) was created in 1914 as a part of a two-pronged effort by Congress to improve enforcement of the antitrust laws. Whereas the Clayton Antitrust Act of 1914 prohibited certain specifically defined types of anticompetitive conduct and provided a broad range of public and private remedies, including private treble damages actions, for its enforcement, the FTC Act broadly prohibited "unfair methods of competition in commerce" and expressly created a specialized agency, having power to issue administrative cease and desist orders, as the exclusive device for its enforcement.

Section 5's prohibition of "unfair methods of competition in commerce" became the linchpin of the FTC's authority to regulate promotional practices. While the Supreme Court initially declared that it was for the judiciary and not the FTC to say what constitutes an "unfair method of competition," it subsequently made it clear that it would give considerable weight to the FTC's opinion. Thus, for all practical purposes, the FTC has had the power not only to prevent "unfair methods of competition" but also to say what that phrase means. This it has done both through administrative adjudication and through the promulgation of administrative rules. The International Trade Commission has more limited authority to issue exclusion orders or cease and desist orders (subject to review by the U.S. Trade Representative and the President) to prevent unfair methods of competition in the import trade of the U.S.

In 1938 the Wheeler–Lea Amendments greatly extended the FTC's authority by amending section 5 of the FTC Act so as to prohibit "unfair or deceptive acts or practices in commerce," thereby allowing the FTC to protect the consumer without having to show any simultaneous threat to competitors. Wheeler–Lea also added a new section (§ 12) specifically empowering the FTC to prevent false advertisements in the promotion of foods, drugs, therapeutic devices or cosmetics, thereby complementing the authority of the Federal Food and Drug Administration (FDA) to regulate the *labelling* of such products. (In 1962, the FDA was given exclusive authority to regulate the advertising as well as the labelling of *prescription* drugs.)

Although the principal purpose of the Wheeler–Lea Amendments was to grant the FTC specific authority to protect the consumer from deceptive acts or practices, the amendments also had the effect of legislatively confirming prior case law which had held that business methods need not threaten a reduction in competition in order to be "unfair methods of competition" within the meaning of the FTC Act. These cases had held that methods which tend to eliminate honesty in competition no less than those which tend to eliminate competition itself are unfair methods of competition.

A number of subsequent legislative enactments have given the FTC specific authority over the labelling of certain products (i.e., wool products, fur products and textile fiber products), the packaging of a variety of consumer products and the regulation of a number of other consumer-related practices (e.g., credit and debt collection practices, credit reporting and consumer warranty practices). Section 5 of the FTC Act, however, remains at the core of the FTC's regulatory authority. Indeed, the single most significant expansion of the FTC's powers occurred in 1975 with the enactment of the Magnuson–Moss Consumer Warranty/Federal Trade Commission Improvement Act (FTC Improvement Act of 1975), which among other things extended the FTC's section 5 authority to include prevention of "unfair methods of competition in *or affecting* commerce and unfair or deceptive acts or practices in *or affecting* commerce." This amendment brings within the FTC's jurisdiction essentially local commercial practices which nevertheless have an adverse impact on interstate commerce. Prior to the FTC Improvement Act of 1975, the interstate commerce requirement constituted a significant jurisdictional limitation on the FTC's power. Although Congress stated that this expansion of the FTC's jurisdiction did not itself in any way preempt state law, the FTC presumably has the authority to administratively preempt state law which conflicts with its enforcement efforts under the Act. But cf. *American Optometric Association v. FTC* (1980) (noting in dictum that the FTC's proposed preemption of state laws on advertising ophthalmic goods and services "at least approached the outer boundaries of its authority and may have infringed on that deference to the state's exercise of their [sic] police powers dictated by the principles of federalism.").

State law often augments rather than undermines the FTC's enforcement efforts. See page 354, supra. Indeed, state statutes prohibiting unfair deceptive or unconscionable practices not only augment the FTC Act but are important in their own right for, unlike the FTC Act, they generally provide consumers (and sometimes competitors) with a private right of action for damages and injunctive relief. See, e.g., *Committee on Children's Television v. General Foods Corp.* (1983), reversing the dismissal of a complaint framed a class action and alleging that the defendant cereal company engaged in deceptive advertising in connection with children-aimed television commercials for sugared breakfast cereals. These allegations were the same as those investigated by the FTC in its controversial "Kid-vid" rulemaking proceeding, see 43 Fed.Reg. 17967 (1978), which the FTC eventually terminated without taking any action after intense Congressional criticism.

In addition to the FTC Act's interstate commerce requirement, a second ostensible jurisdictional limitation on the FTC's power is that its proceedings against an act or practice or method of competition must be "in the public interest." The public interest requirement has been held to mean that the FTC had no jurisdiction over controversies essentially private in nature. Thus, the FTC's jurisdiction over unfair trade practices arguably extends only to those unfair trade practices which pose a substantial threat to the competitive process or the consuming public. The courts, however, have shown great deference to the FTC's public interest determinations and only once has an FTC decision been reversed on this basis. See *FTC v. Klesner* (1929).

While for a time doubt existed as to the power of the FTC to promulgate substantive rules (i.e., rules having the force of law as opposed to interpretative rules merely stating the FTC's understanding of the meaning of its statutory mandate) the power to promulgate substantive rules that define unfair or deceptive acts or practices was judicially recognized in *National Petroleum Refiners Association v. FTC* (1973) (the Octane Posting case) and later legislatively confirmed in the FTC Improvement Act of 1975, which added a new section 18 to the FTC Act, detailing specific rulemaking procedures to be followed in promulgating rules defining unfair or deceptive acts or practices. The Octane Posting case, supra, indicated that the FTC also has power to promulgate substantive rules defining unfair methods of competition, though the informal rulemaking procedures of the Administrative

Procedure Act, rather than the elaborate procedures of section 18, are presumably all that need be followed. Not surprisingly, after 1975 FTC trade regulation rules proliferated.

For violations of an FTC rule or the underlying statute, the enforcement procedure (where neither pre-complaint assurances of voluntary compliance nor a post-complaint consent order are obtained) will take the form of a formal adjudicatory hearing conducted pursuant to the procedures set forth in the Administrative Procedure Act and the FTC Act itself. Where a violation of the FTC Act or an FTC rule is found, various remedial tools are available. For most of its history the FTC was limited to issuing cease-and-desist orders. Although the terms of such orders were largely within the discretion of the FTC, they were only enforceable in civil proceedings brought by the Justice Department in federal court, with a maximum civil penalty of $5,000 per violation of the order. In 1973 the FTC was given power to represent itself in court and the civil penalty was raised to $10,000 per violation. The FTC Improvement Act of 1975 authorized the FTC to seek civil penalties in federal court for violations of trade regulation rules and for conduct known by the defendant to have been determined in a previous cease-and-desist proceeding (whether the defendant was a party to that proceeding or not) to be unfair or deceptive. The FTC Improvement Act also authorized the FTC to seek various forms of consumer redress in state and federal court. The cease-and-desist order, however, remains the chief administrative remedy available for the prevention of unfair methods of competition and unfair or deceptive acts or practices. It can be used to order corrective advertising, where necessary to eliminate the lingering effects of past deceptions. See p. 196 supra.

The FTC's exercise of its expanded enforcement powers under the FTC Improvement Act of 1975, together with its decision to inquire into the fairness of advertising aimed at children, precipitated an almost immediate Congressional reaction. After twice allowing funding for the FTC briefly to run out, Congress in the FTC Improvement Act of 1980 for the first time placed significant legislative limitations on the FTC. The Act required that Congress be given an opportunity to legislatively veto a proposed final FTC rule by concurrent resolution within 90 days of its submission; required the FTC to prepare a detailed cost/benefit analysis for every proposed and final rule; required the FTC to publish agendas listing rules it expects to propose or issue; provided the FTC with only limited authority to investigate and promulgate rules concerning children's advertising, the funeral home industry and the insurance industry; and denied the FTC authority for the next three years to petition for cancellation of a trademark on grounds that it has become generic. The latter provision temporarily halted the FTC's attempt to promote competition among manufacturers of synthetic surfaces by having the trademark "Formica" declared a generic term.

Congress first used its legislative veto to overturn the FTC's controversial proposed rules governing the sale of used cars. The legislative veto was itself declared unconstitutional in not providing for submission to the President for signature, *Consumers' Union v. FTC* (1982), aff'd, 463 U.S. 1216 (1983), and the FTC ultimately adopted a watered down version of the original rules, as well as rules governing the funeral industry.

Notwithstanding the foregoing limitations on the FTC, the core of the FTC's substantive mandate remains intact. That mandate, as we have seen, may be divided into the FTC's authority to prevent deceptive acts and practices and its authority to prevent other unfair acts or practices and unfair methods of competition.

(1) Federal Trade Commission Regulation of Deceptive Acts or Practices

The FTC's authority over deceptive acts or practices encompasses those promotional activities which have the capacity to deceive consumers and to materially affect their purchasing decisions. These two elements comprise the FTC's entire burden of proof in a deceptive practice proceeding.

(a) The Capacity to Deceive. The "capacity to deceive" element is as significant for what it omits as for what it includes. Neither knowledge that an act or practice is deceptive nor intent to deceive need be shown. Nor must the FTC show that the

challenged act or practice actually deceived consumers. *Charles of the Ritz Distributors Corp. v. FTC* (1944). It is enough, according to *Charles of the Ritz,* that the act or practice, taken as a whole, has a capacity to deceive the ordinary consumer. The test for deceptiveness thus bears a strong resemblance to the "likelihood of confusion" test for trademark infringement. See Chapter 4 supra.

Whether the ordinary consumer should be deemed to be credulous and gullible or reasonably prudent and alert is a matter about which the FTC and the courts have vacillated, for the understandable reason that the question admits of no easy answer. On the one hand, the greater the protection provided credulous and gullible consumers the greater the tendency to stifle commercial speech and thus hamper the operation of the competitive process. Taken to extremes, virtually any assertion about a product, service or business would have to be so qualified that it would no longer be commercially advantageous to make the statement at all. (Who, after all, would place an ad which states that: "Caffeine Brand Coffee is ground from the finest coffee beans—but, then, so are most of the competing brands and none of them is particularly good for you.") On the other hand, to limit the law's prohibition against deception to those acts or practices which would deceive a reasonably prudent and alert consumer gives unscrupulous businesses a license to prey on precisely those consumers most in need of protection. A real tension exists, in short, between the FTC's mandate to protect the competitive process and its mandate to protect the consumer.

Although the court in *Charles of the Ritz* held that the FTC should have the discretion to protect even "wayfaring fools" if it so chose, the FTC, after initially choosing to do just that, has since adopted progressively narrower tests for what constitutes deceptive acts or practices. In a 1983 letter to the chairman of a congressional oversight committee, the FTC spelled out its latest enforcement policy with respect to deceptive acts or practices, stating the test to be whether a representation, omission or practice is *likely* to mislead a *reasonable* consumer or a reasonable or ordinary member of an audience, such as children, the elderly or the terminally ill, whose capacity to reason may be impaired. The FTC first applied that test and upheld a finding that the value and performance of an automobile engine attachment had been misrepresented in *Cliffdale Associates, Inc.* (1984), which reprints the 1983 letter as an appendix.

Those acts or practices found to have the requisite capacity to deceive have generally taken one of three forms: (1) direct representations; (2) implied representations; or (3) material nondisclosures. Direct representations are easy enough to identify. The principal difficulty which arises with respect to such representations is whether vague or abstract claims ("New!" "Improved!") are in fact true or false. Identifying what representations are implied or what material facts have been omitted from an advertisement or other promotional activity, on the other hand, is a more difficult task. For example, does the direct representation that a product is "New!" deceptively imply that it is improved or deceptively fail to disclose a material fact by not adding that the "new" product is in fact a watered down version of the old? Faced with such imponderables, the courts have for the most part deferred to the FTC's "expertise" in resolving these questions.

The FTC, for its part, has found implied misrepresentations in cases involving deceptive trademarks, service marks or trade names, deceptive product configurations and trade dress, deceptive illustrations, demonstrations and mockups, inconspicuous or obtuse qualifying statements, ambiguous advertising claims and even technically true statements whose overall implication is nevertheless misleading. The FTC's broadest finding with respect to implied misrepresentations came in its conclusion that *any* advertising claim carries with it the implicit representation that the claimant has a reasonable basis for making the claim and any claim for which no such substantiation in fact exists *at the time the claim was made* is by definition deceptive, whether or not the claim later turns out to be true. The FTC has used this theory, together with its power to prohibit unfair but non-deceptive trade practices as the basis for its advertising substantiation program. See e.g., *Pfizer, Inc.* (1972) (holding it to be an unfair practice to make an affirmative product claim without a reasonable basis for making the claim). See also *American Home Products Corp. v. FTC* (1982) (upholding an FTC requirement of two or more well-controlled clinical studies to substantiate an overt claim of superiority in comparative advertising involving non-prescription drugs where a substantial question exists as to the superiority claim); *Thompson Medical Co. v. FTC* (1986) (upholding the imposition of a similar requirement for a non-comparative efficacy claim for a non-prescription drug). But see FTC Policy Statement Regarding Advertising Substantiation, 49 Fed.Reg. 31000 (1984), in which the FTC reaffirmed its commitment to its advertising substantiation program, but announced that in the future investigations would not take the form of industry-wide "rounds" nor be made public before completion, but would proceed on a case-by-case basis. The FTC also emphasized that post-claim evidence of the truth of a product claim, although not a substitute for pre-claim substantiation, is nevertheless relevant in determining whether it is in the public interest to proceed against a firm or what the appropriate scope of an order against a firm lacking pre-claim substantiation is.

The FTC has never posited an affirmative duty on the part of advertisers to "tell all." Deceptive nondisclosures have thus generally consisted of the omission of those facts which are necessary to make other express or implied representations not misleading. An FTC finding of a deceptive nondisclosure, in other words, is for the most part simply another way of saying that some other express or implied representation is deceptive. The FTC has found material nondisclosures, for example, where advertising contained express or implied half-truths, where well-known products have been changed in a significant yet nonobvious way, and where the appearance of a product is inherently deceptive (e.g., it appears to be new or composed of a certain material but is in fact used or an imitation). These cases complement the FTC's explicit authority under the Wool, Fur and Textile Labelling Acts and the Fair Packaging and Labelling Act to require the affirmative disclosure of information on the labels and packaging of various consumer products.

The most extreme example of deceptive nondisclosure is the FTC's conclusion that goods of foreign origin which are not so marked deceptively fail to disclose a material fact. That conclusion rests on two increasingly questionable assumptions—namely that the ordinary consumer believes that goods sold in this country have been manufactured in this country and that the ordinary consumer prefers American-made goods. While these assumptions may have been true in the immediate post-World War II period, it is becoming less true with every passing trade deficit. A number of GATT signatories have objected that the FTC rule facilitates discrimination against foreign goods, thereby violating GATT's Article IX.

At least one facet of the FTC's concern with preventing material nondisclosures seems to go altogether beyond the prevention of implicit deceptions in the marketing of products and services.

This is FTC's insistence upon at least limited disclosure, in the advertising for a product (and not merely on its label), of any potential dangers to consumer health or safety. Although the mere marketing of a product or service may or may not impliedly represent that the product or service is entirely safe and poses no danger to consumers, the thrust of the FTC's concern is not merely that consumers will be deceptively induced to purchase products or services posing a threat to health or safety but that consumers will be deprived of information needed to use the product or service safely once it is purchased. FTC authority to require disclosure of such information in advertising is as much a function of its power to prevent "unfair" acts or practice as it is a function of its power to prevent deception. See, e.g., *In re International Harvester Co.* (1984), holding that the FTC's deceptiveness authority is but a subset of its unfairness jurisdiction; that not every undisclosed safety problem constitutes a deceptive breach of an implied warranty of fitness; that unfair acts, unlike deceptive acts, must be shown to risk a substantial consumer injury that is not outweighed by any offsetting consumer or competitive benefit and is one consumers could not reasonably have avoided; and that in the case before it a tractor manufacturer's failure to effectively warn tractor operators of a small risk that hot fuel would "geyser" when the fuel cap was loosened did not as a matter of law amount to a deceptive breach of an implied warranty of fitness, but did constitute an unfair act, inasmuch as the failure to disclose risked substantial injury, provided no offsetting benefits and created a risk that tractor operators could not reasonably anticipate and avoid.

The FTC's assertion of its unfairness authority complements other legislative and administrative efforts to require product labels warning the public of potentially dangerous products. The Federal Cigarette Labelling and Advertising Act, 15 U.S.C.A. § 1331 et seq., for example, requires a warning on cigarette packages. At the administrative level, the Consumer Products Safety Commission requires warning labels on a variety of consumer products, while the Food and Drug Administration has authority to prevent the misbranding and adulteration of foods, drugs and cosmetics.

(b) Materiality. A deceptive act or practice is "material" if it is capable of affecting a consumer's purchasing decisions. That definition of materiality, as we shall see, includes *any* representation designed to affect a consumer's decision to purchase a product or service, and not merely those designed to deceive a rational consumer with respect to the inherent qualities of a product, service or business. To understand the full significance of this definition of materiality one must identify the various functions deceptive acts or practices play in affecting consumer choices.

Whatever their particular form, the deceptive acts and practices prohibited by the FTC fall into two broad functional categories: (1) deceptive representations about a product, service or business itself and (2) deceptive representations with respect to "extrinsic" matters in the promotion of a product, service or business. The rationale for prohibiting these two types of deception differs significantly.

The most frequent and least controversial type of deceptive act or practice is that which deceptively describes the content, quality or effectiveness of a product. The misdescription may consist of a direct misrepresentation in advertising or an implied misrepresentation, such as a deceptive trademark. Thus, just as it is deceptive to advertise yellow pine as superior white pine, *FTC v. Algoma Lumber Co.* (1934), so it is deceptive to sell under the trademark "Rejuvenescence" a cream that does not in fact rejuvenate the skin. *Charles of the Ritz Distributors Corp. v. FTC* (1944).

The FTC has likewise been alert to prevent misdescriptions of services and business opportunities. Thus, both franchising operations and correspondence and vocational schools are currently subject to extensive FTC rules designed to prevent consumers from being deceived with regard to the services and opportunities being made available to them. That these regulatory activities protect commercial as well as consumer interests is illustrated by the case of *Branch v. FTC* (1944), which held that the FTC had jurisdiction under section 5 of the FTC Act and also under the Webb–Pomerene Act (which gives the FTC authority to prohibit unfair methods of competition in the export trade) to issue a cease and desist order prohibiting a correspondence school operating in the U.S. from employing fraudulent methods to solicit students in Latin American countries. Although the consumer deception occurred abroad, and was thus beyond the FTC's consumer protection jurisdiction, the court in *Branch* held that the potential detriment to other U.S. businesses competing in the same market was substantial enough to give the FTC jurisdiction to prohibit the school's fraudulent practices as unfair methods of competition.

The prohibition against deceptive product or service descriptions is not limited, however, to misrepresentations as to the inherent quality of the product or service. The FTC and the courts have made it clear that the consuming public is entitled to get what it chooses even though that choice may be dictated by fashion, caprice or mere ignorance. Where a consumer preference exists with respect to a product's origin, composition or price, it is a deceptive act or practice to misrepresent either directly or implicitly the origin, composition or price of the product or service, even though there is no real defect in the inherent quality of the product or service offered. See e.g., *FTC v. Mary Carter Paint Co.* (1965) (upholding an FTC order finding it to be deceptive, where consumers relate price and quality, to advertise a gallon of paint at a price comparable to leading national brands, while consistently offering a second gallon "free" for each gallon purchased, regardless of whether the paint is as good as or superior to the national brands). The FTC has also held it to be a deceptive act or practice to utilize false or deceptive endorsements, certifications, or testimonials. See, e.g., FTC Guides Concerning Use of Endorsements and Testimonials, 16 C.F.R. § 255.1 (requiring that where an ad "represents that the endorser uses the endorsed product, then the endorser must have been a bona fide user of it at the time the endorsement is given"). The FTC has even found, as we have seen, that American consumers have a preference for American-made goods and that consequently it is a deceptive act or practice to market foreign goods without disclosing their origin.

Similar criteria govern the materiality of misdescriptions of businesses. The FTC has determined that consumers prefer to deal directly with manufacturers (in the expectation of a lower price and greater assurance of high quality goods) and to deal with businesses whose operations are on a large scale or well-established. Thus, it is a deceptive act or practice to misdescribe the function a business performs in the distributive chain or the size or length of operation of a business. Trade names which falsely suggest a connection with an established business, a government agency or some other respected organization are likewise materially deceptive.

Some misrepresentations bear no relationship to the quality of goods or services at all—or if they do, are such that the consumer will learn the truth before making a purchase. Bait-and-switch advertising, door-to-door sales methods which utilize fictitious consumer surveys to get a foot in the consumer's door and other "come-on" methods are classic examples of wholly extrinsic misrepresentations.

Extrinsic misrepresentations, like product, service or business misdescriptions which do not misrepresent the inherent quality of a product, service or business, are more designed to break down consumer resistance than to mislead the consumer with respect to whether the product or service, when purchased, will meet the consumer's expectations. Unlike product, service or business descriptions, however, extrinsic misrepresentations are merely designed to establish initial contact with the consumer and not to consummate a sale. Extrinsic misrepresentations may or may not injure consumers in any significant way, but they do materially affect consumer purchasing decisions in the sense that they generate an opportunity for the business making such misrepresentations to overcome consumer buying habits. Deceptive "come-on" tactics are thus a way of overcoming the good will of established products, services or businesses. To allow such deception would jeopardize the good will of established businesses and would put pressure on new and established businesses alike to adopt similar practices.

Extrinsic misrepresentations may be used not only to overcome consumer buying habits but also to overcome consumer scepticism. Hence, the rationale for the FTC's prohibition against the undisclosed use of simulations in place of actual demonstrations. Because a demonstration carries with it the implied assertion that the consumer need not take the advertiser's word on the capabilities of the product, but may witness a demonstration of those capabilities first-hand, it is likely to materially affect the consumer's purchasing decision. See *FTC v. Colgate–Palmolive Co.* (1965) (upholding an FTC order prohibiting the use of a TV ad which, although it purports to show a shaving cream shaving sand paper, is in reality showing a simulation of the test).

(2) Federal Trade Commission Regulation of Unfair Acts or Practices and Unfair Methods of Competition

When the deceptiveness of advertising or other promotional activity appears too attenuated, the FTC may always fall back on its coordinate authority to identify and prohibit a practice as "unfair." As we have seen, the courts give great weight to FTC findings of unfairness and have themselves held that the terms "unfair acts or practices" and "unfair methods of competition" include but are not limited to deceptive practices or practices likely to have anticompetitive consequences within the letter or spirit of the antitrust laws. See *FTC v. R.F. Keppel & Brothers, Inc.* (1934) (upholding an FTC conclusion that selling candy to children by the "break-and-take" lottery method constitutes an unfair method of competition even though no deception was employed and competitors could maintain their market position by adopting similar practices); *Orkin Exterminating Co. v. FTC* (1988) (upholding an FTC conclusion that Orkin's decision to breach over 200,000 contracts providing lifetime guarantees of pest control upon the payment of a stated annual renewal fee constituted on unfair practice).

The FTC, for its part, initially stated that in determining whether a practice which is neither in violation of the antitrust laws nor deceptive is nonetheless unfair, it would consider (1) whether the practice, without necessarily having been previously considered unlawful, *offends public policy* as it has been established by *statutes*, the *common law,* or *otherwise*—whether, in other words, it is within at least the penumbra of some common law, statutory or other established concept of unfairness; (2) whether it is *immoral, unethical, oppressive* or *unscrupulous;* (3) whether it causes *substantial injury* to *consumers* or *other businessmen.* See 29 Fed.Reg. 8324, 8355 (1964), cited with approval in *FTC v. The Sperry & Hutchinson Co.* (1972). But see Letter of FTC, 5 CCH Trade Reg.Rep. ¶ 50,421 (Dec. 17, 1980), (stating that the second test is largely duplicative, that the FTC has never relied on it as an independent basis for a finding of unfairness and will act in the future only on the basis of the other two tests). To determine what constitutes an unfair act or practice or unfair method of competition within the meaning of the

FTC Act it is thus necessary to consider in section 2 below the larger question of what promotional practices have been declared, either by statute, common law or otherwise, to be unfair. Even in the absence of such a declaration, however, practices that cause substantial consumer injury not outweighed by any countervailing benefits to consumers or competition nor reasonably avoidable by consumers will be found to be unfair. See *In re International Harvester Co.* (1984), *Orkin Exterminating Co. v. FTC* (1988), supra.

(3) International Trade Commission Regulation of Unfair Methods of Competition in the Import Trade

The International Trade Commission (ITC) has been given authority under section 337 of the 1930 Tariff Act, 19 U.S.C.A. § 1337, to issue exclusion orders and cease and desist orders to prevent unfair methods of competition connected with the importation of articles into the U.S. or their subsequent sale, where the requisite injury, including destruction of or substantial injury to or prevention of the establishment of an efficiently and economically operated industry in the U.S., or antitrust injury, can be shown. The Omnibus Trade and Competitiveness Act eliminated the injury requirement where a practice involves infringement of a federal statutory intellectual property right. The ITC's authority to prohibit unfair methods of competition in imports has been broadly construed to include not only infringement of statutory intellectual property rights and antitrust violations but also a variety of common law unfair acts, such as passing off and trade secret misappropriation and Lanham Act section 43(a) violations. Although ITC determinations are subject to review by the U.S. Trade Representative and the President as well as by the Court of Appeals for the Federal Circuit (CAFC), presidential rejection of ITC determinations are rare. In *Duracell, Inc. v. U.S. International Trade Commission* (1985), however, the CAFC dismissed a case challenging a presidential rejection of a "grey market goods" case, stating that there is no requirement in section 337 that the President articulate in detail the reasons for rejection and that in the present case it was sufficient that the President disapproved for his own policy reasons, including the desire to avoid conflicting administrative interpretations of existing laws.

2. UNFAIR PROMOTIONAL PRACTICES

A number of promotional practices which are neither violative of the antitrust laws nor deceptive have nevertheless been widely condemned as unfair. These practices may be divided into two groups: (1) purely commercial marketing practices and (2) consumer-aimed promotional practices.

The purely commercial marketing practices which have been held to be unfair generally involve either the coercive use of economic power or the surreptitious offer of bribes. Bribery and coercion amount respectively to "carrot" and "stick" attempts to subvert the competitive process. We have previously described what constitutes actionable and non-actionable coercion. (See Chapter 2, supra) and have described the principal occasion for commercial bribery in competitive (i.e., horizontal) relations—namely the misappropriation of trade secrets. See Chapter 7, supra. What remains to be considered here is the use of bribery as an unfair promotional practice in commercial bargaining (i.e., vertical) relations.

a. Bribery in Commercial Bargaining Relations

Commercial bribery consists of the making of surreptitious payments to the agent or employee of a business in order to induce the agent or employee to act in the course of employment in a way favorable to the briber. The briber is generally either a competitor, customer or supplier of the business whose agent or employee is being bribed. Bribery of a competitor's agent or employee usually occurs in the course of an attempt to obtain the competitor's trade secrets. (See Chapter 7 supra.) Bribery of an agent or employee of a non-competitor, on the other hand, generally has as its object the establishment of a commercial relation or securing more favorable treatment in a commercial relation. More often than not the briber is a supplier seeking to make a sale and the employee is a purchasing agent of a business customer. Where a supplier's goods or services are scarce or unique, a purchaser may seek to bribe an agent or employee of the supplier in order to procure the goods or services or to prevent a competitor from procuring them.

Variants of both forms of bribery occur when the agent or employee is a government official and the bribe is designed to procure a valuable government benefit such as a government contract (in which case the government is the purchaser) or a business license or franchise (in which case the government is the "supplier"). Bribery of a government official, of course, is technically not "commercial" bribery at all but rather bribery in its primary sense—that is, inducing the betrayal of a *public* (as opposed to a *private*) trust. Nevertheless, bribery of government officials generally involves the offering of a bribe for a commercial purpose and thus should be considered along with purely private forms of bribery.

Two other forms of commercial bribery in bargaining and other noncompetitive relations consist of payments made to another's employee or agent to procure the promotion (as opposed to the purchase or sale) of one's product or service (e.g., "payola"—the bribery of a radio disc jockey to promote the playing of a recording company's records) or to procure a particular outcome of an athletic contest or other game of skill.

The practice of commercial bribery has tended to wax and then to wane with the increasing concentration and integration of the economy. Early in this century, large business enterprises at all levels of the traditional tri-level distributive chain relied extensively on sales and purchasing agents. The struggle to establish and maintain trade relations led to widespread commercial bribery. In those areas of the economy where the distributive chain remains unintegrated and competition is keen (e.g., the beer and liquor industries) instances of commercial bribery are still reported. However, the widespread practice of commercial bribery, and hence concern over it, tended to abate as more and more of the economy became both vertically integrated and horizontally concentrated.

Commercial bribery of government officials, on the other hand, has continued to be of concern as government regulation of the economy has increased and the government has become a greater consumer of products and services. The practice of bribing government officials took on international dimensions as domestic businesses entered foreign markets. Evidence of the practice came to light in the Watergate-related disclosures of questionable corporate payments to government officials both at home and abroad. These payments ranged from perfectly legal political contributions to clearly illegal under-the-table payments. While some payments were obviously being extorted by foot-dragging government officials, others were made with little or no government coercion and in some instances clearly constituted bribes.

What all types of commercial bribery have in common is the covert undermining of relationships of trust, with a consequent threat of injury both to the employer of the person being bribed and to the competitors of the briber. The threat of harm to the employer is two-fold: Not only does the bribe deprive the employer of the loyal and unbiased service for which the agent or employee is being paid but, where the business is a purchaser of goods or services, the employer may wind up footing the bill for the bribe, either by paying a higher sales price or receiving poorer quality goods or services than would otherwise be the case. Competitors of the briber, in turn, will be denied an opportunity to compete on equal terms unless they match bribe for bribe. Thus, even those businesses that would not otherwise resort to bribery are virtually compelled to engage in the practice. In addition to these purely private injuries, commercial bribery ultimately harms the consuming public by subjecting it to higher priced or lower quality goods and services.

Given all these adverse effects, it is not surprising that commercial bribery has come in for widespread legal condemnation. Consequently, the victim who is lucky enough to uncover the bribery has a variety of legal remedies, private and public, from which to choose.

Because an employee who accepts a bribe breaches a fiduciary obligation to the employer, by failing to remain loyal to the employer and failing to disclose the bribe, state equity courts have held there to be a right to recover the bribe from the employee in order to prevent the employee's unjust enrichment. Because the briber has induced the employee to breach that fiduciary obligation—which may be thought of as an implied term of the employee's contract with the employer—the employer also has a common-law right to recover from the briber any damages resulting from the briber's having induced the breach of that implied contract. (See Chapter 3 supra.)

It could also be argued that bribes constitute improper interference with the purely prospective relations of the briber's competitors, thereby giving them, as well as the business whose agent is bribed, a common-law claim for relief. (See Chapter 2 supra.) The principal obstacle to recovery on such a theory is establishing that but for the bribe the particular competitor who is bringing the action would have made the sale.

Where a bribe occurs in commerce which the federal government has power to regulate, employers of bribed employees and, more importantly, competitors of the briber have been held to have a cause of action for treble damages under section 2(c) of the Clayton Act, as amended by the Robinson–Patman Act, which prohibits the payment or receipt of unearned commissions, brokerage or compensation. See, e.g., *Fitch v. Kentucky–Tennessee Light & Power Co.* (1943) (upholding a treble damage award in favor of a power company whose president had been paid bribes by the defendant coal company to influence his selection of a coal supplier); *Rangen Inc. v. Sterling Nelson & Sons, Inc.* (1965) (holding that a fish food producer could recover treble damages from a competitor and from a state official whom the competitor had bribed in order to obtain contracts to supply fish food to the state). But see *Stephen Jay Photography, Ltd. v. Olan Mills, Inc.* (1990) (rejecting a claim that a rival photography company violated section 2(c) by donating money to schools in order to persuade them to designate it as the official yearbook photographer). While the principal purpose of Section 2(c) is to prohibit price discrimination disguised as brokerage fees (See Chapter 9 infra), courts have held that section 2(c) is also designed to prevent the undermining of confidence in brokers generally, and thereby to safeguard their role as a valuable market mechanism. The civil liability provisions of the Clayton Act have thus been held to apply wherever a bribe undermines such a relationship, gives one seller an unfair advantage over a competing seller and is associated with the evils which the antitrust laws are designed to prevent (i.e., results in a restraint of trade, monopolization or price discrimination).

In contrast to the provision in the Robinson–Patman Act which prohibits price discrimination per se, the false brokerage provision of the Act is not limited to transactions involving goods intended for resale in the United States, but applies to bribes in foreign as well as interstate commerce. See, e.g., *Canadian Ingersoll–Rand Co. v. D. Loveman & Sons* (1964) (holding that a foreign company had stated a cause of action under section 2(c) against its chief purchasing agent and a U.S. corporation for allegedly conspiring to extract exorbitant prices from the foreign company). *Environmental Tectonics v. W.S. Kirkpatrick, Inc.* (1988), rev'd on other grounds (1990) (holding an American company to have stated a cause of action under section 2(c) against a competitor which allegedly bribed certain Nigerian officials in order to secure contracts to equip a Nigerian air force base medical center). The only limitation on Robinson–Patman Act liability for such bribes is that the bribe must have an effect on U.S. foreign commerce.

The FTC, for its part, has declared commercial bribery to be an unfair method of competition in violation of the FTC Act. While most of the FTC's section 5 proceedings against commercial bribery in domestic trade occurred in the early 1920's, before the Robinson–Patman Act was enacted, the FTC has recently utilized both the FTC Act and the Robinson–Patman Act as the basis for challenging the payment of bribes in U.S. foreign trade where the alleged effect was to exclude other U.S. firms from the foreign market. See, e.g., 43 Fed. Reg. 36973 (1978) (proposed FTC consent order in which three of nation's largest aircraft manufacturers—Lockheed, Boeing and McDonnell–Douglas—agreed not to make payments to commercial customers or foreign governments). In contrast to the Foreign Corrupt Practices Act of 1977, 15 U.S.C.A. § 78 et seq., the FTC Act and Robinson–Patman Act apply to payments to private commercial parties as well as foreign government officials and provide for civil liability as well as criminal sanctions against the practice. For relief from foreign government involvement in or inaction with respect to foreign trade activities, see, pp. 31–33 supra.

b. Consumer–Aimed Promotional Practices

A number of non-deceptive consumer-aimed promotional practices have been condemned as unfair because they constitute "lures to improvidence." These practices may be divided into two groups: the use of lotteries, games and contests, on the one hand, and the use of giveaways, premiums and trading stamps, on the other. All play on the human propensity to get something for nothing, while some play on the gambling instinct as well.

(1) Lotteries, Games and Contests

Lotteries are prohibited by criminal statutes in some states. The objective of much of this anti-lottery legislation has little to do with the protection of trade relations as such. Rather, it is designed to protect the public welfare by discouraging the gambling spirit.

In a number of cases, however, courts have allowed businesses to bring a private action for injunctive relief against competitors who violate such statutes. See, e.g., *United Stations of New Jersey v. Kingsley* (1968) (allowing an operator of gas station to sue major oil distributors and competing retail dealers to prevent certain giveaways allegedly in violation of a statute which prohibited lotteries and "other games of chance" in connection with the sale of motor fuels). Likewise, in *FTC v. R.F. Keppel & Brother, Inc.* (1934), the Supreme Court upheld the FTC's authority to prohibit the "break and take" lottery method of promoting the sale of candy to children as an unfair method of competition, even in the absence of any fraud or deception or conduct likely to grow into violations of the Sherman Act. In so holding, the Court noted that the practice exploited a class of consumers who are unable to protect themselves and was of the sort which the common law and criminal statutes have long treated as contrary to public policy.

While statutory definitions vary from state to state, a lottery may generally be thought of as the non-gratuitous distribution of prizes by lot or chance. A lottery is thus composed of three elements: consideration, chance, and prize. The definition of consideration varies widely from state to state but is generally held to encompass far more than simply the payment of money in return for a chance to win a prize. Consideration may be found, for example, where a customer must be present at a particular location to win a drawing.

If prizes are gratuitously distributed by chance or are not distributed by chance at all but on the basis of a participant's exercise of skill and judgment, on the other hand, the promotional scheme is not a lottery but rather a special type of giveaway (namely a game of chance) or a contest, respectively. In the absence of an express statutory prohibition, games and contests are permissible, so long as no false representations are made in the course of such promotional schemes.

(2) Giveaways, Premiums and Trading Stamps

A number of states have adopted various "anti-premium" statutes which basically outlaw the use of free goods, premiums or trading stamps as a promotional device. Among the rationales given for such statutes are that premiums are a lure to improvidence, appeal to the desire to get something for nothing and force competing sellers to offer similar premiums, resulting in an overall increase in business and consumer costs.

Other states, as we shall see in Chapter 9, have adopted statutes prohibiting sales below cost. Some courts have held that premiums are to be considered in calculating whether a sale is below cost, but that trading stamps are not to be considered in calculating the cost of an item. The U.S. Supreme Court has held that such a distinction does not constitute arbitrary discrimination in violation of the equal protection clause. In *Safeway Stores, Inc. v. Oklahoma Retail Grocers Associ-*

ation, Inc. (1959) the Court found there to be a rational distinction between an across-the-board offer of trading stamps as a cash discount for prompt payment of cash and selective below-cost price cuts—i.e., "loss leader" selling—which is the very evil that the statute was designed to prevent. Why below-cost price cuts are considered an evil which ought to be prevented is a question to be addressed in the next chapter.

CHAPTER NINE
INJURIOUS PRICING PRACTICES

At the heart of the bargaining and competitive processes must be a market in which bargaining over prices and price competition can occur. The basic presupposition of a free market economy is that prices are to be fixed neither by private agreement among competitors nor by government command but rather by the law of supply and demand, as it operates through the myriad bargaining relations that make up the economy. The regulation of pricing practices in a free market economy is thus largely the concern of the law of antitrust, one of whose objectives is to prevent private price fixing, and the law of regulated industries, whose objective is to ensure that, in any areas of the economy where natural monopolies exist or unregulated price competition is deemed inimical to the public interest, prices will be publicly rather than privately fixed.

The common law has generally taken a hands-off approach to pricing practices. Running a business at a loss (i.e., selling below cost) may be evidence of a predatory (i.e., anticompetitive or malicious) purpose, but it is not conclusive evidence. (See Chapter 2, supra.) In the absence of an improper business objective, traders are said to have the right to sell goods or services at whatever price the buyer and seller might agree upon. Only common carriers and innkeepers, which in many instances functioned as monopolies and in any event provided essential public services, were ever judicially required to make reasonable prices equally available to all customers, and even then it was not always clear whether "reasonable prices" meant prices bearing a reasonable relation to costs or merely meant prices which did not vary with similarly situated customers.

The common-law distinction between purely private enterprises and enterprises "affected with the public interest" acquired constitutional significance for a period of time after the Supreme Court indicated in *Munn v. Illinois* (1877) that imposing price regulation on a business not affected with the public interest would constitute an impermissible deprivation of constitutionally protected liberty. The *Munn* view of economic liberty, however, ultimately gave way, beginning with *Nebbia v. New York* (1934), to the currently prevailing view that there is no closed class or category of businesses affected with the public interest, beyond which price regulation cannot extend. Rather, the Court has conceded that the state and federal legislatures have broad authority to regulate economic matters and that judicial review of price or other economic regulation should be limited to determining whether the regulatory scheme is reasonably related to a proper legislative purpose and is neither arbitrary nor discriminatory. The clear import of cases such as *Nebbia* is that it is basically for the legislative branch of government and not the judiciary to balance the relative need for price freedom and price stability.

The Supreme Court did reserve an important albeit more limited role for itself with respect to pricing practices when it held in *Virginia State Board of Pharmacy v. Virginia Citizens Consumer Council* (1976) that a state statute banning the truthful advertising of prescription drug prices constituted an impermissible abridgement of constitutionally protected speech. While that decision has the effect of favoring price freedom over price stability, it merely limits the power of states to regulate price *advertising* and not their power to regulate pricing itself.

Given the legislative power to regulate pricing practices, one might nevertheless ask why, other than to prevent private price fixing by competitors or to regulate natural monopolies, state or federal legislatures might choose to exercise that power. A principal reason for regulating pricing practices, of course, is to achieve overall price stability. Wage and price controls, for example, have been employed on a number of occasions by Congress as a means of combatting inflation.

There may be reasons other than achieving overall price stability for regulating pricing practices. At one time, for example, many states had statutes, euphemistically called "Fair Trade" laws, which permitted manufacturers and wholesalers to engage in vertical resale price maintenance. Although contracts prescribing resale prices had been held by the courts to violate the Sherman Antitrust Act, the 1937 Miller–Tydings Amendment to the Sherman Act legalized vertical minimum resale price maintenance contracts for trademarked commodities sold in any state which permitted such contracts with respect to intrastate sales. The McGuire Act of 1952, in turn, expressly permitted states to enact laws for the enforcement of contracts prescribing stipulated as well as minimum prices and to enforce them against non-signers as well as signers of such contracts. Under such state statutes the price agreement in effect became a covenant which ran with the trademarked goods. The rationale underlying the "Fair Trade" statutes was that because price cutting could injure the good will of a trademarked product, resale price maintenance agreements were a legitimate means of protecting that good will. The interest in the stability of trade relations, in other words, was thought to outweigh the interest in price freedom.

As Congress ultimately recognized, however, the practical effect of the state Fair Trade laws, was to undermine the economic policy which the federal antitrust laws were seeking to further. Thus, in the Consumer Goods Pricing Act of 1975, P.L. 94–145 (Dec. 12, 1975), Congress repealed the Miller–Tydings Amendment and the McGuire Act, thereby removing the antitrust exemption for resale price maintenance agreements. *See California Retail Liquor Dealers Association v. Midcal Aluminum, Inc.* (1980). (State system for wine pricing constitutes resale price maintenance in violation of Sherman Act.)

Repeal of the Fair Trade laws has only served to intensify questions as to the wisdom of other state and federal price regulation statutes which remain in effect. The most notable of these are state and federal statutes prohibiting price cutting (i.e., sales below cost or sales at unreasonably low prices) and price discrimination. To understand the rationale behind these statutes and how the pricing practices they seek to prevent differ, if at all, from the common law's prohibition against predatory pricing, it is necessary to identify the particular trade relations which each body of law seeks to protect and the particular types of interference which each seeks to prevent.

A. TRADE RELATIONS PROTECTED

Running a business at a loss for the sole purpose of injuring or destroying another business or eliminating competition will be actionable at common law regardless of the particular trade relations injured. Because the injury may range from the loss of a few customers to the destruction of the entire business, the common law prohibition against predatory pricing can be said to protect trade relations generally.

State and federal statutes prohibiting price cutting and price discrimination, by contrast, protect narrower classes of trade relations. State sales-below-cost statutes generally prohibit both wholesale and retail sales below cost and thus protect both commercial and retail customer relations of non-pricecutters. The Robinson–Patman Act's prohibition against price discrimination (though not its prohibition against sales at unreasonably low prices) is limited to discrimination among commercial customers and thus protects only commercial customer relations. As these differences in coverage suggest, state sales-below-cost statutes and such anti-price discrimination statutes as the Robinson–Patman Act seek to meet quite different objectives than the common law prohibition against predatory pricing. To pinpoint what the objectives of these bodies of law are, it is necessary to examine precisely what types of pricing practices they make actionable.

B. ACTIONABLE AND PRIVILEGED INTERFERENCE

As we have seen, those pricing practices made actionable at common law or by statute may be divided into two groups: Price cutting and price discrimination. Actually, price discrimination is simply a special form of price-cutting—namely *selective* price cutting. Price cutting and price discrimination are actionable, of course, where they further a predatory purpose—i.e., the lessening of competition or the purely malevolent injury or destruction of another business. Some forms of price cutting and price discrimination, however, may be actionable even though the objective is not predatory. It is the practice itself and not the objective being sought that is deemed unfair.

1. PRICE CUTTING

Only where prices are cut for the sole purpose of injuring or destroying another business is there an action at common law. If the purpose is to eliminate competition, such conduct may violate the antitrust laws as well. (See Chapter 2 supra.) Ostensibly supplementing these two bodies of law are state statutes prohibiting sales below cost and section 3 of the Robinson–Patman Act, which prohibits sales at unreasonably low prices.

a. Sales Below Cost

The main evil sought to be eliminated by statutes prohibiting sales below cost is "loss leader" selling. This promotional practice is said to be unfair not only because it is a destructive means of competition which often leads to price wars, but also because it plays on the gullibility of customers by leading them to expect what is not true, namely, that a store which offers such an amazing bargain must be full of other bargains.

While sales-below-cost statutes vary widely from state to state, they most frequently forbid sales below cost where the intent is to destroy competition or to injure a competitor. Some statutes forbid sales below cost where either the intent or the effect is to destroy competition or to injure a competitor, while a few statutes purport to forbid all sales below cost without regard to intent or the effect on competition or competitors. These prohibitions may apply to all sellers or only those at specified levels of the distributive chain and may extend to sales of all types of commodities or services, to sales of commodities alone, or to sales of selected commodities. Virtually all states explicitly exempt certain transactions, such as clearance, close-out or judicial sales or sales of damaged or deteriorated goods or perishable goods whose sale is forced by the threat of spoilage. Sales to meet a lawful price of a competitor are also exempted.

Enforcement of sales-below-cost statutes is accomplished by means of criminal penalties and civil actions for damages or injunctions. The statutes frequently provide that civil actions may be brought by "any person," which may mean that virtually anyone, and not merely those threatened with injury, may seek to enjoin violations of the act. See, e.g., *Catalina, Inc. v. P. Zwetchkenbaum & Sons, Inc.* (1970). Some courts, however, have required a showing, not only that the plaintiff is a competitor of the defendant, but also that plaintiff suffered actual injury due to the alleged sale below cost. *Heiden v. Ray's Inc.* (1967).

In order for a violation to occur, of course, there must be a nonexempt sale below cost. Reflecting the prevalence of statutes which are limited to sales by wholesalers and retailers, cost is generally defined as invoice or replacement cost plus overhead costs. Where a statute applies to manufacturers, cost for manufacturers is defined as the cost of raw materials, labor and all overhead expenses.

In recognition of the inherent difficulty of computing what share of overhead is borne by an item, the statutes usually contain a provision which either creates a rebuttable presumption that overhead costs are a certain percentage of invoice or material and labor costs or permit introduction of trade association costs surveys as prima facie evidence of overhead costs. The figure arrived at in either of these ways is likely to be an entirely arbitrary estimate of the overhead costs of a particular business. To the suspicious eye the prohibition against sales below such "costs" looks like little more than a legislatively prescribed mandatory markup—that is, a crude form of government sponsored minimum price fixing.

Inclusion of a provision requiring an intent to injure competition or a competitor does little to alleviate the suspicion. Most sales-below-cost statutes, as we have seen, include such a provision and those which do not have frequently been struck down as a matter of state constitutional law—at least where criminal penalties for violation of the statute are provided. Even those statutes which contain an intent to injure requirement, however, do not require a purely malicious intent to injure the competitor. Under a number of statutes, evidence of a sale below cost is presumptive evidence of intent, shifting to the seller the burden of proving a lack of intent to injure a competitor. Since one normally sells below cost for the specific purpose of diverting customers from a competitor, that burden is well-nigh impossible to carry. Not surprisingly, the statutory presumption on more than one occasion has been struck down as unconstitutional. Where statutes have survived constitutional attack, cases involving their violation have tended to rest either solely on a presumed intent to injure or on evidence of nothing more than a competitive purpose on the part of a business to attract a marginal number of a competitor's customers. Thus, in contrast to the common law's limited prohibition against predatory price cutting, sales-below-cost statutes appear as a practical matter to prohibit purely competitive price cutting.

b. Unreasonably Low Prices

Although the principal focus of the Robinson–Patman Act is price discrimination, one provision of the Act does aim specifically at price cutting. Section 3 of the Act, 15 U.S.C.A. § 13a, prohibits sales "at unreasonably low prices for the purpose of destroying competition or eliminating a competitor...." The federal approach to price cutting in the Robinson–Patman Act differs substantially from the approach of the state sales-below-cost statutes.

Not the least of the differences in approach is the more limited means for enforcing the federal provision. Unlike state sales-below-cost statutes (and the price-discrimination provisions of the Robinson–Patman Act), section 3 may only be enforced through criminal prosecution. The Robinson–Patman Act contains no provision for civil enforcement of section 3 by the government and has been held not to be an "antitrust law" whose violation will give rise to a private treble damage action under section 4 of the Clayton Act. See *Nashville Milk Co. v. Carnation Co.* (1958). Not surprisingly, section 3 has been brought to bear on price cutting even less frequently than have state sales-below-cost statutes. Its definition of prohibited price cutting deserves mention, however, if only because it provides a useful contrast to the approach of state sales-below-cost statutes.

Section 3, as we have seen, prohibits sales "at unreasonably low prices for the purpose of destroying competition or eliminating a competitor." Notwithstanding the generality of the language used to define what is, after all, criminal conduct, section 3 has been held to be constitutional, see *United States v. National Dairy Products Corp.* (1963), and, indeed, the generality of section 3 appears to be its chief virtue in comparison with the rigid specificity of state sales-below-cost statutes.

The offense defined by section 3 is composed of two elements: (1) a sale at an unreasonably low price and (2) an intent to destroy competition or injure a competitor. Although each element bears separate examination, it is to be noted that the absence of *either* element will be a complete defense, whether or not the other element has been established. Thus, if one with predatory intent mistakenly charges what is clearly a reasonable price or without predatory intent mistakenly charges what is clearly an unreasonable price, there will be no violation.

In contrast to the state sales-below-cost statutes, section 3 of the Robinson–Patman Act does not prohibit sales below cost as such, but only sales at unreasonably low prices. In theory, at least, a sale below cost might be reasonable and a sale at a slight profit unreasonable, depending on the presence or absence of a legitimate commercial justification for the price in each case. As the Supreme Court in the *National Dairy Products* case made clear, however, the objective of business being to produce profits, a profitless sale will be deemed unreasonable unless justified by a legitimate commercial objective, such as disposing of perishable or outdated goods or meeting prices of a competitor. By the same token, it is unlikely that a sale at a price which produces a profit, however slim, will be held to be unreasonable unless the profit from all like sales is consistently so minuscule in relation to the investment made to produce the profit as to call into question the existence of a legitimate commercial objective. The real index for the reasonableness of a price is thus the seller's intent or purpose in setting it and not its relation to a given definition of cost.

In *United States v. National Dairy Products Corp.* (1963), the case upholding the constitutionality of section 3, the Court held that the prohibition against "unreasonably low prices" was not impermissibly vague, where an indictment for violation of the provision specifically alleged a predatory purpose. The Court thus construed section 3 as requiring that a specific intent to destroy competition or injure a competitor accompany an unreasonably low price for a violation of section 3 to occur. The specific intent required for a violation of section 3 does not appear to differ from the predatory intent required at common law for price cutting to be actionable. Thus, section 3 appears simply to provide a federal criminal remedy for common-law predatory price cutting.

2. PRICE DISCRIMINATION

The Robinson–Patman Act, 15 U.S.C.A. § 13 et seq., is basically an amendment of section 2 of the Clayton Antitrust Act. Although the Robinson–Patman Act is thus technically an antitrust law, both its legislative history and its subsequent judicial construction reflect as much of a concern with protecting businesses from the injurious pricing practices of other businesses as with protecting the competitive process as such. The legislative history of the Act reveals that a particular congressional concern was with protecting independent retailers and wholesalers from attempts by chain retailers to coerce price concessions from or altogether bypass the wholesaler.

The Clayton Act's original section 2 forbade a particular form of predatory price cutting—namely, localized price cutting designed by large nationwide suppliers to force small competitors out of a local market. The amended section 2(a) seeks to limit as well the forcing of price concessions by large volume *buyers*. It does this indirectly, however, by forbidding a seller from discriminating in price between different purchasers of commodities of like grade and quality where the effect of the discrimination may be to lessen, injure, destroy or prevent competition. The indirect approach of section 2(a) was apparently chosen in order to comply with the Supreme Court's then restrictive views on when a buyer, as opposed to a seller, was engaged in commerce which Congress had the power to regulate.

Section 2(a) expressly excepts from its general prohibition any price concession which reflects a cost saving or changing conditions. Section 2(b) goes on to allow any price concession which is a bona fide attempt to meet a competitor's price. Section 2(c) prohibits the granting or receiving of a price concession in the guise of brokerage, commissions or discounts in lieu thereof to the buyer or its agent. Sections 2(d) and 2(e) prohibit a seller from paying for or providing promotional services in lieu of a price concession. Finally, section 2(f) forbids a buyer from knowingly inducing or receiving a price concession prohibited by sections 2(a)–(e). Section 3 of the Robinson–Patman Act, which is not amendatory of the Clayton Act, provides criminal sanctions for three different pricing practices: (1) knowingly discriminating in price by such covert means as discounts, rebates, allowances or advertising service charges; (2) predatory geographic price discrimination; and (3) predatory price cutting.

The civil provisions of the Robinson–Patman Act (sections 2(a)–2(f)) may be enforced either by the federal government or by private parties injured in their business or property as a result of violations of the Act. Although the Federal Trade Commission and the Department of Justice have concurrent power to enforce the civil provisions of the Robinson–Patman Act, the Department of Justice has in practice largely deferred to the Federal Trade Commission, which enforces the Act through judicially enforceable administrative cease and desist orders. The Justice Department retains exclusive power to institute the relatively few criminal proceedings which have been brought under section 3 of the Act.

In addition to government enforcement, the Robinson–Patman Act may be privately enforced through lawsuits for treble damages or injunctive relief. Although government enforcement efforts have been scaled down in recent years, the number of private lawsuits has correspondingly gone up.

While the statutory language of the Robinson–Patman Act is complex, it basically defines three distinct types of price misconduct: (1) Price discrimination per se and price discrimination in the guise of (2) brokerage fees or (3) promotional allowances and services. Defenses which may be raised to charges of price misconduct vary with the particular type of misconduct alleged.

a. § 2(a) Price Discrimination

(1) The Prima Facie Case

In order to make out a prima facie case of price discrimination under section 2(a) of the Clayton Act as amended by the Robinson–Patman Act, it is necessary for the Federal Trade Commission or a private litigant to show that:

(1) a person engaged in commerce

(2) discriminated in price in the course of such commerce

(3) between different purchases of

(4) commodities

   (a) of like grade and quality

   (b) for use, consumption or resale within the United States

(5) where one or more of the purchases was in commerce, and

(6) the substantial effect of the discrimination is to

    (a) lessen competition

    (b) create monopoly, or

    (c) injure, destroy or prevent competition with

        [1] the person who grants the discrimination

        [2] the person who knowingly receives it, or

        [3] the customers of either of them.

Each of these elements has been the subject of considerable litigation. It has been held, for example, that the seller, the discrimination and at least one of the purchases must be "in commerce"—i.e., be involved with the physical movement of a commodity in interstate or foreign commerce. A "discrimination in price" has been held to consist of nothing more than a charging of different prices to two or more contemporaneous purchasers. One does not discriminate, however, by periodically changing prices that one makes uniformly available to all purchasers. "Price" consists of the ultimate cost paid by the purchaser, taking into account any discounts, rebates or allowances. "Purchasers" are limited to those who actually consummate a purchase (as opposed to a lease or rental) of a commodity. A "commodity" is a tangible article of merchandise. Where both commodities and services are involved, the dominant nature of the transaction governs. See, e.g., *First Comics, Inc. v. World Color Press* (1989) (holding that a contract to print comic books was predominantly one for services). Commodities are of "like grade or quality" if they have identical physical qualities. Identical products which are merely packaged in different quantities would thus constitute goods of like grade and quality.

Of particular note is that, in addition to the more general requirement that the discrimination be in commerce, section 2(a) requires the commodities be intended for consumption or resale in the United States. This language has the effect of permitting price discrimination by exporters. It likewise fails to prohibit importers from "dumping" commodities in the U.S. (i.e. selling at lower prices than are charged in other countries), since in order to violate section 2(a) both of the sales being compared must be of commodities for use or resale in the U.S. As we shall see, however, other provisions of the Robinson–Patman Act do prohibit certain forms of price discrimination by exporters and other provisions of U.S. law prohibit dumping by importers.

The most important element for purposes of understanding how section 2(a) of the amended Clayton Act functions as a piece of unfair trade practice legislation is the last element of the prima facie case—namely that which limits actionable discriminations in price to those discriminations whose effect is to bring about one of three types of competitive injury. The first two types of competitive injury (namely the lessening of competition and the creation of monopoly) are simply carried over from the original section 2 of the Clayton Act and reflect the original antitrust goals of that Act. The third type of competitive injury, however, reflects the Robinson–Patman Act's broader concern with preventing injury to individual competitors. Because injury of an individual competitor will generally occur well before any overall lessening of competition or tendency toward monopoly, litigation under the Robinson–Patman Act has largely been concerned with injuries of the third type. As the statutory language indicates, this type of injury can occur at the seller level of competition (i.e. primary line injury), at the buyer level of competition (i.e. secondary line injury), and the level of the favored purchaser's customer (i.e. third line injury). In one case, the Supreme Court has even extended section 2(a) to a fourth line injury—i.e., injury to competitors of the customers of the favored purchaser's customers—where the favored purchaser's customers were shown to have resold to their own subsidiaries. See *Perkins v. Standard Oil Co.* (1969).

At all of these levels the courts and the FTC have had to decide what constitutes a competitive injury within the meaning of the Act. Early Supreme Court dicta suggested that the new provision was intended to equate "injury to competition" with "injury to a competitor disadvantaged by the discrimination." The lower courts and the

FTC have more recently taken the view that the purpose of the Act is to preserve competition and only incidentally to protect individual competitors. While the language of the statute seems to contemplate a uniform standard of competitive injury, regardless of the level at which the competitive injury is said to have occurred, the courts and the FTC have in fact varied the proof requirements for competitive injury, depending on whether a primary line or a second, third or fourth line injury has been alleged.

(a) Primary Line Injury. As we have seen, price discrimination might simply be a form of predatory price cutting—i.e., pricing designed to drive a competitor of the seller out of business. Proof of predatory intent on the part of the discriminating seller will thus be sufficient to establish a prima facie case of primary line competitive injury. The assumption is that where price discrimination is the result of predatory intent, competitive injury is highly likely to have occurred. Such intent may be established by direct documentary or testimonial evidence or may be inferred from such circumstantial evidence as sudden and unexplained price cuts, continuous sales below cost, severe and prolonged undercutting of a competitor's prices, greater competitive strength on the part of the discriminator, or proof that the discriminator has engaged in other anticompetitive or otherwise unfair trade practices.

While proof of predatory intent will be sufficient to establish a prima facie case of first line injury, it is not an essential element of the prima facie case. A discrimination in price could also be rendered actionable by proof that the discrimination has had an adverse impact on competitive conditions in the seller's market. Thus, a seller who simply accedes to a buyer's request for a price concession will violate the act if the price concession can be shown to have had an adverse impact on the seller's market.

At one time it appeared that such an impact could be shown merely by establishing a diversion of sales from one seller to another. Today, diversion of trade is no longer considered sufficient evidence of first line competitive injury, although it remains a relevant factor in determining whether the price discrimination has had an adverse impact on the market in which the discriminating seller operates. Other factors which will be considered relevant to the question of first line competitive injury include the extent to which the discriminating seller dominates the market, the extent and duration of the seller's price cuts, evidence of offsetting price increases in other markets, the overall health of seller's competitors and the relative ease of entry into the market.

A growing number of courts and the FTC itself have been influenced by an article, Areeda and Turner, Predatory Pricing and Related Practices Under Section 2 of the Sherman Act, 88 *Harv. L.Rev.* 697 (1975), which argues that predatory pricing is irrational and thus will not likely occur unless the predator has superior financial resources and there are substantial barriers to entry into the predator's market. In *International Telephone & Telegraph Corp.* (1984) the FTC adopted a set of presumptions suggested by Areeda and Turner—namely that: 1) sales at prices that equal or exceed average variable cost should be strongly, even conclusively, presumed to be legal; 2) sales at prices below average variable cost for a significant period of time should be rebuttably presumed to be anticompetitive; and 3) sales at prices that equal or exceed average total cost should be conclusively presumed to be legitimate. See also *William Inglis & Sons Baking Co. v. ITT Continental Baking Co., Inc.* (1981); (citing and to some extent relying on the Areeda & Turner article and holding that the principles governing proof of predatory intent in an attempt to monopolize claim under section 2 of the Sherman Act are equally applicable to proof of predatory intent in a primary-line Robinson–Patman Act claim). But see *A.A. Poultry Farms v. Rose Acre Farms* (1989) (holding that for a Sherman Act section 2 claim a court need only inquire into the relation between cost and price where market structure makes recoupment of price cuts feasible; and that intent plays no useful role in a predatory price case under the Sherman Act, but indicating in dictum that until the Supreme Court overruled its previous holding that the Robinson–Patman Act prohibits at least some primary-line discrimination that the Sherman Act permits, "predatory intent" coupled with proof of erosion of price levels would continue to be sufficient to state a claim under section 2(a) of the Robinson–Patman Act).

(b) Second, Third and Fourth Line Injury. The principal aim of the Robinson–Patman Act, as we have seen, was to prevent price discrimination induced by the favored buyer. Not surprisingly, most of the litigation under the Act has involved second line competitive injury. In contrast to primary line injury cases, which now require a rather detailed showing of substantial adverse impact on competitive conditions in the discriminating seller's market, second line injury may be established merely by showing a permanent and substantial price differential in the sale of a standardized product to two or more purchasers. Under these conditions the courts and the FTC are apparently willing to assume the likelihood of a private injury and an adverse competitive effect at the purchaser level of competition. But cf. *J. Truett Payne Co., Inc. v. Chrysler Motors Corp.* (1981), in which the Supreme Court held that the victim of an alleged price discrimination is not entitled to "automatic damages" in the amount of the price discrimination but must make a showing of actual injury attributable to something the antitrust laws were designed to prevent. Although such a plaintiff may be entitled to the relaxed standard used in antitrust cases for proof of causation, the Court concluded that the evidence in that case, amounting to little more than evidence of a temporary decline in market share, may not be sufficient to meet even the relaxed standard for proof of causally related injury. See also *Boise Cascade Corporation v. FTC* (1988) (court of appeals holding that

although an inference of competitive injury may be drawn from substantial price discrimination between competing purchasers over time, the FTC erred in rejecting as irrelevant the favored purchaser's evidence suggesting the absence of competitive injury or a reasonable possibility of same). In *Texaco, Inc. v. Hasbrouck* (1990), the Supreme Court stated that a supplier need not satisfy the rigorous requirements of the cost justification defense in order to prove that functional discounts to dual distributor/retailers are reasonable and thus do not cause any lessening of competition between the dual distributor's customers and the supplier's direct customers, but that the functional discounts must constitute reasonable reimbursement for the dual distributor's actual marketing functions. The functional discounts involved in the case did not meet the latter requirement because the dual distributors received a full discount on all their purchases, even though most of their volume was sold directly to consumers.

A price differential is deemed substantial when it is likely to influence the favored customer's resale prices or where it occurs in a market having low profit margins and vigorous competition. Only where price differences are insubstantial in amount or temporary in duration have the courts and the FTC examined the actual competitive effect of the price difference on the market in which the favored purchaser operates.

The prima facie case of third line competitive injury (i.e., injury at the level of customers of the favored purchaser) is essentially the same as a second line injury case except that the favored purchaser must be shown to have reduced his or her resale prices as a result of the discrimination. The prima facie case of fourth line injury is essentially the same as in a third line injury case, with the mere addition of an intermediate customer between the favored purchaser and the customer with whom the disfavored purchaser or its customers is in competition. In practice, few cases of third and fourth line injury have been litigated, further underscoring the Act's preoccupation with second line injury.

(2) Defenses to Section 2(a) Price Discrimination

To the prima facie case of section 2(a) price discrimination, the discriminating seller may raise three affirmative defenses—the cost justification and changing conditions defenses which are provided for in section 2(a) itself, and the meeting competition defense which is separately provided for in section 2(b). If any of these defenses is established, the discriminating seller avoids liability even if the price difference causes competitive injury. The burden of proof as to each defense, however, is on the challenged seller. This allocation of the burden of proof in effect requires a seller in a second line injury case to justify any permanent and substantial price differential—an allocation which stands in marked contrast to the common-law view that pricing practices are presumptively lawful and must be shown to be motivated by predatory intent in order to be held unlawful. All three statutory defenses have been narrowly interpreted by the Federal Trade Commission and the courts, making the task of justifying a substantial price differential all the more difficult. But see *Texaco, Inc. v. Hasbrouck,* supra, stating that a supplier need not satisfy the rigorous requirements of the cost justification defense in order to prove that discounts to dual distributor/retailers are reasonable and thus do not cause any competitive injury.

(a) Cost Justification. Implicit in the Robinson–Patman Act's prohibition against price discrimination is the notion that arbitrary price differentials are unfair because they are likely to be the result of a seller's predatory intent or a buyer's coercive use of bargaining power. Accordingly, price differences which are not arbitrary but merely reflect differences in the seller's costs do not belong under the heading of actionable discrimination. Section 2(a) specifically recognizes that evidence of cost differences will justify a price differential.

For cost justification to be more than a purely illusory defense a degree of approximation in the setting of prices and the calculation of costs must be tolerated. A business cannot be expected to be able to come up with a cost justification for each and every price difference, either before or after the fact. Businesses necessarily deal in averages—the average cost to manufacture and distribute a product or line of products to various classes of customers. So long as the classifications used to cost-justify a particular price difference are sufficiently homogeneous as to make the average cost of selling a line of goods to a class of customers a reasonable approximation of the cost of dealing with each member of the class with respect to each individual product sold, such classifications are likely to be accepted. Evidence that a classification obscures significant cost differences among customers, however, will vitiate a proffered cost justification defense.

(b) Changing Conditions. The changing conditions defense in section 2(a) is basically designed to reassure sellers of perishable or seasonal goods that they are permitted to reduce prices in order to dispose of such goods. To establish the defense, there must be some change, either in the goods themselves or in market conditions, to which a price change is responsive. Where such evidence tends to show that the two purchases being compared were not in fact "contemporaneous," it will provide a basis for negating the prima facie claim that a discrimination has occurred. Section 2(a)'s express proviso on changing conditions thus appears merely to emphasize that even relatively contemporaneous price differences may not necessarily constitute a price discrimination.

(c) Meeting Competition. Just as a seller may cost-justify a price difference or show that it was necessitated by changing conditions, so the seller may show that the price difference is not being used aggressively but defensively. Section 2(b) allows a seller to avoid liability for price discrimination by showing that the lower price was extended

in good faith to meet an equally low price of a competitor.

The good faith requirement serves to prevent a discriminator who fortuitously meets another's price in the course of attempting to undercut it from escaping liability for price discrimination. On the other hand, the meeting competition defense will not necessarily be defeated because one fortuitously beats a competitor's price in the course of a good faith effort to meet it. A margin for error in the effort to meet a price is necessary because a seller cannot always be sure of the accuracy of information (usually provided by a buyer) concerning a competitor's price. The margin for error, however, is small and has been held to be subject to a good faith effort to verify information of questionable accuracy.

A difficulty arises when the only way to verify a price is to contact the competitor whose price is being met. In a number of instances businesses accused of collusive price fixing in violation of the Sherman Act have defended their sharing of price information as necessary in order to avoid violating the Robinson–Patman Act. Consequently, the courts have limited the circumstances in which a seller may lawfully contact a competitor in order to verify a competitor's price. In *United States v. Container Corp. of America* (1969) the Supreme Court held that even an infrequent and irregular exchange of price information was illegal under the Sherman Act. Still more recently the Court cautioned that any exchange of price information—even when putatively for purposes of Robinson–Patman compliance—must remain subject to close scrutiny under the Sherman Act. See *United States v. United States Gypsum Co.* (1978).

While a defendant seeking to establish the "meeting competition" defense need not show that the price being met was itself a legal (as opposed to a discriminatory) price, the courts have made it clear that the meeting competition defense cannot be used to justify copying a competitor's discriminatory pricing scheme which is recognizably illegal. In *FTC v. A.E. Staley Manufacturing Co.* (1945), the Supreme Court emphasized that section 2(b) was not intended to legalize the otherwise illicit conduct of one business just because some other business had done it first. On the other hand, the meeting competition defense is available where, in response to competitive price increases, a brewer *raises* prices in one state that statutorily requires brewers to sell to wholesalers at a single price throughout the state, while not changing prices to wholesalers in adjoining states. *Falls City Industries Inc. v. Vanco Beverage, Inc.* (1983) (Supreme Court reversal of a lower court ruling that the meeting competition defense is available only if the defendant sets its lower price on a customer-by-customer basis and creates the price discrimination by lowering rather than by raising prices).

b. Unearned Brokerage

Section 2(c) of the amended Clayton Act prohibits (1) a person engaged in commerce (2) from paying or receiving a commission, brokerage fee or compensation, or an allowance or discount in lieu thereof (3) except for services actually rendered in connection with a sale of goods (4) where the person paid is not under the direct or indirect control of the person making the payment. The provision was principally designed to outlaw arrangements whereby buyers exacted price concessions disguised as brokerage commissions to their agents or to themselves. As we saw in Chapter 9, supra, section 2(c) has also been held to prohibit commercial bribery in bargaining relations.

Unlike section 2(a), section 2(c) extends liability to the person receiving the payment or discount as well as the seller who offers it and applies to exporters as well as importers and domestic businesses. Further, the language of section 2(c) does not require a showing of price discrimination (i.e., two or more sales) or injury to competition. Nor does the Act allow for a defense of cost justification or meeting competition. The only defense expressly made available is that the brokerage fee was for services rendered. Although the courts seem to have retreated from their early position that a broker not under the control of the party making the payment is inherently incapable of rendering the services contemplated under the statute, they continue to insist that brokerage fees be for services *actually* rendered. To date no broker not under the control of the business making a payment has succeeded in establishing that such services were rendered.

A more difficult case is presented by allowances and discounts in lieu of brokerage. While section 2(c) does not expressly require proof of discrimination (sales at different prices to two or more customers), such evidence may in fact be required in allowance and discount cases to show that the allowance or discount was in fact "in lieu of" brokerage and not simply the result of lower costs. Not all cost savings, however, can be passed along to a purchaser. In *FTC v. Henry Broch & Co.* (1960) the Supreme Court held that a cost justification defense based on saved brokerage was unavailable under section 2(c). The legislative policy of preventing coerced price concessions was apparently viewed as outweighing the uncoerced seller's interest in passing along such cost savings.

c. Discriminatory Promotional Allowances and Services

Sections 2(d) and 2(e) of the amended Clayton Act forbid a seller engaged in commerce from (1) granting promotional payments, services or facilities (2) to or for the benefit of a customer (3) unless made available on proportionally equal terms to all customers who compete in reselling the seller's goods. The purpose of these two sections, like that of section 2(c) is to prevent disguised price discrimination. Despite textual differences between 2(d) and 2(e), the courts have read the two as companion provisions. Thus both have been held to require that the persons and transactions involved be in commerce even though only section 2(d) so specifies. Unlike section 2(c), sections 2(d) and 2(e) normally require a showing of discrimination as a part of the prima facie case. Courts have occasionally required a seller charged with a violation of 2(d) or 2(e) to prove that his conduct is not discriminatory. Unlike section 2(a) price discrimination, however, discriminatory promotional allowances and services are unlawful per se, without any need for a showing of competitive injury. But see *World of Sleep, Inc. v. La–Z–Boy Chair Co.* (1985) questionably citing *J. Truett Payne Co., Inc. v. Chrysler Motors Corp.* (1981), a section 2(a) case, for the proposition that a plaintiff in a section 2(e) case must show that not receiving a promotional allowance affected plaintiff's ability to compete with favored competitors. The only affirmative defense available is the meeting competition defense of section 2(b). The cost-justification defense of section 2(a) is not available.

The effect of sections 2(d) and 2(e) is to flatly prohibit a business from designing a promotion in such a way as to exclude certain of one's customers or attempting to cost-justify offering promotional allowances or services only to certain of one's customers, where they are in competition with each other. On the other hand, promotional allowances, services and facilities need only be made available on proportionally equal terms. Normally this means that some relation can be drawn between the volume of goods purchased and the allowance granted.

d. Buyer Liability for Price Discrimination

Ironically, although the principal impetus behind the Robinson–Patman Act was to prevent chain stores and other large volume buyers from using economic coercion to exact price concessions, the Act focuses primarily on the liability of the discriminating seller and deals only secondarily with the liability of the favored buyer. The reason, as we have seen, is because at the time the Robinson–Patman Act was enacted, the Supreme Court took a restrictive view on the extent to which a buyer is engaged in commerce which Congress is empowered to regulate. Thus, the only sections of the Robinson–Patman Act which apply to a buyer are section 2(c), which makes it unlawful for a buyer to receive unearned brokerage or an allowance in lieu thereof, and section 2(f), which makes it unlawful: (1) for a buyer engaged in commerce (2) knowingly to induce or receive (3) a discrimination in price prohibited by section 2 of the Act. The FTC and the courts have concluded that section 2(f) prohibits the knowing inducement or receipt not only of a per se discriminatory price (i.e. a price violative of section 2(a)) but also of those forms of disguised price discrimination prohibited by sections 2(d) and 2(e). In the alternative, they have held such conduct to be an unfair method of competition within the meaning of section 5 of the FTC Act.

In order to subject a buyer to liability, the FTC or a private plaintiff must first prove that the seller violated the Act and then prove that the buyer had reason to know that the seller's price was illegal. Thus, if a seller in good faith seeks to meet competition within the meaning of section 2(b) of the Act, the buyer will not be liable under section 2(f), even though the buyer knows that the seller is in fact *beating* the competition, see *Great Atlantic & Pacific Tea Co., Inc., v. FTC* (1979), unless the buyer has induced the price concession by misrepresenting to the seller what the competitive price is. See *Kroger Co. v. FTC* (1971).

3. PRICE DISCRIMINATION AND PREDATORY PRICING IN INTERNATIONAL TRADE

Because section 2(a) of the amended Clayton Act is limited to price discrimination which occurs in connection with commodities sold for use, consumption or resale within the United States, it does not prohibit price discrimination by exporters. Sections 2(c), 2(d) and 2(e) and section 3 of the Robinson–Patman Act, on the other hand, contain no analogous limitation, but extend to any payment or acceptance of unearned brokerage, discriminatory payment or furnishing of promotional services, or covert or predatory geographic price discrimination or predatory price cutting which occurs "in commerce." Thus, U.S. law will apply wherever such conduct affects U.S. commerce (e.g., injures a domestic business).

Price discrimination in the import trade is of far greater domestic concern than price discrimination in the export trade. Not only does section 2(a) of the amended Clayton Act prohibit an importer from discriminating among U.S. purchasers, but a number of other federal statutes provide relief against a special form of import price discrimination, known as "dumping."

Dumping occurs when a foreign manufacturer sells goods in the United States for less than fair value—i.e., less than it charges for the same goods at home or other markets. The Tariff Act of 1930, 19 U.S.C.A. § 1202 et seq., as amended by the Trade Agreements Act of 1979 (which repealed the earlier Antidumping Act of 1921) and the Trade and Tariff Act of 1984 (which extensively amends the antidumping sections of the 1930 Act), provides for a special antidumping duty to be assessed and collected on imports of a product which is being or is likely to be dumped in the United States and is causing or threatening material injury to a U.S. industry or retarding its establishment.

The Omnibus Trade and Competitiveness Act of 1988 added a further provision allowing a U.S. party to attack so called "input" dumping that is occurring in a foreign country that is a signatory of the General Agreement on Tariffs and Trade and its associated Antidumping Code, where the goods being dumped are incorporated into a product that is then exported to the U.S. Section 1317 of the Act authorizes domestic producers of such input "like product" to petition the Office of the U.S. Trade Representative who may, in turn, seek remedial action by the government of that country against the unfair imports.

In the U.S., the International Trade Administration (ITA) of the Commerce Department, acting on behalf of the Secretary of Commerce, is responsible for making a determination as to whether a product is being dumped. If the Secretary so finds, the International Trade Commission (ITC) must then determine whether the dumping is causing or threatening a material injury or retarding establishment of a U.S. industry. A finding of such injury results in the assessment and collection of a special duty in the amount of the difference between the home market price (or the price on other foreign markets) and the price at which the goods are sold in the United States. Any interested party, such as a foreign government or business or a U.S. business, labor union, or trade association, who is a party to the ITC's administrative proceedings may seek judicial review before the Court of International Trade (formerly the U.S. Customs Court), and may appeal its final decisions to the Court of Appeals for the Federal Circuit.

Price discrimination in the import trade may also occur indirectly through foreign government subsidization of certain of its exports. In such cases section 303 of the Tariff Act of 1930, 19 U.S.C.A. § 1303, as amended by the Trade Agreements Act of 1979, and the Trade and Tariff Act of 1984, provides for imposition of countervailing duties in the amount of the government subsidy. Here, as with dumping duties, the existence and amount of the subsidy is determined by the ITA, while the existence of competitive injury is determined by the ITC.

Section 337 of the Tariff Act of 1930, 19 U.S.C.A. § 1337, forbids unfair methods of competition or unfair acts in the import trade. While the principal use of this provision has been to prevent the importation of articles which infringe U.S. intellectual property rights, the ITC has also used this provision to assert jurisdiction over various types of antitrust claims, including predatory pricing. Where such conduct threatens or prevents the establishment of a U.S. business, the imported articles may be excluded from this country or the ITC may issue a cease and desist order. Either action of the ITC may be overturned by the President within 60 days. The ITC may not use its section 1337 authority to deal with dumping or countervailing duty cases.

INDEX

References are to pages

ADVERTISING
See also False and Deceptive Advertising; Promotional Practices

Children's advertising, 371, 374
Cigarettes, 382
Comparative, 160, 362–364
Corrective, 196, 374
Deceptive Price Advertising, 384–385
Drug prices, 183, 404
Foods, drugs and cosmetics, 369
Franchising, 63, 106
Real estate ads, 108
Regulation,
    Federal Food and Drug Administration, 369, 382
    Federal Trade Commission, 368–387
Slogans, 105, 127, 181, 197
Substantiation, 378–379
Truthful, 25, 404

ANTI-DILUTION STATUTES
See Dilution

ANTITRUST LAWS
See also Conspiracies; Federal Trade Commission; Pricing Practices; Refusal to Deal

Clayton Act,
    Amended by Robinson–Patman Act, 57, 395, 414–416, 417, 419–420, 431, 435–436

ANTITRUST LAWS—Cont'd
Clayton Act—Cont'd
 Enforcement and remedies, 368
 Relation to unfair trade practice law, 24
 Scope of act, 57
 Treble damage provision, 368, 396
Concerted group conduct, 41–42, 65–67, 70–71
Exclusive dealing, 57, 78
Export trade, 30–31
Extraterritorial application, 32
Federal Trade Commission Act,
 FTC Improvement Act of 1980, p. 374
 Magnuson–Moss Consumer Warranty/FTC Improvement Act of 1975, pp. 370–371, 372–374
 Relation to unfair trade practices law, 24
 Scope of act, 57, 333–334, 368–375, 387–389, 397–398
 Unfair methods of competition, 368–369, 387–389, 397–398, 399, 434
 Unfair or deceptive acts or practices, 369–370, 375–389
 Wheeler–Lea Amendments, 369–370
Import trade, 30
Monopolization, 56, 62, 66, 69–70
Patent licensing, 225–226
Per se violations, 56
Pricing practices, 402
Refusal to deal, 62
Relation to unfair trade practice law, 23–24
Resale price maintenance, 71, 405–406
Restraints of trade,
 Conspiracies, 56
 Contracts, 56, 405–406
Robinson–Patman Act,
 Amendment to Clayton Act, 57, 395, 414–416, 417, 419–420, 431, 435–436
 Bribery, 395–397
 Buyer liability, 434–435
 Discriminatory promotional allowances and services,
  Defenses, 433
  Elements of prima facie case, 432–433
  Enforcement, 416–417
  Extraterritorial application, 31, 396–397, 435–436
 Price discrimination,
  Competitive injury, 420–426
  Defenses, 426–430
  Elements of prima facie case, 417–418

ANTITRUST LAWS—Cont'd
Robinson–Patman Act—Cont'd
  Price discrimination—Cont'd
    Extraterritorial application, 419
    Relation to unfair trade practice law, 24
    Sales at unreasonably low prices,
      Constitutionality, 412, 414
      Intent, 412–414
      Reasonableness of price, 412–413
  Scope of Act, 407
  Section-by-section summary, 415–416
  Unearned brokerage,
    Allowances and discounts in lieu of brokerage, 432
    Bribery, 395–397
    Defenses, 431
    Elements of prima facie case, 431–432
    Extraterritorial application, 31, 396–397, 431
Sherman Act,
  Association membership rules as violation, 298–299
  Consumer Goods Pricing Act, 405
  Exchange of price information, 429–430
  Extraterritorial application, 32
  McGuire Act, 405
  Miller–Tydings Amendment, 405
  Per se violations, 56
  Relation to unfair trade practice law, 23–24
  Resale price maintenance, 405–406
  Rule of reason, 56
  Scope of Act, 56
  State antitrust laws, 81
  Tie-ins and tying arrangements, 57, 156
  Trademark licensing, 156

ATTORNEY'S FEES
See Remedies

BAIT AND SWITCH
See Promotional Practices

BERNE CONVENTION
See International Agreements

BOYCOTTS
See Refusal to Deal

BRIBERY, 30, 54–55, 93, 221, 334, 391–398
Athletic contests, 392

BRIBERY—Cont'd
Commercial bribery,
    Defined, 391–392
    Effects, 394–395
    Types, 391–394
Common-law remedies, 395
Federal statutory remedies, 395–397
Foreign commerce, 44, 396
Foreign Corrupt Practices Act, 31, 398
Government officials, 392–394
Interference with contractual and precontractual relations, 93, 395
Law governing, generally, 334
Misappropriation of trade secrets, 321, 391
Payola, 392
Robinson–Patman Act violations, 395–396
Treble damages, 395

CALIFORNIA RESALE ROYALTIES ACT, 244

CERTIFICATION MARKS
    See also Lanham Act; Marks and Names
Cancellation, 153–154
Defined, 105–106
Lanham Act protection of unregistered marks, 357
Registration, 105, 130–131

CHARACTERS
See Literary and Artistic Characters

CLAYTON ACT
See Antitrust Laws

COERCION
    See also Refusal to Deal
Common-law condemnation, 5, 53–55
Concerted group conduct, 65–72, 92–93
Conditioned refusal to deal, 65, 68, 69
Contractual relations,
    Inducing breach, 84
    Inducing modification, 53, 65, 89–90
    Inducing termination, 53, 69
Privileged, 54, 71–72

COLLECTIVE MARKS
See Marks and Names

COMBINATIONS AND CONSPIRACIES
See Conspiracies

COMMON LAW
See Contracts and Contractual Relations; Torts and Tort Law

COMPUTER PROGRAMS
Copyright protection, 230, 234, 237, 249–250
Patent protection, 218–219
Trade secret protection, 312

CONCERTED GROUP CONDUCT
See Antitrust Laws; Coercion; Conspiracies; Contracts and Contractual Relations; Refusal to Deal

CONSPIRACIES
See also Concerted Group Conduct; Refusal to Deal
Common-law, 5, 53, 67–68
Sherman Act, 56

CONSTITUTION, U.S.
Commerce clause, 18, 21, 23, 29
First Amendment and,
    Commercial Speech, 25
    Copyright, 236
    Defamation, 337–340, 341
    Dilution statutes, 183
    Disparagement, 344–346
    Misappropriation, 26, 299–300
    Right of publicity, 264
    Trademarks and trade names, 26, 107–108, 137, 183
    Truthful advertising, 25, 183, 404
Fourteenth Amendment,
    Due process clause and economic liberty, 25, 403–404
    Equal protection clause and civil rights statutes, 62, 400–401
Patent and copyright clause, 18, 20, 137, 211–212, 235
    Discoveries, 217, 235
    Writings, 228–229, 235, 260
Supremacy clause, 18–19, 27, 212
    State law, 18–19, 137, 212
    Treaties, 27
Thirteenth Amendment, 96

CONSUMER TESTING AND RATING ORGANIZATIONS, 349–350

CONTRACTS AND CONTRACTUAL RELATIONS
See also Franchising; Licensing; Torts and Tort Law

CONTRACTS AND CONTRACTUAL RELATIONS—Cont'd
Breach, 3
Client relations, 55
Coerced, 53
Commercial, 34, 75
Employment, 34, 41, 73–75, 313, 315–316
Exclusive dealing, 73, 74, 78
Express, 35, 76–81
    Covenants not to compete, 77, 78–81, 314–315
    Covenants of confidentiality, 80, 313–314
    Warranties of title or merchantability, 75–76
Illegal, 77
    Gambling, 77
    Restraint of trade, 53, 77
    Usurious, 77
Implied, 81–83
    Covenants not to solicit former customers, 82
    Covenants of confidentiality, 82, 314–315
    Covenants of loyalty, 82
Interference, 4–5, 41–42, 73, 83–94
    Bribery, 54–55, 93, 395
    Coercing modification, 65, 89–90
    Concerted group conduct, 92–93
    Groundless litigation, 54
    Inducing breach, 65, 73, 83, 84–88, 395
    Inducing termination, 90–91
    Malice, intent, recklessness, 73–74, 84–85
    Negligence, 86–87
    Soliciting clients, 55, 93–94
    Term contracts, 76, 85
    Terminable at will contracts, 75, 76, 85, 91, 92
    Unenforceable contracts, 77
Post-contractual covenants, 78–81
Preemption of state contract law, 21, 309
Specific performance, 95–96
Statute of frauds, 77
Trade secrets, 5
Void, 77

CONTRIBUTORY INFRINGEMENT
Copyrights, 283, 285
Mask works, 288–289
Patents, 269
Trademarks, 184–185

COPYRIGHT

See also Computer Programs; Constitution, U.S.; Contributory Infringement; *Droit Moral*; Literary and Artistic Characters; Literary and Artistic Works; Preemption of State Law: Remedies; Shopright Doctrine

Architectural Works Copyright Protection Act of 1990, pp. 230, 231–232, 238

Assignments, 244–245, 247

Berne Convention, 29, 241, 242, 245–246

Berne Implementation Act of 1988, p. 246

Common law, 5, 213, 231, 240
    Advantages over federal law, 240
    Infringement damages, 358
    Shopright doctrine, 244
    Trade secrets and ideas, 311

Computer Software Rental Amendments Act, 230, 274

Copyright Act of 1909,
    Compared with 1976 Act, 230–235, 239–241, 246–247
    General publication, 239–240
    Literary titles, 135–136
    Preemption of state law, 244
    Renewal right, 241–242, 246–247
    Term, 241–242

Copyright Act of 1976,
    Compared with 1909 Act, 230–235, 239–241, 246–247
    Compulsory licensing, 245–246, 273, 276–277
    Exclusive rights, 271–278
    Preemption of state law, 134–135, 240, 258–262, 264, 275, 300
        Non-equivalent rights, 260–262
        Non-preempted subject matter, 134–135, 260, 264
    Specific sections,
        § 101, pp. 233, 243
        § 102, pp. 231, 234, 236, 250–251, 261, 296
        § 103, pp. 235, 262
        § 104, pp. 241, 252
        § 106, pp. 272–273, 286
        § 106A, p. 272
        § 107, pp. 277, 280, 281
        § 108, p. 273
        § 109, pp. 274–275
        § 110, p. 276
        § 111, p. 276
        § 115, p. 273
        § 116, pp. 246, 276
        § 116A, p. 246

COPYRIGHT—Cont'd
Copyright Act of 1976—Cont'd
  Specific sections—Cont'd
    § 117, pp. 234, 275
    § 201, pp. 242–243
    § 203, p. 308
    § 204, p. 244
    § 205, p. 244
    § 301, pp. 19, 260–261, 272
  Subject matter protected and excluded, 231–234, 249, 250
  Term of protection, 241–242
  Termination of transfers, 246–247
Copyright defined, 212
Copyright Office,
  Compulsory license applications and royalties, 245–247, 273, 276, 277
  Deposit of copyrighted work and registration, 241, 312–313
  Recording assignments and exclusive licenses, 244
  Recording terminations of transfers, 247
  Registration of mask works, 255
Copyright Remedy Clarification Act, 230, 302
Copyright Royalty Tribunal, 246
Fair use privilege, 277–278, 280–285
  Burlesque, parody and satire, 283–284
  Library photocopying, 284–285
  Teacher and classroom copying, 277–278
  VCR copying, 283
Federal copyright generally, 212–214
First sale limitation, 274–275
Infringement, 271, 278–281
  Imported goods, 30, 303
  Mutilation, 207–208
  Plagiarism, 204
Licensing, 244–247
Literary titles, 135–136
Notice requirement, 241
Owners protected, 242–243
Preemption of state law, 19–21
  Common law copyright, 240
  Misappropriation, 120, 258–262, 300
  Right of publicity, 264
  Shrink wrap license laws, 275
  Unfair competition, 134–135
Renewal right, 241–242, 246–247
Subject matter protected and excluded, 231–234, 249, 250

INDEX

COPYRIGHT—Cont'd
Term of copyright, 241–242
Termination of transfers, 246–247
Territorial scope of copyright, 212–213
Universal Copyright Convention, 28–29, 242, 252–253
Visual Artists' Rights Act, 230, 272

COURT OF APPEALS FOR THE FEDERAL CIRCUIT, 112, 222, 227–228

COURT OF CUSTOMS AND PATENT APPEALS, 112

COVENANTS NOT TO COMPETE
See Contracts and Contractual Relations

CUSTOMER LISTS
Casual memory rule, 325
Implied covenant not to use or disclose, 82
Trade secret protection, 316

DAMAGES
See Remedies

DECEIT
See Misrepresentation

DECEPTIVE ADVERTISING
See False and Deceptive Advertising

DECEPTIVE PROMOTIONAL PRACTICES
See False and Deceptive Advertising; Promotional Practices

DEFAMATION
Common-law origin, 4, 49, 52
Damages, presumption and proof, 336, 338
Defenses, 336–341
Defined, 335–336
Group defamation, 340–341
Libel, 336
Malice, common-law and constitutional, 337, 340
Private plaintiffs, 339–340
Public figures, 338, 340, 344
Public officials, 337
Remedies,
    Damages, 336, 338
    Injunctive relief, 346
Slander, 336
Trade disparagement,

INDEX
References are to pages

DEFAMATION—Cont'd
Trade disparagement—Cont'd
Distinguished, 341–342

DILUTION
First Amendment limits, 183
Model State Trademark Act, 179–180
State antidilution statutes, 26–27, 109, 160, 179–184
State power to prevent, 136

DISPARAGEMENT
See Torts and Tort Law; Trade Disparagement

DROIT MORAL, 29, 208
See also Copyright, Visual Artists' Rights Act

DUMPING
See Pricing Practices

EQUITABLE DEFENSES
Acquiescence, 187, 188, 189, 190, 209, 301, 302
Laches, 72, 187, 188–190, 209, 301, 302
Unclean hands, 72, 187, 188, 189–190, 209, 301, 302

EQUITABLE REMEDIES
See Remedies

EUROPEAN ECONOMIC COMMUNITY, 253, 254

EXCLUSIVE DEALING
See Antitrust Laws; Contracts and Contractual Relations

FALSE AND DECEPTIVE ADVERTISING
See also Advertising; Federal Trade Commission; Promotional Practices
Common-law, 17, 350–353
Designations of geographic origin, 351–352
Single source requirement, 350–351
Lanham Act, section 43(a), pp. 23, 354–366
Deceptive non-disclosure, 364–365
Disparagement of a product, service or business, 355, 363
Failure to identify country of origin, 364
False or misleading descriptions of representations of fact, 354, 355, 356, 358, 361–363
False or misleading designations of origin, 354, 356, 358–360
Product, service or business misidentification, 355
Remedies, 365–366
Standing to sue, 356–358

INDEX

References are to pages

FALSE AND DECEPTIVE ADVERTISING—Cont'd
Public regulation,
    FDA regulation, 369
    FTC regulation, 369–370, 375–387
    State regulation, 353–354, 367, 371
    Unfair Trade Practices and Consumer Protection Law, 354
    Uniform Deceptive Trade Practices Act, 353

FEDERAL PREEMPTION OF STATE LAW
See Preemption of State Law

FEDERAL TRADE COMMISSION
    See also Advertising; Antitrust Laws; Bribery; False and Deceptive Advertising; Promotional Practices
Advertising substantiation program, 378–379
Corrective advertising, 196, 374
Creation, 368ff
Enforcement procedure, 373–374
FTC Act,
    Children's advertising, 371, 374
    Deceptive acts or practices, 369, 375–387
    Export trade, 31, 383
    Funeral home industry, 374, 375
    Insurance industry, 374
    Unfair methods of competition, 299, 368, 387–389, 397, 399
        Bribery, 397
        Lotteries, 399
Jurisdiction,
    Interstate commerce, 370
    Public interest, 372
Legislative veto, 374–375
Preemption of state law, 370–371
Robinson–Patman Act, 397, 416
Rulemaking, 372–373
Statutory authority, 24

FIRST AMENDMENT
See Constitution, U.S.

FOOD AND DRUG ADMINISTRATION, 369, 582

FOREIGN CORRUPT PRACTICES ACT
See Legislation

FRANCHISING
Business and service misdescriptions, 383
Coercive or oppressive franchisor conduct, 91

FRANCHISING—Cont'd
Contracts, 75
Termination, statutes regulating, 64–65
Trademarks and service marks, 106
    Licensing, 155–156
Types, 63–64

GAMBLING
Contracts, 77
Games of chance, 398–400
Lotteries, 398–400
Refusal to deal with gamblers, 72

GENERAL AGREEMENT ON TARIFFS AND TRADE (GATT)
See International Agreements

GENERICIDE, 143–144
See also Marks and Names; Trademarks

GOOD WILL
    See also Trademarks
Assignment of trade symbols and, 154
Contracts for sale of, 75, 79
Contractual protection,
    Express covenants not to compete, 78–80
    Implied covenants,
        Not to derogate, 82
        Not to solicit former customers, 82
Creation by use of trade symbols, 107
Definition, 35
Diversion by deceptive "come on" tactics, 386
Product and business good will; diversion by palming off, 198–199
State "Fair Trade" law protection of, 405
Trade symbols as embodying, 99–100

GREY MARKET GOODS
See International Trade Practices; Lanham Act

IDEAS
As intangible business asset, 35
Assignment, 319–320
Legal protection, scope and limits of,
    Common law of ideas, 310, 317–319
    Contractual protection, 310, 313–316
    Copyright law,
        Common law, 311

IDEAS—Cont'd
Legal protection—Cont'd
  Copyright law—Cont'd
    Federal, 234, 236–237, 279–280
    Misappropriation law, 299–300
    Patent law, 218
Licensing, 63, 319–320

INJUNCTIONS
See Remedies

INTELLECTUAL PROPERTY, 16, 31, 193, 215, 269, 302, 306
See also Copyright; Patents; Trade Names; Trade
  Secrets; Trademarks

INTERNATIONAL AGREEMENTS
Berne Convention, 29, 241, 242, 245–246
General Agreement on Tariffs and Trade (GATT), 29, 33, 380, 437
Paris Convention, 28, 117, 223
Patent Cooperation Treaty, 28, 213
Treaty on the Protection of Intellectual Property in Respect of Integrated Circuits, 254
Universal Copyright Convention, 28–29, 242, 252–253

INTERNATIONAL TRADE COMMISSION, 179, 192, 302–303, 330, 368, 369, 389–390, 437, 438
Copyright infringement, 303
Dumping, 437–438
Patent infringement, 302
Trademark infringement, 179, 192
Unfair methods of competition in the import trade, 369, 389–390

INTERNATIONAL TRADE PRACTICES
  See also Bribery; Pricing Practices
Bribery, 396
Copyright infringement, 303
Dumping, 436–438
Government subsidization, 437–438
Parallel imports (Grey market goods), 175–179, 390
Patent infringement, 302
Predatory pricing, 435–436
Price discrimination, 435–436
Trademark and trade name infringement, 111, 113–114, 175–179

INDEX

JOINT VENTURES, 34, 75

LABELLING
See Product Labelling

LABOR LAW, FEDERAL, 16, 21, 41–42

LABOR UNIONS
Dumping, standing to complain, 437
Identifying marks, 106
Labor disputes, 16, 21, 41–42

LANHAM ACT
    See also False and Deceptive Advertising; Marks and Names; Trademark Act of 1905; Trademarks
Definitions,
    Certification mark, 105–106
    Collective mark, 106
    Service mark, 105
    Trade name, 101–102, 105
    Trademark, 101, 105
False advertising, private action for, 23, 114
    Deceptive mutilation of a TV script, 208, 360
    False designations of origin, 154, 333, 354–355, 358–360, 364
    False or misleading descriptions or representations, 333, 354–355, 358–359, 361–363, 364
    Literary and artistic titles, 359
    Palming off, 355, 359
    Product configurations, 193–194
    Remedies, 360, 365–366
    Standing to sue, 356–358
    Trade disparagement, 355, 363
    Trade names, 361
Infringement of registered marks,
    Contributory infringement, 184–185
    Defenses, 186–191
    Likelihood of confusion, 161, 162–163
    Non-competing goods, services, or businesses, 166–172
    Parallel imports, 175–179
    Remedies, 192–196
Paris Convention, implementation, 117
Preemption of state law, 22, 108
Purpose of Act, 357–358
Registration, 23, 110–114
    Abandonment,
        Misuse, 151, 153–156

INDEX

References are to pages

LANHAM ACT—Cont'd
Registration—Cont'd
  Abandonment—Cont'd
    Misuse—Cont'd
      Assignments in gross, 154–155
      Naked licensing, 155–156
      Non-use, 151–153
  Acquired distinctiveness (secondary meaning), 118, 119, 121, 123, 128, 138–139, 148, 150
  Benefits, 112–114
  Cancellation,
    Certification marks, 130–131, 153–154
    FTC authority, 374
    Generic terms, 141–146, 157
  Color, 147–149
  Concurrent registration, 174–175
  Deceptive and misdescriptive marks and names, 118–119, 120–125, 128–131
  Deceptive marks, 122, 128–129, 140
  Deceptively misdescriptive marks, 128–130
  Disparaging marks, 126, 190
  Foreign marks, and names, 30, 114, 115–117
  Historical names, 126–127
  Incontestability, 113, 114, 157, 186–187, 189
  Inherently distinctive marks and names, 119–120, 129
  Patent and Trademark Office proceedings, 110–111, 188–189
  Personal names, 125–128
  Prerequisites,
    Foreign registration, 115, 116–117
    Secondary meaning, 118, 119, 121, 123–124, 128, 148
    Use of marks, actual or intended, 115–117
  Principal Register, 110, 112–113, 115–116, 124, 125, 127, 138
  Product configurations and containers, 137–138
  Slogans, 127
  Suggestive marks, 120, 122
  Supplemental Register, 110, 117, 127, 150
  Titles, 138–139
  Trade names, 101–105, 114
Relation to state law, 22
Specific sections,
  § 2(a), pp. 127, 128, 140
  § 2(c), p. 127
  § 2(d), pp. 114, 122, 140, 174
  § 2(e), pp. 120, 122, 123, 125, 128, 141
  § 2(f), pp. 121, 123

LANHAM ACT—Cont'd
Specific sections—Cont'd
- § 14, pp. 130, 141, 144, 153, 157, 186
- § 15, pp. 114, 139, 145, 157, 186
- § 19, p. 188
- § 23, p. 127
- § 32, p. 161
- § 33, pp. 187, 189, 190
- § 34, pp. 187, 366
- § 35, pp. 187, 194, 195, 366
- § 36, p. 366
- § 39a, p. 108
- § 42, pp. 114, 176, 178, 192
- § 43, pp. 23, 114, 132, 146, 184–185, 193, 208, 333, 334–366, 390
- § 44, p. 114
- § 45, pp. 105, 127, 146, 152, 357, 358

Trade names, protection provided, 114
Trademark Clarification Act of 1984, pp. 145–146
Trademark Revision Act of 1988, pp. 116, 354, 358

LEGISLATION
> See also Antitrust Laws; California Resale Royalties Act; Copyright; Federal Trade Commission; Lanham Act; Model or Uniform Acts; Patents; Semiconductor Chip Protection Act of 1984; Trademark Act of 1905; Trademark Counterfeiting Act of 1984

Federal,
- Administrative Procedure Act, 372–373
- Automotive Dealers' Franchise Act, 64
- Consumer Goods Pricing Act, 405
- Export Trading Company Act of 1982, p. 31
- Federal Cigarette Labeling and Advertising Act, 382
- Federal Petroleum Marketing Practices Act, 64
- Federal Trade Commission Improvement Acts of 1975, 1980, pp. 370–374
- Foreign Corrupt Practices Act, 31, 398
- Omnibus Trade and Competitiveness Act of 1988, pp. 31, 32, 192, 270, 330, 389, 436
- Patent Variety Protection Act of 1970, pp. 220–221
- Racketeer Influenced and Corrupt Organizations Act (RICO), 366–367
- Tariff Act of 1930, pp. 30, 176, 177, 179, 192, 302, 303, 436, 438
- Tariff and Trade Act of 1984, pp. 30, 32, 192, 436, 438

INDEX

References are to pages

LEGISLATION—Cont'd
Federal—Cont'd
Trade Act of 1974, pp. 30, 31, 32, 192
Trade Agreements Act of 1979, pp. 30, 192, 436, 438
Webb–Pomerene Act, 31
Wheeler–Lea Amendments, 369
State,
California Civil Code, 266, 267
California Resale Royalties Act, 244
Fair Trade Laws, 404–406
New York Civil Rights Law, 262, 263
Shrink-Wrap Licensing Laws, 274

LICENSING
See also Copyright, Compulsory Licensing; Franchising
Contracts, 75
Copyrights, 243–244
Franchising, 63
Ideas, 63
Patents, 213, 224–225, 226–227
Trade secrets, 319
Trademarks and trade names, 154, 155–156

LITERARY AND ARTISTIC CHARACTERS, 136–137, 197

LITERARY AND ARTISTIC WORKS
See also Copyright; Titles, Literary and Artistic
California Resale Royalties Act, 244
Characters, 136–137
Common-law protection, 197, 213, 231
Mutilation, 207–209, 360
Plagiarism, 204–205, 295–296

LITERARY TITLES
See Titles, Literary and Artistic

LOTTERIES
See also Promotional Practices
Definition, 399
Federal Trade Commission authority, 387–388, 399
Law governing, 334, 399
Private remedies, 399
Trademarks used in association with, 190

MALICE
See also Predatory Conduct or Purpose; Pricing Practices
Constitutional and common-law definitions, 337, 338, 340

MALICE—Cont'd
Defamation, 337, 338, 340
Infliction of pecuniary harm, 11, 43, 57–61
Interference with contracts, 5
Malicious competition, 9–11, 58–60
Nuisance, 10
Pleading and proof, 58–60
Privileged conduct, 11, 13, 61–62
Selling below cost, 60, 407–408, 411
Trade disparagement, 342, 345

MARKS AND NAMES
See also Certification Marks; Secondary Meaning; Service Marks, Trade Names; Trademarks

Abandonment, 151–157
    Misuse, 151, 153–156
    Non-use, 151–153
    Recapture, 145
Assignment, 154–155
Collective marks, 106
Color, 147–149
Distinctive product and business features, 131–138
Family of marks or names, 107, 165
Generic terms, 119, 141–146, 182
Genericide, 143–146
Geographic terms, 124, 193
House marks, 107
Infringing and non-infringing uses,
    Collateral uses, 159–160, 182
    Contributory infringement, 184–185
    Defenses,
        Absolute, 186
        Equitable, 186, 187–190
    Dilution, 26–27, 109, 160, 179–184
    Non-competing goods, services and businesses, 166–172
    Palming off distinguishing, 6–7, 98–99, 197
    Parallel imports, 175–179
    Priority, 116, 158–159
    Remedies, 192–196
Inherently distinctive terms, 119–120
Legal protection,
    Federal,
        Private right of action, 359–361
        Registration, 23, 104–108, 110–114
        Regulation, 370

MARKS AND NAMES—Cont'd
Legal protection—Cont'd
　Prerequisites,
　　Actual or intended use, 116–118
　　Distinctiveness, 118–139
　　Foreign Registration, 116–117
　　Secondary meaning, 121ff
　State,
　　Common-law protection, 100–104
　　　Personal names and likenesses, 125–127, 262, 263
　　　Trade names, 107
　　Registration, 114–115
Licensing, 155–156
Misdescriptive terms, 128–131
Personal names, 125–128, 193, 262, 263
Policing, 157–158
Secondary meaning, 118, 119, 121, 123, 128, 138–139, 148, 150
Slogans, 105, 127
Suggestive, 120, 122

MASK WORKS
See Semiconductor Chip Protection Act of 1984

MISAPPROPRIATION
　See also Copyright; Ideas; Publicity, Common-Law Right of; Trade Secrets
Competition requirement, 297–299
Conduct constituting,
　Bribery, 296, 321
　Copying news, 256
　Interference with contract, 295
　Invasion of commercial privacy, 295
　Palming off, 294–295
　Plagiarism, 295–296
　Unauthorized broadcasts, 256, 264, 295
　Unauthorized recording, 256, 294–295
　Videotaping, 26
Defenses, 303
Elements of Prima facie case, 293
First Amendment limits, 300, 303
Historical development, 8–9, 16, 133, 214, 256–262
Preemption,
　Federal copyright law, 258–262, 300
　Federal patent law, 134, 258–259
Remedies, 303
Right of publicity and, 263

MISAPPROPRIATION—Cont'd
Subject-matter protected,
- Dress designs, 256, 258
- Human cannonball act, 26, 264, 300
- News, 214, 256–257, 296
- Personal name and likeness, 263
- Phonograph records and tapes, 256, 261
- Sales staff, 93
- Trade secrets, 304ff

MISREPRESENTATION
See Torts and Tort Law

MODEL AND UNIFORM ACTS
Little FTC Acts, 354
Model State Trademark Act, 114, 179
Printers Ink Model Statute, 367
Unfair Trade Practice and Consumer Protection Law, 354
Uniform Deceptive Trade Practices Act, 353–354
Uniform Trade Secrets Act, 316, 321, 327

NEGLIGENCE
See Torts and Tort Law

NUISANCE
See Torts and Tort Law

OMNIBUS TRADE AND COMPETITIVENESS ACT OF 1988
See Legislation

PACKAGING
See Trade Dress and Packaging

PALMING OFF
See Product Substitution and Alteration; Torts and Tort Law

PARALLEL IMPORTS
See International Trade Practices; Lanham Act

PATENT AND TRADEMARK OFFICE
Patent applications,
- Confidentiality, 318
- Procedure, 221–223

Trademark registrations,
- Procedure, 110–114, 186, 188

PATENT COOPERATION TREATY
See International Agreements

PATENTS
Application procedure, 221–223
    Confidentiality, 318
Assignments, 213, 224–227
Contracts for sale of, 75
Defined, 212
Federal law generally, 16, 19–21
Infringement, 268–271
    Defenses, 301
    Imported goods, 30
    Remedies, 301–302
Invalidation, 227–228
Licensee estoppel doctrine, 225
Licensing, 213, 224–225, 226–227
Patent and Trademark Office, 221–224
Patent Law Amendments Act of 1984, pp. 269–270
Preemption of state law, 19–21
    Trade secret law, 308–310
    Unfair competition law, 133–134
Purpose, 212
Rights conferred, 224, 268
    Priority, 222–223
    Termination, 227–228
    Territorial scope, 212–213
Shopright doctrine, 226
Subject-matter protected,
    Designs, 220
    Inventions, 217–220
    Plants, 220, 223, 224
Utility patents, 218–220

PLAGIARISM
See Literary and Artistic Works; Misappropriation; Product Substitution and Alteration

PLANT PROTECTION, 220–221, 223, 224

PREDATORY CONDUCT OR PURPOSE, 9–12, 43
See Concerted Group Conduct; Contracts and Contractual Relations; Malice; Refusal to Deal

PREEMPTION OF STATE LAW
Administrative preemption, 370–371
Constitutional basis, 18
Express legislative preemption, 19
Federal law,

PREEMPTION OF STATE LAW—Cont'd
Federal law—Cont'd
Antitrust law, 23–24, 395–396
Copyright law, 19, 20–21, 134–135, 258–262, 300
Labor law, 21–22
Lanham Act, 108
Patent law, 19–20, 21, 133–134
Trademark law, 22–23
Judicial preemption, 19–21
Non-preempted areas,
California Resale Royalties Act, 244
Contract law, 21, 309, 329–330
Right of publicity, 261–264
Trade secrets, 261, 308–310, 327–329
Trademarks and trade dress, 133
State law affected,
Common-law copyright, 231
Direct Molding statutes, 21, 299
Misappropriation, 257–262
Regulation of real estate broker advertising, 108
Shrink-wrap licensing laws, 275
Trade secrets, 21, 261, 308–310, 327–329
Trademark law, 133–134
Unfair competition, 133–134

PRICING PRACTICES
Coercing price concessions, 89–90
Deceptive price advertising, 384–385
Drug price advertising, 25, 183, 404
Dumping,
> Generally, 30

Defined, 419, 436
Statutes prohibiting, 30, 436–437
Predatory pricing,
Common-law remedies, 402–403, 406
Federal criminal sanctions, 412–414
Price cutting, 12, 25
Sales at unreasonably low prices, 407, 411–414
Sales below cost, 27, 407, 408–411
Cost, 410
Intent, 409–410, 410–411
Loss-leader selling, 408
Premiums and trading stamps, 400–401
Price discrimination,
Buyer liability, 415, 434–435

INDEX

References are to pages

PRICING PRACTICES—Cont'd
Price discrimination—Cont'd
  Competitive injury, 418, 420
    Primary line injury,
      Impact on competition, 422
      Intent, 421–422
    Second line injury, 424–425
    Third and fourth line injury, 425–426
  Damages, 424
  Defenses, 426ff
    Changing conditions, 428
    Cost justification, 427–428
    Meeting competition, 428ff
      Good faith, 429
      Price verification, 429–430
      Recognizably illegal prices, 430
  Defined, 415, 418
  Discriminatory promotional allowances and services,
    Defenses, 433
    Scope, 432–434
  Dumping, 436–438
  Foreign trade, 419, 435–438
  Predatory price discrimination, 421–424
  Seller liability, 415
  Unearned brokerage, 431ff
    Allowances and discounts in lieu of brokerage, 432
    Bribery, 395–397
    Export trade, 31
    Services-rendered defense, 431–432
Price fixing, 56, 402, 404
  Resale price maintenance, 71, 405–406
Wage and price controls, 404

PRIMA FACIE TORT
See Torts and Tort Law

PRINCIPAL REGISTER
See Lanham Act

PRIVACY
See Torts and Tort Law

PRODUCT AND BUSINESS FEATURES
  See also Copyright; Lanham Act; Secondary Meaning;
    Trademarks
Color, 147–149

PRODUCT AND BUSINESS FEATURES—Cont'd
Common-law protection, 102
Federal trademark protection, 131–139, 146–150
Functional features, 132, 146–150
Non-functional features, 131–139

PRODUCT LABELLING
See also Trade Dress and Packaging
Copyright protection, 239
Regulation,
    Consumer Product Safety Commission, 382
    Federal Cigarette Labelling and Advertising Act, 382
    Federal Trade Commission, 370, 380
    Food and Drug Administration, 369, 382

PRODUCT SUBSTITUTION AND ALTERATION
Product alteration, 205–209
    Adulterated goods, 207
    Foods, drugs and cosmetics, 382
    Literary and artistic works, 207–209
    Reconditioned goods, 205–207
Product substitution, 200–205
    Inferior quality goods, 203–204
    Less well known goods, 200–203
    Plagiarism, 204–205
    Seconds, 203–204, 205

PROMOTIONAL PRACTICES
See also Bribery; Coercion; False and Deceptive Advertising; Federal Trade Commission; Lotteries
Deceptive acts or practices,
    Bait-and-switch advertising, 385–386
    Business misdescriptions, 385
    Demonstrations, 387
    Direct representations, 377–378
    Endorsements, certifications and testimonials, 385
    Export trade, 383–384
    Implied misrepresentations, 377–378
    Inherent product qualities, 382–384
    Irrational consumer preferences, 384–385
    Non-disclosure, 379–382
Unfair practices and methods of competition,
    Bribery, 391–398
    Coercion, 53–54, 89–92, 391
    Giveaways, premiums and trading stamps, 334, 400–401
    Lotteries, games and contests, 334, 398–400

INDEX

References are to pages

PROMOTIONAL PRACTICES—Cont'd
Unfair practices and methods of competition—Cont'd
    Mass breach of contract, 388

PUBLICITY, COMMON-LAW RIGHT OF
    See also Misappropriation; Torts and Tort Law, Invasion of
        Privacy
Descendibility, 265–267
Duration, 266, 267
Relation to copyright law, 214, 263–264
Relation to misappropriation, 214, 263
Right to privacy distinguished, 263

RECORD AND TAPE PIRACY
See Misappropriation

REFUSAL TO DEAL
    See also Coercion; Concerted Group Conduct; Conspiracies
Anticompetitive purpose, 62
Concerted group conduct (group boycott), 11, 13, 66, 68–72
Conditioned, 65, 68, 69
Malicious, 11, 13
Privileged, 11, 13, 61, 71–72
Public utility or public calling, 62
Racially motivated, 62, 69
Secondary boycott, 68
Statutory limits on, 62–67
Unconditioned, 11, 13, 61, 69
Unilateral, 11, 13, 71

REMEDIES
Damages,
    Attorney's fees,
        Copyright infringement, 302–303
        False and deceptive advertising, 353, 366
        Trademark infringement, 195
    Compensatory damages,
        Breach of confidential relationship, 91
        Copyright infringement, 302–303
        Defamation, 336–339
        False and deceptive advertising, 353, 365–366
        Interference with contractual relations, 87, 94
        Interference with precontractual relations, 72
        Misappropriation,
            Publicly disclosed trade values, 300, 303
            Trade secrets, 329–330

INDEX

REMEDIES—Cont'd
Damages—Cont'd
  Compensatory damages—Cont'd
    Nuisance, 45
    Palming off, 209
    Special damages,
      Defamation, 336
      Interference with contractual relations, 87, 95
      Trade disparagement, 342–345
      Trademark infringement, 162, 194, 196
  Profits,
    Breach of confidential relationship, 91
    Copyright infringement, 302–303
    Fraud, 91
    Patent infringement, 302
    Trademark infringement, 162, 194–195
  Punitive damages,
    Contract claims, 95
    Defamation, 337, 339
    Interference with contractual relations, 95
    Tort actions, 95
    Trademark infringement, 162, 195
  Statutory damages, 303
  Treble damages,
    Anti-trust violations, 368, 395–396, 416
    Patent infringement, 302
    Trademark infringement, 195
Injunctive relief,
  Breach of employment contract, 95–96
  Copyright infringement, 274, 283
  Defamation, 346
  False and deceptive advertising, 352, 353, 365–366
  Interference with precontractual relations, 67, 72
  Misappropriation, 300, 303
  Nuisance, 45
  Product substitution or alteration, 214
  Trade disparagement, 346–348
  Trade secret misappropriation, 328–329
  Trademark and trade name infringement, 162, 167, 168–169, 192–194
Restitution, 95, 194–195

RIGHT OF PUBLICITY
See Publicity, Common–Law Right of

ROBINSON–PATMAN ACT
See Antitrust Laws

SALES BELOW COST
See Pricing Practices

SECONDARY MEANING
See also Marks and Names; Trademarks
Defined, 102, 121
Geographic terms, 129–130
Misdescriptive marks and names, 128–129
Personal names, 125
Product and business features, 131, 138
Proof, 123–124
Titles and characters, 136, 138–139

SECURITIES LAWS, 41, 52n

SEMICONDUCTOR CHIP PROTECTION ACT OF 1984
Generally, 214–215, 248
Exclusive rights, 285–293
    Assignment, 251
    Contributory infringement, 288–289
    Duration, 285
    Knowingly inducing infringement, 286, 288–289
    Licensing, 251
    Limitations on,
        First sale, 289
        Innocent infringement, 289–290, 292–293
        Reverse engineering, 215, 289–292
    Nature, 215, 285–286
        Distribution right, 286, 288
        Importation right, 285
        Reproduction right, 285, 286–288
Mask works,
    Generally, 215
    Described, 248–249
    Infringement, 285–293
    Originality, 250, 291
Notice, 255–256, 292–293
Owners protected, 251–254
Registration, 255, 285
Relation to other law,
    Copyright, 215, 250, 251, 252, 286, 287, 288, 289, 291–292
    Patent, 215, 250–251, 289
    Trade secret, 215

SEMICONDUCTOR CHIP PROTECTION ACT OF 1984—Cont'd
Specific sections,
- § 901, pp. 248, 251, 255, 288, 293
- § 902, pp. 248, 250, 251, 252, 253, 291
- § 904, p. 285
- § 905, pp. 285–289
- § 906, pp. 289, 290, 291
- § 907, p. 292
- § 908, p. 255
- § 909, pp. 255, 293
- § 914, p. 253

SERVICE MARKS
See also Marks and Names
Athletic services, 165
Defined, 105
Entertainment services, 139
Infringement, 165
Non-competing services, 165
Registration, 105

SHOPRIGHT DOCTRINE
Copyright law, 244
Patent law, 224
Trade secrets, 323–324

STATUTES
See Legislation

STATUTES OF FRAUDS
See Contracts and Contractual Relations

STRICT LIABILITY
See Torts and Tort Law

TITLES, LITERARY AND ARTISTIC
See also Copyright; Literary and Artistic Works; Marks and Names; Misappropriation; Trademarks
Deceptive titles, 359
Legal Protection,
   Common law, 102, 135–136, 197
   Federal trademark law, 105, 136, 138–139, 359
Unavailability of copyright protection, 135, 234

INDEX

TORTS AND TORT LAW
See also Bribery; Coercion; Concerted Group Conduct; Contracts and Contractual Relations, Interference; Defamation; False and Deceptive Advertising; Malice; Misappropriation; Pricing Practices; Product Substitution and Alteration; Publicity, Common-law Right of; Refusal to Deal; Trade Disparagement; Trade Names; Trademarks; Unfair Competition

Common law generally, 2–5
Conversion, 9
Disparagement, 4, 14, 52
Interference with contractual relations, 4–5, 41–42, 73, 83–94
Invasion of privacy, 5, 127, 214, 262–263
Misrepresentation,
  Deceit, 49–50, 98
  Fraud, 91, 225
  Negligence, 50–51, 91, 225
  Strict liability, 57n
Negligence,
  Infliction of pecuniary loss, 47–49
  Interference with contractual relations, 86–88
  Misrepresentation, 50–51, 91, 225
Nuisance, 3, 4, 10, 45–47
Palming off, 6–7, 53, 98–99, 102, 197ff
Prima facie tort, 12–15, 205, 296
Slander of title, 52–53
Strict liability,
  Contract breach, 87
  Economic losses, 87
  Federal securities law violations, 52n
Trespass, 3, 83
Unfair competition, 2, 5–11, 16, 18, 20–21

TRADE ASSOCIATIONS
Contracts involving, 75
Dress designers, 70
Interference with trade relations, 67–70
Lumber retailers, 68
Policing schemes, 70
Standing,
  Dumping, 437
  False advertising, 356–357

TRADE DISPARAGEMENT
See also Torts and Tort Law
Actual malice requirement, 342, 345

TRADE DISPARAGEMENT—Cont'd
Constitutional limitations, 344–346
Consumer testing and rating organizations, 345, 349
Defamation distinguished, 341–344
Historical origins, 4, 14, 52
Lanham Act, 362–363
Privilege, 349
Puffing, 348–349
Remedies,
    Private,
        Injunctive relief, 346–347
        Special damages requirement, 342, 343–344
    Public,
        FTC authority, 347

TRADE DRESS AND PACKAGING
Common-law protection, 102, 103
Deceptive substitution of services, 198
Lanham Act protection, 359
Trademark and service mark protection, 105

TRADE LEGISLATION
See Legislation

TRADE MARKS
See Marks and Names; Trademarks

TRADE NAMES
Definition,
    Common-law, 101–104
    Statutory, 105
Infringement,
    Deceptive substitution of services, 198
    Intent, 108–109
    Palming off distinguished, 102
    Scope of injunctive relief, 103
Law governing,
    Common-law protection, 102–103
    Federal protection, 114
    Foreign legal systems, 114
    State prohibition of use of, 26
Nicknames, 127

TRADE RELATIONS
Agency relations, 391
Bargaining relations, 34
    Franchise relations, 63–65

TRADE RELATIONS—Cont'd
Consumer relations, 34, 75
Employment relations, 34, 40, 41, 75, 391–392
Fiduciary relations, 48, 50, 395
Owner relations,
    Joint ventures, 34, 75
    Partner relations, 34, 75
    Shareholder relations, 34, 41, 75
Public relations, 34

TRADE REPRESENTATIVE
See U.S. Trade Representative

TRADE SECRETS
  See also Ideas; Misappropriation
Appropriation,
    Misappropriation,
        Breach of contract or confidence, 320
        Defenses, 305, 322–323, 324–325, 327
        Improper acquisition, 47, 307–308, 316–318
        Inducing breach, 82, 321
        Knowing use or disclosure, 325–327
        Unauthorized use or disclosure, 323–325
    Privileged appropriation, 322–323, 324–325
    Remedies,
        Injunctive relief, 306, 327–329
        Monetary relief, 328, 330
Assignment, 319–320
Contracts for the sale of, 75
Contractual protection, 313–316, 319
    Covenants not to compete,
        Commercial, 78–80, 314
        Employee, 79–81, 315
    Covenants not to disclose,
        Commercial contracts, 314
        Employment contracts, 80, 315, 323–325
    Covenants not to solicit customers, 314, 315–316, 323–325
Defined, 316–317
Law governing,
    Common law, 5, 213, 304–310, 311–313
    Constitutional law, just compensation, 306, 307
    Copyright, 311–312
    Origin, 304–306
    Relation to federal law,
        Copyright law, 261, 311–312
        Patent law, 21, 213, 308–310

TRADE SECRETS—Cont'd
Law governing—Cont'd
  Shopright doctrine, 323–324
  Subject-matter protected, 316–317, 318–319
Licensing, 319
Theories for legal protection, 306–308

TRADEMARK ACT OF 1905
  See also Lanham Act
Infringement, 166, 167–168, 169
Registration, 166, 168–169
Scope, 104, 120

TRADEMARK COUNTERFEITING ACT OF 1984, pp. 191, 195

TRADEMARKS
  See also Lanham Act; Marks and Names
Definition,
  Common-law, 101–104
  Statutory, 104–106
Dilution, 26–27
Formats protected, 105
Law governing,
    Generally, 6–7
  Federal law, 22–23
    Constitutional basis, 22–23
    Relation to state law, 22–23
  State law,
    Antidilution statutes, 26–27
    Common law, 6–7, 98–99, 100–104
    Fair Trade laws, 404–406
Relation to product good will, 35
Technical, 6, 101–103, 104, 119, 131, 142

TRADING STAMPS
Anti-premium legislation, 400–401
Exchanges, 299
Federal and state law governing, 334

TREATIES
See International Agreements

UNFAIR COMPETITION
See Torts and Tort Law

UNIFORM ACTS
See Model and Uniform Acts

U.S. TRADE REPRESENTATIVE, 31, 32, 193, 302–303, 390, 457

WORLD INTELLECTUAL PROPERTY ORGANIZATION, 254